Vedic Investigations

PAPERS OF THE 12TH WORLD SANSKRIT CONFERENCE
Vol. 1

Vedic Investigations

Edited by
ASKO PARPOLA
PETTERI KOSKIKALLIO

MOTILAL BANARSIDASS PUBLISHERS
PRIVATE LIMITED • DELHI

Papers of the 12th World Sanskrit Conference Held
In Helsinki, Finland, 13-18 July 2003
Vol. 1

General Editors:
PETTERI KOSKIKALLIO & ASKO PARPOLA

*First Edition: Delhi, **2016***

ISBN: 978-81-208-4030-0

Also available at:
Motilal Banarsidass
41 U.A. Bungalow Road, Jawahar Nagar, Delhi 110 007
8 Mahalaxmi Chamber, 22 Bhulabhai Desai Road, Mumbai 400 026
203 Royapettah High Road, Mylapore, Chennai 600 004
236, 9th Main III Block, Jayanagar, Bengaluru 560 011
8 Camac Street, Kolkata 700 017
Ashok Rajpath, Patna 800 004
Chowk, Varanasi 221 001

Printed in India
by RP Jain at NAB Printing Unit,
A-44, Naraina Industrial Area, Phase I, New Delhi–110028
and published by JP Jain for Motilal Banarsidass Publishers (P) Ltd,
41 U.A. Bungalow Road, Jawahar Nagar, Delhi-110007

PREFACE

That the papers of a conference session appear thirteen years after the event may be something like a world record, but a record for which we are not particularly proud. We sincerely apologize to the authors for having withheld their contributions from becoming accessible to colleagues at large for such a long time. Usually conference proceedings so much delayed do not appear at all, so the final appearance of this volume may give some consolation to everybody involved. But the shame for this delay is ours, the editors of this volume.

Asko Parpola volunteered to organize the 12th World Sanskrit Conference in Helsinki in July 2003 in order to boost the profile of Indology at Helsinki University, where the future of the chair of Indological and South Asian Studies was going to be deliberated after his impending retirement in 2004. Besides a university lectureship in Indian languages (occupied by Dr Bertil Tikkanen until 2015, and from 2015 onwards by Dr Mikko Viitamäki), this professorship was the only position for teaching and research in this field at Helsinki University and in Finland at large. We trust that the 12th WSC substantially helped in inducing the Faculty of Arts to establish a five-year professorship in South Asian Studies; it was internationally advertized, and filled in 2006, Dr Klaus Karttunen occupying the position until 2012. Thereafter a tenure-track chair was established, and Dr Xenia Zeiler was chosen to the associate professorship in South Asian Studies in 2014.

The programme of the 12th World Sanskrit Conference with the names and affiliations of the participants and the titles and abstracts of their papers were published in booklets delivered to the participants during the conference. In this first volume of the Proceedings, we complement those booklets by publishing, as an appendix, the Closing Address delivered by Asko Parpola on Friday the 18th of July 2003. As that address makes plain, the two of us collaborated very closely in organizing the 12th WSC. Essentially, AP's task consisted in getting the funding and receptions for the conference, while planning it was done together and PK was chiefly in charge of the practical arrangements. We believe that, with the help of a number of student volunteers, and blessed with a good weather, we were fairly successful in our task as far as holding the conference is concerned.

We had collaborated in a similar fashion already in organizing the 12th international conference 'South Asian Archaeology 1993', held at Helsinki University in July 1993 and in publishing its 887-paged proceedings in record time in 1994. We both further collaborated with Dr Christian Carpelan in arranging the much smaller international symposium on 'Early Contacts between Uralic and Indo-European: Linguistic and archaeological considerations' at the Tvärminne Marine Research Station of Helsinki University in 1999, and in publishing its proceedings in 2001.

The plan to publish the proceedings of the entire 12th World Sanskrit Conference was a most ambitious one. Only few organizers of the WSC have also published papers presented in them, and even then not comprehensively. We could get funds for a publication agreement with Motilal Banarsidass, securing that the volumes would be published on good paper at a reasonable price, and that every author would get a free copy of the volume where his or her paper was published, and that the editors of the volumes would in addition each get a copy of all the volumes. But we got only a very small allowance for language checking and editing, and these funds were soon exhausted. Our plan was to ask a prominent Sanskrit scholar of the respective field who was a native speaker of English to act as one of the editors of each volume and on voluntary basis to revise the contributions of colleagues whose native language was not English. On the whole, this plan worked very well.

Professor Stanley Insler, who participated in the 12th World Sanskrit Conference without presenting a paper, is a leading authority in Vedic studies. He most kindly promised to act as an editor of this volume, and also read a couple of the papers that we edited soon after the conference. Professor Masato Fujii, with whom Asko Parpola arranged the thematic panel 'Fieldwork on Vedic manuscripts, recitation and ritual traditions' in the Vedic session, was also to be one of the editors of this volume. Thus Asko Parpola, Masato Fujii and Stanley Insler were initially planned to be the editors of this volume, and this information has been repeated over the years in the advertisements of the publication series. Thus the names of Fujii and Insler have unintentionally become associated with the shameful delay of this volume. We sincerely apologize to these two eminent scholars and hope we shall succeed in clearing their names with this apology and clarification.

As already stated, the blame is all ours, as the two of us alone have been responsible for the editing of these papers and the delay of their publication. The main reason for this postponement is that Petteri Koskikallio, who has been responsible for the technical formatting of the contributions, has over the years always had his hands full, first, of earning his bread, and then, of editing other volumes of the 12th WSC on voluntary basis without monetary compensation. Asko Parpola has been responsible, also on voluntary basis, both for revising the language of the non-native speakers of English (though he himself belongs to the same category) and for checking the contributions also otherwise.

Altogether thirty papers were presented in the Vedic section of the 12th World Sanskrit Conference. Several participants did not submit their papers for publication in this volume. Among them was Werner Knobl's exciting paper on the 'nonce-formations' of Ṛgvedic poets, afterwards integrated in his doctoral dissertation

(Leiden University, 2009), entitled *A Surplus of Meaning: The Intent of Irregularity in Vedic Poetry*, available for download at http://hdl.handle.net/1887/14036. Two submitted papers could not be published in this volume due to their shortcomings. It remains to briefly introduce the nineteen contributions included.

Shrikant Bahulkar is one of the leading Atharvaveda scholars. During his longer stays at Varanasi, he has with interviews and study of literature collected all presently available information on the history of Atharvavedic recitation, ritual practice and study in this holy city. The result is a very detailed and clear exposition of the topic.

Didhiti Biswas collects information about ancient grammarians whose rules and opinions are quoted in Prātiśākhyas and Śikṣās, but whose (grammatical) works have otherwise not been preserved, Vyāḍi being a possible exception.

Joel Brereton has written an important monograph on the Āditya deities (1981) and translated into English the entire Ṛgveda in collaboration with Stephanie Jamison (2014). His paper focuses on the problematic nature of the two groups of gods called *deva* and *asura*: in the later Vedic texts, the *asura*s are devilish enemies of the *deva*s worshipped by Vedic people, while in the Iranian tradition of the Avesta, *ahura*s are the good gods fighting against demonic *daēva*s. In the Ṛgveda, such an obvious opposition between the two groups is lacking, as both terms can qualify some deities, yet some scholars insist on an opposition even in the Ṛgveda. Brereton concentrates on the dialogue hymn 10.124 that has figured quite a lot in the argumentations.

Clemens Cavallin's doctoral dissertation (2003) dealt with the correspondences that according to the Brāhmaṇa texts exist between different ritual, human and cosmic entities. The breaths form an important category of entities in this system of correspondences. They are intimately connected with the internalization of Vedic sacrificial actions, a ritual process that Cavallin discusses thoroughly in his paper.

Tatyana Elizarenkova (1929–2007) translated the entire Ṛgveda and Atharvaveda into Russian and published in English a book on *Language and Style of the Vedic Ṛṣis* (1995). Here she offers a comprehensive and richly illustrated semantic and syntactic analysis of the two words used for the concept of 'body' in the Ṛgveda, *tanū́-* (f.) and *śárīra-* (n.).

László Fórizs criticizes earlier translations and interpretations of the Ṛgvedic hymn 1.143 by Dīrghatamas, and offers his own solution to the problems associated with this laudation of Agni and Apāṃ Napāt.

Masato Fujii and Asko Parpola have for many decades been tracing and photographing manuscripts of texts belonging to the rare Jaiminīya school of Sāmaveda. Their paper records the results of their campaigns in 2002–2006, including their identification of the entire contents (i.e. also non-Sāmavedic works) of the private libraries of some important Jaiminīya Brahmins.

Cesary Galewicz has written a monograph (2009) on Sāyaṇa, the medieval commentator of the Veda. He has also made an impressive documentary film *Anyonyam* on the Keralan ritual competition in Vedic recitation (2002), shown at the 12th WSC. Galewicz examines the relatively recent compendium of the Āśvalāyana Ṛgvedins of Maharashtra and Konkan called *Ṛgvedadaśagrantha*. He focuses on the final portion entitled *Khila-Upaniṣad,* said to be a part of the *Yāmalāṣṭakatantra.* Here Śiva reveals to Pārvatī the most important part of the Veda by enumerating would-be Vedic Khilas and Upakhilas.

Ute Hüsken's doctoral thesis was on the behavioral rules for the Buddhist nuns (1996), whereafter she has mainly studied the rituals of the Vaiṣṇava communities of South India. The theme of her paper, dealt with more extensively in a monograph published in 2009, is 're-invention' of a ritual tradition in response to novel circumstances. She considers what does the *vaidikatva* of the Vaikhānasa Vaiṣṇavas mean and involve, in particular with reference to the rivaling sect of Pāñcarātra Vaiṣṇavas and to some life cycle rites.

Jan E. M. Houben has published, among other things, on the Vedic *pravargya* ritual and on Bhartṛhari's philosophy of language. Here he focuses on the meaning of the *nihnavana* rite, which is a minor component of the Vedic *soma* sacrifices, stated to be an entirely meaningless act by Frits Staal. Houben has dedicated his study to Staal, whose notion of 'the meaninglessness of ritual' he also studies here in depth.

Gabriela Ilieva attempts to find out what did it entail to be a woman in ancient India of Ṛgvedic times. She analyzes three of the four hymns in which a female voice directly addresses the gods with a wish, the hymns of Ghoṣā (ṚV 10.39–40) and Apālā (ṚV 8.91).

Stephanie Jamison is a leading scholar of Vedic studies, who has translated the entire Ṛgveda into English in collaboration with Joel Brereton (2014), and the author of several penetrating monographs. In her keynote paper she defends the nowadays often contempted traditional philology and its methods – close reading of texts with alert attention to every grammatical, lexical and semantic detail. She marshals fascinating examples to prove that philology can reveal aspects of ancient India that are not overtly mentioned in our only available sources for reconstructing social history. We learn about the methods of teaching in Ṛgvedic times, including brahmanical recital and animal fables, about ancient obstetrics, and changing attitudes towards women as agents in the law texts.

Joanna Jurewicz's publications include a book on monism in Indian philosophy (in Polish, 1994) and a book entitled *Fire and Cognition in the Rigveda* (2010). Her present essay is related to the latter theme. Etymologies presented in Brāhmaṇa texts have often been considered senseless. A case in point is the derivation of the word *agni-*, 'fire', from the word *agri-*, which does not otherwise exist (ŚB 2.2.4.2). Applying cognitive linguistics, Jurewicz shows that this etymology has a rational motivation, the idea of 'fire's precedence' that dominates the Ṛgvedic conception of this divinity.

Mieko Kajihara has since her doctoral thesis (Harvard 2002) concentrated on the themes of *brahmacarya*, initiation and study of the Veda. Here she presents a very thorough analysis of the references to the 'renewed initiation' (*punarupanayana*) in Vedic texts, from the Atharvaveda Saṁhitās over the Brāhmaṇas to the Gṛhyasūtras.

Guni Hesting Kirchheiner (1932–2007) was not a professional scholar of the Veda, but a lover of Indian music. She presents her project of recording recitation of the four Vedas: the inspiration behind the project, its purpose, how it was carried out, and the results.

David M. Knipe is well known for his many penetrating studies of Vedic and Hindu ritual. He has just published a book on his long-continued field work on the *śrauta* traditions of coastal Andhra (2015). The present essay, where 'now' means 'in 2003', has as its theme *sōmidēvamma*, the wife (*patnī*) of an Andhra *soma* sacrificer. It focuses on the problem of her being called *somapītinī*, 'one who has drank *soma*', though she has not actually partaken of this sacred drink. This induces Knipe to deal at large with various aspects in the life and death of the Vedic Brahmins he has studied in the field, particularly their union in the daily *agnihotra*, and the funeral rites of *brahmamedha* and *mūsiyāvanam*.

Timothy Lubin is an authority in the Gṛhya- and Dharmasūtras and the customary Indian law. He has updated the present prolegomena to his forthcoming critical edition and annotated translation of the *Baudhāyanagṛhyasūtra* and its supplements, the *Baudhāyanagṛhyaparibhāṣāsūtra* and the *Baudhāyanagṛhyapariśeṣasūtra*. These much neglected texts contain a lot of interesting and in part unique material that illuminate the transition from Vedic to classical Hindu cult. Lubin reviews the current state of research on these texts, particularly their relationship to the *Baudhāyanaśrautasūtra* and its appendices, and to the other Gṛhya texts. He also surveys the manuscripts and other material available to the new critical edition.

Manjula Devi discusses various aspects of the *dakṣiṇā*, the 'honorarium' that the *yajamāna* has to present to the sacrificial priests of the *śrauta* rite performed on his behalf. The paper considers only statements made in primary sources, without referring to other recent research on this important topic.

Frederick Smith's thesis was on the Bhāskara Miśra's Mīmāṁsā exegesis of Vedic ritual (1984), but he has also written a major book on spirit possession in South Asia (2006). During his extensive fieldwork on the living tradition of Vedic *śrauta* sacrifices in Maharashtra, Gujarat and South India, Smith has over the years collected much ephemeral material, some of which he presents in this paper. One of his objects is to understand the motivations of late 20th- and early 21st-century *yajamāna*s to have such rare and expensive rituals performed.

All in all, these papers make a substantial volume that retains its value in spite of the long delay, for which we editors once more sincerely apologize. We also thank the contributors for their wonderful patience and belief in the ultimate appearance of the book. Only Fred Smith has submitted a revised version of his paper for publication elsewhere, but has kindly permitted us to retain here the original version.

Helsinki, November 2015

ASKO PARPOLA
PETTERI KOSKIKALLIO

CONTENTS

CONTRIBUTORS

S. S. BAHULKAR
Bhandarkar Oriental Research Institute
812 Shivaji Nagar
Pune 411 004
INDIA
e-mail: shrikant.bahulkar@gmail.com

DIDHITI BISWAS
Department of Sanskrit
University of Calcutta
87/1 College Street
Kolkata 700 073
INDIA
e-mail: didhiti2007@yahoo.co.in

JOEL BRERETON
Department of Asian Studies
The University of Texas at Austin
120 Inner Campus Drive, G9300
Austin, TX 78712-1251
U.S.A.
e-mail: jpb@austin.utexas.edu

CLEMENS CAVALLIN
Department of Literature, History of Ideas, and Religion
University of Gothenburg
Box 200
40530 Gothenburg
SWEDEN
e-mail: clemens.cavallin@lir.gu.se

LÁSZLÓ FÓRIZS
European Buddhist Training Center
Börzsöny utca 11
Budapest 1098
HUNGARY
e-mail: info@ebtc.hu

MASATO FUJII
Institute for Research in Humanities
Kyoto University
Yoshida-Honmachi, Sakyo-ku
Kyoto 606-8501
JAPAN
e-mail: fujii@zinbun.kyoto-u.ac.jp

JAN E. M. HOUBEN
École Pratique des Hautes Études
Sciences historiques et philologiques
54, rue Saint-Jacques
CS 20525 – 75005 Paris
FRANCE
e-mail: johannes.houben@ephe.sorbonne.fr

GEZARY GALEWICZ
Department of Languages and Cultures of India & South Asia
Jagiellonian University Cracow
al. Mickiewicza 3
31-120 Cracow
POLAND
e-mail: cezarygalewicz@yahoo.com

UTE HÜSKEN
Department for Culture Studies and Oriental Languages
University of Oslo
Box 1010
Blindern
N-0315 Oslo
NORWAY
e-mail: ute.huesken@ikos.uio.no

GABRIELA NIK. ILIEVA
Department of Middle Eastern and Islamic Studies
New York University
50 Washington Square South
New York, NY 10012
U.S.A.
e-mail: gni1@nyu.edu

STEPHANIE W. JAMISON
The Department of Asian Languages & Cultures
UCLA College
290 Royce Hall
Box 951540
Los Angeles, CA 90095-1540
U.S.A.
e-mail: jamison@humnet.ucla.edu

JOANNA JUREWICZ
Chair of South Asia
Faculty of Oriental Studies
University of Warsaw
ul. Krakowskie Przedmieście 26/28
00-927 Warsaw
POLAND
e-mail: j.jurewicz@uw.edu.pl

MIEKO KAJIHARA
Graduate School of Humanities and Sociology
University of Tokyo
7-3-1 Hongo, Bunkyo-ku
Tokyo 113-0033
JAPAN
e-mail: kajihara@l.u-tokyo.ac.jp

DAVID M. KNIPE
Faculty of Asian Languages and Literatures
University of Wisconsin, Madison
Van Hise Hall, 1220 Linden Drive
Madison WI 53706
U.S.A.
e-mail: dmknipe@wisc.edu

TIMOTHY LUBIN
Department of Religion
Washington and Lee University
Baker Hall 118
Lexington, VA 24450
U.S.A.
e-mail: lubint@wlu.edu

MANJULA DEVI
Department of Sanskrit
Gauhati University
Guwahati, Assam 781 014
INDIA
e-mail: sanskrit.gauhati.ac.in

ASKO PARPOLA
Asian and African Studies
Department of World Cultures
University of Helsinki
Box 59
00014 University of Helsinki
FINLAND
e-mail: asko.parpola@helsinki.fi

FREDERICK M. SMITH
Division of World Languages, Literatures & Cultures
111 Phillips Hall
Iowa City, IA 52242-1323
U.S.A.
e-mail: frederick-smith@uiowa.edu

ABBREVIATIONS

(Some more abbreviations are given in the bibliographies)

Texts

ĀgGS	*Āgniveśyagṛhyasūtra*
AB	*Aitareyabrāhmaṇa*
AiĀ	*Aitareya-Āraṇyaka*
ĀpDhS	*Āpastambadharmasūtra*
ĀpGS	*Āpastambagṛhyasūtra*
ĀpŚS	*Āpastambaśrautasūtra*
ĀśvGS	*Āśvalāyanagṛhyasūtra*
ĀśvŚS	*Āśvalāyanaśrautasūtra*
AV	*Atharvaveda(saṃhitā)*
AV(P)	*Atharvavedasaṃhitā*, Paippalāda recension
AVPr	*Atharvavedaprātiśākhya*
AV(Ś)	*Atharvavedasaṃhitā*, Śaunaka recension
BĀU	*Bṛhadāraṇyaka-Upaniṣad*
BhārGS	*Bhāradvājagṛhyasūtra*
BDhS	*Baudhāyanadharmasūtra*
BGPS	*Baudhāyanagṛhyaparibhāṣā(sūtra)*
BGS	*Baudhāyanagṛhyasūtra*
BGŚS	*Baudhāyanagṛhyaśeṣasūtra*
BŚS	*Baudhāyanaśrautasūtra*
ChāgU	*Chāgaleya-Upaniṣad*
ChU	*Chāndogya-Upaniṣad*
CS	*Carakasaṃhitā*
GauDhS	*Gautamadharmasūtra*
GB	*Gopathabrāhmaṇa*

GGS	*Gobhilagṛhyasūtra*
HGS	*Hiraṇyakeśigṛhyasūtra*
HGŚeṣaS	*Hiraṇyakeśigṛhyaśeṣasūtra*
HŚS	*Hiraṇyakeśiśrautasūtra*
JB	*Jaiminīyabrāhmaṇa*
JGS	*Jaiminigṛhyasūtra*
JUB	*Jaiminīya-Upaniṣadbrāhmaṇa*
KaṭhB	*Kaṭhabrāhmaṇa*
KaṭhB(*u*)	*Kaṭhabrāhmaṇa (Upanayanabrāhmaṇa)*
KāṭhGS	*Kāṭhakagṛhyasūtra*
KauṣGS	*Kauṣītakagṛhyasūtra*
KauśS	*Kauśikasūtra*
KauṣU	*Kauṣītaki-Upaniṣad*
KB	*Kauṣītakibrāhmaṇa*
KhGS	*Khādiragṛhyasūtra*
KS	*Kāṭhakasaṃhitā*
KŚS	*Kātyāyanaśrautasūtra*
LGS	*Laugākṣigṛhyasūtra*
LŚS	*Lāṭyāyanaśrautasūtra*
Manu	*Manusmṛti*
MGS	*Mānavagṛhyasūtra*
MS	*Maitrāyaṇīsaṃhitā*
MŚS	*Mānavaśrautasūtra*
MuU	*Muṇḍaka-Upaniṣad*
P	Pāṇini's *Aṣṭādhyāyī*
PB	*Pañcaviṃśabrāhmaṇa*
PGS	*Pāraskaragṛhyasūtra*
PraśU	*Praśna-Upaniṣad*
ṚDG	*Ṛgvedadaśagrantha/Ṛgvedīyadaśagrantha*
ṚP	*Ṛkprātiśākhya*
ṚV	*Ṛgveda(saṃhitā)*
ṚVKh	*Ṛgvedakhila*
ŚĀ	*Śāṅkhāyana-Āraṇyaka*
ŚB	*Śatapathabrāhmaṇa*

ṢB	*Ṣaḍviṃśabrāhmaṇa*
ŚGS	*Śāṅkhāyanagṛhyasūtra*
ŚŚS	*Śāṅkhāyanaśrautasūtra*
SuśS	*Suśrutasaṃhitā*
SVB	*Sāmavidhānabrāhmaṇa*
TĀ	*Taittirīya-Āraṇyaka*
TB	*Taittirīyabrāhmaṇa*
TP	*Taittirīyaprātiśākhya*
TS	*Taittirīyasaṃhitā*
TU	*Taittirīya-Upaniṣad*
VaiGS	*Vaikhānasagṛhyasūtra*
VaiSmS	*Vaikhānasasmārtasūtra*
VārGS	*Vārāhagṛhyasūtra*
VāsDhS	*Vāsiṣṭhadharmasūtra*
ViSm	*Viṣṇusmṛti*
VP	*Vājasaneyiprātiśākhya*
VS	*Vājasaneyisaṃhitā*
YATKU	*Khila-Upaniṣad* 'of the *Yāmalāṣṭakatantra*'

Journals, publishers, series, etc.

ABORI	*Annals of the Bhandarkar Oriental Research Institute*, Poona
HOS	Harvard Oriental Series
JA	*Journal Asiatique*
JAOS	*Journal of the American Oriental Society*
MLBD	Motilal Banarsidass
OUP	Oxford University Press
WZKS	*Wiener Zeitschrift für die Kunde Süd* (*und Ost-*) *asiens*

General

Pt.	Pandit
V.S.	*vikrama-saṃvat*, Vikrama era (= AD 57–)

The Tradition of the Atharvaveda in Varanasi

S. S. BAHULKAR

1. BACKGROUND

Since ancient times, the city of Varanasi is known as a sacred place of pilgrimage for the Hindus and a seat of learning, particularly of the Vedas and Śāstras. There are several works highlighting the religious and cultural importance of this city. The *Kāśīkhaṇḍa* of the *Skandapurāṇa* is devoted to the description of Varanasi. In modern times, Indian as well as western scholars have written a number of books on the history of Varanasi. Some scholars such as Pt. Gopīnāth Kavirāj, Pt. Baladev Upādhyāy and others have collected valuable information about the scholarly tradition of Varanasi. In recent years, Wayne Howard, in his book *Veda Recitation in Vārāṇasī* (1986), has brought to light the contemporary tradition of Vedic studies in Varanasi. There exists a tradition of the study of all the four Vedas in Varanasi. There are a few books and articles giving information on the tradition of Vedic study in Varanasi.

In the particular case of the Atharvaveda (= AV), it has always been difficult to gather reliable and sufficient information. This Veda has always been looked down upon by the followers of the first three Vedas and its tradition has become almost extinct in various parts of India. In Varanasi, some followers of the AV have made commendable efforts to continue and promote the study of the AV, but the scholarly community is not aware of the history and the present day position of the study of the AV in Varanasi.

Against this background, it is important to collect whatever information is available at present. If such documentation is not done, even this information will be lost forever. The present paper is an outcome of a survey of the tradition of the AV in Varanasi, based on information available in various documents and personal communication.

The paper deals with three aspects of the study: 1) history of the study of the AV in Varanasi, 2) the ritualistic tradition of the AV in Varanasi and 3) manuscripts and published works related to the AV.

2. HISTORY OF THE STUDY OF THE ATHARVAVEDA

There are several works studying the history of Varanasi. According to the authors of these works, from ancient times, the holy city of Varanasi was a seat of learning. In his book *Varanasi Down the Ages* (1974), Kuber Nath Sukul gives a brief account of the tradition of the study of the Vedas in Varanasi. According to him, Varanasi was a university colony in the midst of forest. There were specialists in each of the four Vedas. The seals discovered in the Rājghāṭ excavations mention names of Vedic schools (*caraṇa*): the *bahvṛcacaraṇa* for the teaching of the Ṛgveda and the *caraka-caraṇa* for the teaching of the Kṛṣṇa Yajurveda. As for the Sāmaveda, there were several institutions. There are as many as six seals which mention the name Chāndogya on the obverse. There is also mention of a *caturvidyācaraṇa*, an institute devoted to the teaching of all the four Vedas, and a *traividyācaraṇa* for the teaching of the first three Vedas. In addition, there was a school teaching all aspects of the Vedas (*sarvatravidyācaraṇa*) (Sukul 1974: 90).

In the Pāli scriptures, the Kosiya and Tittira Jātakas mention that the teachers at Varanasi taught the three Vedas and eighteen crafts (Sukul 1974: 88).

That the Gāhaḍvāl kings of Varanasi had been granting villages to learned men in Varanasi and that these men were learned specialists is evident from the following appellations connected with their names: *ṛgvedacaraṇa*, *caturvedin*, *yajurvedacaraṇa*, *atharvavedacaraṇa*, *dvivedin*, *chāndogyacaraṇa* (Sukul 1974: 93).

K. Chandramouli has written a book on Varanasi with the title *Kashi: The City Luminous* (1995)., He tries to establish a connection between Varanasi and the AV. Both recensions of the AV, i.e., the Śaunaka (= AV(Ś)) and the Paippalāda (= AV(P)) contain a verse that mentions river Varaṇā́vatī (AV(Ś) 4.7.1 = AV(P) 5.8.8). Chandramouli (1995: 7) thinks that the name refers to the river Varaṇā only. It is learnt that the name Vārāṇasī denotes the region between the two rivers Varuṇā and Assī. Chandramouli further points out that the name Kāśī occurs for the first time in the AV. In a hymn to *takmán*, the seer says:

> *gandhā́ribhyo mū́javadbhyó 'ṅgebhyo magádhebhyaḥ* |
> *praiṣyán jánam iva śevadhíṃ takmā́naṃ pári dadmasi* || (AV 5.22.14)
>
> To the Gandhāris, the Mūjavants, the Aṅgas, the Magadhas, like one sending a person a treasure, do we commit the fever. (Trans. Whitney 1905: 261, with the emendation *préṣyan*)

The Paippalāda recension of the AV however has a variant where the word *aṅgebhyaḥ* has been replaced by the word *kāśibhyaḥ* (AV(P) 13.1.12) 'to the Kāśis'. Chandramouli (1995: 12) thinks that 'the region of Kāśi was Aryanised in the time span between the two śākhās of the AV'. Sukul too has made a reference to the mantra quoted above and has argued in the same manner.

Motīcandra's book in Hindi with the title *Kāśī kā itihās* ('The History of Kāśī', 1985) is one of the sources consulted frequently. In that book, Motīcandra refers to Dayā Rām Sāhnī's article 'Chandravati Plates of Chandra-Deva: V.S. 1150 and 1156' (Sāhnī 1917–18). The copper plate of V.S. 1156, i.e. 14th April AD 1100, bears the record of grants donated to 500 learned brahmins. Among those brahmins, there was a brahmin named Chīhāla who belonged to the *atharvacaraṇa*, Bhāradvāja *gotra* and was a *dvivedin*, i.e., 'expert in two Vedas' (Motīcandra 1985: 133).

All these references show some possible connection of Varanasi with the AV, but are too scanty to lead to any conclusion. It appears that several families of learned pandits had gone to Varanasi from different parts of India and had settled there. These families, particularly from Kanauj, South India, Uttarāñcal, Gujarat and Maharashtra have enriched the tradition of the study of both the Vedas and the Śāstras in Varanasi. Once upon a time, the tradition of Vedic study might have been well-established. However, it had begun to decline in the 19th century AD. I may quote a passage from M. A. Sherring's book *The Sacred City of the Hindus in Ancient and Modern Time* (1868). He says:

> At the present moment, I have been given to understand that not twenty families of Brahmans in all Benares are devoted to the study of the Vedas, and that, if those which engage in this peculiar study, there is not one indigenous to Benares, but all are of the Bhaṭṭ Brahmans from Gujerat. I cannot, however, vouch for the absolute truth of this statement, although I believe it is quite true that the study of the Vedas has very much fallen off in Benares. (Sherring 1868: 347)

Sherring further tries to find the reason of this decline of the Vedic study. According to him, the pandits studying the Vedas were supported by kings and rich people,

> but, for several years past, especially since the mutiny, the amount of that support has greatly diminished. The consequence is that the pandits, in many instances, have abandoned the close study of Sanskrit, and, with it, the instruction of their pupils, and have largely directed their attention to other more profitable pursuits. (Sherring 1868: 347)

In his book *Veda Recitation in Vārāṇasī*, Wayne Howard has collected information on the tradition of Veda recitation on the basis of the relevant books and personal communication. He has given a good account of the Vedic heritage of Varanasi and has shown how ancient Varanasi, the capital of the kingdom of Kāśī, had association with Vedic recitation performed at Vedic sacrifices, particularly the *aśvamedha* sacrifice. The name of Kāśī occurs in connection with Veda recitation in the *Śatapathabrāhmaṇa*. The passage in question refers to the horse sacrifice performed by king Dhṛtarāṣṭra (Howard 1986: 1). The famous Daśāśvamedha Ghāṭ marks the site where the Bhāraśiva, a ruling dynasty, took ceremonial baths at the completion of the *aśvamedha* observances near the end of the 2nd century AD. Howard further assumes that interest in Vedic lore and the performance of Vedic sacrifices continued during subsequent centuries, with intermittent interruptions (Howard 1986: 6).

The great majority of the brahmins who were instrumental in enriching the tradition of Vedic and Śāstric learning were from the southern parts of India, including Maharashtra. In Uttar Pradesh, even the region of Maharashtra is considered to be southern. An important work, the *Gādhivaṃśānucarita*, composed by Śaṅkara Bhaṭṭa, describes the tradition of the southern brahmins in Varanasi. Mahāmahopādhyāya Haraprasād Śāstrī has given the contents of this work (Śāstrī 1912). The colony of southern pandits was established by Nārāyaṇa Bhaṭṭa, son of Rāmeśvara from Pratiṣṭhāna, modern Paiṭhaṇ on the banks of the Godāvarī in Maharashtra. Nārāyaṇa's son, Śaṅkara, wrote the history of the Gādhi or Bhaṭṭa family. Haraprasād Śāstrī mentions as many as seven families of the southern pandits: Śeṣa, Dharmādhikārī, Gādhi or Bhaṭṭa, Bhāradvāja, Pāyaguṇḍe, Caturdhara (or Chowdharī) and Puṇtāmkar (Puṇtāmbekar). The credit of establishing Sanskrit *pāṭhaśālā*s goes mostly to these southern pandits. The oldest of such schools was that of Dinkar Aṇṇā Jośī. Other *pāṭhaśālā*s were those of Vināyak Bhaṭṭ Ḍoṅgre, Rājarām Kaśelkar, Śrīkṛṣṇa Deodhar, Bālkṛṣṇa Nene, Bābū Dīkṣit, Yajñeśvar Candraśekhar Dravid̤, Gaṇeś Bāpaṭ and Somnāth Bāpaṭ. These *pāṭhaśālā*s imparted education in Vedic recitation.

It may be noted that instruction in the recitation of the AV was not a speciality of any of these *pāṭhaśālā*s. The teachers belonged to the first three Vedas and there was hardly any one who was born in an Atharvavedic family. In this situation, the efforts made by some pandits for the survival and the propagation of the study of the AV deserve our attention. For some reasons, these efforts have not yet been brought to light. Howard has confined his study to a brief comparison of the recitation of a verse from the hymn for peace (AV(Ś) 19.9.1), performed by two Atharvavedins, namely, Pt. Lakṣmīśaṅkar Gaurīśaṅkar Rāvaḷ of Bhāvnagar, Gujrat, and Pt. Nārāyaṇ Śāstrī Raṭāṭe of Varanasi.

Howard does not elaborate his remarks on the tradition of the AV in Varanasi, saying that he does not wish to intrude on the work of another researcher, who is planning 'a detailed study of Atharvavedic traditions' (Howard 1986: 110). This study has however not been published yet, even after the lapse of thirty years. During my stay in Sarnath from 1993 to 1995, I was fortunate to have frequent meetings with Dr. Viśvanāth Vāman Dev and other pandits of Varanasi who gladly supplied me with whatever information they possessed. The present study is an outcome of my survey of the AV tradition in Varanasi during those two years and subsequently the summer of 1998.

Atharvaveda *pāṭhaśālā*s

In Varanasi, there are at least two well-known *pāṭhaśālā*s which have made sincere efforts to establish the study of the AV. They are: 1. Śrīvallabharāma-śāligrāma-sāṅgaveda-vidyālaya, popularly known as the Sāṅgaveda Vidyālaya and 2. Nigamāgama Darbhaṅgā Saṃskṛta Vidyālaya or Darbhaṅgā Vidyālaya.

Sāṅgaveda Vidyālaya

The Sāṅgaveda Vidyālaya was established on Sunday, the thirteenth day of the bright half of the month of Māgha, V.S. 1977 (AD 1920), at the hands of Śrī Prabhu Nārāyaṇ Siṃh, the then king of Kāśī. The school was founded with the financial support from Śrī Bihārīlāl Mehtā who was a great supporter of Sanskrit learning, Vedas as well as Śāstras. The first principal of the school was Pt. Lakṣmaṇ Śāstrī Draviḍ, a famous pandit who went to Varanasi from Tamil Nadu. At the very beginning, the school appointed teachers for the teaching of the Ṛgveda, the Mādhyandina and the Kānva recensions of the Śukla Yajurveda, the Kṛṣṇa Yajurveda (the Taittirīya recension), the Sāmaveda (the Kauthuma recension) and the AV (the Śaunaka recension) as well as the Śāstras of *vyākaraṇa* and *nyāya*. The record available at the Sāṅgaveda Vidyālaya mentions the names of the teachers and their tenure as a teacher in that school. The teachers for the AV were:

1) Pt. Bhagavānīlāljī (V.S. 1977–84)
2) Pt. Lābhśaṅkar Jhā (V.S. 1988–90).

In subsequent years, Pt. Rāmcandra Śāstrī Raṭāṭe and Dr. Manoharlāl Dvivedī shouldered the responsibility of teaching the AV.

Nigamāgama Darbhaṅgā Vidyālaya

This school was established at the instruction of Maharṣi Svāmī Viśuddhānandjī under the patronage of Śrī Lakṣmeśvar Siṃh, the then king of Darbhanga. The exact year of its establishment is not available. In a booklet on the history of this school written by Pt. Nārāyaṇ Śāstrī Raṭāṭe, it is mentioned that the school is 'very ancient' (Raṭāṭe 1988: 11). The school was shifted to Lohana, Darbhanga, for some years and consequently the teachers had to find their livelihood in the Government Sanskrit College and elsewhere in Varanasi. The school was re-established in Varanasi under the patronage of Śrī Rāmeśvar Siṃh, King of Darbhanga, and renamed as Nigamāgama Darbhaṅgā Vedavidyālaya on the fourth day of the bright half of the month of Bhādrapada of V.S. 1983 (AD 1926). This day is a special one, known as *gaṇeśacaturthī*, the first day of the Gaṇeśa festival. The school started with the appointments of three teachers: Pt. Bābū Dīkṣit Jaḍe for the Ṛgveda, Pt. Śaṅkararām Sāmavedī for the Sāmaveda and Pt. Rāmcandra Śāstrī Raṭāṭe for the AV. At that time, Pt. Raṭāṭe was teaching at the Sāṅgaveda Vidyālaya. He was requested to join the Darbhaṅgā Vidyālaya. These teachers were paid twenty Rupees per month by way of remuneration (Raṭāṭe 1988: 21). The school was supported by the king of Darbhanga before the independence of India. After the independence, since 1957, the State Government of Uttar Pradesh sanctioned annual grants to the school. This school is now affiliated to the Sampūrṇānand Sanskrit University, Varanasi.

Atharvaveda teachers

Pt. Jayadevāśram

The first name in the list of the teachers of the AV in Varanasi should be Pt. Jayadev Pañcolī who was better known as Jayadevāśram, after he became a *saṃnyāsin*. He was one of the few Atharvavedins by birth. Pt. Jayadevāśram belonged to the family of the Atharvavedins in the Nāgara community of Gujarat, while others belonged to some other Vedas and studied the AV in addition to their own *śākhā*. No detailed information regarding this scholar is available. My remarks are based on Pt. Baladev Upādhyāy's book *Kāśī kī pāṇḍityaparamparā* ('The scholarly tradition of Kāśī', 1993), annual reports of the Sāṅgaveda Vidyālaya and personal communication with the late Pt. Viśvanāth Vāman Dev, a renowned *ghanapāṭhin* and scholar of the Ṛgveda from Varanasi. It is not certain whether Pt. Jayadevāśram taught at that school, but it is evident that he had a number of disciples, who in turn continued to teach the AV in Varanasi, Gujarat and elsewhere. He was supposed to be the greatest of all Atharvavedins in the latter half of the 19th century and the first half of the 20th century (Kālviṇṭ 1968: 54; Upādhyāy 1993: 703). Pt. Jayadevāśram was appointed as *purohita*, a priest well-versed in the Atharvavedic ritual, by the Mehtā family that was instrumental in establishing the Sāṅgaveda Vidyālaya.

Besides the propagation of the AV, Pt. Jayadevāśram also tried to re-establish the Śāṅkhāyana *śākhā* of the Ṛgveda by arranging the performance of sacrificial rites according to that *śākhā* (Draviḍ 1936: 9). Pt. Jayadevāśram was born in 1857 and died in 1935.

Bhagavānīlāl Agnihotrī

Bhagavānīlāl Agnihotrī was a Nāgara brahmin belonging to the Śāṅkhāyana school of the Ṛgveda. In his childhood, he lived in the Bānswāḍā State in Gujarat. He first studied his own *śākhā*, i.e. the Śāṅkhāyana *śākhā* of the Ṛgveda and then turned his attention to the study of the AV, which he studied with Pt. Lakṣmīśaṅkar Dvivedī, an Atharvavedin and an expert in Mantraśāstra at Bānswāḍā. Pt. Bhagavānīlāljī came to Varanasi at the age of 14 with his teacher Pt. Lakṣmīśaṅkar Dvivedī and soon enjoyed the reputation as an excellent Vaidika in Varanasi. Pt. Bhagavānīlāljī taught the following students: Gaṅgādhar Taṅgirāl (Andhra Pradesh), Nāthūlāl Pañcolī (Bānswāḍā), Bhagavānīlāl Pañcolī (Bānswāḍā), Narmadāśaṅkar Pañcolī (Bānswāḍā), Nārāyaṇ Ghuḷe (Varanasi), Paraśurām Rāmḍohkar (Varanasi), Jagannāth Ghuḷe (Varanasi), Rāmcandra Āṭhavale (Varanasi) and Manoharlāl Dvivedī (Varanasi).

Pt. Lābhśaṅkar Jhā

Lābhśaṅkar Jhā was the son-in-law of Pt. Jayadevāśram and was the teacher of the AV at the Sāṅgaveda Vidyālaya in V.S. 1988–90. He was the teacher of Pt. Lakṣmīśaṅkar Gaurīśaṅkar Rāvaḷ of Bhāvnagar, whose recitation has been recorded and utilized by Howard (1986: 109–110).

Pt. Rāmcandra Śāstrī Raṭāṭe

Rāmcandra Śāstrī Raṭāṭe was one of the best Atharvavedins of Varanasi. He was born in a Mahārāṣṭrīya family and was a Ṛgvedin, but studied all the four Vedas. He was known as 'the universal master of the Vedas' (*vaidikacakravartin*). His brother-in-law was an Atharvavedin and was appointed by the king of Ayodhyā. Pt. Raṭāṭe studied the AV with Pt. Gaṇeś Bhaṭṭ Mārtaṇḍ. Later he was appointed as the teacher of the AV by the king of Ayodhyā in place of his brother-in-law due to the sudden death of the latter. He spent four years in Ayodhyā. He studied the remaining portion of the AV with Pt. Thatte, a Mahārāṣṭrīya pandit of Ayodhyā (Phaḍke

1968: 103). After his return to Varanasi, he taught the AV first at the Sāṅgaveda Vidyālaya for some years and then took up the position of the Atharvaveda teacher at the Darbhaṅgā Vidyālaya where he taught the AV for 35 years (Phaḍke 1968: 103). He was also Honorary Professor at the Saṃpūrṇānand Sanskrit University from 1978 until his death (Raṭāṭe 1988: 41). Among his pupils were Sakhārām Bhaṭṭ Vaidya (who later became the teacher of the AV at the Goyaṅkā Vidyālaya, Varanasi), Nārāyaṇ Bhaṭṭ Ghuḷe, Rāmcandra Āṭhavale, Ḍhuṇḍhirāj Raṭāṭe, Nārāyaṇ Raṭāṭe (son), Śrīmāneśvar Jhā, Śukadev Jhā, Jagannāth Ghuḷe, etc. Pt. Raṭāṭe was a great scholar of the Ṛgveda and the AV. When Pt. S. D. Sātavaḷekar edited the Saṃhitās of the Ṛgveda and the AV, he consulted Pt. Raṭāṭe for the correct reading of the texts (Upādhyāy 1993: 707).

Pt. Śrīkṛṣṇa Dev

Pt. Śrīkṛṣṇa Dev belonged to the Ṛgveda and was one of the great Ṛgvedins of Varanasi. Dr. Viśvanāth Dev informed me that Pt. Śrīkṛṣṇa Dev also studied the AV and performed some Atharvavedic rites.

Pt. Jagannāth Śāstrī Pāṭhak

Jagannāth Śāstrī Pāṭhak was a scholar of the Ṛgveda, *vyākaraṇa* and *nyāya*. In his old age, he studied the entire Saṃhitā of the AV with Pt. Lele of Ayodhyā.

Pt. Nārāyaṇ Śāstrī Raṭāṭe

Pt. Rāmcandra Śāstrī's son Pt. Nārāyaṇ Śāstrī continued his tradition of the study of the AV. He too taught the AV at the Darbhaṅgā Vidyālaya. He wrote a brief history of the Darbhaṅgā Vidyālaya in which he gave a biographical sketch of Pt. Rāmcandra Śāstrī. He has edited and written some books on the AV ritual, the information about which is given below. He was honoured with the title Atharvavedamārtaṇḍa by the Kāśī Paṇḍita Sabhā in 1952 and with the title Vedapaṇḍita by the Uttar Pradesh Sanskrit Akademi for the year 1979–80. He has written about thirty research articles in Hindi and Sanskrit on Vedic topics. In 1984, the All India Radio of Varanasi made audio recordings of the recitation by Pt. Raṭāṭe. Guru Gaṅgeśvarānand Pratiṣṭhān of Nāsik made the video recording of his recitation of the Saṃhitā. The duration of this recording is 18 hours (Raṭāṭe 1988: 49).

Pt. Manoharlāl Dvivedī

Pt. Manoharlāl Dvivedī was the eldest son of Pt. Bhagavānīlāljī. He also studied the basic AV ritual, namely, the domestic *darśapūrṇamāsa* or *ājyatantra* and *pākatantra* with Pt. Jayadevāśram (personal communication from Dr. Dvivedī). He was the teacher of the AV at the Sāṅgaveda Vidyālaya and Saṃpūrṇānand Sanskrit University. Dr. Dvivedī has also written a book *Kātyāyanayajñapaddhativimarśa* on the ritual according to the *Kātyayanaśrautasūtra* (Upādhyāy 1993: 704).

3. THE RITUALISTIC TRADITION OF THE ATHARVAVEDA

As there was no community of Atharvavedins in Varanasi, there was not much scope for the performance of the AV ritual. Even in Gujarat, I observed that some of the AV priests studied the Śukla Yajurveda and performed some domestic rites for the persons belonging to that school. In Varanasi, Pt. Jayadevāśraṃ had performed some Atharvavedic rites for his patron Pt. Muralīlāljī Mehtā (Draviḍ 1936: 9). Pt. Rāmcandra Śāstrī Raṭāṭe had performed the *kuśakaṇḍikā* or the basic domestic ritual and *madhuparka* according to the AV for Śrī Rāmeśvar Siṃh, King of Darbhanga. I came to know from Pt. Viśvanāth Dev that his elder brother, Pt. Śrīkṛṣṇa Dev had performed some rites of the AV, the details of which are not available. It appears that some of the Atharvavedins in Varanasi were engaged in some sort of sorcery practices, particularly those connected with the *Pratyaṅgirākalpa*.

I have obtained a copy of one such manuscript from Dr. Viśvanāth Dev.

At present, there are very few Atharvavedins in Varanasi. Howard mentions three of them: Pt. Nārāyaṇ Śāstrī Raṭāṭe, Rāmcandra Āṭhavale and Gaṅgādhar Dev. Pt. Raṭāte passed away some years ago. Pt. Gaṅgādhar Dev is now a teacher of AV at the Saṃpūrṇānand Sanskrit University and engaged in the propagation of Sanskrit.

4. MANUSCRIPTS AND PUBLISHED BOOKS

There are several manuscripts belonging to the AV tradition available in Varanasi. The Sarasvatī Bhavan Library of the Saṃpūrṇānand Sanskrit University has several manuscripts of the *Śaunakasaṃhitā*, the *padapāṭha*, the *Gopathabrāhmaṇa*, the Prayogas and other works related to the AV. The library of the Sāṅgaveda Vidyālaya and the Viśvanātha Library of Śrī J. M. Goyaṅkā Vidyālaya also has some manuscripts. Besides, there are private collections belonging to the families of Pt. Raṭāṭe, Pt. Manoharlāl Dvivedī, Pt. Rāmcandra Śāstrī Āṭhavale, Pt. Śrīkṛṣṇa Dev and Dr. Viśvanāth Dev. Some of the manuscripts belonging to Pt. Sakhārām Vaidya are seen with Pt. Rāmcandra Śāstrī Āṭhavale's son, Śrī Haribhān Āṭhavale. However, it is very difficult to obtain exact information about the manuscripts in those collections. Dr. Viśvanāth Dev was very kind to show me some manuscripts of the *Pratyaṅgirākalpa* of the AV. Dr. Manoharlāl Dvivedī claimed that he possessed rare manuscripts of Atharvavedic works, but did not show them to me. Pt. Nārāyaṇ Śāstrī Raṭāṭe has published the *Pratyaṅgirāstotra* in the Śaunaka tradition and has written an article on the *Ātharvaṇaśānti*. In a short biographical sketch of Pt. Nārāyaṇ Śāstrī Raṭāṭe, W. K. Lele mentions that Pt. Raṭāṭe had prepared a press copy of his edition and translation of several Atharvavedic works, namely, the *Viniyogamālā*, the *Kauśikapaddhati* and the *Caturādhyāyī* and had corresponded with the Government of India in order to get them published (Raṭāṭe 1988: 41). It is not known whether these works were ever published. Pt. Nārāyaṇ Śāstrī announces the forthcoming publication of some unpublished rare works belonging to the Śaunaka *śākhā*: (1) *Gaṇasaṃhitā*, a collection of mantras employed in the *śāntika*, *pauṣṭika* and *ābhicārika* rites, and (2) *Bhaiṣajyādhyāya*, the fourth chapter (*kaṇḍikās* 25.1–32.27) of the *Kauśikasūtra*, dealing with remedies for various ailments.

The libraries and the personal collections have manuscripts of a number of Prayogas yet unpublished. A special mention must be made of the Prayogas of the *ājyatantra* and *pākatantra* and the *madhuparka* composed by Devabhadra Balabhadra Pāṭhaka who also has composed Prayogas of domestic ritual of the Sāmavedins. He calls himself 'an author of Prayogas' (*prayogakāra*) and describes these Prayogas following the *Kauśikasūtra*. He says, 'Since there are no Prayogas following the Sūtra, I have composed this Prayoga, quoting the *sūtras*' (Bahulkar 1978: 33). In his book *Kāśī yā Banāras*, Bālmukund Varmā mentions that Devabhadra Pāṭhaka composed in the 17th century commentaries on Śrauta and Smārta works and *Subodhinī*, a commentary on the *Vedāntasāra* (Varma 1935: 46). Devabhadra Pāṭhaka was a resident of Varanasi. Dr. Viśvanāth Dev informed me that Devabhadra Pāṭhaka's house was close to his own and was known in that vicinity as 'the house of Pāṭhakjī' (*pāṭhak jī kī havelī*). From the colophon at the end of the Prayoga of *madhuparka*, it appears that Devabhadra probably belonged to the Mādhyandina *śākhā* of the Śukla Yajurveda (Bahulkar 1978: 34).

Another work of special interest is the commentary *Bālabodhavivekinī* on the Hymn to Pratyaṅgirā (AV(Ś) 10.1). The author is Vāsudeva Dvivedī. There is also a commentary by the same author on a similar hymn, which does not belong to the AV(Ś), but is claimed to be from the Paippalāda *śākhā* of the AV (Bahulkar 2004: 16–17). The hymn does not belong to the extant Saṃhitā available in the Kashmirian as well as the Orissan transmissions of the AV(P), but bears affinity with a *khila* hymn in the Ṛgveda tradition (*Khilasūktāni*, *Ṛgvedasamhitā*, *adhyāya* 4, *khila* 5). Both of these commentaries are important, as there is no commentary of Sāyaṇa on the tenth *kāṇḍa* of the AV(Ś) to which the hymn to Pratyaṅgirā belongs. There are some manuscripts of these commentaries deposited in the Sarasvatī Bhavan Library, Sāṅgaveda Vidyālaya and private collections. It appears that the actual performance of sorcery was in vogue some decades ago and that the Atharvavedins in Varanasi possessed manuscripts of this commentary. There are also some other Prayogas devoted to *abhicāra*, with the titles *Āṅgirasakalpa*, *Pratyaṅgirākalpa*, *Pratyaṅgirāsūktavidhāna*, *Kṛtyānirhaṇasūktavyākhyā*, etc.

These remarks would show that the tradition of the AV in Varanasi was never a genuine one. There were hardly any Atharvavedins who belonged to that Veda by birth, with the exception of one or two. Most of the Atharvavedins belonged to the Ṛgveda or the Śukla Yajurveda and hailed from Maharashtra or Gujarat. As Howard rightly points out, there is close similarity between the recitation of the Maharashtrian Ṛgveda and that of the Atharvaveda. The pandits from Maharashtra and Gujarat made efforts to re-establish the tradition of the Atharvaveda in Varanasi out of genuine love for that Veda and also to fulfil professional needs. Their efforts had not been brought to light so far. I hope that the information presented here will be useful for further research.

REFERENCES

AV = *Atharvavedasaṃhitā*. Edited by S. D. Sātavaḷekar. Pārḍī: Svādhyāy maṇḍal, 1957.

Atharva-Veda Saṃhitā. Trans. by W. D. Whitney. (HOS, 7–8.) Cambridge, Mass.: Harvard University Press, 1905.

BAHULKAR, S. S. 1978. The Prayoga-dīpa of Devabhadra: a brief survey. *Journal of the University of Poona*, Humanities Section, 43: 31–35.

—— 2004. The apocryphal (?) hymn to Pratyaṅgirā. In: Arlo Griffiths & Jan E. M. Houben (eds.), *The Vedas. Texts, Language and Ritual. Proceedings of the Third International Vedic Workshop, Leiden, 2002*: 15–22. Groningen: Egbert Forsten.

CHANDRAMOULI, K. 1995. *Kashi: The City Luminous*. Calcutta: Rupa and Co.

DRAVIḌ, Rājeśvar Śāstrī (ed.) 1936. *Śrī Vallabharām Śāligrām Sāṅgaveda Vidyālay kā ṣoḍaś vārṣik vivaraṇ*. Varanasi: Muralīlāl Mehtā & Giridhārīlāl Mehtā.

HOWARD, Wayne 1986. *Veda Recitation in Vārāṇasī*. Delhi: MLBD.

KĀLVINṬ, D. V. 1968. Kāśī kī vaidik evaṃ śrautādi paramparā. In: Phaḍke 1968: 141–160.

KAVIRĀJ, Gopīnāth 1965. *Kāśī kī sārasvat sādhanā*. Patna: Bihār rāṣṭrabhāṣā pariṣad.

MOTĪCANDRA 1985. *Kāśī kā itihās*. Varanasi: Viśvavidyālaya prakāśan.

PHAḌKE, Anant Śāstrī (ed.) 1968. *Caturvedavid-agnihotri-śrīmad-rāmacandra-raṭāṭe-mahodayānāṃ smṛtigranthaḥ*. Varanasi: Śrī-vedamūrti-raṭāṭe-smṛtigrantha-prakāśana-samiti.

RAṬĀṬE, Nārāyaṇ Śāstrī 1988. *Kāśīstha Nigamāgama Darbhaṅgā Vidyālay kā saṃkṣipt itihās evam ātharvaṇaśāntiḥ*. Varanasi: Śrī Sītārāmcandra (Raṭāṭe) smṛti lekhamālā prakāśan.

SĀHNĪ, Dayā Rām 1917–18. Chandravati plates of Chandra-Deva: V.S. 1150 and 1156. *Epigraphia Indica* 14: 192–209.

ŚĀSTRĪ, Haraprasād 1912. Dakshini pandits at Benares. *The Indian Antiquary* 41: 7–13.

SHERRING, Matthew Atmore 1868. *Benares. The Sacred City of the Hindus in Ancient and Modern Timès*. London: Trubner & Co.

SUKUL, Kuber Nath 1974. *Varanasi Down the Ages*. Patna: Kameshwar Nath Sukul.

UPĀDHYĀY, Baladev 1993. *Kāśī kī pāṇḍitya paramparā*. Varanasi: Viśvavidyālaya prakāśan.

VARMĀ, Bālmukund 1935. *Kāśī yā Banāras. Silver Jubilee of His Majesty the King Emperor Souvenir Volume*. Banaras: Bālmukund Varmā.

Some Forgotten Scholars in Prātiśākhyas and Śikṣās

DIDHITI BISWAS

INTRODUCTION

A number of famed grammarians are known to have had different approaches on various linguistic issues. Yet one feels confused about these rules and their application. The available quotations of these grammarians are scattered in ancient texts, and their collection and the correlation of the rules remain interesting tasks. One can observe that these scholars form schools, which follow particular sets of rules and that they defend these rules in their own ways. Scholars can be considered as forgotten if they are either associated with rules that are not familiar or not much used, or are referred to by name only in texts that contain rules similar to theirs, and besides not a single text attributed to these scholars has come down to us. In this paper an attempt is made to list and study the opinions and prescriptions of some such forgotten scholars found in Prātiśākhyas and Śikṣās.

ŚĀKAṬĀYANA

Among the scholars studied in this paper, Śākaṭāyana is the only one referred to in all the available Prātiśākhyas. He is quoted in the *Ṛkprātiśākhya* (ṚP 1.16) in the discourse of optional views regarding the terminal sound of a *pada*. It was one of the controversial issues in the Prātiśākhyas that involves much debate. Śākaṭāyana prefers the first and the fifth mute as the final sound. In this connection the ṚP (1.15) does not fail to quote the opinion of Gārgya, who wants the last and the third mute to be the final sound. The *Atharvavedaprātiśākhya* (AVPr 1.8) in its discussion of this issue says that Śaunaka wants the first and the third mute to be the last sound.

According to Śākaṭāyana, the first half of all the four diphthongs is *a*, and its combination with *i*, *u*, *ī* and *ū* produces *e*, *o*, *ai* and *au* (ṚP 13.39). He also teaches that the *visarjanīya* when followed by one of the first two labials becomes the *upadhmānīya*, and when followed by one of the first two gutturals is changed into the *jihvāmūlīya* (*Vājasaneyiprātiśākhya* 3.12). Śākaṭāyana observes that the *visarjanīya* becomes homogeneous with the following sibilants *ś*, *ṣ* and *s* (VP 3.9). Śākalya deviates from him, being in favour of an unchanged *visarjanīya* before sibilants (VP 3.10). Later Pāṇini (P 8.3.36) combines these two views in the sūtra *vā śari*.

Along with Kāśyapa, Śākaṭāyana recommends the elision of *m* and *n* in sandhi when followed by *r* or any sibilant and the nasalisation of the penultimate vowel (VP 4.4). The ṚP (4.7) and the *Āśvalāyanaśrautasūtra* (1.2.17) allow this sandhi in the case of semivowels (*y*, *l*, *v*) only. Pāṇini recommends this optionally (P 8.4.29 *vā padāntasya*).

The Prātiśākhyas in general recommend the elision of final *y* or *v* followed by a vowel barring a few exceptional cases. These *y* or *v* form part of the syllables *ay*, *āy*, *av*, *āv*, the converted forms of *e*, *ai*, *o* and *au*. Śākaṭāyana here comments that *y* and *v* are not totally omitted but are pronounced indistinctly (AVPr 2.24). The same observation is attributed to Śākaṭāyana by Pāṇini also (P 8.3.18 *vyorlaghuprajatnatarah śākaṭāyanasya*). The *Taittirīyaprātiśākhya* (TP 10.23) attributes the same view to Vātsapra, whose name is only once mentioned in the Prātiśākhyas and Śikṣās. Śākaṭāyana probably was in favour of the elision as he comments that the *v* of *asau* is not dropped before a vowel not having the same place of articulation (VP 4.127). This elision, according to Pāṇini, is recommended by Śākalya (P 8.3.19 *lopaḥ śākalyasya*). Actually this issue invites a great debate among scholars of different schools. The TP wants the elision if the *y* and *v* is preceded by *a*. Mācākīya prefers the elision if the *y* and *v* are followed by *u* or *o* only (TP 10.22). Sāṃkṛtya modifies this rule as he prescribes the elision of *v* only (TP 10.21), but Ukhya is completely against any elision (TP 10.20).

The opinion of Śākaṭāyana is also found recorded in VP 4.191, in the context of the *kramapāṭha*, where this scholar holds that *su* joined to the next word should be repeated with *iti* in *krama*.

Yāska (1.12) refers to Śākaṭāyana as a grammarian when he introduces the different conflicting opinions regarding the radical origin of all the substantives: *tatra sarvāṇi nāmāny ākhyātajānīti śākaṭāyanaḥ nairuktasamayaś ca*. The connective particle *ca* indicates that Śākaṭāyana belonged to the school of grammar. In the following section he is also referred to as establishing his own view with examples. Śākaṭāyana is also quoted as opposing the current view of the Nirukta school that the prepositions do carry their meanings independently: 1.3 *na nirvaddhā upasargā arthān nirāhur iti śākaṭāyanaḥ*.

Śākaṭāyana's personality no doubt enjoyed a respectable position in the Vedāṅga literature as his opinions are often referred to in Prātiśākhyas of different Vedas. Even on one and the same issue, he prescribes different rules for different Vedas, as we saw in the case of the elision of *v*. His observations on various issues being respectfully remembered and collected by Yāska and Pāṇini also indicates his great command of the different schools. However, in all probability all these Śākaṭāyanas are not one and the same person, so one may take his name as a patronymic. In that case all the various Śākaṭāyanas repeatedly referred to in the singular may be understood to be followers of a school of grammar and phonetics founded by one Śākaṭāyana. The ascription of the

Uṇādisūtras to this school and its acceptance by Pāṇini support also this assumption.

ŚĀKALA AND ŚĀKALYA

Two other names of authorities which one often comes across are Śākala and Śākalya. The ṚP occasionally refers to these two names, while the *Vājasaneyiprātiśākhya* once refers to Śākalya alone. Probably they signify two different authorities, who however belonged to one and the same tradition. The word Śākala is known as a school of the Ṛgveda, and the observations going by this name probably indicate rules to be followed in this school. These Śākala statements are enlisted below.

1) The followers of the Śākala school recommends that words ending in *a*, *ā*, *ṛ*, *ṝ*, *i*, *ī*, *u*, *ū* and not designated as *pragṛhya* become nasalised and prolated with three moras (ṚP 1.64). In this connection the opinions of Śāṅkhāyana and Kāṇḍamāyana recorded in the TP (15.7) can be mentioned. These two scholars recommend nasalised pronunciation of a prolated *samānākṣara* (but not *pragṛhya*) as a final. Śāṅkhāyana is a well-known personality of the Ṛgvedic school, but he is not referred to as a grammarian in the *Ṛkprātiśākhya*: the single grammatical observation ascribed to him and noted above occurs in the Prātiśākhya of the Taittirīya school of the Black Yajurveda.

2) According to the Śākala school, the single *u* is *pragṛhya* and when it is connected with *iti*, it becomes nasalised and long: *ū ity ū̐* (ṚP 1.75).

3) Challenging the view of ṚP 6.1 that a consonant is repeated after a vowel, Śākala observes that a conjunct after a long vowel is not repeated (ṚP 6.14).

4) The pronunciation of *l* before a sibilant is indistinct (ṚP 6.20) and it should be separately pronounced (ṚP 6.24). This rule means that before uttering the sibilant one should pause and

then pronounce the *l* indistinctly. This way of pronunciation was followed by some as an alternative while pronouncing a conjunct, irrespective of the quality of the sound concerned (ṚP 6.27).

5) If two successive changes occur in a chain reaction in the *kramapāṭha*, then ignoring the usual rule that two words are to be uttered at a time, one should utter four words; for instance, *u du ṣu ṇaḥ* (ṚP 11.19). Gārgya, however, prefers the repetition of three words at a time (ṚP 11.26).

6) In the *saṃhitāpāṭha*, occasional changes like metrical lengthening take place in words. Some scholars prefer to restore the original form of the word and combine it with the following words in the *kramapāṭha*. Some others utter the word unchanged and then restore the original form adding *iti* after it. According to the Śākala school, however, the word is not only to be restored but to be repeated with *iti* as well (ṚP 11.61).

The name of Śākalya is well-known in Vedic texts. Traditionally he is taken to be the maker of the *Ṛgvedapadapāṭha*. Interestingly, none of the views attributed to Śākalya in the ṚP and the VP concern the *padapāṭha* rules, whereas Śākala makes a number of comments on this topic.

Regarding the accent, Śākalya and other scholars observed that a *pracaya* accent, if followed by an acute or circumflex, becomes grave (ṚP 3.22). This phenomenon is recorded in Pāṇini's rule 8.4.67 in a slightly different way: *nodāttasvaritodayamagārgya-kāśyapagālavānām*. According to this rule, Gārgya, Kāśyapa and Gālava think that a grave accent following an acute will always become a circumflex, irrespective of the following accent. Āgniveśyāyana quoted in TP 14.32 agrees with these views recorded by Pāṇini.

In regard to the consonant sandhi, Śākalya says that *n* and *t* followed by *ś* become *ñ* and *c* respectively, while *ś* remains unchanged (ṚP 4.13).

ṚP 4.4 records an observation attributed to the father of Śākalya (Śākalyapitā), according to which *ś* preceded by the first mute becomes *ch*. Disagreeing with Śākaṭāyana, Śākalya opines that the *visarjanīya* remains unchanged before *ś*, *ṣ* and *s* (VS 3.10). Śākalya Sthavira observed that *a* after *e* and *o* should be pronounced as *e* and *o* respectively (ṚP 2.8).

References to Śākala and Śākalya occur in various Brāhmaṇa texts, where they are great personalities, but not specifically grammarians. Śākalya's views concerning symbolic interpretation of the *saṃhitā* are recorded in the *Aitareya-Āraṇyaka* (3.1.2) and the *Śāṅkhāyana-Āraṇyaka* (7.3). Another important reference to Śākalya is in Yāska's *Nirukta* 6.28, where this father of the Padapāṭha is criticised for incorrectly splitting up the single word *vāyo*. Pāṇini records five of Śākalya's observations in his rules. One of them concerns the *padapāṭha*: P 1.1.16 *sambuddhau śākalyasyetāv anārṣe*. The other opinions of the grammarian Śākalya recorded by Pāṇini are not attributed to him in any of the earlier texts. Nevertheless it is clear that this great grammarian and before him the authors or compilers of the Prātiśākhyas rated high the opinions of the grammatical tradition that was associated with the name of Śākalya. The antiquity of this school is indicated by such authority names as Sthavira Śākalya and Śākalyapitā. Apart from the Padapāṭha, no grammatical text of this school is available now, but its importance is clear from all the references mentioned above. It will not be out of place to mention that Śākalya is mentioned in the *Āśvalāyanagṛhyasūtra* (3.4.4) among the 33 teachers to whom water libations are to be offered.

ŚAUNAKA

Śaunaka was a historical person, and many texts are ascribed to him. Tradition considers him to be the author of the ṚP, of the fifth chapter of the *Aitareya-Āraṇyaka* and of the *Āśvalāyanaśrautasūtra*. Opinions that go by the name of Śaunaka are twice quoted in non-Ṛgvedic Prātiśākhyas. One is in the AVPr (1.8); it concerns the final sound of a word and has already been discussed above. The other one in the VP (4.120) relates to the euphonic combination. According to Śaunaka, a first class mute is changed into a second class mute when the following sound is *ś*, *ṣ* or *s*, but not of the same position. Thus *anuṣṭup śāradī* is changed into *anuṣṭuph śāradī*, but *tat savituḥ* remains unchanged as *t* and *s* are both dentals. This view of Śaunaka has found full support from Bāḍabhīkāra, a less-known scholar quoted in TP 14.13, as he differs from the Taittirīya opinion, which does not retain the condition of *asamānasthāna*.

GĀRGYA

Gārgya is referred to in the *Ṛkprātiśākhya* only. His opinion regarding the terminal sound of a word (ṚP 1.15) has already been discussed above. Gārgya allows anaptyxis in some particular cases. The ṚP (6.33) observes that if the first mute is followed by the fifth mute, then the first one is repeated and that is called *yama*. According to Gārgya, anaptyxis takes place somewhat resembling the *ṛkāra* after this repetition (ṚP 6.36).

Yāska in *Nirukta* 1.12 refers to Gārgya as a preceptor of the Nirukta school, who does not advocate the theory of radical origin of all substantives. Yāska also quotes Gārgya's opinion that the prepositions have their own meanings (1.3).

Pāṇini also refers to Gārgya in three of his sūtras. But Gārgya is a very common name in the entire Vedic literature. The reference to it in various contexts from ritual to grammar indicates that this school trotted a vast area.

VYĀḌI

Vyāḍi is three times quoted in the ṚP. In one of these cases he prescribes the mode of pronouncing the *anusvāra*: either through the mouth and nose, or through the nose only (ṚP 13.37). The other two observations are related with accent. When a word is repeated being connected with *iti* in *padapāṭha* or *kramapāṭha*, then the grave accent of that word will not be changed into *pracaya* after the circumflex of *i*, but will remain grave (ṚP 3.23). Vyāḍi remarks that while the prolation of *upari svid āsīt* (ṚV 10.129.5) and *bhīr iva vindatī* (ṚV 10.146.1) is recited, the last mora is to be recited as acute (ṚP 3.28).

The name Vyāḍi is not found in any other Vedic text, but it is associated with a book called 'Saṃgraha', which is basically a review of Pāṇini's sūtras in 100,000 verses. Vyāḍi is known to have composed also Vikṛtipāṭha, a very small treatise on the various modes of reciting Vedic mantras. It is difficult to ascertain if there is any relation between the Vyāḍi of the ṚP and the Vyāḍi of Saṃgraha and Vikṛtipāṭha.

JĀTŪKARṆYA

Jātūkarṇya, a well-known ritualist of the Ṛgvedic school is referred to three times in the VP. According to Jātūkarṇya, the two words *pārāvātān* and *āgnimāruta* are separated with *avagraha* in *padapāṭha* (VP 5.22). This scholar is connected with the rule *kaśyapasyānārṣeye* (VP 4.158). According to the commentator, this means that the elision of *y* and the doubling of *ś* result in *ch* in the word *kaśyapa* when its sense is not that of a sage. This raises the question, did *kaśyapa* originally carry the meaning of *kacchapa*, that is, 'tortoise'. In VP 4.123, Jātūkarṇya observes that in a conjunct, *h* remains unchanged if it is followed by *ṛ* and preceded by a mute other than the fifth one. The commentator adds that the preceding sound is also not changed into the third class.

One Jātūkarṇya, the son of Kātyāyanī, is quoted in the *Śāṅkhāyana-Āraṇyaka* (8.10) commenting that the splendour of the *vīṇā* is the *saṃhitā*. The Āraṇyaka text explains that the skilled playing of *vīṇā* is just like the utterance of speech by a skilled speaker. The Kāṇva recension of the *Bṛhadāraṇyaka-Upaniṣad* (2.6.3; 4.6.3) records Jātūkarṇya as a pupil of Āsurāyaṇa and Yāska. In the Mādhyandina recension of the *Bṛhadāraṇyaka-*

Upaniṣad (2.5.21; 4.5.27) he is a student of Bhāradvāja. Actually Jātūkarṇya was a common patronymic (it denotes a 'descendant of Jātūkarṇa'), and there were many Jātūkarṇyas. Vedic texts quoted off and on these scholars with different identities; some of them were ritualists, some grammarians.

MĀṆḌUKEYA

The opinion of Māṇḍukeya is quoted once only in the Prātiśākhyas, and that in the ṚP in connection with the accent of *praśliṣṭasandhi*. According to Śākalya, in the *praśliṣṭasandhi* of *i* and in the *kṣaiprasandhi* and *abinihitasandhi*, if the preceding vowel is acute and the following one is grave, then the combined accent will be circumflex (ṚP 3.13). The Māṇḍukeyas accept the circumflex in principle in all types of *praśliṣṭasandhi*, but do not actually pronounce it so (ṚP 3.14 *māṇḍukeyasya sarveṣu praśliṣṭeṣu tathā smaret*). Probably due to their deep respect of the tradition, they continue to pronounce it as acute, but they cannot deny the legitimacy of the circumflex.

The views of the Māṇḍukeya school regarding the philosophical and symbolical interpretation of *saṃhitā* are mentioned in the *Aitareya-Āraṇyaka* (3.1.1). Different scholars of the same family maintained different opinions and the Āraṇyaka texts do not miss to quote them. Thus we come across the views of Śauravīra (AiĀ 3.1.1) and his son Dīrgha (ŚĀ 7.2), and also of Hrasva Māṇḍukeya (AiĀ 3.2.1; ŚĀ 8.1), who makes an important observation regarding the different types of sounds. The views of the Māṇḍukeyas seem to have been widely accepted in their time, since the famous preceptor Sthavira Śākalya agreed with Hrasva Māṇḍukeya about the symbolization of *saṃhitā* propagated by the Māṇḍukeya school (AiĀ 3.2.6).

Hrasva Māṇḍukeya notes that there is a space between the former and the latter half of a euphonic combination in the shape of the accent and mora of these two sounds. Madhyama, the son of Hrasva Māṇḍukeya and Pratībodhī, says that the combination of mora and different accents should be done perfectly following the rules (AiĀ 3.1.5).

All these references indicate that the school of Māṇḍukeya, though only once referred to in the ṚP, represented a well-known grammatical tradition of the Ṛgveda. The *Aitareya-Āraṇyaka* spent two complete chapters (AiĀ 3.1.1 and 5) to the views of different scholars of this school on the discourse of grammar, though in a philosophical fashion.

UKHYA, UTTAMOTTAMĪYA, SĀṂKṚTYA

The observations of Ukhya, Uttamottamīya and Sāṃkṛtya are recorded in the TP. The opinions of these three scholars are associated with some specific words. Ukhya holds that the *ai* of the word *raṃkhai* should be pronounced with excessive effort (TP 16.24). Elsewhere, Ukhya says that the word *eṣṭaḥ* becomes *eṣṭu* before *r* (TP 8.22), while according to Sāṃkṛtya it should be *eṣṭo* (TP 8.21) and Uttamottamīya prefers the form *eṣṭa* (TP 8.20).

Recoding of observations by different preceptors on one and the same issue indicates the existence of different schools of the Black Yajurveda. Keith in the preface of his *Taittirīyasaṃhitā* translation (Keith 1914: xc) says that the Taittirīyas appear to be a separate school with two subdivisions, the Aukhīyas and the Khāṇḍikīyas. I would like to suggest that Ukhya might belong to the Aukhīya school. This hypothesis can perhaps be confirmed if manuscript of this school are found.

ŚAITYĀYANA, ĀTREYA AND OTHERS

The TP records the controversy among some scholars regarding such basic points as the pronunciation of vowels and consonants. According to Śaityāyana, special effort should be made in uttering all kinds of sounds (TP 17.7). Ātreya on the other hand says that a syllable should be uttered neither very distinctly nor very indistinctly (TP 17.8).

Another observation by Ātreya is quoted in the discussion of sandhi. According to this scholar, when the final *n* or *m* of the preceding word becomes *l*, then the vowel preceding the *l* becomes nasalised (TP 5.31 *uttamalabhāt pūrvo 'nunāsika ity ātreyaḥ*).

Ātreya is a patronymic derived from Atri. In the *Śatapatha-brāhmaṇa* (4.3.4.21), Atri appears as the Hotṛ, so the descandants of this *ṛṣi* are supposed to belong to the school of the Ṛgveda. In the *Bṛhadāraṇyaka-Upaniṣad* (2.6.3; 4.6.3), Ātreya is the pupil of Māṇṭi. In the Kāṇḍānukrama, Ātreya is referred to as a branch of the Taittirīya school, and Keith (1914: xxxiii) remarks that 'there is no reason to suppose that the Ātreya of the Kāṇḍānukrama is not the Ātreya of the Prātiśākhya, though of course no absolute proof of identity can be expected'. It might be proved if an Ātreya *śākhā* of the Yajurveda could be found.

In the utterance of the *anusvāra* and other nasal sounds, Śaityāyana recommends stronger nasal quality (TP 17.1). The son of Kauhalī (Kauhalīputra) says that the utterance will be the same everywhere, which probably means that no extra effort should be made for the nasalisation of these sounds (TP 17.3). Bhāradvāja observes that the utterance of the *anusvāra* should be soft (TP 17.3). This is the only occasion where Bhāradvāja, a very popular name in the entire Vedic literature, is referred to as a grammarian.

Regarding the accent of *o* of *om*, the most significant word in the Veda, the opinions of the authorities differ. Vālmīki thinks that it should be acute (TP 18.6), Plākṣi and Plākṣāyaṇa prefer it to be circumflex (TP 18.5), Kauṇḍinya takes it to be dhṛtapracaya (TP 18.3), while Śaityāyana is liberal in this context as he says it can be any one of the acute, grave and circumflex accents (TP 18.2). The word *dhṛtapracaya* in Kauṇḍinya's quoted view is a bit confusing, as it is explained as the fourth musical note in the *Tribhāṣyaratna* and as the third musical note in the *Vaidikābharaṇa*. This explanation in turn anew opens up the question whether the Vedic accent is pitch or stress.

PAUṢKARASĀDI

Pauṣkarasādi is a well-known name in the TP, being mentioned five times in this text. Pauṣkarasādi advocates uttering the circumflex and *vikrama* with great effort (TP 17.6). The TP (19.1) designates as *vikrama* the low tone (*nīca*) between two acutes, between two circumflexes or between an acute and a circumflex. Kauṇḍinya holds that the low tone also becomes *vikrama* when a *pracaya* precedes (TP 19.2).

According to Kauṇḍinya, a mute is doubled in pronunciation when it follows a *l* or *v* (TP 14.2). So *kalpa* becomes *kalppa* according to this scholar. Pauṣkarasādi holds that *l* following a *prakṛtasvara* is converted into *ḍ* (TP 13.6), e.g., *mṛḍāṭīdṛśe*. The commentators think that the reference to Pauṣkarasādi is out of respect and not to show any optional view.

The scope of conversion of *ś* into *ch* while *ś* is preceded by a mute is limited by Pauṣkarasādi, as he notes that this conversion does not take place if the *ś* is followed by a consonant (TP 5.37). Vālmīki, in any case, prohibits this conversion when the preceding mute is *p* (TP 5.36). It may be noted that traditionally a vyākaraṇa text is ascribed to Vālmīki.

Pauṣkarasādi is not mentioned in other Vedic texts, except in the *Śāṅkhāyana-Āraṇyaka* (7.8) in connection with the symbolic interpretation of sandhi. Probably this scholar and his followers were chiefly grammarians belonging to the Yajurveda, who did not miss the chance to philosophise grammatical rules, finding eventually a place in the ŚĀ too on account of their wide acceptability. Later Kātyāyana as well in his Vārtika refers to one Pauṣkarasādi (*cayo dvitīyāḥ śari pauṣkarasāder iti vācyam*).

PLĀKṢI AND PLĀKṢĀYAṆA

There are three references to Plākṣi and Plākṣāyaṇa as jointly maintaining the same view. Their observations regarding the accent of *om* (TP 18.5) have been mentioned above (see Śaityāyani).

According to the TP (14.1), a consonant preceded by a vowel and followed by another consonant becomes doubled. These two scholars deviate a little from this view, as according to them, this doubling does not take place if the preceding consonant is a spirant and the following consonant is a first mute (TP 14.17). They prohibit the conversion of the *visarjanīya* into a spirant when it is followed by a guttural or labial mute or a sibilant (TP 9.6). Āgniveśa and Vālmīki prohibit this conversion only when the *visarjanīya* is followed by a guttural or a labial mute (TP 9.4). Kāṇḍamāyaṇa observes that the *visarjanīya* is dropped when it is followed by a spirant that is immediately followed by a surd sound (TP 9.1).

The views of Plākṣi and Plākṣāyaṇa differ only once in the TP, and that regarding the pronunciation of a spirant surd and a mute together. Plākṣi says that after a spirant surd followed by a surd is inserted a first mute of the same position as the following surd (TP 14.10 *aghoṣe plākṣeḥ*), e.g., *niṣkkevalya*. According to Plākṣāyaṇa, this insertion takes place only when the following sound is the fifth mute (TP 14.11 *uttamaparāt tu plākṣāyaṇasya*), e.g., *snāti* > *stnāti*. Another interpretation of this sūtra is that the insertion occurs when a sonant spirant is followed by a fifth mute, e.g., *ahnām* > *ahtnām*.

The *Taittirīya-Āraṇyaka* (1.7.2) tells of one Śaptakarṇa that his name was Plākṣi and that he saw seven suns. Plākṣi means 'son of Plakṣa', while Plākṣāyaṇa denotes a 'follower of Plākṣi'. Hence it is but natural that Plākṣi and Plākṣāyaṇa would agree on most points. The single case of a difference in opinion might be due to the influence of local pronunciation, possibly suggesting their settlement in different places.

STHAVIRA KAUṆḌINYA

Some quotations of Kauṇḍinya in the TP and their contexts have already been communicated earlier in this paper. One Sthavira Kauṇḍinya is cited in connection with the nasalisation. According to this scholar, when *n* is converted into *r* or into a sibilant, or into y which is later omitted, and when *m* is dropped, the preceding vowel becomes nasalised, and this nasalisation becomes successively more and more distinct in each of these cases (TP 17.4). Kauṇḍinya is associated with the Yajurveda alone. Probably the Kauṇḍinyas were popular in this school, as Kauṇḍinya's opinions are quoted four times in the TP. According to the *Bṛhadāraṇyaka-Upaniṣad* (2.6.1), Kauṇḍinya was the disciple of Śāṇḍilya.

KĀṆVA

The name Kāṇva is mostly associated with the Yajurveda, and a school of this Veda is ascribed to Kāṇva. Other Vedic texts also do not miss a chance to refer to the views of this scholar in connection with different rituals. Among the Prātiśākhyas it is only the VP that records opinions of Kaṇva, in connection with the accent. According to Kāṇva, when a grave precedes a circumflex, the reciter indicates it with the oblique position of his hand (VP 1.123). In another comment, Kāṇva says that when *iti* is followed by a word that has an acute accent in the middle or at the end, the word is pronounced as *tiryaññīca*, i.e., grave (VP 1.149).

DĀLBHYA

Dālbhya or Dārbhya, a patronymic meaning 'descendant of Dalbha or Darbha', occurs mostly in Sāmavedic texts, in ritualistic contexts. In the single reference to this scholar in the VP (4.15), he does not approve of the insertion of *k* and *t* between *ṅ* and *s* and *t* and *s* respectively. This insertion is recommended not only in the VP (4.14), but also in the AVPr (2.9) and the TP (5.32–33). Pāṇini (P 8.3.28) prescribes such an insertion optionally.

HĀRITA

Hārita is referred to only once in the TP. This text prescribes that a consonant is doubled when preceded by a vowel and followed by another consonant (TP 14.1). Hārita reduces the scope of this rule by noting the a surd spirant is not doubled (TP 14.18), for instance in *vaiśya*, *manuṣyānām*, *asya*. Hārita is a patronymic derived from Harita, and Harita is quoted in the *Yājñavalkyaśikṣā* (101).

SOME SCHOLARS MENTIONED IN THE ŚIKṢĀS

In the *Nāradaśikṣā* (2.3.8) a teacher called Somaśarman notes that a mora (*mātrā*) should be measured according to the accents of a *ṛkmantra*. The same text (2.8.5) quotes another teacher, Audabrajin, who prescribes shoots of the trees *khadira*, *kadamba*, *karavīra* and *karañja* for brushing the teeth. The *Nāradaśikṣā* (1.7.17) introduces Nārada as the originator of the musical note *pañcama* and Tumburu as that of *dhaivata* and *niṣāda*. Nārada, Tumburu, Vasiṣṭha and Viśvavārā are said not to have determined specific rules for *sāman* notes due to their difficult character.

The *Pāṇinīyaśikṣā* (56) names one Dākṣīputra as a preceptor who received the knowledge from Śaṅkara. The *Yājñavalkyaśikṣā* records the names of some predecessors but not their opinions. According to this text (4), the acute accent belongs to Bhāradvāja, the grave to Gautama, and the circumflex to Gārgya. Similarly, the *ākhyāta* belongs to the Bhāradvājagotra, the *nāma* to the Bhārgavagotra, the *upasarga* to the Vāsiṣṭhagotra, and the *nipāta* to the Kāśyapagotra.

CONCLUSION

From the above discussion it emerges that the two most debatable points in the Prātiśākhyas involved as many as five divergent opinions. These two points were (1) the status of *y* and *v* as parts of *ay*, *āy*, *av* and *āv* in sandhi (AVPr, TP), and (2) the accent of *om* (TP).

Other points where at least three different opinions are mentioned are (1) the final sounds of a word (ṚP, AVPr), (2) the utterance of nasals (VP, ṚP, TP), (3) the conversion of the *vi-*

sarjanīya into a spirant (TP), and (4) one particular case of sandhi: *eṣṭaḥ rāya* (TP).

Two authorities are consulted on two points: (1) the conversion of *ś* into *ch* (TP) and (2) the position of *pracaya* followed by a circumflex and acute (ṚP, TP).

Among the Prātiśākhyas it is the *Taittirīyaprātiśākhya* that most frequently records the views of different scholars. In fact all the rules but one in the 17th chapter of this text record observations made by different scholars. The TP refers to 21 authorities, the ṚP to 8, the VP to 7, and the AVPr to just 2. Of all the scholars it is Śākaṭāyana who is respectfully mentioned in all the Prātiśākhyas. Śākalya is mentioned in the ṚP and the VP. Other authorities quoted in the Prātiśākhyas are confined to one text only, and some of them are mentioned just once. Thus Uttamottamīya, Kāṇḍamāyana, Kauhala, Plākṣāyaṇa, Bāḍabhīkāra, Vyāḍi, Śaityāyana, Śāṃkṛtya and Vātsapra do not occur in any available text other than the TP, and Uttamottamīya, Bāḍabhīkāra, Gautama, Bhāradvāja, Mācākīya, Vātsapra, Śāṅkhāyana and Hārita are mentioned in the TP just once, and so is Dālbhya in the VP.

The mention of so many scholars by name in the Prātiśākhyas and Śikṣās clearly shows that linguistic study had separate importance among the academic circles of the society in India at least two thousand years ago. Some of these names are found in various Brāhmaṇa texts as well, in connection with specific ritualistic points. But we need not think that the persons were identical only on account of the identity of their names. It is a common problem with the teachers of the Veda. It is also difficult to associate them with a particular Veda. Actually there was a time when the students studied all the Vedas, irrespective of their lineage. Later they were left with the option of studying any three, two or at least one Veda, according to their ability and will. So the association of a name like Śākaṭāyana with different Vedas probably indicates his earlier date.

The scholars referred to in different Prātiśākhyas and Śikṣās are quite numerous. Their works have been quoted in ancient texts in a wide number of contexts, but the original works from which these quotations were taken could not be traced. So in a way present-day researchers have to depend on ancient but basically secondary sources and on their relatively scanty references to have some idea of these lost works. These scholars are forgotten in that sense. But there is no doubt that the study of these quotations of the Prātiśākhyas and Śikṣās helps to trace missing lines in the history of grammar.

REFERENCES

AiĀ = *Aitareya-Āraṇyaka*. See Keith 1909.

AVPr = *Atharvavedaprātiśākhya*. See Whitney 1862.

BISWAS, Didhiti (ed. & trans.) 2000. *Nāradīyā Śikṣā (with Bengali Translation and Annotation)*. Kolkata.

KEITH, Arthur Berriedale 1908. *The Śāṅkhāyana Āraṇyaka. With an Appendix on the Mahāvrata.* (Oriental Translation Fund, New Series, 18.) London: The Royal Asiatic Society.

—— (ed.) 1909. *The Aitareya Āraṇyaka. Edited from the Manuscripts in the India Office and the Library of the Royal Asiatic Society, with Introduction, Translation, Notes, Indexes and an Appendix Containing the Portion hitherto Unpublished of the Śāṅkhāyana Āraṇyaka.* (Anecdota Oxoniensia, Aryan Series, 9.) Oxford: Clarendon Press.

—— 1914. *The Veda of the Black Yajus School Entitled Taittirīya Sanhitā translated*, I–II. (HOS, 18–19.) Cambridge, Mass.: Harvard University Press.

RANGACHARYA, P. K., & R. SHAMA SASTRI (eds.) 1906. *The Taittirīya-Prātiśākhya with the Commentaries of Somayārya and Gārgya Gopālayajvan.* (Bibliotheca Sanskrita, 33.) Mysore: Government Branch Press. [Reprinted with an introduction by J. L. Shastri as: R. Shama Sastri & P. K. Rangacharya (eds.), *The Taittirīya-Prātiśākhya with the Commentaries Tribhāṣyaratna and Vaidikābharaṇa*. Delhi: Motilal Banarsidass, 1985.]

RASTOGI, Indu (ed.) 1967. *The Śuklayajuḥ-Prātiśākhya of Kātyāyana. Critically edited from Original Manuscripts with English Translation of the Text.* (The Kashi Sanskrit Series, 179.) Varanasi: The Chowkhamba Sanskrit Series Office.

RP = *Ṛkprātiśākhya*. See Śastrī 1931 and Vyāsa & Śarmā 1903.

ŚĀ = *Śāṅkhāyana-Āraṇyaka*. See Keith 1908.

ŚASTRĪ, Maṅgaladeva (ed.) 1931. *Śrīśaunakīyam ṛgvedaprātiśākhyam with the Commentary of Uvaṭa.* Allahabad: The Indian Press.

SHARMA, V. Venkaṭarāma (ed.) 1934. *Vājasaneyi Prātiśākhya of Kātyāyana: Sanskrit Text, Edited.* (Madras University Sanskrit Series, 5.) Madras: University of Madras.

TP = *Taittirīyaprātiśākhya.* See Whitney 1871; Rangacharya & Shama Sastri 1906.

VP = *Vājasaneyiprātiśākhya.* See Rastogi1967; Sharma 1934.

VYĀSA, Yugalakiśora (ed.) 1893. *Śikṣāsaṃgraha. A Collection of Śikṣās by Yājñavalkya and others, with Commentaries on Some of Them, Edited and Annotated.* (Benares Sanskrit Series, Work 13, nos. 35, 40, 42, 44 and 46.) Benares: Braj Bhushan Das & Co.

VYĀSA, Yugalakiśora & Prabhudatta ŚARMĀ (eds.) 1903. *Śaunaka's Prātiśākhya of the Rigveda, with the Commentary of Uvvaṭa, Edited and Annotated. Maharṣiśaunakapraṇītam ṛkprātiśākhyam uvvaṭakṛtabhāṣyayutam.* (Benares Sanskrit Series, Work 13, nos. 48, 59, 64, 79.) Benares: Braj B. Das & Co.

WHITNEY, William D. 1862. The Atharva-Veda-Prātiçākhya, or Çāunakīyā Caturādhyāyikā: Text, translation, and notes. *Journal of the American Oriental Society* 7: 333–615. [Reprinted as a book: New Haven: The American Oriental Society, 1862; reprinted again: (The Chowkhamba Sanskrit Studies, 20), Varanasi: The Chowkhamba Sanskrit Series Office, 1962.]

—— 1871. The Tāittirīya-Prātiçākhya, with its commentary, the Tribhāshyaratna: Text, translation, and notes. *Journal of the American Oriental Society* 9: 1–469. [Reprinted as a book: New Haven: The American Oriental Society, 1871; reprinted again: Delhi: Motilal Banarsidass, 1962, 1973.]

Reconstructing Ṛgvedic Religion: *Devas*, *Asuras*, and Rites of Kingship

JOEL BRERETON

As part of their descriptions of the Ṛgvedic divine world, scholars often posit a fundamental division between two distinct groups of supernatural beings, the *devás* and the *ásuras*. There are at least two excellent reasons for conjecturing such an opposition in the *Ṛgveda*. The first is that such an opposition clearly exists in later Veda, whose narratives tell of recurrent conflict between *devás* and *ásuras*.[1] The second is the well-established contrast in Iran between *daēuuas* and *ahuras*. However, there is a critical problem in drawing a direct line between Iranian religion and the later Veda: the negative and positive values of these terms are reversed in the two cultures. While in India, from the middle Vedic period onward, *devás* are gods and *ásuras* demonic antigods, throughout Iranian history, the *daēuuas* are devilish, while *ahura* names the Zoroastrian supreme deity and those powers that support his rule.[2] Still, despite their very different fates in India and Iran, Indo-Iranian **asura* and **daiva* might have designated two different groups of supernatural beings. So then, if there were an opposition of *devá*

---

[1] The conflict between the *devás* and *ásuras* is a frequent, and frequently discussed, motif in the Brāhmaṇas. See, for example, Lévi 1898: 42ff. and Hale 1986: 170ff.

[2] Cf. Yasna 30.9, translated in Insler 1975: 35: 'Therefore may we be those who shall heal this world! Wise One and ye other lords [*ahura*], be present to me with support and with truth.'

and *ásura* before the *Ṛgveda* and since they certainly are opposed after the *Ṛgveda*, an opposition between them could reasonably be assumed for the *Ṛgveda*.

But the *Ṛgveda* presents a difficulty for this view. In it, *devá* always and *ásura* usually are positive terms (one is not good and the other evil), and they are not in obvious opposition to one another, since the same divine being can be called both *devá* and *ásura*.[3] For those who see an archaic division between *devá* and *ásura*, therefore, the problem is to explain the absence of their consistent opposition in the *Ṛgveda*. Various scholars addressed this problem, but I would like to consider one particularly influential and careful analysis, that of F. B. J. Kuiper, who set forth his views in several publications that appeared in the 1970s.[4]

In Kuiper's understanding, during the Ṛgvedic period, the *ásura*s comprised a group of gods associated with the first stage of creation. According to his reconstruction of Vedic cosmogony, at the beginning of time, the world was only water with a mound of earth floating on its top, and this rudimentary world was governed by the *ásura*s. In a second stage of creation, Indra, the leader of the *devá*s, anchors the primeval mound and opens it, freeing the waters to flow onto the earth. In order to break open the mound, Indra kills the dragon Vṛtra, the personified power of 'resistance' to his rule. Indra's victory over Vṛtra, Kuiper argues, must have been also a defeat for the *ásura*s, who, because they embodied the old order, would have been part of the resistance to Indra and his new order.

After his victory, Indra props up heaven and thereby creates the dual world of heaven and earth. This division of the world is reflected in the spatial division of its deities: the *devá*s take the upper world, and the *ásura*s retreat to the lower. But the *ásura*s are fur-

---

[3] Cf. Gonda 1960: 75.

[4] The critical essays that lay out his theory are conveniently collected in Kuiper 1983, and his views are developed in Kuiper 1979. For general syntheses of his views, see especially Kuiper 1975 and 1979: 10ff. For a thorough review of different interpretations of *ásura* and different theories of the relationship between *devá*s and *ásura*s, see Hale 1986: 1ff.

ther weakened by the defection of the chief *ásura*s, including Varuṇa, Agni, and Soma, who join the *devá*s in heaven. In this way, Kuiper can explain how the same gods can be both *ásura*s and *devá*s: they were once *ásura*s, but now they have joined the ranks of *devá*s.

Kuiper acknowledges that the *Ṛgveda* itself says little about the struggle between *devá*s and *ásura*s. It does not, he explains, because the *Ṛgveda* is concerned with Indra and the new order, after the establishment of the *devá*s in heaven. The poets are simply not interested in the first stage of creation, and therefore refer to it only occasionally and obliquely. It is in the later Veda that the interest in this struggle revives, and the ancient conflict of *ásura*s and *devá*s returns within Vedic narrative.[5]

The most searching critique of Kuiper's reconstruction and of similar ones based on a primal division between *ásura*s and *devá*s is a study of the term *ásura* by Wash Edward Hale (1986). After examining the occurrences of *ásura* in the *Ṛgveda*, Hale concluded that there is little to support the theory that either in the Indo-Iranian period or in the Ṛgvedic period the *ásura*s formed a distinct group of deities, whose identity or worship was separate from and in opposition to that of the *devá*s.[6] The term *ásura*, he argued,

---

[5] In the end, the *Ṛgveda* itself offers only fragments and shards in support of of Kuiper's theory. Hale (1986: 1ff.) gives a summary of Kuiper's views and a persuasive critique of them. Kuiper draws on evidence from the *Ṛgveda*, but it is very carefully chosen evidence. Yes, Indra does prop heaven and earth apart, but so do other gods, such as Varuṇa, Soma, the Maruts, and Agni. Other contrary evidence is not considered. Why, asks Hale, if Vṛtra is an *ásura* is he never called an *ásura* in the *Ṛgveda*? And still other Ṛgvedic evidence is used inaccurately. Kuiper argues that when, in ṚV 8.96.9, *ásura*s are called *adevá*s, the verse refers to *ásura*s who are no *devá*s. However, as Hale rightly points out (here and later on pp. 83f.), *adevá* is likely an adjective. The verse rather refers to *ásura*s that are ungodly, who do not worship the gods. Indeed, Hale concludes, the starting point for Kuiper's reconstruction is not so much the *Ṛgveda*, but much more the model of ancient Near Eastern cosmologies and the opposition of *devá* and *ásura* in later Indic literature.

[6] The *ásura*s are not a group of gods or a group of demons. For that matter, in the core *Ṛgveda* the term *ásura* never occurs in the plural, but only in the singular to denote specific gods or human rulers.

means a 'lord',[7] and this term could be applied either to gods (that is, to *devás*) or to humans. Except possibly and partially in the very latest stratum of the *Ṛgveda*,[8] there is no fundamental division of Ṛgvedic divine world into exclusive categories of *devá* and *ásura*. Hale's searching review of all Ṛgvedic attestations of *ásura* has convinced me that he is right.

However, one hymn of the late *Ṛgveda* has been repeatedly invoked as evidence for a Ṛgvedic struggle between *ásura*s and *devás*. This is ṚV 10.124, which, according to Kuiper, presents the narrative of the defection of a few deities from the side of the *ásura*s to that of the *devás*. This interpretation is by no means original to Kuiper. Indeed already in 1919, W. Norman Brown declared that, although many details of this hymn remained contested, there was 'unanimous assent' that the hymn 'is a dialogue containing an invitation from Indra to Agni to leave the Asuras and serve at the sacrifice of the Devas' (Brown 1919: 100). The consensus declared by Brown is also embodied in Geldner's translation of the hymn and continued in Oberlies' recent study of Ṛgvedic religion (Oberlies 1998: 391).[9]

Hale (1986: 86ff.), of course, rejected this interpretation of ṚV 10.124, since it is completely incompatible with his view that *ásura*

---

[7] EWAia I, pp. 147f. derives *ásura* from IE *$*h_2n̥s$* attested in Hittite */has-/* 'give birth' and */hassu-/* 'king' and YAv *ahu-* 'lord'. Oberlies (1999: 222, n. 5) offers a complementary analysis that tries to account for the form of *ásura*. Following a suggestion of Thieme, Oberlies derives the word *vandhúra* from an IE root **uendh* 'plait' through an *-u*-derivative, **vandhú* 'the plaited', and a suffix *-ra* indicating 'largeness'. The term *vandhúra*, which designates the body of a chariot, is thus literally the 'great basket'. Perhaps in a similar fashion, an *asu-ra* was originally a 'great lord'. Since all lords might be called 'great', *ásura* eventually entirely displaced **asu* 'lord'. This is a convenient analysis for the view I will present, but I am doubtful about it. More likely, *-ra* functioned simply as an adjectival suffix and that *ásura* originally meant 'lordly'. An original adjective *ásura* assumed a nominal function, displaced the noun **asu*, and ultimately gave rise to a second adjectival form, *asuryà*. For objections to such an analysis, however, see Schlerath 1968, which argues that the *-ra*-suffix is used for primary, not secondary derivation.

[8] Cf. Hale 1986: 85f.

[9] Among the dissenting voices, however, is Oldenberg (1885: 68ff.).

does not designate a group of deities. He does not help his case, however, when he concludes:

> I confess that I do not understand this hymn. None of the interpretations I have summarized seems adequate, but I have no better alternative to offer. (Hale 1986: 91f.)

But some alternative is surely necessary. For him not to give one simply leaves too large a gap in his theory. Therefore, I propose to reexamine this hymn and to suggest an alternative interpretation that accords with Hale's analysis of *ásura*.

ṚV 10.124 is a dialogue hymn. As is typical in such hymns, the identity of the speakers is unclear, and unfortunately, much depends who speaks which verses. The hymn begins with the sacrificer's voice:

> *imáṃ no agna úpa yajñám éhi páñcayāmaṃ trivṛ́taṃ saptátantum* I
> *áso havyavā́ḷ utá naḥ purogā́ jyóg evá dīrgháṃ táma ā́śayiṣṭhāḥ* II
> (ṚV 10.124.1)
>
> [Sacrificer:] Come near, Agni, to this sacrifice of ours, with its five tracks, three turns, and seven threads.[10] You will be the conveyor of oblations and the one that goes in front of us. Already for a long time, you have lain in long darkness.[11]

In assigning this verse to the sacrificer, I am already at odds with the scholarly consensus, which holds the speaker to be Indra.[12] But were it not for the interpretation of this hymn as a summons to turncoat *ásuras*, lines a–c would be read as a fairly standard invitation to Agni to be present at the sacrifice and to ensure its success. It is only the last line that is unusual: Agni has been invisible and in darkness. That is to say, the ritual fire has apparently been extin-

---

[10] According to Geldner (1951), these typical numbers express the great variety of the forms of sacrifice.

[11] For *ā́śayiṣṭhāḥ*, cf. Hoffmann 1967: 156f. According to his analysis, in conjunction with *jyók*, the aorist indicative describes an action which continued from the distant past until the present moment.

[12] Cf. Geldner 1951. It is an assignment adopted even by Hale.

guished. Why might Agni have been away? Why might the ritual fire have disappeared? The fire could have gone out, or it may have been put out either for travel or for renewal.[13] Or it might have been extinguished because of the death of the sacrificer, for the later Veda prescribes that the fires of the sacrificer should be put out after his death and cremation.[14] This last is a natural ritual response, since the ritual fire is the alter ego of the sacrifice (Heesterman 1993: 27, 29) – he is dead, so it is gone. In its other occurrence in 1.32.10, the expression long darkness' is a Ṛgvedic metaphor for death,[15] and therefore, although it is here applied to the sacrificial fire, the phrase could also make oblique reference to a sacrificer's death. Let me then follow this trail: that the hymn is a summons to the fire to return after the death of a sacrificer. If so, then the sacrificer of this rite and the speaker of this verse must be a successor to the old sacrificer.

The voice of the second verse, which responds to the call to Agni, is naturally that of Agni himself:

> *ádevād deváḥ pracátā gúhā yán prapáśyamāno amṛtatvám emi* |
> *śiváṃ yát sántam áśivo jáhāmi svā́t sakhyā́d áraṇīṃ nā́bhim emi* |
> (ṚV 10.124.2)

> [Agni:] Going in hiding and in secret away from one who is no god, I, a god, looking forward, go toward life.[16] When, unkind, I leave him, although he is kind, I go to an alien navel, away from our mutual companionship.

---

[13] The later ritual system provides for just such exigencies in the *punarādheya*, the ritual reinstallation of a sacrificer's fire.

[14] Heesterman 1993: 115. Not surprisingly, since the *Ṛgveda* hardly touches upon funeral rites (except, of course, for a late funeral hymn, ṚV 10.18), this custom is not directly attested in the *Ṛgveda*.

[15] Dīrghatamas appears twice in the *Ṛgveda* (1.158.6 and 8.9.10). Since the *Bṛhaddevatā* ([Macdonell 1904] 4.11ff.), at least, the name has often been taken as signifying the sage's blindness. But this interpretation may not be applicable to the *Ṛgveda* at all and surely is not applicable to 1.32.10 and 1.124.1.

[16] Cf. Thieme (1952: 29), who translates *amṛtatvá* as 'Lebenskraft'. That is, the meaning of *amṛtatvá* may not be 'immortality', precisely, but rather the absence of death.

That death was the reason for Agni's absence is suggested by his departing from one who was 'no god', that is, who could (and did) die. Agni himself is a god and rather than accompanying his old companion in death, turns away from death and toward life. He turns toward his own renewed life as the sacrificial fire and also, perhaps, toward one who is alive, that is, toward a new sacrificer. Agni calls himself 'unkind' because he abandons the 'kind' sacrificer who once tended the sacrificial fires and goes to an alien 'navel'.[17] In connection with Agni, this 'navel' is perhaps the sacrificial area or even the fire place, similar to the *uttaranābhi* in the later *soma* sacrifice. For Ṛgvedic parallels, see, for example, ṚV 3.5.5c *pā́ti nā́bhā saptáśīrṣāṇam agníḥ* 'Agni protects the seven-headed in the navel', where the 'navel' is the place of the sacrifice, even though the identity of the 'seven-headed' is not clear.[18] A second passage addresses the Maruts:

> *nā́bhā yátra prathamáṃ saṃnásāmahe tátra jāmitvám áditir dadhātu naḥ* ||
> (ṚV 10.64.13cd)
>
> At the navel where we first reach home together, there let Aditi establish our kinship.

Here the 'navel' is, at one level at least, the place of the sacrifice.[19] Thus in 10.124.2, Agni appears once more in a new ritual place or in the ritual place of a new sacrificer, no longer the old ritual place of his old companion.

The new sacrificer then responds to Agni:

---

[17] Kuiper (1979: 21) renders the word *nābhi* as 'lineage', which is possible. The translation is similar to that of Geldner (1951), who translates it 'clan' ('Sippe') and who is followed by Hale. Renou (1965: 29) has 'appurtenance'.

[18] Here Geldner (1951) has 'im Nabel (der Erde?)' but ultimately he identifies the navel as the sacrifice or the sacrificial place. The 'seven-headed', he suggests, recalls the 'sevenheaded recitation' (*arká*) of 8.51.4 or the 'insight' (*dhī́*) of 10.67.1.

[19] Cf. Geldner 1951: '*nā́bhi* doppelsinnig: das Opfer als Nabe! der Welt (1,143.4 u. ö.) und das Symbol der Verwandtschaft.'

páśyann anyásyā átithiṃ vayā́yā ṛtásya dhā́ma ví mime purū́ṇi |
śáṃsāmi pitré ásurāya śévam ayajñiyā́d yajñíyam bhāgám emi ||
(ṚV 10.124.3)

[Sacrificer:] Looking at the guest of the other branch, I measure out the many domains of truth. I proclaim a kindness for the father and lord. I go from that not belonging to the sacrifice to a portion in the sacrifice.

The 'guest' is the fire. Once the divine guest of the departed sacrificer, Agni has now come as the guest of a new sacrificer. This new sacrificer measures out 'the many domains of truth', the places where fire will be installed,[20] as in 1.95.9ab

urú te jráyaḥ páry eti budhnáṃ virócamānam mahiṣásya dhā́ma |
(ṚV 1.95.9ab)

Your broad expanse encompasses your base, the glowing domain of the buffalo.[21]

More problematic is the reference to 'the other branch'. Perhaps the old sacrificer was another branch of the same tree, that is, of the same family, as that of the new sacrificer.[22] That the old sacrificer is a relative of the new is supported by *pāda* c, in which the new sacrificer calls the old sacrificer 'lord' and 'father'. This 'father' might be his biological father or a paternal uncle[23] or perhaps even

[20] Renou (1965: 29) translates 'maintes positions-rituelles'. The *dhā́mans*, he says (98) are similar to the seven *dhā́mans* of the sacrifice in 10.122.3. On that verse (97), he says that the 'positions' are 'les mansions' of the sacrifice, as one speaks elsewhere (10.189.3) of the 'thirty *dhā́mans*' or stations (of the day).

[21] Geldner (1951) translates *jráyaḥ* as 'Lauf' and comments that this refers either to the *paryagnikaraṇa* or the course of the sun. Renou (1964: 26), however, opts for a ritual reference in this verse. Agni's 'expanse' might refer to the distribution of the fires about the sacrificial area or possibly the space of the fire place occupied by fire.

[22] While on the previous verse, I argued that *nā́bhi* designates the fire place of Agni, it is possible that the phrase 'alien navel' suggests a paradox or irony. Agni goes to an alien location, no longer the sacrificer's own (*nítya*, the opposite of *áraṇa*, cf. EWAia I, p. 107). However, the use of *nā́bhi* 'navel' to describe this new location might suggest a kinship between the new and the old locations or a kinship between the old and new sacrificers.

[23] Cf. Böhtlingk & Roth 1855–75: IV, 715, definition 3b *sub pitar*, with examples.

a respected, older man, but in some way, the new sacrificer represents his 'son' and successor.

This is not the only reference to a human 'lord' and 'father' in the *Ṛgveda,* although the parallel occurs in another controversial hymn. ṚV 10.56 is often understood as a funeral hymn for a horse,[24] but, in accordance with Indian tradition, it is more likely a funeral hymn for man. In vs. 6, the poet describes the mutual support of the living and the dead:

> *dvídhā sūnávó 'suraṃ svarvídam ā́sthāpayanta tṛtī́yena kármaṇā* I
> *svā́m prajā́m pitáraḥ pítryaṃ sáha ā́vareṣv adadhus tántum ā́tatam* II
> (ṚV 10.56.6)
>
> In their two ways, (first) the sons made the sun-finding lord to mount [Agni] by the third (ritual) act; (and second,) the fathers have placed their own offspring, their paternal strength, here among those later, as their extended thread.

That is to say, the sons have acted in a way that transport their father, 'the sun-finding lord', to heaven, and the ancestors have continued their thread, their lineage, in their offspring.[25] As in 10.124, the 'lord' here is the late father. In 10.56, however, the concern is that the sons perform the correct funeral rites for their lord; whereas 10.124 is concerned with the issue of succession.[26]

---

[24] Cf. Geldner 1951 and Oldenberg 1909–12, *ad loc.*

[25] The 'third act' in line b is not clear to me. Geldner (1951) thinks that Sāyaṇa is right that it is the act of begetting children. In explanation, Sāyaṇa points to the later concept of the man's three debts, of which the third is the obligation to have offspring. Since I associate the 'third act' with the sons, however, I would take it as some, perhaps concluding, ritual act that is part of funeral rites.

[26] In general, the role of fatherhood appears to be closely connected to an *ásura*. In addition to 10.124.3 and 10.56.6, see also 3.3.4; 5.83.6, and AVŚ 4.15.11f.; 5.11.1. The *Atharvaveda* has a revealing example of how literal an *ásura*'s fatherhood can be: AVŚ 4.15.11–12a *prajā́patiḥ salilā́d ā́ samudrā́d ā́pa īráyann udadhím ardayāti* I *prá pyāyatāṃ vṛ́ṣṇo áśvasya réto 'rvā́ṅ eténa stanayitnúnéhi* II *apó niṣiñcánn ásuraḥ pitā́ naḥ* 'Raising the waters from the salt sea, Prajāpati will shake the water-bearing cloud. Let it overflow: the semen of the bull, the stallion. Come near with that thunder, pouring down the waters as

The son of 10.124 declares a kind thing to this father, and *pāda* d could be that kind word, although then it is puzzling why his receiving a sacrificial share would be a kindness to the father. Perhaps with his father's death, the younger sacrificer inherits both the sacrificial benefit and also the sacrificial responsibility. The kindness to the father might reflect the father's dependence on his son's continued ritual performance, since his son's offerings help guar-

---

our lord and father.' Prajāpati sends down the rain as his seed to give birth to all beings, and through this act, he is 'lord and father'.

Such an association of lordship and fatherhood may also explain the poets' reference to the god Heaven as an *ásura*. Heaven is infrequently invoked in the *Ṛgveda*, but following hoary Indo-European tradition, Heaven is Father Heaven, Dyaus Pitar. It may be because Heaven is the divine Father that Heaven may be also a divine Lord (cf. 1.54.3, 131.1; 3.29.14, 53.7, 56.8; 6.20.2; 10.10.2, 31.6, 67.2). I garland this statement in double uncertainty, because although there are nine passages in which the 'lord' mentioned might be Heaven, in few of them (perhaps only one, 1.131.1) is that identification completely secure. One of the likely instances is 10.67.2, which illustrates the concatenation of Heaven, lord, and fatherhood: *ṛtáṃ śáṃsanta ṛjú dī́dhyānā divás putrā́so ásurasya vīrā́ḥ* | *vípram padám áṅgiraso dádhānā yajñásya dhā́ma prathamám mananta* 'Reciting the truth, reflecting rightly, the sons of Heaven, the heroes of the lord, the Aṅgirases, creating their inspired track, conceived the first establishment of the sacrifice.' To be sure, however, the lord in this verse need not be Heaven – Renou (1966: 70) takes him to be Bṛhaspati – and heaven, for that matter, need not be the god Heaven, although it is more natural to understand it as such.

Finally, although I am reluctant to make too much of an uncertain and distant etymological connection, *ásura* is likely related to Hittite *has* 'engender' and *hassu* 'king' (EWAia I, p. 148), which again might suggest a link between fatherhood and kingship. Puhvel (1991: 245) elaborates on the possible significance of the derivation of *hassu* from *has*: 'Thus *hassu-* ... had a Proto-Anatolian sense of "Born One" or "Begotten One", as a nominal *u*-stem derivative from *has(s)-* (< **ḫamsu-* reflecting either **E₂m̥su-* or *E₂omsu-*). The parallelism of the Germanic words for king derived from the root **genE-* ..., seen in e.g. ON *konr* prince (<**gnyos*...), is reinforced by inner-Hittite data ... Or perhaps, granted the ambiguity of the diathesis, the proto-sense was alternatively related to that of Lat. *genius* (<**genyos* or **gynos*) "numen of potency", with the king as the embodiment and epitome of male procreative powers at the apex of the socioreligious order.' Puhvel's second explanation would imply an association of fatherhood and lordship. I asked my colleague Gary Beckman to evaluate the Hittite data and, unimpressed, he replied (personal comment) that this 'all seems rather useless to me, since there is nothing in Hittite texts suggesting that the king is uniquely well-born or studly'.

antee the father's life and prosperity in the realm of the ancestors.[27] Or perhaps the speaker's kindness is simply unstated and irrecoverable. But in one way or another, the new sacrificer offsets Agni's unkind abandonment by the kind thing that he declares.

In the interests of full disclosure, I need to say that this translation and discussion of the verse depart rather far from more typical interpretations of it. The consensus, both ancient and modern, is that the *ásura* here is not a human,[28] but a god, although there is considerable disagreement on which god: Varuṇa? Heaven? Rudra?[29] Geldner suggests that this Father Asura might be Vṛtra,[30] but Vṛtra is never called an *ásura* in the *Ṛgveda* – never[31] – and therefore I see no reason to presume he ever was an *ásura* in the *Ṛgveda*. To regard the *ásura* in this verse as either a god or a demon, therefore, does not lead to any clear or compelling alternative.

In vs. 4, Agni once again replies:

> *bahvī́ḥ sámā akaram antár asminn índraṃ vṛṇānáḥ pitáraṃ jahāmi* |
> *agníḥ sómo váruṇas té cyavante paryā́vard rāṣṭráṃ tád avāmy āyā́n* ||
> (ṚV 10.124.4)

> [Agni:] For many years, I have acted[32] within it [/him].[33] Choosing Indra for my own, I leave the father.[34] Agni, Soma, and Varuna – these are in motion. The kingship has turned around, and I help it as I come here.

---

[27] As in 10.56.6, above. Cf. also 10.15.14 and Oberlies 1998: 477.

[28] For other examples of human *ásuras*, see Hale 1986: 47f., 76f.

[29] For these different possibilities and their advocates, see Hale 1986: 89f.

[30] See also Geldner's introduction to this hymn and his more extended comments in Pischel & Geldner 1897: 293f.

[31] Cf. Hale 1986: 90, citing Hillebrandt. Given the large number of times Vṛtra is mentioned in the *Ṛgveda*, one would reasonably expect that the overlord of the *ásuras* would at least once be called an *ásura*.

[32] Cf. Hoffmann 1967: 156f.: 'viele Jahre habe ich (bis jetzt) bei ihm gewirkt'. Kuiper (1979: 16 and n. 38) does not find Hoffmann's translation adequate, and, although admitting that the precise sense of *kṛ* here is unclear, prefers to take it in this context to mean 'pass (time)' (as does Sāyaṇa): 'Many years have I passed within him ...' This interpretation is possible. Even Hoffmann, while he questions Geldner's translation of a parallel passage, reproduces it: 1.33.15c *jyók cid átra tasthivā́ṃso akran* 'schon lange hatten sie hier verweilend

Agni witnesses that he once acted within the sacrifice or within the domain of the old sacrificer, but now he chooses Indra. This is the key verse for those who see this hymn as the story of old *ásura*s' transformation into *devás*. According to Kuiper, Agni here leaves an *ásura* (interpreters often let this slip over into 'he leaves the *ásura*s'), and he chooses the *devá* Indra, bringing along with him the *ásura*s Soma and Varuṇa.

There are a number of difficulties with this view. Most notably, as Hale (1986: 70) has argued at length, if Indra is the representative of the *devás* and *devás* are not *ásura*s, then Indra himself can-

---

gesäumt'. But it is not a necessary interpretation, since the line may simply state that Agni performed his ritual functions for many years.

[33] The phrase *antár asmin* is problematic. In my view, it most likely means within the sacrifice that is obliquely mentioned in vs. 3. In this interpretation, Agni acted within the ritual when he was the fire of the previous sacrificer. Parallel would be the collocation *vidáthe antár* in 5.59.2d *antár mahé vidáthe yetire nárah* 'The fine men [= the Maruts] have taken their places within the great ritual distribution' and 2.27.8b *trī́ṇi vratā́ vidáthe antár eṣām* 'Three are their [= the Ādityas'] commands within the ritual distribution.' Cf. also 3.55.12c *ṛtásya té sádasīḷe antár* 'Within the seat of truth, I invoke those two (cows)', where the 'seat of truth', on at least one level, likely refers to the ritual. However, the explanation adopted by most interpreters is that *antár asmin* means 'within the *pitár asura*'. According to Kuiper (1979: 16–18), for example, Agni was once enclosed within Father Asura, that is, Varuṇa, in the primordial world before the creation of the organized world. I find that this and similar interpretations create a rather substantial construction out of an ambiguous phrase. But if *antár asmin* should be translated 'within him', it might mean only that Agni acted for many years within the sphere or authority of the old sacrificer. The possible parallels involving the god Varuṇa point to this interpretation rather than that of Kuiper. Cf. 7.86.2b *kadā́ nv àntár váruṇe bhuvāni* 'When shall I be within Varuṇa?' and 7.87.5a *tisró dyā́vo níhitā antár asmin* 'Three heavens are hidden within him [= Varuṇa].' In both these examples 'within Varuṇa' means in obedience to the command or authority (*vratá*) of Varuṇa (cf. Brereton 1981: 84f.). This is particularly clear in the first example in which the speaker hopes to be restored to obedience to Varuṇa and to the favor of Varuṇa, after having been the object of the god's anger. However, this interpretation of 'within' as 'within (the authority of)' may be possible only with Varuṇa, since *váruṇa* is etymologically related to *vratá* (Brereton 1981: 70ff.) and therefore *váruṇe* might be an abbreviated expression for *vraté váruṇasya*.

[34] If there is a mythological precedent invoked here, it may be Indra's displacing his own father, although in that case, Indra succeeded his father apparently by killing him.

not be an *ásura*. But in the *Ṛgveda*, Indra is an *ásura*,[35] though admittedly not in the core *Ṛgveda* and admittedly not often.[36] One example is 1.174.1 in which Indra is an *ásura* and invoked along with the *devás*:

> *tvám rā́jendra yé ca devā́, rákṣā nṝ́n pāhy àsura tvám asmā́n* I
> *tvám sátpatir maghávā nas tárutras, tvám satyó vásavānaḥ sahodā́ḥ* II
> (ṚV 1.174.1)
>
> May you as king, Indra – (also those) who are gods – guard (our) men; may you protect us, o lord. You, the master of the dwellings and our surpassing benefactor, you are the real possessor of goods and giver of strength.

If 1.174 is a late hymn, so is 10.124, and if an *ásura* Indra is rare, he nonetheless exists. But if there are difficulties for Kuiper's view, there are difficulties for mine as well.

If Agni is actually talking about his transition to the sacrifice of a new sacrificer, then 'Indra' in this verse must be that sacrificer. But is this possible? Can Indra the god be represented in a human being? Yes, I think he can.[37] Happily, we have another hymn in the *Ṛgveda*, in which a king takes on the role and name of Indra. This is *Ṛgveda* 4.42, the 'coronation hymn' of King Trasadasyu. As Lommel (1951) demonstrated, in assuming his role as king, Trasadasyu declared himself to be both Varuṇa and Indra. In vss. 2–3, Trasadasyu declares:

> *ahám rā́jā váruṇo máhyaṃ tā́ny asuryā̀ṇi prathamā́ dhārayanta* I
> *krátuṃ sacante váruṇasya devā́ rā́jāmi kṛṣṭér upamásya vavréḥ* II
> (ṚV 4.42.2)
>
> I am king Varuṇa. For me they uphold these foremost lordly (powers). The gods follow the will of Varuṇa. I am king of the boundary of the highest cover.

---

[35] Cf. also 8.90.6; 10.99.12, and 10.96.11, on which Hale (1986: 70) says that it is 'fairly certain' that the *ásura* is Indra.

[36] On the other hand, he is rather frequently called *asuryà* 'lordly' or he possesses *asuryà* 'lordliness'. Cf. 2.23.2, of Indra as Bṛhaspati, and 4.16.2; 6.20.2, 30.2, 36.1; 7.21.7, 22.5; 10.50.3, 54.4, 105.11.

[37] See also on vs. 6 below.

ahám índro váruṇas té mahitvórvī́ gabhīré rájasī suméke | (ṚV 4.42.3ab)

I am Indra, am Varuṇa. By my greatness, these two realms, wide and deep, are well-supported.

Trasadasyu is Varuṇa and Indra because he embodies in himself the two aspects of kingship that these two gods represent. Indra primarily is the king as warrior and Varuṇa, the king as governor presiding over society and social relations. As Lommel points out, this conception of kingship continues in the later rite of royal consecration, in which the newly installed king is compared to Varuṇa *dharmapati* and to Indra *vṛtrahan*.[38]

In 10.124, we also have the identification of the new sacrificer as Indra, because that new sacrificer is also the new king, or, at any rate, someone who stakes a claim to be the new king. He is or would be an Indra among humans. In this case, then, the new sacrificer is not only claiming his father's ritual responsibilities but, assuming his father was the old king, also his father's rule. In the second half of vs. 4, Agni affirms that other gods, including Varuṇa, are also present to help maintain the sacrificer's rule. 'The kingship has turned around', Agni declares, for indeed there is a new king, and Agni promises to do what he can to help in the institution of that king's new rule.

To this, the new sacrificer and king replies, now addressing Varuṇa who has been made present by Agni:

nírmāyā u tyé ásurā abhūvan tváṃ ca mā varuṇa kāmáyāse |
ṛténa rājann ánṛtaṃ viviñcán máma rāṣṭrásyā́dhipatyam éhi ||
(ṚV 10.124.5)

[Sacrificer:] And these lords have come to be without craft. If you will love me, Varuṇa, sifting untruth from truth, o king, come here to the governance of my rule.

He thus invites Varuṇa to govern his kingdom. For the moment, the strategy of this aspiring king differs from that of Trasadasyu. Rather than identifying himself with both Indra and Varuṇa as

---

[38] Cf. also Schmidt 1992.

Trasadasyu did, this king embodies Indra and then invites the help of Varuṇa.

But who, then, are the *ásura*s that appear in this verse? They are other lords, rival rulers, or perhaps even other claimants to the rule that our sacrificer claims. Elsewhere the *Ṛgveda* also attests such hostile 'lords', as in 8.96.9bc *kás ta indra práti vájraṃ dadharṣa | anāyudhā́so ásurā adevā́ḥ* 'Who has dared your mace, Indra? Weaponless are the godless lords', and 1.108.6b *ayáṃ sómo ásurair no vihávyaḥ* 'This Soma must be invoked by us in competition with the lords.'[39] In the first of these two verses, the 'lords' here are not non-*devá*s, but rather humans who lack the gods.[40] In the second, *vihávya* refers to the rivalry among lords and sacrificers for the attention and support of the gods.[41] In both cases, the *ásura*s are human rivals.

One other note on 10.124.5: the end of this verse is problematic for those who wish to see this hymn as the story of leading *ásura*s going over to the side of the *devá*s. If the god Indra were speaking for himself, it is odd that he invites Varuṇa to assume 'the governance' (*ā́dhipatya*) of his 'kingdom' (*rāṣṭrá*). We might expect Indra to invite Varuṇa to become part of his rule, but surely not to take charge of it. Such a request makes more sense coming from a human king, who looks to establish the authority of his rule by asserting divine support for it.

Kuiper (1979: 22–32) is well aware of the problem presented by this verse and discusses it carefully. He argues that *ā́dhipatya* (or *ádhipatya*)[42] here does not refer to 'governance' in general, but

---

[39] Hale also cites other instances in which *ásura* in the sgl. refers to a particular human enemy (Hale 1986: 47f., 76f.). I think he is correct, but it is difficult to know when the *Ṛgveda* is referring to a human enemy and when to a demonic one, or indeed whether human enemies do not become demonic ones.

[40] The grammatical distinction between *ádeva* 'who are no gods' and *adevá* 'who have no gods' is clear.

[41] As Kuiper (1979: 103f.) has shown, the term *vihavá* means to invoke in competition with others.

[42] Kuiper (1979: 25, n. 73) defends the reading *ádhipatya*, which follows the *Padapāṭha*, instead of *ā́dhipatya*, as Oldenberg (1909–12) argues.

rather to rule over a specific part of the world.[43] In his reading, the governance that Indra offers to Varuṇa 'is the *ádhipatya* over the waters and the western quarter' (Kuiper 1979: 29), that is, over the spheres that are typically Varuṇa's in the later Veda. Such a characterization of Varuṇa and limitation of his rule is an anachronism, however. There is nothing in the *Ṛgveda* that assigns Varuṇa's authority to a specific direction, and while Varuṇa does govern the waters, especially the rain waters, he does so in his capacity as lord of the world, not as a god whose sphere is restricted to the waters.[44]

At this point, I have laid out the features of my interpretation of this hymn. Let me simply add that I believe that the dialogue between Agni and the sacrificer ends with verse 6. In that verse, the new sacrificer and king again explicitly identifies himself with

---

[43] Kuiper 1979: 27: 'In Vedic cosmogony, ... *ádhipati* is the specific term for a god or group of gods who, in the system of classification, have the function of protector(s) of one of the points of the compass.'

[44] Oberlies (1998: 354) has suggested a different way of reading this verse. He has adopted, with some modifications, Kuiper's view of the *ásura*s as old gods displaced by new gods, the *devá*s. And also like Kuiper and others, he understands this hymn to tell of the abandonment of the *ásura*s by Agni, Varuṇa, and Soma. On this verse, however, he invokes another theory that he has developed at length. Indra and Varuṇa, he says, represent two different kinds of kingship: Indra is the war-king (Kriegskönig) and Varuṇa he calls the peace-king (Friedenskönig) (cf. Oberlies 1998: 348ff.). This complementary concept of kingship reflects the alternation between *yóga*, which describes the community's trek, its cattle-raiding, and its encounters with hostile peoples, and *kṣéma*, its settled life. Oberlies suggests that in Vedic society two different kings ruled during these two periods. Just as Varuṇa is not Indra, so the peace-king was not the war-king. It is in this light that he interprets this verse. When Indra (who in his view is the speaker of this verse) invites Varuṇa to assume the 'governance' of his kingdom, this represents the handing over of power from the war-king to the peace-king.

While I think he is right to read this verse as involving kingship, I doubt that there are really two kings. As we have already seen, the coronation hymn of Trasadasyu anoints one person as both Indra and Varuṇa, and thus, in Oberlies' terms, as both war- and peace-king. Second, if we understand this verse as a transfer of power from a war-king to a peace-king, then, according to Oberlies' interpretation, we would have a myth in which Varuṇa abandons the *ásura*s and comes over to the side of Indra, and then Indra immediately gives up his power to Varuṇa.

Indra, here by assuming Indra's most characteristic deed, the destruction of Vṛtra. The final three verses are in the voice of a priestly narrator. In vs. 7, he identifies the new king also with Varuṇa by attributing to him the deeds of that god. Thus, the king's reinstallation of the fire becomes Varuṇa's act of hanging the sun, 'the sign in heaven', and the king's duty to guarantee the fertility of the land through seasonable rain with Varuṇa's release of waters.[45] In vs. 8, the new king once again becomes Indra, or rather, possesses the preeminence that belongs to Indra. And finally, in verse 9, the 'poet-sages', the priests, recognize Indra. And where do they perceive him? In the king,[46] who acts in accordance with the praise that follows him.[47]

> *idáṃ svàr idám íd āsa vāmám ayám prakāśá urv àntárikṣam* |
> *hánāva vṛtráṃ niréhi soma havíṣ ṭvā sántaṃ havíṣā yajāma* ||
> (RV 10.124.6)
>
> [Sacrificer:] Here is the sun – right here has the prized one come to be and (over) here, his appearance throughout the broad midspace. We two will smash Vṛtra – come out, Soma! We (all) will sacrifice with an oblation to you [= Soma], though you are an oblation.
>
> *kavíḥ kavitvā́ diví rūpám ā́sajad áprabhūtī váruṇo nír apáḥ sṛjat* |
> *kṣémaṃ kṛṇvānā́ jánayo ná síndhavas tā́ asya várṇaṃ śúcayo bharibhrati* ||
> (RV 10.124.7)

[45] In a similar way, in 4.42.4, Trasadasyu, speaking in the person of Varuṇa, says *ahám apó apinvam ukṣámāṇā dhāráyaṃ dívaṃ sádana ṛtásya* 'I swelled the splashing [or 'growing', cf. Kiehnle 1979: 170] waters. I uphold the heaven on the seat of truth.' I find this reference to the release of the waters somewhat puzzling. It is certainly true that Varuṇa controls the waters, but the release of the waters is typically associated with the destruction of Vṛtra by Indra. Perhaps this merging of the acts of Indra and Varuṇa reflects the merging of the two gods in the person of the king. Note also that this hymn and especially this verse turn on the repetition of /v/'s: Vṛtra, Varuṇa, *varṇa, vṝ, vi-vic, vāma*. Again, is this an indication of the integration of Varuṇa into the rule of the new king?

[46] There are alternatives to this interpretation. The 'wild goose' could also be Soma (cf. Scarlata 1999: 638, n. 900).

[47] Or, more exactly, lines ab refer to the heavenly Indra, Indra the god, and lines cd to the earthly Indra, Indra represented in the king.

[Narrator:] The poet-sage through his poetic craft has suspended the sign in heaven. With no domination (of them), Varuṇa has let loose the waters. Making for themselves a peaceful dwelling, like wives, are the rivers. These (rivers), flame-bright, carry its [=the sun's] color here and there.

tā́ asya jyéṣṭham indriyáṃ sacante tā́ īm ā́ kṣeti svadháyā mádantīḥ |
tā́ īṃ víśo ná rā́jānaṃ vṛṇānā́ bībhatsúvo ápa vṛtrā́d atiṣṭhan ||
(ṚV 10.124.8)

Those [waters] follow his preeminent character as Indra. He dwells peacefully among them, who find invigoration through (his) independent power.[48] In choosing him, like clans their king, those stood away from Vṛtra, being averse (to him).

bībhatsū́nāṃ sayújaṃ haṃsám āhur apā́ṃ divyā́nāṃ sakhyé cárantam |
anuṣṭúbham ánu carcūryámāṇam índraṃ ní cikyuḥ kaváyo manīṣā́ ||
(ṚV 10.124.9)

They say that the wild goose is the yokemate of those averse (to Vṛtra), as it roams in companionship with heavenly waters. As he roams here and there, following the verse of praise, Indra (it is that) the poet-sages recognized through their inspired thought.

To recapitulate, then, 10.124 is not the only evidence cited for a myth in which Soma, Agni, Varuṇa and other *ásuras* go over to the side of the *devás*. But it is the only hymn in which this narrative has been thought to appear in more than allusions and fragments. A possible alternative is that this hymn asserts a claim of succession and a claim to rule. Unlike Trasadasyu, the claimant here seems to have opposition, which would have made the ritual affirmation of his rule all the more essential. In this interpretation, *ásura* dissolves as a designation for a group of gods. In its two occurrences, in the singular in vs. 3 and in the plural in vs. 5, *ásura* refers to humans, not to gods or antigods or old gods. And not only does it refer to humans, but to quite different humans: in vs. 3, to the predecessor of the sacrificer and in vs. 5, to the sacrificer's enemies or rivals.

I realize that even if this interpretation of 10:124 is persuasive, there remain a galaxy of other questions, of which I will briefly ad-

---

[48] Or possibly 'through (their) independent power'.

dress just two. First, what kind of 'lord' is an *ásura*, both in this hymn and elsewhere? Hale (1986: 48) suggests that he was a leader in war, but this view is based largely on an unlikely interpretation of the term *sátpati*, which occurs alongside *ásura*. This term *sátpati* is probably not related to *sátvan* 'warrior' as Hale maintains, but more likely to *sádas*, a 'seat' or 'dwelling place' and refers to the 'master of the dwelling' or 'dwellings'.[49] In 1.174.1, quoted above, the *ásura* and *sátpati* Indra is less a warrior than, as Oberlies (1999: 177) describes him, the king as protector and giver of peaceful dwelling places. In general, an *ásura* is a ruler as governor, rather than a ruler as warrior. For this reason, *ásura* often describes Varuṇa and Mitra, the gods who govern relations among humans, and Agni, the god who governs the ritual relations between humans and gods. This interpretation of *ásura* can also explain why Indra, who typically is a warrior-ruler, is only occasionally called *ásura* or *asuryà*.

A second question is how, if there were no ancient, defined class of *ásuras*, *ásura* became a name for the antigods in the later Veda. The great advantage of a theory of a primordial opposition between *ásura* and *devá* is its ability to avoid a gap between the Ṛgvedic and the later Vedic conceptions of an *ásura*. In attempting to explain how such a transformation might have arisen, I follow Hale's lead.

Already in 10.124 we have seen that *ásura* is essentially a neutral term. There can be good lords and bad, lords that are friends and lords that are enemies. Also, like every other term for a ruler – *rā́jan* 'king', *viśpáti* 'clan-master', *gṛhápati* 'house-master', *sátpati* 'master of the dwellings' and the like – *ásura* can describe both humans and gods. It is among the human *ásura*s, or humanlike *ásura*s, rather than among divine *ásura*s that the origins of the *ásura*s as antigods likely rest (cf. Hale 1986: 77). In the *Ṛgveda*, evil *ásura*s are typically enemies of the sacrificers and of Indra,

[49] Cf. EWAia II, p. 690, which briefly sets out the different etymological possibilities.

whom the poets invoke in battle against their rivals. So, for example, the poet of 7.99 declares Indra and Viṣṇu's power to defeat Śambara and the lord, the *ásura*, Varcin:

> *índrāviṣṇū dṛṃhitā́ḥ śámbarasya náva púro navatíṃ ca śnathiṣṭam |*
> *śatáṃ varcínaḥ sahásraṃ ca sākáṃ hathó apraty ásurasya vīrā́n ||*
> (ṚV 7.99.5)
>
> Indra and Viṣṇu, you pierced the nine and ninety firm fortifications of Śambara. You strike the hundred and the thousand of Varcin, the heroes of the lord, all at once, without opposition.

Or again, in 10.138.3, the enemy is the lord, the *ásura*, Pipru:

> *dṛḷhā́ni píprar ásurasya māyína índro vy ā́syac cakṛvā́ṁ ṛjíśvanā ||*
> (ṚV 1.138.3cd)
>
> Those that are firm, that belong to Pipru, the crafty lord, has Indra cast away, having worked with Ṛjiśvan.

Ṛjiśvan is a king who elsewhere offers Indra *soma* and receives Indra's help in battle (1.101.1 2; 5.29.11; 10.99.11, 138.3).

In the *Ṛgveda*, it is not always possible to distinguish evil humans from demons. Such enemies of Indra as those mentioned here – Śambara, Varcin, and Pipru[50] – are or become composite figures, partly demon, partly human. According to Witzel (1995: 325), many of these enemies were human originally, but the poets demonize them 'through a clever mix of myth and reality'. He compares their demonization to the Chinese description of Europeans as 'foreign devils' or the late Ayatollah's characterization of the United States as the 'Great Satan'. From such beginnings, those demonic enemies can become demon enemies. And once demonization of *ásura*s led to demon *ásura*s,[51] the *ásura*s could become a class of beings in opposition to the gods.

It is difficult to say when or where this process of recreating the *ásura*s finally reached its end, but there is one particular Vedic tra-

---

[50] And likewise others, such as Cumuri, Dhuni, and Śuṣṇa.

[51] Cf. Hale 1986: 77f., commenting on 10.138.3.

dition, the Maitrāyaṇī *śākhā*, that attests in fairly dramatic form the ultimate crystallization of demon *ásuras*. The *Maitrāyaṇīsaṃhitā*, for the first time in Vedic literature, explicitly identifies the great enemy of the gods, Vṛtra, as an *ásura* (MS 4.3.4).[52] This identification was suggested by Geldner for the *Ṛgveda*, but it is only well into the post-Ṛgvedic period that a text finally, actually, says that Vṛtra was an *ásura*. Also for the first time, the *Maitrāyaṇī-Upaniṣad* 6.35 attests the word *sura* for a god. As has been long recognized, this word is a back-formation, extracted from *ásura*.[53] These two developments – the identification of Vṛtra as an *ásura* and the creation of an opposition *asura* (antigod) / *sura* (god) – witness the full conception of *ásuras* as opponents of the gods. That both these developments take place within the same school suggests that it may have been within that tradition that the opposition between *devás* and *ásuras* fully achieved its classical formulation.

ADDENDUM

Since this paper was submitted, Theodore Proferes published a superb study, *Vedic Ideals of Sovereignty and the Poetics of Power* (New Haven, Conn.: American Oriental Society, 2007). In it, on pp. 106–113, he offers a translation and interpretation of 10.124, which advance our understanding of the hymn. His analysis is still cast within the framework of a narrative in which the gods Agni, Soma, and Varuṇa abandon Father Asura to follow Indra. However, he also says that the hymn's fundamental theme is Indra's royal unction: 'Anointed with water by Varuṇa, Indra is transformed into a solar figure and becomes king.' (p. 106) I find this to be an important insight. I interpret the royal rite in the hymn to be the consecration of a human king who assumes the role of Indra rather than of Indra himself, but especially since Indra is the model

---

[52] Cf. especially 42:14 and Hale 1986: 171f.

[53] Cf. EWAia I, p. 148 *sub ásura-*.

of a human king, our interpretations head in similar directions. On the other hand, we differ on the role of Varuṇa in the hymn. In my view not only Indra but also Varuṇa is embodied in the king; for Proferes Varuṇa is rather the instrument of a king's unction. We also differ in many other details, but I believe Proferes has rightly seen and emphasized the centrality of the solar symbolism and of fire and water in the unction rite and in the hymn. For further I urge readers to consult Proferes's illuminating discussion.

REFERENCES

BÖHTLINGK, Otto & Rudolph ROTH 1855–75. *Sanskrit-Wörterbuch*, I–VII. St. Petersburg: Kaiserliche Akademie der Wissenschaften.

BRERETON, Joel P. 1981. *The Ṛgvedic Ādityas*. (American Oriental Series, 63.) New Haven: American Oriental Society.

BROWN, W. Norman 1919. Proselytizing the Asuras. *JAOS* 39: 100–103.

BUITENEN, J. A. B. van 1962. *The Maitrāyaṇīya Upaniṣad*. The Hague: Mouton & Co.

EWAia = MAYRHOFER, Manfred 1986–2001. *Etymologisches Wörterbuch des Altindoarischen* I–III. (Indogermanische Bibliothek, Zweite Reihe: Wörterbücher.) Heidelberg: Universitätsverlag Carl Winter.

GELDNER, Karl F. 1951. *Der Rigveda, aus dem Sanskrit ins Deutsche überstezt* I–III. Cambridge, Mass.: Harvard University Press.

GONDA, Jan 1960. *Die Religionen Indiens* I: *Veda und älterer Hinduismus*. (Die Religionen der Menschheit. 11.) Stuttgart: W. Kohlhammer.

HALE, Wash Edward 1986. Ásura in *Early Vedic Religion*. Delhi: Motilal Banarsidass.

HEESTERMAN, J. C. 1993. *The Broken World of Sacrifice*. Chicago: The University of Chicago Press.

HOFFMANN, Karl 1967. *Der Injunktiv im Veda. Eine synchronische Funktionsuntersuchung*. (Indogermanische Bibliothek, Dritte Reihe: Untersuchungen.) Heidelberg: Carl Winter Universitätsverlag.

INSLER, S. 1975. *The Gāthās of Zarathustra*. (Acta Iranica, 8, 3. série: Textes et mémoires, 1.) Téhéran: Bibliothèque Pahlavi.

KIEHNLE, Catharina 1979. *Vedisch* ukṣ *und* ukṣ/vakṣ. *Wortgeschichtliche und exegetische Untersuchungen*. (Alt- und Neu-Indische Studien, 21.) Wiesbaden: Franz Steiner Verlag.

KUIPER, F. B. J. 1975. The basic concept of Vedic religion. *History of Religion* 15: 107–120.

—— 1979. *Varuṇa and Vidūṣaka. On the Origin of the Sanskrit Drama.* (Verhandelingen der Koninklijke Nederlandse Akademie van Wetenschappen, Afd. Letterkunde, N. R. 100.) Amsterdam: North-Holland Publishing Co.

—— 1983. *Ancient Indian Cosmogony. Essays,* selected and introduced by John Irwin. New Delhi: Vikas Publishing House.

LÉVI, Sylvain 1898. *La doctrine du sacrifice dans les Brāhmaṇas.* (Bibliothèque de l'École Pratique des Hautes Études, Sciences religieuses, 11.) Paris: Ernest Leroux.

LOMMEL, Herman 1951. Vedische Skizzen. In: *Beiträge zur indischen Philologie und Altertumskunde. Walther Schubring zum 70. Geburtstag dargebracht von der deutschen Indologie* (Alt- und Neu-Indische Studien, 7): 25–38. Hamburg: Cram, De Gruyter & Co.

MACDONELL, A. A. 1904. *The Bṛhad-Devatā Attributed to Śaunaka: A Summary of the Deities and Myths of the Rig-Veda,* I–II. (HOS, 5–6.) Cambridge, Mass.: Harvard University Press.

OBERLIES, Thomas 1998. *Die Religion des Ṛgveda. Erster Teil: Das Religiöse System des Ṛgveda.* (Publications of the De Nobili Research Library, 26.) Wien: Institut für Indologie der Universität Wien.

—— 1999. *Die Religion des Ṛgveda. Zweiter Teil: Kompositionsanalyse der Soma-Hymnen des Ṛgveda.* (Publications of the De Nobili Research Library, 27.) Wien: Institut für Indologie der Universität Wien.

OLDENBERG, Hermann 1885. Ākhyāna-Hymnen im Ṛgveda. *ZDMG* 39: 52–90.

—— 1909–12. *Ṛgveda: Textkritische und exegetische Noten* [I–II]. (Abhandlungen der Königlichen Gesellschaft der Wissenschaften zu Göttingen, Philologisch-historische Klasse, N.F. 11.5 & 13.3.) Berlin: Weidmannsche Buchhandlung.

PISCHEL, Richard & Karl GELDNER 1897. *Vedische Studien,* II. Stuttgart: Verlag von W. Kohlhammer.

PUHVEL, Jaan 1991. *Hittite Etymological Dictionary,* III: *Words beginning with H.* (Trends in Linguistics: Documentation, 5.) Berlin: Mouton de Gruyter.

RENOU, Louis 1964. *Études védiques et pāṇinéennes,* XII. (Publications de l'Institut de Civilisation Indienne, Série in-8°, 20.) Paris: Institut de Civilisation Indienne de l'Université de Paris.

—— 1965. *Études védiques et pāṇinéennes,* XIV. (Publications de l'Institut de Civilisation Indienne, Série in-8°, 23.) Paris: Institut de Civilisation Indienne de l'Université de Paris.

—— 1966. *Études védiques et pāṇinéennes,* XV. (Publications de l'Institut de Civilisation Indienne, Série in-8°, 26.) Paris: Institut de Civilisation Indienne de l'Université de Paris.

SCARLATA, Salvatore 1999. *Die Wurzelkomposita im Ṛg-Veda*. Wiesbaden: Dr. Ludwig Reichert Verlag.

SCHLERATH, B. 1968. Altindisch *asu-*, awestisch *ahu-* und ähnlich klingende Wörter. In: J. C. Heesterman, G. H. Schokker, & V. I. Subramoniam (eds.), *Pratidānam: Indian, Iranian and Indo-European Studies Presented to Franciscus Bernardus Jacobus Kuiper on His Sixtieth Birthday* (Janua Linguarum, Series Maior 34): 142–153. The Hague: Mouton & Co.

SCHMIDT, Hanns-Peter 1992. The place of Ṛgveda 4.42 in the ancient Indian royal ritual. In: A. W. van den Hoek, D. H. A. Kolff & M. S. Oort (eds.), *Ritual, State and History in South Asia: Essays in Honour of J.C. Heesterman* (Memoirs of the Kern Institute, 5): 323–349. Leiden: E. J. Brill.

THIEME, Paul 1952. *Studien zur Indogermanischen Wortkunde und Religionsgeschichte*. (Berichte über den Verhandlungen der Sächsischen Akademie der Wissenschaften zu Leipzig, 98.5.) Berlin: Akademie-Verlag.

WITZEL, Michael 1995. Ṛgvedic history: poets, chieftains and politics. In: George Erdosy (ed.), *The Indo-Aryans of Ancient South Asia: Language, Material Culture and Ethnicity* (Indian Philology and South Asian Studies, 1), 307–352. Berlin: Walter de Gruyter.

Interiorisation of Ritual in the Brāhmaṇas: Role of the Breaths in the Vedic System of Ritual Correspondences

CLEMENS CAVALLIN

THOUGHT AND ACTION

In her book *Ritual Theory, Ritual Practice* (1992), Catherine Bell stresses the central role that the opposition between thought and action (or merely bodily movements) plays in the relatively new interdisciplinary subject of Ritual Studies.[1] This dichotomy is akin to the traditional divisions between body and soul, spirit and matter, thus implying ontological issues. In the analysis of ritual action, the dichotomy often emerges as an opposition between inner and outer aspects of ritual acts. The outer aspects are those which reveal themselves directly to the senses of the scholar, while the inner aspects are those parts of the ritual act which have to be inferred from the outer aspects, for example the intentions of the ritual practitioners or the symbolical meanings of the actions.

---

[1] See Bell 1992: ix, 6, 19, 48. She does not clearly state, however, how to overcome this dichotomy, but one could interpret her launching the notion of ritualisation as a way of, if not solving, then at least circumventing the problem, cf. Bell 1992: 7f. Cf. also her use of the notion of ritual practice, Bell 1992: 74–88. But while discussing the relation between secularisation and ritual studies, she writes: 'A strategic dichotomizing of thought and action may well be basic to the pragmatic negotiations of "self" and "society" in such secular cultures' (Bell 1992: 222).'

INTERIORISATION

The so-called internalised or interiorised rituals constitute an interesting category of rituals, and ritual speculation, for they illuminate and challenge some features of the division between outer and inner aspects.[2] Such rituals result from processes of interiorisation in which the emphasis has been shifted from the outer to the inner aspects of a ritual.

Ritual interiorisation has figured in scholarly discussions of the development of Vedic religion and ritual in the Vedic period, especially in discussions of the emerging asceticism and the doctrines associated with it. For example, J. C. Heesterman sees the *śrauta* sacrifices and their treatment in the Brāhmaṇa texts as results of a ritual reform, a move away from the dangerous agonistic sacrifices to the secure and transcendental classical Vedic rituals. Sacrifice became a ritual that turned its back to the concerns of the world, and this 'transcendental' perfect order became personified in the ritual officiator, who, nevertheless, still tried to mediate between the unsafe world of everyday life and the ritually established absolute realm. The renouncer, however, in contrast to the ambivalent stance of the ritualist, drew the logical conclusion and tried to cut

---

[2] Ritual internalisation should, however, not be confused with the psychological notion of internalisation, which primarily denotes the internalising of the *norms* of parents or of society. In some contexts, the demarcation line between these two senses of internalisation tends to become blurred. Cf. Gade 2002, with a theoretical discussion and a case study (Qur'ānic recitation) and Kugle 2003. For the sake of conceptual clarity, 'ritual interiorisation' will henceforth be reserved for the tendency of emphasising the inner aspects (material or mental) of an action, while 'internalisation', on the other hand, primarily denotes the assimilation of norms for (ritual) action. Bisschops 1999 is an example of the use of the term ritual internalisation in the sense of ritual interiorisation. I have previously in a conference paper (Cavallin 2003b) also used the phrase ritual *internalisation* instead of ritual *interiorisation*.. Furthermore, these two processes (internalisation and interiorisation) could be part of the same ritual practice, as indicated by Gavin Flood (2002) in his discussion of the tantric ritual of the purification of the body. The concept of interiorisation has also been introduced within psychoanalysis as a technical term for the patient's interiorisation of analytical dialogue. However, while discussing this phenomenon, Moshe Spero (1999: 172) alternatively uses the notions of internalisation and interiorisation.

his ties to society. For Heesterman, the driving force behind these two roles was the individualisation of the sacrifice, i.e. the abolishing of the opponent in the ritual battle. He writes:

> The principle is the individualization of the ritual, which could not but lead to its interiorization (Heesterman 1985: 41).

Brian K. Smith, on the other hand, emphasises the discontinuity between the thinking of the Brāhmaṇas and that of the Upaniṣads,[3] and the interiorisation of ritual is, according to Smith, primarily a device for depicting the new ideal of the renouncer as essentially something old, or perhaps more correctly as the perfection of the old well-known order of the sacrifice.[4]

The question of ritual interiorisation in the Vedic context seems to be connected to questions of religious and ritual change, and thus to the question of continuity contra radical change. However, regarding the prototypically interiorised ritual, viz. the *prāṇāgnihotra*, Bodewitz argues in his study *Agnihotra and Prāṇāgnihotra* that this ritual was not only the concern of ascetics, but also of Vedic householders.[5]

Bodewitz, moreover, touches upon some issues of general importance for the discussion of ritual interiorisation. I would like to elaborate on these issues, and then continue with a discussion of *prāṇa* and the *prāṇa*s in the *brāhmaṇa* system of ritual correspondences (i.e. the *bandhus*), and their connection with ritual interiorisation.[6]

---

[3] Smith 1989: 194f., 209f.

[4] Smith 1989: 211. For a similar interpretation of 'ritual interiorization' in the Vedic context, see Eliade 1958: 111–114.

[5] Bodewitz 1973: 293–305.

[6] Bodewitz (1973: 213) thus has to deal with the difference between mental sacrifices and the *prāṇāgnihotra* which is concretely performed and among other ritual acts contains the pouring of water on the big toe of the ritual performer's right foot (BDhS 2.12.11 = *praśna* 2, *adhyāya* 7.11)). Furthermore, he has to address the role of interiorisation in giving up ritual, and the fact that interiorised ritual moments coexist with exterior ritual utterances and gestures.

As one of the final statements of his study, Bodewitz presents the following basic observation:

> In using the term 'interiorization' one should be aware of the fact that several disconnected phenomena are covered by this rather vague word (Bodewitz 1973: 330).

Before actually analysing examples of interiorisation, we, therefore, have to make the taxonomy of interiorisation more clearcut, and thus to explore the causes of vagueness. I would like to address the following two issues: 1) the nature and relation between these two dichotomies: outer–inner, and physical–mental, and 2) are there different types of interiorisation?

OUTER–INNER AND PHYSICAL–MENTAL

If we begin with the pair outer and inner, it seems evident that it primarily concerns spatial qualities. In the discussion of rituals, however, it has a secondary meaning, viz. the opposition between physical and mental. This latter meaning is based on the characterisation of the outer as that which can be observed, and the inner as the hidden, which can be known only indirectly. We could therefore define the opposition between the outer and the inner aspects of an action as basically an epistemological question. However, certain ritual proceedings can be performed concretely within the body, as in the case of the *prāṇāgnihotra*, and these acts thereby become invisible for an outsider's senses and one normally has to infer their existence on the basis of outer aspects, which are more directly observable. Although these acts are not mental they are thus on the inner side of the outer and inner dichotomy. The inner aspects of ritual acts, or in order to emphasise the epistemological dimension, the hidden or the indicated aspects, can thus be both physical and mental. We therefore have to consider that the two dichotomies, outer and inner, physical and mental, only partly coincide. We can furthermore pose the question whether it would be possible that the mental could be on the outer side, i.e. whether we can gain access to it in a direct way. The issue is thus whether mental phenomena are absolutely inner or only inner in a relative way as physical processes are. In this context, it could be interesting to reflect on the different viewpoints of the participants in a ritual. A participant, let us say, the *hotṛ* of a Vedic *śrauta* ritual, has a more or less direct access to some of his own inner processes in a way which the other participants, such as the *adhvaryu* or the *udgātṛ*, do not have. 'Inner' from the vantage point of the individual does therefore have two meanings: firstly, in regard to his own inner processes, mental and physical, which are more or less hidden from the notice of the other participants; secondly, 'inner' signifies those processes of his fellow ritual participants which are hidden from his view. Interiorisation could bring about problems, as indicated by PB 4.9. This passage states that after the mental (*manasā*) singing of the *sarparājñī* verses has been concluded, the *adhvaryu* should be notified with a look, as he otherwise cannot know when the mental singing is finished.

DIFFERENT TYPES OF INTERIORISATION

After this brief indication of the problematic relation between the dichotomies of outer–inner and physical–mental, we can turn to the second issue, viz. the different types of interiorisation. Initially we have to distinguish between three different levels of interiorisation. The first is normative interiorisation, which is constituted by norms prescribing the ways in which rituals should be performed in order to be efficacious, e.g. they should be performed mentally, or with specific intentions. The second level is that of interiorising interpretations, according to which concrete rituals are interpreted as dealing mostly with interior principles, such as the breaths or the mind. These first two levels are both of a meta-ritual character, while the third consists of interiorising ritual performances, performing certain ritual acts solely in the mind. These three levels can be interconnected in several different ways, and can be characterised as respectively: norm, description and action.

Regarding the question of different kinds of interiorisation, an attempt will be made in the following to differentiate between five different types. The first two deal with the efficacy of the ritual act, shifting the basis of the supposed ritual efficacy to interior principles.

1) *Interiorisation with a focus on intentionality*[7]

In this case, the efficacy of the ritual is ultimately attributed not to the ritual utterances and gestures, but to the mental attitude of the performer.

2) *Interiorisation with a focus on knowledge*

As in the case of intentionality, the ritual efficacy is believed to be dependent on the mental make-up of the performer, but in this case specifically on the knowledge of the performer.

The following two types of interiorisation deal with the mode of performance:

3) *Mental performance*

This type is involved when Vedic ritualists use the word *manasā* 'with the mind'.

4) *Physical interiorisation*

This type is perhaps best illustrated by the *prāṇāgnihotra*, in which food is sacrificed into the interiorised ritual fires.

---

[7] In this type the efficacy of ritual is considered to depend upon certain qualities of the relation between consciousness and the purpose of the ritual (or, for instance, the relation to the recipient of a sacrificial oblation). It might be helpful to differentiate between intentions and motives, as Rickman does while discussing Dilthey's hermeneutical philosophy, to differentiate between intentions and motives. Rickman argues that actions undertaken primarily for achieving some objective, and not for communication, express in a clear way the intention of the actor, i.e. what he intends to bring about. He thus defines the intention as 'the agent's immediate goal' which is different from the motive according to which he undertakes the action. (Rickman 1988: 51.) Ritual interiorisation with a focus of intentionality could thus be of two different types depending upon if the focus is on the intention (e.g. obtaining heaven or eliminating the foe) or the motive (doing ones duty, love etc.).

The fifth and final type of interiorisation concerns the result or the aim of the ritual, which can be either of a mental or of a more physical character. In other words, instead of being directed to an intersubjectively accessible result, the ritual is geared to cause effects within the human person.

5) *Interiorisation of the effects, or the aim, of the ritual*

We cannot here engage in a general and detailed discussion of these five different types of interiorisation, but it is important to point out that the epistemological character of the inner aspects give to interiorisation an ambivalence or a duality of meaning: the inner aspects could be of a concrete physical character as well as more mentally constructed. Interiorisation processes are therefore in some measure dependent upon how the human person is thought to be constituted. In Vedic ritual thought and practice, this feature forms a link between interiorisation and the breaths, or the vital powers.

THE BREATHS

In the system of Vedic ritual correspondences (the so-called *bandhus*), the breaths are conspicuous both quantitatively and qualitatively. For example, in statistical studies they have emerged as the most important category within the system of ritual correspondences of the Brāhmaṇa texts.[8] In the first place, this testifies to a tendency of interiorisation of the fifth type mentioned above, viz. the interiorisation of the effects of the ritual. Brāhmaṇa texts often mention placing of the breaths into the *yajamāna* as the aim of a given ritual.[9] The *bandhus* are used to establish the desired links between the ritual and the inner principles of man. In that

[8] See Mylius 1976: 150; Cavallin 2003a: 123, 158.

[9] E.g. in ŚB 7.2.2.18 the gods put (*dadhur*) breath into Prajāpati, and this is imitated by the ritual performer (*dadhāti*). In AB 2.30.5, the act of pouring (*samavanayati*) the remains of the libations for the *dvidevatyas* in the *hotṛ-camasa*, is correlated to the pouring (*samavanayate*) of the breaths into the body.

way,the *bandhus* function as interiorising interpretations of actual ritual proceedings, giving them an aim, which perhaps was not evident from the ritual itself.

If the aims of Vedic rituals were to some extent interiorised through the use of ritual correspondences, then this is also true in regard to the views on ritual efficacy. Ritual efficacy, i.e. the stipulated capacity of the ritual to achieve some specific aim, was in the Brāhmaṇa period viewed as largely dependent upon the *bandhus*, which formed causal links enhancing the supposed potency of Vedic sacrifices. But, ritual efficacy was also, in a secondary way, believed to be dependent on the knowledge of the *bandhus*. The recurrent phrase *ya evaṃ veda*, 'he who knows thus', points out that if the ritual performer possesses the knowledge expounded in the preceding Brāhmaṇa passage, certain results are sure to be produced. For example, AB 4.14.7–8 states:

> *yo vai saṃvatsarasya prāṇodānau veda, sa vai svasti saṃvatsarasya pāraṃ aśnute. 'tirātro vā asya prāyaṇīyaḥ prāṇa, udāna udayanīyaḥ. svasti saṃvatsarasya pāram aśnute ya evaṃ veda ya evaṃ veda.*
>
> He, who knows the exhalation and the inhalation of the year, attains in safety the other side of the year. The introductory Atirātra is its expiration, the concluding the inhalation. In safety he reaches the other side of the year, who knows thus.[10]

The supposed efficacy of the Vedic sacrifices became thereby not merely dependent upon the proper performance of the rituals, but also on the knowledge of the performer. If both the efficacy and the aim of a ritual become interiorised, then a development in which the outer aspects are bypassed is not unlikely to occur. The causal link is then established directly between knowledge and the desired effects within the human person, bypassing the outer aspects of ritual activity.

---

[10] The translation deviates from that of Keith (1920) only in two details: *udāna* is translated as 'inhalation' instead of 'ending breath', and the word *asya* is translated as 'its' instead of being left untranslated.

In the Brāhmaṇas, *bandhus* involving the vital powers figure also in the third category of interiorisation, that of mental performance. In several places in the Brāhmaṇas and in the Śrautasūtras, we come across references to mental performances of a part of a given ritual.[11] One example is the mental singing of verses to the serpent queen (*sarparājñī*) on the tenth day of the *dvādaśāha*.[12] This mental laud is followed by the audible recitation of the interesting *daśahotṛ* formula[13] which correlates mainly different mental entities with various ritual implements and priests, thus presenting a picture of a complete mental ritual.[14] In the series of interior principles mentioned in the *daśahotṛ*, the focus is not on the different respiratory breaths, which, however, are referred to in the phrase *prāṇo haviḥ*, 'The oblation is the breath', but on mental processes of thinking and willing, evidenced by such concepts as intelligence (*citti*), thought (*citta*), the object of thought (*ādhīta*) and will (*keta*). Nevertheless, in ĀpŚS 14.13.4, where the ritual of the thirteenth day of the special sacrifice of the *hotṛ* formulas is described, the recitation of the *daśahotṛ* is connected to ritual inhalations and

---

[11] E.g. ĀśvŚS 8.13.21, translated by Mylius as 'Nachdem der *adhvaryu* im Geist den (Soma)Becher ergriffen hat, bringt er im Geist die (Opfer)speise herbei', or ĀpŚS 14.14.10 translated by Caland as 'In Gedanken opfere er für einen, der den Himmelsraum zu erreichen wünscht.

[12] For a description of the ritual see ĀśvŚS 8.13.3–9. For *brāhmaṇa* discussions see AB 5.23, KB 27.7 (27.3 in Keith's translation), PB 4.9 and TS 7.3.1.2. The verses are from RV 10.189, a short hymn, the dedication of which is not settled, see Geldner 1951: III, 403. In the edition of van Nooten and Holland (1994: 573), it is given as 'To Sārparājñī or Sūrya from Sārparājñī'. An interesting fact is that it contains one reference to breathing, namely in verse 2b *asya prāṇād apānatī*, 'breathing in from its breath'.

[13] For the mental recitation of the *daśahotṛ* in the mythological context of Prajāpati creating, see TB 2.2.1.1. Prajāpati 'saw' the *daśahotṛ* and through the mental recitation of it and a sacrifice on a bunch of grass he created. For the other *hotṛ* formulas see KS 9.16.

[14] ĀpŚS 21.10.6–7 seems to prescribe not only the *daśahotṛ*, but also the *catur-*, *pañca-*, *ṣaḍ-* and *saptahotṛ*. For discussions of the various *hotṛ* formulas, see Hillebrandt 1897: 165–166 and Mylius 1993.

exhalations.[15] Furthermore in TB 2.2.1.7 and KS 9.16, the *daśahotṛ* formula is connected to the practice of black magic, and the destructive act is made possible through the numerical correspondence between the nine breaths plus the navel on the one hand and the *daśahotṛ* on the other. The breaths of the foe could thus be extinguished (KS: *upadāsayati*) or bewitched (TB: *abhicarati*).[16]

The breaths, moreover, play a part in the fourth type of interiorisation, that of physical interiorisation. As previously mentioned, the best example of this is perhaps the *prāṇāgnihotra* sacrifice, in which an offering of food is made into the breaths, i.e. the interiorised ritual fires.[17] However, it is not necessary that the theme of substitution, which is salient in the *prāṇāgnihotra,* should be present for this type of interiorisation to occur. The inner side of the body is in most religious ritual traditions to some extent ritualised. This is the case in several Vedic rituals without substitution being implied. Actual ritual breathings form an interesting category in this regard, as the respiration provides an interface between outer and inner, and between micro- and macrocosmos.[18] Furthermore, as in the *prāṇāgnihotra* ritual, consumption of food stuffs or potions is a common way in most ritual systems of extending ritualisation to the interior of the human body. A further example of this, in the Vedic context, is naturally the consumption of *soma*. But also the eating of the *iḍā* (a sacrificial cake in the *darśapūrṇamāsa iṣṭi*) is of interest. It is linked with the breaths as recipients of oblations, fulfilling the function of the ritual fires in the *prāṇāgnihotra.*[19] In ŚB 1.8.1 the consumption of the *iḍā* by

---

[15] According to Caland (1924: 386, note 2 on ĀpŚS 14.13.4), the sense is that he thus sacrifices the exhalation in the inhalation.

[16] See also ĀpŚS 14.15.1.

[17] For the description of the *prāṇāgnihotra*, see BDhS 2.12 (*adhyāya* 7); for the interiorisation of the ritual fires in the ritual of renunciation, see BDhS 2.17.26 (*adhyāya* 10.26).

[18] See e.g. ŚB 11.8.3.6, with Eggeling's footnote, ĀśvŚS 5.21, ĀpŚS 17.1.12–13, ŚB 8.3.4.

[19] For a description of the ceremony of consuming the *iḍā* in the *darśapūrṇamāsa*, see ĀpŚS 3.2. AB 2.30 discusses the relation between the drinking

some of the priests and the *yajamāna* is described as an offering into the breaths:

> *tāṃ vai prāśnantyeva nāgnau juhvati ... prāṇeṣveva hūyate hotari tvad yajamāne tvad adhvaryau tvad* (ŚB 1.8.1.38–39)
>
> They (the priests and sacrificer) eat it (the *iḍā*), and do not offer it up in the fire ... In the vital airs rather it is offered, partly in the Hotṛ, partly in the Sacrificer, partly in the Adhvaryu.[20]

SUMMING UP

Summing up the discussion of interiorisation, we could say that evidence or traces of four of the five types of interiorisation mentioned in this paper can be found in the middle Vedic literature. The Vedic concept of the breaths, or the vital powers, cover almost all interior principles, both material and mental, and therefore naturally play an important part in all these forms of ritual interiorisation. The translation of *prāṇāḥ*, in some contexts, as 'vital powers', furthermore, points to focusing on the principles of human life in respect to the conceptual pair of outer and inner; rather than on the strict epistemological division of the observable and the non-observable. Ritual interiorisation, in its many forms, was thus combined with an investigation of the fundamental principles of the human person; an investigation which was mainly carried out within the discourse of ritual correspondences. However, we must note the absence of the first type of interiorisation, namely that which in respect of ritual efficacy places importance

---

of *soma* and the consumption of *iḍā*. The cups of two deities (*dvidevatya*) are connected to the breaths, while the *iḍā* is connected to cattle; for the ritual proceedings see ĀśvŚS 5.5–6. In the context of the consumption of the *iḍā* in the *darśapūrṇamāsa*, ĀśvŚS 1.7.2 describes the rite of anointing first the upper lip and then the lower lip with the index finger smeared with cleared butter whilst uttering the following two formulas: 'Of thee, offered by the lord of the mind, I eat for sap, for out-breathing' and 'Of thee, offered by the lord of speech, I eat for strength, for inbreathing' (ŚB 1.8.1.14–15, translated by Eggeling).

[20] Eggeling's translation.

on the intentionality of the performer, i.e. the view maintaining that it is not only necessary to perform the rituals according to the rules, but that a special mental attitude (such as faith or selflessness) should also be present to make the ritual work. Such a deficiency on the part of the Brāhmaṇa texts could be taken as evidence of an automatic or mechanistic view of ritual action, but this is not absolutely necessary. This feature could instead be interpreted in the light of the general theory of ritualisation formulated by Caroline Humphrey and James Laidlaw in their book *The Archetypal Actions of Ritual* (1994). The principle which they call 'the ritual commitment' was still very much alive in the Vedic ritual system. According to the theory of Humphrey and Laidlaw, ritual entails the abolishment of individual intention in favour of following the rules.[21] Therefore among the types of ritual interiorisation discussed in this paper, the type emphasising intentionality is that which is most clearly subversive to ritual as such. Interiorisation could thus be in conformity with ritualisation, i.e. when following the rules and suspension of individual intention are central. But interiorisation could also break up the very fundament of ritual action, i.e. when the ritual commitment is modified or challenged by processes of interiorisation.

REFERENCES

Sanskrit Texts and Translations

AB = *Aitareyabrāhmaṇa*

– *Das Aitareya Brāhmaṇa, mit Auszügen aus dem Commentare von Sāyaṇācārya und anderen Beilagen herausgegeben* von Theodor Aufrecht. Bonn: Adolph Marcus, 1879.

– *Rig-Veda Brāhmaṇas* ... translated ... by Arthur Berriedale Keith. (HOS, 25.) Cambridge, Mass.: Harvard University Press, 1920.

[21] This fundament of their theory is akin to Frits Staal's hypothesis of the meaninglessness of ritual. See Staal 1990; Stausberg 2002: 24.

ĀpŚS = *Āpastambaśrautasūtra*

– *The Śrauta Sūtra of Āpastamba ... with the Commentary of Rudradatta*, edited by Richard Garbe, I–III. (Bibliotheca Indica, 92.) Calcutta: Asiatic Society of Bengal, 1882–1902.

– *Das Śrautasūtra des Āpastamba, 1.–7.* Buch aus dem Sanskrit übersetzt von W. Caland. (Quellen der Religionsgeschichte, Gruppe 7: Indische Religionen, 8.) Göttingen: Vandenhoeck & Ruprecht – Leipzig: J. C. Hinrichs, 1921.

— *Das Śrautasūtra des Āpastamba, achtes bis fünfzehntes Buch* aus dem Sanskrit übersetzt von W. Caland. (Verhandelingen der Koninklijke Akademie van Wetenschappen te Amsterdam, Afdeeling Letterkunde, Nieuwe Reeks 24:2.) Amsterdam: Koninklijke Akademie van Wetenschappen te Amsterdam, 1924.

— *Das Śrautasūtra des Āpastamba, sechszehntes bis vierundzwanzigstes und einunddreissigstes Buch* aus dem Sanskrit übersetzt von W. Caland. (Verhandelingen der Koninklijke Akademie van Wetenschappen te Amsterdam, Afdeeling Letterkunde, Nieuwe Reeks 26: 4.) Amsterdam: Koninklijke Akademie van Wetenschappen te Amsterdam, 1928.

ĀśvŚS = *Āśvalāyanaśrautasūtra*

– *Āśvalāyana-Śrautasūtra*, erstmalig vollständig übersetzt, erläutert und mit Indices versehen von Klaus Mylius. (Reihe Texte und Übersetzungen, 3.) Wichtrach: Institut für Indologie, 1994.

BDhS = *Baudhāyanadharmasūtra*

– *Das Baudhāyana-Dharmasūtra*, herausgegeben von E. Hultzsch. Zweite verbesserte Auflage. (Abhandlungen für die Kunde des Morgenlandes, 16.2.) Leipzig: Deutsche Morgenländische Gesellschaft, 1922.

– *Dharmasūtras: The Law Codes of Āpastamba, Gautama, Baudhāyana, and Vasiṣṭha*. Annotated text and translation by Patrick Olivelle. Delhi: MLBD, 2000.

KB = *Kauṣītakibrāhmaṇa*

– *Kauṣītaki-Brāhmaṇa*, I: *Text*. Herausgegeben von E. R. Sreekrishna Sarma. (Verzeichnis der orientalischen Handschriften in Deutschland, Supplementband 9.1.) Wiesbaden: Franz Steiner Verlag, 1968.

KS = *Kāṭhakasaṃhitā*

– *Kāṭhakam: Die Saṃhitā der Kaṭha-çākhā*, herausgegeben von Leopold von Schroeder, I–III. Leipzig: Deutsche Morgenländische Gesellschaft, 1900–10.

PB = *Pañcaviṃśabrāhmaṇa*

– *The Tāṇḍyamahābrāhmaṇa*, ... edited ... by A. Chinnaswāmi Śāstrī (II: and Paṭṭābhirāma Śāstrī), I–II. (Kāshi Sanskrit Series, 105.) Benares: The Chowkhamba Sanskrit Series Office, 1934–35.

– *Pañcaviṃśa-Brāhmaṇa. The Brāhmaṇa of Twenty Five Chapters*. Trans. by Willem Caland. (Bibliotheca Indica, 255.) Calcutta: The Asiatic Society of Bengal, 1931.

RV = *Ṛgveda*

– *Rig Veda: A Metrically Restored Text with an Introduction and Notes*, ed. by Barend A. van Nooten & Gary B. Holland. (HOS, 50.) Cambridge, Mass.: Department of Sanskrit and Indian Studies, Harvard University, 1994.

– *Der Rigveda aus dem Sanskrit ins Deutsche übersetzt und mit einem laufenden Kommentar versehen* von Karl F. Geldner. I–III. (HOS, 33–35.) Cambridge, Mass.: Harvard University Press, 1951.

ŚB = *Śatapathabrāhmaṇa*

– *The Çatapatha-Brāhmaṇa in the Mādhyandina-çākhā with Extracts from the Commentaries of Sāyaṇa, Harasvāmin and Dvivedaganga*, ed. by Albrecht Weber. Berlin: Ferd. Dümmler's Verlagsbuchhandlung – London: Williams and Norgate, 1855. [Reprint: (The Chowkhamba Sanskrit Series, 96) Varanasi: The Chowkhamba Sanskrit Series Office, 1964.]

– *The Śatapatha-Brāhmaṇa According to the Text of the Mādhyandina School*, trans. by Julius Eggeling, I–V. (Sacred Books of the East, 12, 26, 41, 43, 44.) Oxford: Clarendon Press, 1882–1900. [Reprint: Delhi: MLBD, 1963.]

TS = *Taittirīyasaṃhitā*

– *Die Taittirīya-Saṃhitā*. herausgegeben von Albrecht Weber, I–II. (Indische Studien, 11 & 12.) Leipzig: F. A. Brockhaus, 1871–72.

TB = *Taittirīyabrāhmaṇa*

– *The Taittirīya Brāhmaṇa with the Commentary of Bhaṭṭabhāskaramiśra*, ed. by A. Mahadeva Sastri, R. Shama Sastry and L. Srinivasacharya, I–IV. (Government Oriental Library Series, Bibliotheca Sanskrita, 36, 57, 38, 42.) Mysore: Government Branch Press, 1908–21.

Secondary Literature

BELL, Catherine 1992. *Ritual Theory, Ritual Practice*. New York: OUP.

BISSCHOPS, Ralph 1999. Metaphor as the internalisation of ritual – With a case study on Samuel Holdheim (1806–1860). In: Ralph Bisschops & James Francis (eds.), *Metaphor, Canon and Community. Jewish, Christian and Islamic approaches*: 284–307. Bern: Peter Lang.

BODEWITZ, H. W. 1973. Agnihotra and Prāṇāgnihotra. In: H. W. Bodewitz, *Jaiminīya Brāhmaṇa I, 1–65. Translation and Commentary*. (Orientalia Rheno-Traiectina, 17): 213–338. Leiden: E. J. Brill.

—— 1986. Prāṇa, apāṇa and other prāṇa-s in Vedic literature. *Adyar Library Bulletin* 50: 326–348.

BROWN, George William 1990. Prana and Apana. *Yoga Mimamsa* 29.3: 50–61. [Reprint from *JAOS* 39 (1919): 104–112.]

CAVALLIN, Clemens 2003a. *The Efficacy of Sacrifice. Correspondences in the Ṛgvedic Brāhmaṇas*. (Skrifter utgivna vid Institutionen för religionsvetenskap, Göteborgs Universitet, 29.) Göteborg: Göteborg University, Department of Religious Studies.

—— 2003b. Sacrifice as action and actions as sacrifices: The role of breath in the internalisation of sacrificial action in the Vedic Brāhmaṇas. In: Tore Ahlbäck (ed.), *Ritualistics*: 19–35. Åbo: Donner Institute for Research in Religious and Cultural History.

—— 2013. *Ritualization and Human Interiority*. Copenhagen: Museum Tusculanum Press.

ELIADE, Mircea 1958. *Yoga. Immortality and Freedom*. (Bollingen Series, 56.) Princeton: Princeton University Press. [Originally published in French in 1954.]

FLOOD, Gavin 2002. The purification of the body in Tantric ritual representation. *IIJ* 45: 25–43.

GADE, Anna 2002. Taste, talent, and the problem of internalization: A Qur'ānic study in religious musicality from Southeast Asia. *History of Religions* 41.4: 328–366.

HEESTERMAN, J. C. 1985. *The Inner Conflict of Tradition. Essays in Indian Ritual, Kingship and Society*. Chicago: The University of Chicago Press.

HUMPHREY, Caroline & James LAIDLAW 1994. *The Archetypal Actions of Ritual. A Theory of Ritual Illustrated by the Jain Rite of Worship*. Oxford: Clarendon Press.

KUGLE, Scott A. 2003. The heart of ritual is the body: Anatomy of an Islamic devotional manual of the nineteenth century. *Journal of Ritual Studies* 17.1: 42–60.

MYLIUS, Klaus 1976. Die vedischen Identifikationen am Beispiel des Kauṣītaki-Brāhmaṇa. *KLIO Beiträge zur Alten Geschichte*, Band 58, Heft 1: 145–166.

—— 1993. Wesen und Funktion der Hotṛ-Formeln. *ABORI* 72–73 (The Amṛtamahotsava volume): 113–135.

RICKMAN, H. P. 1988. *Dilthey Today. A Critical Appraisal of the Contemporary Relevance of His Work*. (Contributions in Philosophy, 35.) New York: Greenwood Press.

SMITH, Brian K. 1989. *Reflections on Resemblance, Ritual, and Religion*. New York: OUP. [Reprint: Delhi: MLBD, 1998.]

STAAL, Frits 1990. *Rules without Meaning. Ritual, Mantras and the Human Sciences*. (Toronto Studies in Religion, 4.) New York: Peter Lang.

SPERO, Moshe Halevi 1999. A brief note on Ingram's (1997) concept of interiorization. *The American Journal of Psychoanalysis* 59.2: 171–174.

STAUSBERG, Michael 2002. Ritteorier och religionsteorier. In: *Riter och ritteorier: Religionshistoriska diskussioner och teoretiska ansatser*: 13–37. Nora: Nya Doxa.

On the Meaning of Words Signifying 'Body' in the Ṛgveda

T. YA. ELIZARENKOVA (†)

There are two words signifying 'body' in the Ṛgveda: *tanū́-* f. and *śárīra-* n. They are of different frequency: *tanū́-* is found 208 times, *śárīra-* only 7 times (Lubotsky 1997: I, 584–586; II, 1386). They also have a different semantic volume. *Tanū́-* is a substantive derived from the verb *tan-* 'to extend, spread, stretch',[1] which represents the body as an extent or stretch in both temporal and spatial sense. It is a polysemantic word, implying not only the physical structure of the body, but its spiritual aspect as well, which explains its use as a reflexive pronoun. It is a fairly frequent word often found in vague contexts. The sense of the other denomination of the body, *śárīra-* (etymology not quite established), is much more narrow: it designates only the physical body, usually as a firm structure.

According to Grassmann's dictionary, the principal meanings of *tanū́-* are 'body', 'person', and 'self' (Grassmann 1875: 519–520). 'Body' is the main and most frequent meaning of the word. *Tanū́-* designates any kind of body: the body of mortals and of gods, both anthropomorphic and non-anthropomorphic. Here are some examples, first about human beings.

---

[1] *Tanū́-* is not a feminine to the adjective *tanú-* 'thin, slender, small', as proposed by Debrunner (Wackernagel [& Debrunner] 1954: 493). The independent and direct development of *tanū́-* from the verbal root *tan-* was demonstrated by Pinault (2001).

6.75.12 *ṛ́jīte pári vṛndhi nó | 'śmā bhavatu nas tanū́ḥ*

Spare us, O weapon flying true to its mark; let our body be stone (O'Flaherty 1981: 237).

10.85.27 *enā́ pátyā tanvàṃ sám sṛjasva-*

Mingle your body with that of your husband (O'Flaherty 1981: 270).

Then about gods.

10.72.8 *aṣṭáu putrā́so áditer | yé jātā́s tanvàs pári*

There are eight sons of Aditi, who were born of her body (O'Flaherty 1981: 39).

3.48.4 *yathāvaśáṃ tanvàṃ cakra eṣáḥ*

He created his body the way he liked [said about Indra].

The body or many bodies are regularly mentioned in connection with Agni.

3.18.4 *marmṛjmā́ te tanvàm bhū́ri kṛ́tvaḥ*

Many times we have embellished your body.

3.20.2 *tisrá u te tanvò devávātās | tā́bhir naḥ pāhi gíro áprayuchan*

You have also three bodies agreeable to the gods, with them protect attentively our songs.

Some bodies of Agni are benevolent to men, others are destructive. Uṣas, the Morning Dawn, is proud of her body (1.123.10, 124.6); she is showing it, so that people might see and enjoy it (1.123.11). The Maruts are shining brightly with their bodies adorned with golden ornaments (5.60.4, etc.). Even Soma, the deified juice, enjoys a body:

9.70.8 *śúciḥ punānás tanvàm arepásam | ávye hárir ny àdhāviṣṭa sā́navi*

The pure one, clarifying his stainless body, the tawny one trickled down to the surface of the woollen strainer.

An absolutely abstract deity, of whom it is only known that she has got loops to punish the sinners, is addressed in

10.59.5 *ghṛténa tvám̩ tanvàm̩ vardhayasva*

Increase your body by means of ghee!

Now the question arises about the kind of denotatum to which *tanū́-*, the physical body, is referred. Was it only the trunk, or the physical structure, the trunk together with the limbs and the head? The contexts of the Ṛgveda differ in this respect. While many of them are not diagnostic, there are some where the difference between *tanū́-* and the limbs is clearly expressed, for instance:

2.39.5 *hástāv iva tanvè śámbhaviṣṭhā | pā́deva no nayatam̩ vásyo ácha*

Like the two hands most helpful for the body, like the two feet bring us to happiness [an Aśvin hymn].

2.16.2 *jaṭháre sómam̩ tanvì sáho máho | háste vájram bhárati śīrṣáṇi krátum*

He carries Soma in his belly, strength and might in his body, the thunderbolt in his hand, will in his head [an Indra hymn].

1.89.8 *sthiráir áṅgais tuṣṭuvā́m̩sas tanū́bhir | vy àśema deváhitam̩ yád ā́yuḥ*

Having praised (you), we would like to attain the life-span fixed (for us) by the gods, possessing (still) firm limbs and bodies.

In 4.2.13, Agni is asked to reward the priest who has toiled during the ritual. And the next verse runs:

4.2.14 *ádhā ha yád vayám agne tvāyā́ | padbhír hástebhiś cakṛmā́ tanū́bhiḥ | rátham̩ ná kránto ápasā bhuríjor | ...*

And therefore, O Agni, loving you, we have toiled with our feet, hands, bodies, with the work of the two arms like those who build a chariot ...

But at the same time it is clear from the passages dealing with a dead man who is to unite with his new body in the highest heaven, that *tanū́-* here implies the complete body, including also the limbs and the head. It is known from the funeral hymns of the Ṛgveda that the corpse, the dead body, is regarded as an oblation that Agni should bring to the gods. the oblation fire 'prepares', 'cooks' this sacrifice which should be complete.[2] The meaning of it is that if the body is somehow damaged, Agni should put it in order:

10.16.6 *yát te kṛṣṇáḥ śakuná ātutóda*
pipīláḥ sarpá utá vā śvā́padaḥ |
agníṣ ṭád viśvā́d agadáṃ kṛṇotu
sómaś ca yó brāhmaṇā́m̐ āvivéśa ||

Whatever the black bird has pecked out of you, or the ant, the snake, or even a beast of pray, may Agni who eats all things make it whole, and Soma who has entered the Brahmins (O'Flaherty 1981: 50).

The concept of the 'new body' with which a dead man should unite in the realm of Yama is a rather vague one (cf. O'Flaherty 1981: 46–49), but one thing is clear about it: in order to be able to unite with it, the dead man should retain at the cremation his whole body, comprising all his limbs and his head. The union with the new body is mentioned also in connection with the deified horse; cf. the funeral speech to the horse:

10.56.1 *saṃvéśane tanvàś cā́rur edhi.*| *priyó devā́nām paramé janítre*

By merging with a body, grow lovely, dear to the gods in the highest birthplace (O'Flaherty 1981: 94).

Attention should also be drawn to the general concept of a physical body, expressed by *tanū́-*. The Vedic *ṛṣi*s regarded the physical body in a way somewhat different from a modern man. Their concept was wider, and it might always comprise the penetration of some abstract notions into the physical structure. A number of examples of this kind are found in the hymns of the Ṛgveda:

---

[2] In the funeral hymn 10.16, two kinds of Agni are distinguished in this situation: Agni *kravyā́d*, the cremation fire, who burns the dead body, and Agni *jātávedas*, who conveys the deceased to the highest heaven (cf. verse 9).

1.55.8cd *ā́vṛtāso 'vatā́so ná kartṛ́bhis | tanū́ṣu te krátava indra bhū́rayaḥ*

Like the wells covered by those who have made them, there are many resolutions[3] (hidden) in your bodies, O Indra.

8.39.2 *ny àgne návyasā vácas | tanū́ṣu śáṃsam eṣām*

O Agni, by means of (our) new song re(tain) the praise in the bodies of those (people).

10.56.4 *sám avivyacur utá yā́ny átviṣur | áiṣāṃ tanū́ṣu ní viviśuḥ púnaḥ*

They have gathered together (all their deeds) that were shining, and these have entered their bodies again. ['They' are the divine horses, and 'their bodies' seem to be the 'new' bodies acquired in the highest heaven.]

A greater degree of 'spiritualization' of *tanū́-* is found in those contexts, where this word means 'person', that is, form, image, manifestation of a man or a god. This meaning implies not only the corporal form, but also some mental peculiarities. This meaning is rarely expressed distinctly (hence the interpreters in their comments of these passages contradict each other), but it exists.

8.96.10 *gírvāhase gíra índrāya pūrvī́r | dhehí tanvè kuvíd aṅgá védat*

Present songs to Indra, who is fond of praise, to his person, many praise songs. Of course, he will appreciate them!

8.100.1 *ayáṃ ta emi tanvā́ purástād | víśve devā́ abhí mā yanti paścā́t*

I am going here in front of you in my own person, all the gods go behind me.

10.83.5 *táṃ tvā manyo akratúr jihīḷāháṃ | svā́ tanū́r baladéyāya méhi*

I have irritated you, O Manyu, without intention. Come to me in your own person so as to give (me your) force![4]

---

[3] Geldner (1951: I, 72) translates 'Ratschlüsse', Renou (1969: 21) 'pouvoirs d'agir'.

[4] Grassmann (1875) gives some more examples that illustrate this meaning, but they are too vague.

This meaning is closely related to a much more frequent and well-defined meaning of *tanū́-*, namely that of a reflexive pronoun, 'self', 'one's own'. For example, when all the gods admired Indra in his battle with the dragon, it is said:

6.18.14 *káro yátra várivo bādhitā́ya | divé jánāya tanvè gṛṇānáḥ*

... where, being lauded, you created free space for the oppressed sky, for the people, for yourself.

8.44.15 *yó agníṃ tanvò dáme devám mártaḥ saparyáti*

which mortal honours in his own[5] house Agni, the god ...

7.86.5 *áva drugdhā́ni pítryā sṛjā nó | 'va yā́ vayáṃ cakṛmā́ tanū́bhiḥ*

Release us from sins committed by fathers, re(lease) us from those that we have committed ourselves.[6]

In this connection one should keep in mind an important observation of Pinault (2001: 188):

L'emploi de *tanū́-* tend vers celui d'un réfléchi, sans jamais atteindre le statut d'un simple réfléchi renvoyant au sujet grammatical de la phrase.

Used in this meaning, *tanū́-* is often found in combination with the pronominal indeclinable *svayám* 'self' and the pronominal adjective *svá-* 'one's own'. For instance:

6.51.7 *svayáṃ ripús tanvàṃ rīriṣīṣṭa*

Let the deceiver hurt himself.

7.86.2 *utá sváyā tanvā̀ sáṃ vade tát*

And I say it to myself.

Tanū́- refers to the generation of the ego ('ourselves') when it is used in combination with words denoting 'offspring, descendants',

---

[5] Literally, 'in the house of the body' (*tanvò* is in the genitive case).

[6] O'Flaherty (1981: 214) translates: '... we have committed with our own bodies'.

such as *tán-*, *tánaya-* (derived from the same root as *tanū́-*: *tan-* 'to stretch', here in the temporal sense), *toká-* and *prajā́-*. For instance:

6.49.13 *rāyā́ madema tanvā́ tánā ca*

We want to enjoy the riches for ourselves and for (our) offspring.

10.4.7 *rákṣā ṇo agne tánayāni tokā́ | rákṣotá nas tanvò áprayuchan*

Protect, O Agni, our descendants, (our) offspring, and also protect attentively ourselves!

In this connection one should be reminded that the names of the god Agni include the compound word *tánūnápāt*, literally 'offspring of himself', because the fire is born from the fire.

The difference between the reflexive meaning and the meaning 'body' is sometimes quite subtle, and there are cases where the context does not give sufficient grounds for a certain choice.

3.1.1 *śamāyé agne tanvàṃ juṣasva*

... während ich ... den Dienst versehe, o Agni – finde du an dir selbst Wohlgefallen! (Geldner 1951: I, 332)

... je fais le travail-rituel: ô Agni, apprécie (l'oblation versée en) ton propre corps! (Renou 1964: 48)

3.15.2 *jánmeva nítyaṃ tánayaṃ juṣasva | stómam me agne tanvā́ sujāta*

Agni, freu dich am eignen Leibe über mein Loblied wie über die Geburt des leiblichen Sohnes, du, Edelgeborener (Geldner 1951: I, 351).

Apprécie par toi-même, ô Agni, mon corps-de-louagne comme (on apprécie) la naissance, (à savoir celle d'un fils, d') un descendant (qui nous soit) propre, ô (dieu) bien né! (Renou 1964: 60–61)

Sometimes the authors of the hymns are simply playing with *tanū́-*:

1.165.11 *ámandan mā maruta stómo átra*
yán me naraḥ śrútyam bráhma cakrá |
índrāya vŕ̥ṣṇe súmakhāya máhyaṃ
sákhye sákhāyas tanvè tanū́bhiḥ ||

Your praise has made me rejoice, lordly Maruts, the sacred chant worthy of hearing that you made here for me – for Indra the bull, the good fighter – that you my friends made in person for me, your friend, in person (O'Flaherty 1981: 169)[7]

There are contexts in the Ṛgveda where *tanū́-* is synonymous, in some respects, to the word *ātmán-/tmán-* 'breath, soul, the principle of life, self, person, the living body as a unity, etc.' (Monier-Williams 1899: 135). The two words are usually synonymous when they are members of the formula 'We ourselves and our descendants'. For instance:

1.114.6 *tmáne tokā́ya tánayāya mṛla*

Have mercy upon ourselves, (our) children (and) grandchildren! [The hymn is addressed to Rudra].

1.183.3 ... *rátho* ... I *yéna narā nāsatyeṣayádhyai* I *vartír yāthás tánayāya tmáne ca*

... the chariot ... on which you, O lords of men Nāsatyas, drive on your journey so as to strengthen – for the sake of (our) offspring and ourselves. [= 6.49.5]

1.184.5 *yātáṃ vartís tánayāya tmáne ca*

Ride on your journey for the sake of (our) offspring and ourselves.

Besides, there is a context where *ātmán-* has a pronominal meaning:

9.113.1 *śaryaṇā́vati sómam* I *índraḥ pibatu vṛtrahā́* I *bálaṃ dádhāna ātmáni* I ...

Let Indra the killer of Vṛtra drink Soma in Śaryaṇāvat, gathering his strength within himself ... (O'Flaherty 1981: 133).

---

[7] Here O'Flaherty follows Geldner's interpretation: 'dem Freund die Freunde in eigener Person meiner Person' (Geldner 1951: I. 240). But Renou understands it in a different way: ... pour moi (votre) ami, (vous qui êtes des) amis, pour moi-même, (la Formule élaborée) par vous-mêmes' (Renou 1962: 55). In his comments on this passage, Renou stresses the 'Insistance sur l'idée pronominale, *me* ... *máhyam* ... *tanvè*' (Renou 1962: 116).

Compare this with

> 1.55.86b *ásāḷhaṃ sáhas tanvì śrutó dadhe*
>
> The famous one has gathered irresistible power in his body [or: within himself].

At last, in the late maṇḍala 10 there is a spell against the *yákṣma-* disease (consumption), where the healer says, after having enumerated the organs and parts of body from which he tears away the *yákṣma-*:

> 10.163.12–13 *yákṣmaṃ sárvasmād ātmánas | tám idáṃ ví vṛhāmi te*
>
> Yákṣma from all the body – now I tear it away for you [cf. Zysk 1985].

There is no doubt that *ātmán-* in this context designates the physical body.

Meanwhile, there are a few passages in the Ṛgveda where *tanū́-* and *ātmán-* are opposed to each other. In a hymn dedicated to the sacrificial horse it is said:

> 1.162.20 *mā́ tvā tapat priyá ātmā́piyántam | mā́ svádhitis tanvà ā́ tiṣṭhipat te*
>
> Let not your own soul burn you as you go away. Let not the axe do lasting harm to your body. (O'Flaherty 1981: 91)[8]

The final verse of an Indra hymn states:

> 8.3.24 *ātmā́ pitús tanū́r vā́sa | ojodā́ abhyáñjanam ...*
>
> Food is the soul, clothes the body, unguent is granting power.[9]

[8] Geldner (1951: I, 224) translates *priyá ātmā́* 'das liebe Leben'. Renou comments: 'Noter *ātmán-* en regard de *tanū́-*, le premier étant atteint moralement, le second atteint physiquement' (Renou 1967: 87).

[9] Renou's explanation of these lines is: '... càd. le corps opp. à âme et symbolisé par le vêtement opp. à la nourriture: images pré-upaniṣadiques' (Renou 1966: 173).

One should keep in mind that the opposition of body and soul was not yet established in the Ṛgveda. The hymns of this *saṃhitā* show only the very beginning of the process that led to this distinction. One can see how the function of the reflexive pronoun gradually passes to *ātmán-*; as noted by Wackernagel and Debrunner (1930: 489), this testifies to the fact that the perception as to the essence of personality was changing. In the later development of the language, *tanū́-* was ousted by *ātmán-* from the function of a reflexive pronoun.

The case paradigm of *tanū́-* comprises all the cases in the singular and plural, as well as one dual form. The singular occurs almost twice as frequently (136 times) as the plural (71 times). The nominative is a rare case (8 occurrences in the singular and 4 in the plural). The reflexive meaning is not found with the nominative case. This case usually (in 11 cases out of 12) indicates the subject of a sentence, while the predicate is an intransitive verb, a verb in the middle voice or a noun. For instance:

6.24.7 *vṛddhásya cid vardhatām asya tanū́*

Though he has increased, his body should increase (more)! [This hymn is addressed to Indra.]

3.20.2 *tisrá u te tanvò devávātās*

There are also three bodies of you, desired by the gods. [This is an Agni hymn.]

The accusative is the most frequent of cases (46 in the singular, 21 in the plural). This is the case of the direct object governed by a transitive verb. The list of verbs used with *tanvàm* or *tanvàḥ* is significant in many respects. Only some of these verbs are connected with a distinct meaning of *tanū́-*; many of them admit various meanings of this substantive. Most frequent with *tanū́-* as a direct object are the verbs *śu(m)bh-* 'to adorn' (8 times): Agni is adorning his body (or bodies), the Maruts, the mortals; and *vṛdh-* 'to increase, to strengthen' (4 times): the devotees are strengthening the bodies of their gods by their oblations and laudatory songs. Both verbs refer to physical bodies. The same reference is characteristic of a group of verbs meaning 'to copulate, to mingle one's body with another body': *(tanvàm) ā viś-*, *(tanvàṃ) ric-*, *(tanvàṃ) sám pṛc-*, *(tanvàṃ) sám sṛj-* (the story of Yama and Yamī; the wedding hymn). But there is also another group of verbs governing *tanū́-* in the accusative. The gods are asked to protect (*rakṣ-*) the bodies of their devotees or the devotees themselves, not to harm (*riṣ-*) their bodies or their persons. Agni is described as finding pleasure (*juṣ-*) in his body or in himself.

Some of these verbs deserve special attention. The combination *tanvàṃ yaj-* 'to sacrifice the body' is found twice in connection with Agni.

6.11.2 *yájasva tanvàṃ táva svā́m*

Sacrifice your own body!

10.7.6 *yáthā́yaja ṛtúbhir deva devā́n | evā́ yajasva tanvàṃ sujāta*

How you have sacrificed to the gods, O god, at the appointed times, the same way sacrifice for yourself, O nobly born!

There is a close connection between the semantic fields of the verbal roots *yaj-* and *tan-* and their derivatives in the hymns of the Ṛgveda. It is known that 'to make an oblation, to sacrifice' is expressed by the combination *yajñáṃ tan-*, which is well testified in this *saṃhitā* (about 20 times). This combination may serve as a key to the semantic motivation, that is, to the mythological background of *tanū́-*. It is used twice in the Puruṣasūkta:

10.90.6 *yát púruṣeṇa havíṣā | devā́ yajñám átanvata*

When the gods spread the sacrifice with the Man as the offering

10.90.15 *devā́ yád yajñáṃ tanvānā́ | ábadhnan púruṣam paśúm*

... when the gods, spreading the sacrifice, bound the Man as the sacrificial beast (O'Flaherty 1981: 30-31).

Puruṣa was a victim whose body was bound to the sacrificial post and dismembered. By means of the sacrifice his body spread out in all directions and filled the whole cosmos (the moon, the sun, the middle realm, the sky, the earth, etc., were born from the parts of his body). The mythological idea of a body (*tanū́-*) acquired in the Ṛgveda the image of spread, stretch, extension; it comprises all the parts and has no limits. That was the model for the usual *tanū́-*.

It is significant that twice in the Ṛgveda the accusative is governed by the verb *ví tan-* 'to spread out, to extend':

5.15.3 *aṃhoyúvas tanvàs tanvate ví*

They are spreading out their bodies, which ward off troubles'

6.46.12 *yátra śū́rāsas tanvò vi tanvaté | priyā́ śárma pitṝṇā́m | ádha smā yacha tanvè tane ca chardír | ...*

Where the heroes are spreading out their bodies (and) the favourite shields of (their) fathers, there grant a screen for ourselves and for (our) offspring!

In the latter example, there is a play with the derivates of the root *tan-*.

After the accusative, next in frequency is the instrumental case (43 times, 34 in the singular, 9 in the plural). The instrumental is either governed by verbs or used adnominally. Among the verbs governing this case the most frequent is *vṛdh-* 'to increase, to strengthen, to grow'. For instance, it is said about Agni:

6.9.4 *... jajñe ... [á]martyas tanvā́ vár̥dhamānaḥ*

... he is born immortal, growing with his body.

Indra is addressed in

8.19.11 *tanvā́ vāvṛdhasva*

Strengthen your body!

These are, of course, references to the physical body. The same can be said about a group of verbs such as *śad-* 'to show off one's body' (Uṣas), *śumbh-* 'id.' (the Aśvins), *ruc-* and *bhrāj-* 'to shine (with the body)'; and verbs meaning 'to mingle one's body with another one', such as *sáṃ gam-* and *sám pṛc-*.

But there are verbs which do not require one definite meaning of *tanū́-*; the ability of the instrumental case to express both the instrument of an action and the subject of it makes it possible to play with various meanings of *tanū́-*. For instance, the verb *mad-* 'to rejoice, be glad, exult, intoxicate; to be drunk':

3.41.6 *sá mandasva hy ándhaso | rā́dhase tanvā́ mahé*

So, intoxicate your body with the beverage, for the great granting of gifts.

So berausche dich denn in eigner Person am Tranke ... (Geldner 1951: I, 384)

Tel (étant) enivre toi donc du breuvage ..., par toi-même! (Renou 1969: 84)

There are examples where *tanū́-* with the reflexive meaning is in the singular, though it refers to a denotatum in the plural:

6.49.13 *rāyā́ madema tanvā́ tánā ca*

We would like to rejoice at the riches, ourselves and our offspring.

Here the verb is in the plural, *tanvā́* is in the singular. Compare the already above (pp. 91–92) given example 1.165.11 with concord in number between the subject and the reflexive pronoun: The lordly Maruts made the sacred chant by themselves (*tanū́bhiḥ*).

The dative case of *tanū́-* (found in the hymns 22 times, 21 in the singular, 1 in the plural) is mostly represented by the dativus commodi, 'to do something for the sake of somebody', and almost half of all the examples has the meaning of the reflexive pronoun ('to do for oneself'):

1.84.17 *kás tokā́ya ká íbhāyotá rāyé | 'dhi bravat tanvè kó jánāya*

Who will speak in favour of the offspring, who in favour of the household and of the riches, who in favour of ourselves (and) of the people?

The dative singular *tanvè* is sometimes referred to the denotatum in the plural:

8.68.12 *urú ṇas tanvè tána | urú kṣáyāya nas kṛdhi*

Create us wide space, for ourselves and for the offspring, (create) wide space for us to settle! [*tanvè* singular, *nas* plural].

The ablative case of *tanū́-* is very rare (3 times in the singular), while the genitive is rather frequent (16 times in the singular, 15 in the plural). The literal meaning of the physical body is most frequent of the genitive of *tanū́-*. It is illustrated by a variety of nominal constructions, such as: *tanvò rakṣitár-* 'protector of the body', *tanvò ... gopā́* 'id.', *trātár- tanū́nām* 'defender of the bodies', *avitár- tanū́nām* 'sustainer of the bodies', *rása- tanū́nām* 'juice of the bodies', *bálāni tanvàḥ* 'powers of the body', *śrī́- tanū́nām* 'beauty of the bodies'; *jarás- tanū́nām* 'old age of the body', *tanvò rápaḥ* 'injury of the body'.

The meaning of a reflexive pronoun is much rarer in the genitive constructions (1/5 of all the cases). For instance:

2.9.2 *ágne tokásya nas táne tanū́nām | áprayuchan dī́dyad bodhi gopā́ḥ*

O Agni, shining brightly, be our attentive protector for the lasting of our offspring and of ourselves!

Sometimes it is difficult to say whether the meaning of *tanvàḥ* in these constructions is reflexive or rather 'person':

2.17.7 *daddhí bhāgáṃ tanvò yéna māmáhaḥ*

Give a lot to myself (or: to my person) with which you will make (me) happy!

Locative is the only case in the paradigm of which the plural forms (21) prevail over the singular ones (8). *Tanū́-* in the locative constructions designates as a rule a physical body. For instance:

6.74.3 *sómārudrā yuvám etā́ny asmé | víśvā tanū́ṣu bheṣajā́ni dhattam*

Soma-and-Rudra! Bring all these remedies for our bodies!

But the concept of a physical body can sometimes include also 'non-physical' abilities, as, for instance, in a description of the Maruts:

8.20.26 *víśvam páśyanto bibhṛthā tanū́ṣv ā́ | ténā no ádhi vocata*

Seeing everything, you carry (it) on your bodies. Speak in our favour with it!

The reflexive meaning is rare (4 times). Once the reflexive *tanvī̀* in the singular refers to the denotatum in the plural:

10.65.7 *yajñám janitvī́ tanvī̀ ní māmṛjuḥ*

Having generated the sacrifice, they took it to themselves [they = the gods].

Epithets attributed to *tanū́-* are very few, especially those expressed by qualitative adjectives. They usually have a positive meaning: *priyá-* 'dear' (but more frequently 'one's own'), ***arepás-*** 'spotless', *rúśat-* 'bright', *yajñíya-* 'worthy of sacrifices', ***aṃhoyú-*** 'warding off troubles'. The only frequent epithet is the pronominal adjective *svá-* 'one's own', as in

5.4.6 *vadhéna dásyuṃ prá hí cātáyasva | váyaḥ kṛṇvānás tanvè svā́yai*

Drive away the Dasyu with your deadly weapon, creating energy for your body!

Also rather frequent are constructions with the genitive case of the personal pronouns (mostly of their enclitic forms), having the possessive meaning:

6.40.4 [*á*]*thā te yajñás tanvè váyo dhāt*

And the sacrifice will give energy for your body.

There are a number of compounds with *tanū́-*. All of them but one have *tanū́-* as the first member. *Tanū́-* as a part of a compound has a reflexive meaning in *tánūnápāt* 'offspring of himself', the name of Agni (found 8 times, regularly in the second verse of the Āprī hymns). In most other compounds with *tanū́-*, the meaning of this word should be understood widely: it is not only the physical body, but also some abstract substance. It is not by chance that Böhtlingk in volume three of his dictionary translates a group of these compounds in the following way:

> *tanūkṛ́t-* 'Leib und Leben erhaltend', *tanūkṛthá-* 'Erhaltung des Leibes und Lebens', *tanūtyáj-* 'Leib und Leben hingebend', *tanūpā́-* 'Leib und Leben schirmend' (Böhtlingk 1882: 8).

In this respect he follows the interpretation of Grassmann (1875: 520). The semantics of *tanū́-* is vague and should be interpreted from the context:

> 1.31.9 *tanūkṛ́d bodhi prámatiś ca kāráve*
>
> Be creator of the body (or: of the person?) and protector for the singer! [This is an Agni hymn.]

Geldner (1951: I, 35) translates *tanūkṛ́t* 'leiblicher Erzeuger', Renou (1964: 5) 'un géniteur', and comments: '*tanūkṛt* est moins 'fabriquant le corps' ... que 'creant un être de son groupe' — **svakṛt* ...' (Renou 1964: 77).

> 8.79.3 *tvám soma tanūkṛ́dbhyo*
> *dvéṣobhyo nyákṛtebhyaḥ* |
> *urú yantā́si várūtham* ||
>
> You, O Soma, are the giver of vast protection against hostile actions made by ourselves (and) by the others.

Tanū́- as a member of *tanūrúc-* 'shining with one's body' and *tanū́śubhra-* 'id.' signifies a physical body.

The second member of all these compounds is derived from one of those verbal roots that can govern case forms of *tanū́-* in a syntactic construction: *kṛ-*, *tyaj-*, *pā-*, *ruc-*, *śubh-*. There exists also one compound in which *tanū́-* forms a second member: *átaptatanū-* 'whose body is not heated'.

One may conclude that *tanū́-* as a member of compounds possesses the same variety of meanings as in independent use, and its semantics remains ambiguous.

The other denomination of 'body', *śárīra-*, is much simpler. It is a substantive of the neutral gender, meaning 'the body, bodily frame, solid parts of the body (pl. the bones)'. Its etymology remains undecided: the connection with the root *śar- śṛṇā́ti* 'to divide, break, smash, destroy' is not definitely established (cf. Mayrhofer 1997: 618). It is a rare word in the Ṛgveda, found in the hymns only 7 times, once is a 'family' maṇḍala, 6 times in the late part of the *saṃhitā* (maṇḍalas 10 and 1).

The word *śárīra-* designates the bodies of mortals, gods, the deified horse and the dragon Vṛtra. But there is also a difference between *tanū́-* and *śárīra-*: *tanū́-* is the name either of the living body which can be bright, full of strength, the person itself, or of the 'new body' with which the dead man unites in the highest heaven, while *śárīra-* twice out of the seven examples denotes a dead body. The following verse refers to the dead body of Vṛtra among moving waters:

1.32.10 *átiṣṭhantīnām aniveśanā́nām | kā́ṣṭhānām mádhye níhitaṃ śárīram*

In the midst of the channels of the waters which never stood still or rested, the body was hidden (O'Flaherty 1981: 150).

This verse is a request to Agni as the cremation fire:

10.16.1 *máinam agne ví daho mā́bhí śoco | mā́sya tvácaṃ cikṣipo mā́ śárīram*

Do not burn him entirely, Agni, or engulf him in your flames. Do not consume his skin or his flesh. (O'Flaherty 1981: 49)

The funeral hymn 10.16 is rather instructive in respect of mutual relations between *tanū́-* and *śárīra-*. In the above quoted verse 1, *śárīra-* belongs to the dead man. Verse 3 is addressed to the dead man who is cremated:

10.16.3 *óṣadhīṣu práti tiṣṭhā śárīraiḥ*

Take root in the plants with your limbs (O'Flaherty 1981: 49)

Setz dich in den Pflanzen fest mit deinen Gebeinen (Geldner 1951: III, 148).

In verse 4, Agni is asked thus:

10.16.4 *yā́s te śivā́s tanvò jātavedas | tā́bhir vahainaṃ sukṛ́tām u lokám*

With your gentle forms, O knower of creatures, carry this man to the world of those who have done good deeds (O'Flaherty 1981: 49)[10]

And verse 5 runs as follows:

10.16.5 *ā́yur vásāna úpa vetu śéṣaḥ | sáṃ gachatāṃ tanvā̀ jātavedaḥ*

Let him reach his own descendants, dressing himself in a life-span. O knower of creatures, let him join with a body. (O'Flaherty 1981: 49–50)

So, *śárīra-* is here the denomination of a dead body and its parts, while *tanū́-* designates the living moving body of Agni or the 'new' body of the deceased which is necessary for a happy life in heaven.

There is one verse, where both *śárīra-* and *tanū́-* are used:

6.25.4 *śū́ro vā śū́raṃ vanate śárīrais | tanūrúcā táruṣi yát kṛṇváite*

But a hero conquers a hero with his firm limbs, when the two (adversaries) with bright bodies struggle for superiority.[11]

The usual meaning of *śárīra-* in the plural is 'bones', sometimes according to the context the 'firm limbs' or the 'firm parts of the body' are meant:

---

[10] Geldner (1951: III, 148) has: 'deine freundlichen Leiber'.

[11] Geldner (1951: II, 124) translates *śárīrais* with 'durch seine Leibes(stärke)'. In this context *śárīra-* symbolizes physical strength, while *tanū́-* gives a hint at a bright personality.

10.99.8 *úpa yát sī́dad índuṃ śárīraiḥ | śyenó 'yopāṣṭir hanti dásyūn*

When he sits down near the (Soma-)juice with his firm limbs, the eagle with iron claws kills the Dasyus.

Here 'he' and 'the eagle' is Indra. Sāyaṇa glosses *śárīraiḥ* with *svaśarīrāvayavair aṅgaiḥ* (ṚV 1946, IV: 664).

There is a context where *śárīra-* is definitely opposed to the mind. In a hymn lauding the deified horse that is partly identified with the sun-horse the poet says:

1.163.11 *táva śárīram patayiṣṇv àrvan | táva cittáṃ vā́ta iva dhrájīmān*

Your body is flying, O courser, your mind is gliding like the wind.

In another context this opposition is implicit. The long-haired ascetics, who have mounted the wind, imply that their souls completely escape the mortals when they say:

10.136.3 *śárīréd asmā́kaṃ yūyám | mártāso abhí paśyatha*

Our bodies are all you mere mortals can see (O'Flaherty 1981: 138).

The paradigm of *śárīra-* consists of three cases: the nominative (in the singular), the accusative (once in the singular, once in the plural) and the instrumental (3 times in the plúral). So the instrumental case appears to be the most frequent, the meaning being 'bones' or 'limbs'.

There is only one case where *śárīra-* is defined by an adjective:

1.155.6 *bṛháccharīra-*

having a vast body. [This compound is an epithet of Viṣṇu.]

In conclusion one can say that the complicated and ambiguous notion of *tanū́-*, which comprises the ideas of a material and a mental substance, played a much more prominent part in the hymns of the Ṛgveda than the narrow and well-defined *śárīra-*. This certainly reflects the world view of the Vedic poets.

In the later development of the Indo-Aryan languages, *tanū́-* looses its polysemantic character. The New Indo-Aryan languages have reflections of both *tanū́-* and *śárīra-*, but only with the meaning of a physical body (cf. Turner 1966: 321, 715).

REFERENCES

BÖHTLINGK, Otto 1882. *Sanskrit-Wörterbuch in kürzerer Fassung*, III: *ta–na*. St. Petersburg: Kaiserliche Akademie der Wissenschaften.

GELDNER, Karl F. 1951. *Der Rigveda aus dem Sanskrit ins Deutsche übersetzt und mit einem laufenden Kommentar versehen*, I–III. (HOS, 33–35.) Cambridge, Mass.: Harvard University Press.

GRASSMANN, Hermann 1875. *Wörterbuch zum Rig-Veda*. Leipzig: F. A. Brockhaus.

LUBOTSKY, Alexander 1997. *A Ṛgvedic Word Concordance*, I–II. (American Oriental Series, 82–83.) New Haven: American Oriental Society.

MAYRHOFER, Manfred 1997. *Etymologisches Wörterbuch des Altindoarischen*, II. (Indogermanische Bibliothek, Reihe 2: Wörterbücher.) Heidelberg: Universitätsverlag Carl Winter.

MONIER-WILLIAMS, Monier 1899. *A Sanskrit-English Dictionary. Etymologically Arranged with Special Reference to Cognate Indo-European Languages*. New edition. Oxford: Clarendon Press.

O'FLAHERTY, Wendy Doniger 1981. *The Rig Veda: An Anthology. One Hundred and Eight Hymns, Selected, Translated and Annotated*. (The Penguin Classics.) Harmondsworth: Penguin Books.

PINAULT, Georges-Jean 2001. Védique *tanū́-* et la notion de personne en indo-iranien. *Bulletin de la Société de linguistique de Paris* 96.1: 181–206.

RENOU, Louis 1962. *Études védiques et pāṇinéennes*, X. (Publications de l'Institut de Civilisation Indienne, Série in-8°, 17.) Paris: Institut de Civilisation Indienne de l'Université de Paris.

—— 1964. *Études védiques et pāṇinéennes*, XII. (Publications de l'Institut de Civilisation Indienne, Série in-8°, 20.) Paris: Institut de Civilisation Indienne de l'Université de Paris.

—— 1966. *Études védiques et pāṇinéennes*, XV. (Publications de l'Institut de Civilisation Indienne, Série in-8°, 26.) Paris: Institut de Civilisation Indienne de l'Université de Paris.

—— 1967. *Études védiques et pāṇinéennes*, XVI. (Publications de l'Institut de Civilisation Indienne, Série in-8°, 27.) Paris: Institut de Civilisation Indienne de l'Université de Paris.

—— 1969. *Études védiques et pāṇinéennes*, XVII. (Publications de l'Institut de Civilisation Indienne, Série in-8°, 30.) Paris: Institut de Civilisation Indienne de l'Université de Paris.

ṚV 1946 = *Ṛgveda-saṃhitā* [*with the Commentary of Sāyaṇācārya*], IV. Ed. by V. K. Rajwade et al. Poona: Vaidika Saṁśodhana Maṇḍala, 1946.

TURNER, Ralph L. 1966. *A Comparative Dictionary of the Indo-Aryan Languages*. London: Oxford University Press.

WACKERNAGEL, Jakob, [& Albert DEBRUNNER] 1930. *Altindische Grammatik*, III: *Die Nominalflexion – Zahlwort – Pronomen*, von Albert Debrunner und Jacob Wackernagel. Göttingen: Vandenhoeck & Ruprecht.

WACKERNAGEL, Jakob, [& Albert DEBRUNNER] 1954. *Altindische Grammatik*, II.2: *Die Nominalsuffixe*, von Albert Debrunner. Göttingen: Vandenhoeck & Ruprecht.

ZYSK, Kenneth G. 1985. *Religious Healing in the Veda. With Translations an Annotations of Medical Hymns from the Ṛgveda and the Atharvaveda and Renderings from the Corresponding Ritual Texts.* (Transactions of the American Philosophical Society, 75.7.) Philadelphia: The American Philosophical Society.

Apāṃ Napāt, Dīrghatamas and Construction of the Brick Altar: Analysis of Ṛgveda 1.143

LÁSZLÓ FÓRIZS

INTRODUCTION

In this paper[1] I translate and interpret Ṛgveda 1.143, which presents a newer and stronger vision of Dīrghatamas. In the arrangement of the surviving Śākalya recension of the ṚV, 1.143 belongs to the Dīrghatamas cycle, a group of 25 hymns traditionally attributed to Dīrghatamas. Vedic scholars have been frustrated about the hymn, and no consensus on its significance and meaning has been reached. It is a laudation of Agni and Apāṃ Napāt. I will show that the intertwining imagery of the hymn gives Agni a unique cosmological significance unparalleled in contemporary sacerdotal poetry.

SOME PRINCIPLES CONCERNING THE TRANSLATION

The following principles concerning the translation may seem trivial but are important.

---

1 This research has been supported by The Hungarian Scientific Research Fund, OTKA T 21224, The Pro Renovanda Cultura Hungariae, and The Gate of Dharma Buddhist Fund.

1) A solution that does not violate the grammar is preferable to a solution that does. For example, a nominative is not an accusative, even if it occurs in a difficult Vedic passage. Cf. Sāyaṇa's interpretation of ṚV 1.143.3.
2) A solution that does not misuse the vocabulary (e.g., by introducing *ad hoc* meanings) is preferable to a solution that does. Cf. Geldner's 'Elefant' in ṚV 1.143.7.
3) A solution that does not replace a whole word by another one in order to get the 'required' meaning is preferable to a solution that does. Cf. Ludwig's replacement of *ajarāḥ* by *amarāḥ* in ṚV 1.143.3.
4) A solution that does not modify the grammatical form of a word forcefully to get a 'more desirable' form (e.g., a word with a different ending) is preferable to a solution that does. Cf. the replacement of *aktúr* (masc. sing. nom.) by *aktū́n* (masc. pl. acc.) in ṚV 1.143.3 by Oldenberg and later on by Geldner, Mylius, etc. (Renou and Elizareṇkova tried to avoid this kind of abuse in two different ways.)
5) A solution that does not violate the metre is preferable to a solution that does. Cf. ṚV 1.149.3 *ā́ yáḥ púraṃ nā́rmiṇīm ádīded* in the metrically restored (!) edition of van Nooten and Holland (1994: 91).
6) A solution that does not destroy (alter) the integrity of the original text is preferable to a solution that does. Cf. The insertion of the refrain *nábhantām anyaké same* in ṚV 8.41 by the redactors. Nevertheless, such an early intrusion can provide us useful information.

[7) A profound solution is preferable to a simplistic one.]

ANALYSIS OF ṚV 1.143

A Newer and Stronger Vision to Agni

Let us start the analysis with an important observation: the hymn differs from the usual patterns of Ṛgvedic poetry with regard to its poet (his metronymic name/maternal lineage)[2], its theme (Apāṃ Napāt, *iṣṭi*, anointment of the cosmic/creative Agni), and its poetic form (application of pure rhymes in 1ab, 1cd, 2ab, *agnáye – bhare*, *priyó – ṛtvíyaḥ*, *víomani – mātaríśvane*). The hymn is Dīrghatamas' newer and stronger vision to Agni/Apāṃ Napāt:

> I bring forward a stronger and newer vision (praise) to Agni, a hymn of Vāc to the son of strength; [he is] Apāṃ Napāt, the beloved *hotā*, who together with the Vasus has sat down on the Earth observing the appointed time. (ṚV 1.143.1.)

The Problem of Apāṃ Napāt

The most important and most difficult part of the vision is verse 3. So I will discuss it in greater detail. Without taking into account the complex roles that Apāṃ Napāt (and Agni) could play, a proper understanding of the subtle imagery of the verse is not possible.

Apāṃ Napāt is encountered only in a few hymns of the Ṛgveda: in 1.22.6a, 143.1c; 2.31.6d, 35.1c, 35.2c, 35.3d, 35.9a, 35.10b; 3.9.1c; 6.50.13b, 52.14b; 7.34.15a, 47.2b; 10.30.3b, 30.14d, 92.13b. There is an entire hymn of the Gṛtsamada clan (2.35) that lauds Apāṃ Napāt exclusively. An alternative appellation is *apā́ṃ gárbhaḥ* that occurs in 1.70.3a, 164.52b; 3.1.12d, 1.13a, 5.3b; 7.9.3d; 9.97.41b. This alternative form does not occur in the 2nd Maṇḍala. Neither Apāṃ Napāt nor *apā́ṃ gárbhaḥ* is found in the

---

[2] Dīrghatamas is called Māmateya in four different hymns of the Ṛgveda. RV 1.147.3 and 1.152.6 are probably self-references. One reference, 4.4.13, is in a hymn of the Vāmadevas. In addition, in a controversial biographical hymn that vividly describes the dramatic end of his long and fruitful life, Dīrghatamas is called not only by his metronym Māmateya (1.158.6), but also twice by his patronym Aucathya (1.158.1). I plan to discuss the intricacies of this important hymn and the life and work of Dīrghatamas in another paper.

4th, 5th and 8th Maṇḍalas. The 9th Maṇḍala has only *apā́ṃ gárbhaḥ*. We can see that in the 1st, 3rd and 7th Maṇḍalas both forms occur. The Dīrghatamas cycle has Apāṃ Napāt only in 1.143, while *apā́ṃ gárbhaḥ* occurs at the end of the Riddle hymn (1.164.52b).

The problematic nature of Apāṃ Napāt is evident from the discrepancies between his numerous scholarly interpretations: sun, lightning, moon, water spirit, Soma, Varuṇa, god of waters, the horse-shaped sun-fire in the waters (Findly 1979; Parpola 2005). In his quest for a sound interpretation, Dumézil turned to Indo-European mythology for clues. Findly summarizes the results of her comparative analysis in the following way:

> We can see ... that the myths from the Old Irish, Roman, and Iranian sources have four major themes: 1) a burning or glowing element 2) hidden in the midst of the waters 3) attainable only by those who are qualified and forbidden to those who are not, 4) but whose illegitimate attempts to claim the element result in the overflowing of the waters (Findly 1979: 176).

What Findly tries to show is that all these four major themes can also be found in the Ṛgveda, but with a gradual shift of emphasis from the 'natural' water forms (streams, rivers, lakes, seas, rains, and snows) to the 'ritual' ones (the water used in the preparation of oblations and other kinds of liquid offerings, i.e., milk, ghee, Soma, and honey), culminating in the ritual mixing of the *vasatīvarī* and *ekadhanā* waters in the course of the *aponaptrīya* ceremony of the Soma ritual.

Some Remarks on the *aponaptrīya* Ceremony

The following questions arise naturally: What ritual activities precede its performance and what activities follow it? What (if any) special ritual constructions are present in the scene in the course of the *aponaptrīya* ceremony?

At the time of the *Śatapathabrāhmaṇa* the Soma ritual has two ritual enclosures. Besides the *vedi*, there is also an *uttaravedi* (U). The old *āhavanīya* (OA) has already become the new *gārhapatya*

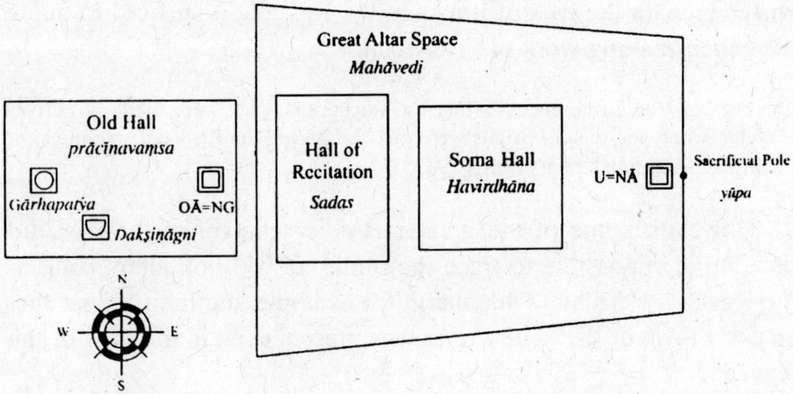

Fig. 1. Ritual enclosures for Soma rituals

(NG) (see Fig. 1). However, the new domestic altar is square-shaped and constructed of bricks (*gārhapatyaciti*) in the place of the old offering altar, which was made of clay.[3]

Whether any of the fireplaces or altars was made of bricks at the time of the hymn discussed remains an open problem, but we know that in later times not only the new domestic altar, but also the new bird-shaped fire-altar in the east (*agniciti*) was made of bricks. Since what time have brick constructions been present in Vedic rituals? The answer to this question is not known.

3 One of the main themes of the *aponaptrīya* rite is the mixing of the old and the new: '"Water hath united with water, plants with plants!" the sap of the sacrifice which was fetched yesterday and that fetched today, both kinds he thereby mixes together' (ŚB 3.9.3.29). There is another possible connotation here: mixing of the old ritual and the new one. I think the two ritual enclosures and the 'strange' (square-shaped) form of the new domestic altar clearly indicate that rituals have grown together. I intend to discuss this problem complex in another paper.

I am well aware that present-day scholars of the Veda apparently agree on the lack of bricks in the Ṛgveda; it suffices to quote the epoch-making work of Frits Staal:

> The Ṛg-Vedic references to houses indicate that they were made of perishable wood and thatch. Bricks were thus not part of the Ṛg-Vedic technical or ritual accomplishments (Staal 1983: I, 131).

However, some of the greatest Vedic scholars of the past did not find it impossible to trace the piling up of brick altars back to the Ṛgveda. Hermann Oldenberg, for example, did not rule out that an early form of the *agnicayana* was present even in the time of the Ṛgveda:

> Perhaps we may conjecture ... that the *agnicayana* rite in its simplest form was known already in the Ṛgveda period (Oldenberg 1988: 286).

For Eggeling (1897: xiii–xviii), this was possible also in the context of the Puruṣasūkta (ṚV 10.90). Interestingly enough, Geldner saw a possible reference to it even in our present hymn (ṚV 1.143).[4]

From the above comments we can conclude that at least indirectly the *aponaptrīya* ceremony is connected with the construction of a brick altar during the performance of a Soma ritual. But since what time has the construction of a brick altar been part of the Soma ritual? Where does it come from?

Vedic Fireplaces and the *uttaravedi*: Evidence of ṚV 1.140.1, 2.35.5 and 1.149.3

Instead of just relying on the situation that prevailed at the time of the *Śatapathabrāhmaṇa*, we have to find evidence for any of these constructions in the Ṛgveda, at the time of Dīrghatamas.

---

[4] Cf. Geldner's note on ṚV 1.143.4: 'In den Nabel der Erde = den Feueraltar' (Geldner 1951: 201).

There is some Ṛgvedic evidence on the *uttaravedi*. In a hymn of the Dīrghatamas cycle, Agni is called *vediṣád* (ṚV 1.140.1). This means that Agni sits on the *vedi*, but in this case Agni can sit only on the *uttaravedi*, as Hillebrandt noted already long ago:

> Because Agni is called *vediṣád* in RV. 1.140.1, thus corresponding to the *uttaravedi* of the ritual ... (Hillebrandt 1980: 379).

The most problematic word of verse 5 of the Apāṃ Napāt hymn ṚV 2.35 is *kṛ́tā*.[5] It occurs only here in the Ṛgveda. For Geldner, the reading (*kṛ́tā iva*) is only one of the probable options, and he did not try to translate it (cf. Geldner 1951: 321, n. 1). Nor did Renou: 'le mot reste mysterieux' (Renou 1965: 103). Mayrhofer did not give a clear derivation either. For him, the word was still 'nicht voll geklärt'. As an excuse, he made a reference to the failure of Geldner and Renou. Bailey's tentative suggestion is 'girl'. He identified the word with *Vīdēvdād* 19.30 (*srīra*) *kərəta*, and translated it as '(beautiful) girls/maidens', but according to Mayrhofer (1992–2001: I, 390) this was 'ohne erkennbare philologische Begründung'. On the other hand, Mayrhofer (ibid.) got very close to the solution when he tried to think over Bailey's rather *ad hoc* conjecture:

> A.a.O. auch zum Etymon von iir. **kṛ́tā-* 'Mädchen'; wenn es existiert hat, dann ist es eher erotischer Slang aus '*Spalte'.

The most probable meaning of *kṛ́tā* is 'holed' or 'something/somebody with a hole', e.g., holed fireplaces. (At that time, the Vedic innovations concerning fireplaces, such as those of the *āhavanīya*, were still waiting to take place.) So the translation is:

> Three women, goddesses, desire to bestow (*didhiṣanti*, desiderative of *dhā-* 'to give') food upon the immovable (or unshakeable, *avyathyá*, fut. part. pass. (gdv.) of *vyath-* 'to waver') god. [It seems] as if he stretches forth (*úpa prasarsré*, pr. intens. sg. 3, of (*úpa*) *pra+sṛ-*, 'to extend, stretch forth to') to

---

5. ṚV 2.35.5 *asmaí tisró avyathiyā́ya nā́rīr devā́ya devī́r didhiṣanti ánnam | kṛ́tā ivópa hí prasarsré apsú sá pīyū́ṣaṃ dhayati pūrvasū́nām* ||

the holed ones (the holed fireplaces) in the waters while he sucks the milk of those who have brought forth [life] for the first time.

The problem of ṚV 1.149.3 is an old one.[6] Geldner (1951: 207) translates 'die Burg *Nārmiṇī*'. Witzel repeats this with a question mark: '*Nārmiṇī* "a fort?"' (Witzel 1999: 361). For the meaning of *pur* one has to consult Wilhelm Rau:

> The evidence ... does not fit the cities of the Indus civilization. It rather suggests the existence of numerous, frequently concentric, mud or stone ramparts of round or oval ground-plan, – many times hastily erected – and reinforced by wooden defences, enclosing thatched timber sheds to serve at best as temporary homes but more often to shelter men and their cattle in times of war, water supply and provisions being, therefore, of vital importance (Rau 1976: 52; cf. also Parpola 1988: 211–217).

According to Mayrhofer (1992–2001: II, 38), '*nā́rmiṇī-*, f., Name (oder Beiwort) einer *púr-* (s.d.; ṚV 1,149,3)', is of uncertain interpretation: he refers, with reservation, to the explanation 'nicht trümmerhaft' (*na-* + *árma-*). In my view, interpreting *ná* as a negative particle is problematic, among other things because in this case *púraṃ ná árminīṃ* would become *púraṃ nā́rmiṇīm* in speech; but if we interpret it as a particle of comparison, the problem disappears.

> *Ná* is used in V. (very commonly in ṚV., comparatively rarely in AV., but never in B.) as a particle of comparison, exactly like *iva* 'as, like'. This *ná*, being in sense closely connected with the preceding word, never coalesces in pronunciation (though it does in written Sandhi) with a following vowel, whereas *ná* generally does. This *ná* always follows the word of comparison to which it belongs; or if the simile consists several words, then *ná* generally follows the first word, less commonly the second. (Macdonell 1916: 236)

Interestingly enough, the 'metrically reconstructed' text of van Nooten and Holland (1994: 592) does not even mention the problem, while Oldenberg (1897: 177) does:

---

[6] ṚV 1.149.3 *ā́ yáḥ púraṃ ná árminīm ádīded átyaḥ kavír nabhanýo ná árvā | sū́ro ná rurukvā́ñ chatáātmā* ||

> We do not know what *nārmiṇī* is. Possibly in this word two words, *ná ármiṇī*, are contained, so that the particle *ná* would be repeated in each of the three Pādas. The translation would then be: 'he who lighted up the *ármiṇī* (?) like a stronghold'.

Though Oldenberg did not give a solution for the word *ármiṇī*, and we do not agree with him in the details of his translation, the interpretation of *ná* as a particle of comparison (even if it was only a hypothetical suggestion) goes beyond all the other tentative solutions.

My solution is the following:

1) In spite of the text of van Nooten and Holland (1994: 91) the first line is: *ā́ yáḥ púraṃ ná ármiṇīm ádīded.*
2) In the comparison, *pur* denotes a (possibly fortified) ceremonial centre, a kind of sanctuary rather than a fort, the emphasis being on the sacred character of the place rather than on its fortified nature. This agrees both with the newly found fortified ceremonial centre at the BMAC settlement in the oasis of Dashly-3 in northern Afghanistan and with the *agnicayana* portion of the *Śatapathabrāhmaṇa* (ŚB 6.3.3.24–25).
3) According to my reading, the problem of *ármiṇī* is connected with the interpretation of *armaká* (ṚV 1.133.3) and *árma* (TS, TB+). I think the most probable meaning for *ármiṇī* (as well as *armaká*) is 'fire-well', i.e., 'a holed (fire-)place made of mud or clay'. As already noted, the Vedic innovations concerning fireplaces, such as those of the *āhavanīya*, were still waiting to take place. Cf. Mayrhofer:

> *árma-* m. (TS, TB +), dazu *armaká-* m. (RV [1,133,3]+; s. Hoffm, ZDMG 110 [1960] 68 Anm. 2 = HoffmA 124 Anm. 2): wohl 'Brunnen' (Bedeutungsbestimmung nach K. T. Schmidt, StIdgW 290ff.). – Wenn richtig bestimmt, dann identisch mit toch. B *ālme* 'Brunnen' (und Flußnamen Europas wie *Almus*, *Alma* usw.) < idg. *$^*h_2el$-mo-*; dazu vṛddhiert *$^*h_2\bar{e}l$-mo-* in toch. B *yolme* 'Teich,' Schmidt, a.a.O. (Mayrhofer 1992–2001: I, 120)

4) The fire-well (and the sacred place) is illuminated by the hundredfold *ātman* (*sū́ro ná rurukvā́ñ chatáātmā*) (and not set aflame by it/him).

So the translation is:

> Who illuminates the fire-well like a sanctuary/fort, the sage (seer, *kaví*) runs like a neighing steed, the hundredfold *ātman* shines like the Sun.

The Cosmic, Creative Role of Apāṃ Napāt

Although Findly talks about ṚV 2.35 in great detail in her paper (Findly 1979), she omits three important verses of this hymn. The first omitted verse[7] clearly states:

> Apām Napāt, the true [Lord][8], has with his Asuric power (*asuríyasya mahnā́*) created all the creatures (2.35.2.cd).

Remarkably enough, in a late Avestan text we find a passage that strengthens this evidence:

> ... We worship the great lord ... Apąm napā̊ ..., the strong one, ... who created men ..., the god who dwells in the waters, and who is the first to hear when he is worshipped. (Yašt 19.51, transl. Hillebrandt 1980)

Of course, such a creative activity and cosmological role is incompatible with the Avestan fire cult, even if the name, Apąm napā̊, is Avestan. Taking into account the fact that Yašt 19 belongs to the later part of Avestan texts (Witzel 2001: 4), the situation is remarkable. Attributing the creation of men to a subordinate Yazata, Apąm napā̊, is in clear conflict with the usual Zoroastrian concepts of creation.[9]

---

[7] ṚV 2.35.2 *apā́ṃ nápād asuríyasya mahnā́ víśvāni aryó bhúvanā jajāna.*

[8] '*aryó*,' of course, refers to the creator god and not to the creatures. (Contrary to this, e.g., O'Flaherty 1981: 105.)

[9] Hillebrandt was among the first scholars who realized the problem. In spite of his obsession with lunar interpretations, he was well aware of the problems presented by this aspect of Apāṃ Napāt.

In view of the Iranian evidence the omission of the verse 2.35.2 by Findly is even more problematic. Findly should have analyzed the evidence instead of covering up the tracks. The second omitted verse ṚV 2.35.12[10] leads us to another important aspect of Apāṃ Napāt that Findly's analysis failed to touch: the concrete, earthly form of the god:

> I rub its back, I would like to bestow it[11] with the holed ['fireplaces'] and food, and praise it with stanzas.[12]

To summarize: Findly's paper seems to be a well balanced analysis but there are at least two aspects of Apāṃ Napāt it fails to do justice to, namely, (1) its cosmic, creative role and (2) its concrete earthly form. The lack of these themes in the Indo-European heritage does not mean that these are negligible or unimportant aspects of the Apāṃ Napāt complex. It can only be interpreted as a sign that they came from another background.

Analysis of the Available Renderings of ṚV 1.143.3

ṚV 1.143.3 has caused endless frustration among scholars since the time of Sāyaṇa. No sound interpretation has been achieved yet.

Sāyaṇa takes *tveṣāḥ* in the sense of *dīptayaḥ* (*'asya stūyamānasyāgneḥ tveṣā dīptayaḥ'*) and construes *asyá tveṣā́ ajárāḥ* as a clause by itself. According to him, *bhānávaḥ* is the subject of the next clause; *susaṃdṛ́śaḥ* and *sudyútaḥ* are nominative plurals agreeing with *bhānávaḥ* and forming the predicate of the clause; *suprátīkasya* is in construction with *asya.* In explaining the second

---

[10] ṚV 2.35.12 *asmaí bahūnā́m avamā́ya sákhye yajñaír vidhema námasā havírbhiḥ | sáṃ sā́nu mā́rjmi dídhiṣāmi bílmair dádhāmi ánnaiḥ pári vanda ṛgbhíḥ* ||

[11] The demonstrative, of course, refers to Apāṃ Napāt, but in this case to its visible, touchable, concrete earthly form (referred to by 'it' instead of 'him').

[12] The third verse omitted by Findly, ṚV 2.35.15, also refers to an important aspect of Apāṃ Napāt shared by the Ṛgveda and the Iranian myth, namely the contest theme. However, it is fair to say that Findly paid due attention to this aspect of the Apāṃ Napāt complex in her analysis.

line Sāyaṇa 'takes refuge in the absurdity' that the nominative perhaps stands here for the accusative (cf. Peterson 1888: 89–91 for this and the next three paragraphs.)

Roth takes *bhā́tvakṣasaḥ* (which occurs only here in the Ṛgveda) as a genitive and apparently (cf. Böhtlingk & Roth 1852: 91, under *ati*) connects it with *sindhavaḥ*. He explains that form as an anomalous genitive (*sindhavaḥ* = *sindhvaḥ* = *sindhoḥ*). He takes *ati* to be a preposition governing the genitive in the sense of 'over': 'on the surface of'. Accordingly, the translation in Geldner and Kaegi's *Siebenzig Lieder* (1875) is 'Like the shimmer which floats on the surface of the stream'.

Ludwig (1876–88) takes *bhā́tvakṣasaḥ* with *agneḥ*: 'who has light for his strength', and takes *atyaktuḥ* to mean 'all night through'. He takes *ajarāḥ* in both places as an adjective and avoids the apparent tautology by changing the second *ajarāḥ* to *amarāḥ*. In this way, Agni resembles the rivers as far as he, like them, is in constant motion day and night.

Grassmann follows Sāyaṇa in taking *bhā́tvakṣasaḥ* and *sindhavaḥ* as nominative plurals. He takes *ati* as an adverb with *rejante*. For *sindhavaḥ* in the sense of 'streams of light' he instances ṚV 1.52.14 *sindhave rajasaḥ* as a somewhat similar metaphor. He translates the sentence as

> Die Flammenströme flimmern, wie das Tageslicht, die lichtgewalt'gen, nimmer schlummernd, ewig jung[13] (Grassmann 1876: 148).

Oldenberg proposes: 'Probably we should read *áti aktū́n*; comp. 6.4.5. *áti eti aktū́n*' (Oldenberg 1897: 158). He translates:

> His flames are fierce; never ageing are the flames of him who is beautiful to behold, whose face is beautiful, whose splendour is beautiful. The never sleeping, never ageing (rays) of Agni whose power is light, roll forward like streams across the nights(?). (Oldenberg 1897: 157)

---

[13] 'The flame-streams shine like the daylight (*áti aktúr*), full of light, never slumbering, ever young.'

It seems straightforward, but comes at the price of abusing the (orally transmitted) text. Soon we will see how much this 'little change' costs.

Geldner: '... zittern die Nacht über gleich dem Farbenspiel der Flüsse' (Geldner 1951: 201), with the same abuse of the original.

Mylius (along with the same lines as Geldner and Oldenberg):

> Seine funkelnden, nicht alternden, seine Strahlen des schönen Anblick gewährenden, schönantlitzigen, schön leuchtenden, leuchtkräftigen Agni bewegen sich zitternd die Nacht über, wie die Flüsse nicht schlummernd, nicht alternd (Mylius 1978: 16).

Renou:

> *aktú* 'Farbenspiel' de Gld. est tentant, mais non confirmé (Atkins JAOS. 70 p. 35 proposait 'flot'); peut-être un ancien *aktū́n ná síndhavaḥ* (*aktū́n* en liaison avec *áti* comme 1.36.16, 6.4.5) a-t-il été remplacé par *aktúḥ* sous l'influence du type *sindhur ná kṣódaḥ* (Renou 1964: 105).[14]

Renou's effort is quite remarkable, but it is evident that he had difficulty in grasping the meaning of the verse:

> Ses (flammes) étincelantes, à l'abri de vieillir, les rayons de ce (dieu) beau à contempler, au beau visage, au bel éclat, / vigoureux en brillance, tremblent par delà (les nuits) comme la surface-ointe (des) fleuves, (ses rayons) exempts de sommeil, exempts de vieillir. (Renou 1964: 35)

Let us have a look at the second (and most interesting) part of his rendering:

> les rayons ... tremblent par delà (<u>les nuits</u>) comme la surface-ointe (<u>des</u>) fleuves – 'the rays tremble beyond (<u>the nights</u>) as the surface-ointment (<u>of</u>) the streams.'

---

[14] 'The "*Farbenspiel*" of Geldner (for *aktú*) is tempting but it is not confirmed (Atkins, JAOS. 70, p. 35 proposed "*flot*", 'wave'); perhaps an ancient *aktū́n ná síndhavo* (*aktū́n* in connection with *áti* as in 1.36.16, 6.4.5). A replacement of *aktū́n* with *aktúḥ* under the influence of the type *sindhúr ná kṣódaḥ*.'

He is almost there, but the final conclusion is still much ado about (almost) nothing. Although he interprets *aktú* as 'ointment/anointing', he could not escape from the bondage of the preconceptions of his predecessors; even the nights came back in the backdoor of the first brackets; and, what is (grammatically) worse, Roth's spirit also appeared in the coat of the second brackets.

In fact, Oldenberg was one of the first scholars who argued that *aktú* could also mean 'ointment' in the Ṛgveda. Cf. the Index of words in Oldenberg 1897: *aktú*, night, 1.36.16, 68.1, 94.5; 2.10.3; 3.7.6; 4.10.5; *áti aktúḥ* (conj. *áti aktū́n*), 1.143.3; *aktú*, ointment: *aktúbhiḥ ajyate*, 3.17.1. In a note to 3.17.11, Oldenberg stated: 'I do not believe that the existence of a Vedic word *aktú*, "ointment", should be denied.' Nevertheless, he did not think this possibility over, or more probably, he did try, but failed.

Elizarenkova: She too is almost there (in the first line, at least): Его искрящиеся нестареющие (языки пламени), его лучи' – but then she falls into the same kind of trap as all of her predecessors:

> (У этого) прекрасного видом (бога) с прекрасным обликом, с яркой вспышкой, / Сильные (своим) блеском (лучи), трепещут, словно реки / Сквозь ночь, о Агни, недремлющие, нестареющие (Elizarenkova 1989: 182).

Even if she quotes the original in note 3c: '... трепещут, словно реки *сквозь ночь* (*áty aktúr na sindhavo*) ...' (Elizarenkova 1989: 633), the problem is still there: the preposition (*áti*) requires an accusative! Anyway, she is honest like Peterson (who left this verse untranslated in his English rendering of the poem): 'Сравнение остается неясным. Предлагались разные эмендации текста, но ни одна из них не очевидна.'[15] It seems to me that Elizarenkova, while struggling towards the understanding of the structure and meaning of the complex imagery of the verse, relied too much on the simplistic approach of her predecessors.

---

[15] 'The simile seems to be unclear. Many emendations of the text have been suggested, but none of them is obvious/clear.'

The strange thing is that the language of this particular hymn is not that difficult. The same holds true for the majority of the hymns of the whole Dīrghatamas cycle. A clear exception is, for example, ṚV 1.158; but in this case the authorship of Dīrghatamas is more than questionable. As a matter of fact, almost all the obscurities concerning the grammar and the meaning of words have already been removed by the above mentioned scholars. However, no proper understanding of the complex imagery of the poem has been achieved yet. It is the overall picture, the integrity of the vision that is lost. In order to solve the difficulties, one has to understand not only the grammar and the proper meaning of the words, but also the intertwining images and the overall context of the poem. The (probably) unconscious application of pure rhymes in ṚV 1.143.1ab, 1cd, 2ab (*agnáye – bhare, priyó – ṛtvíyaḥ, víomani – mātaríśvane*) is in agreement with the importance of the poet's vision about the emergence of a newer and stronger Agni. The poetical form of the hymn reflects the intensity of the poet's penetration into the depth of the mystery of creation.

My Solution of ṚV 1.143.3

The first line is a nominal sentence; the subject is put at the end of the phrase as in the case of Pāṇinean Sanskrit: *asyá tveṣā́ ajárā asyá bhānávaḥ* 'His rays are his unageing (ceaseless, not decaying) stimulations/ incitements'. The second line can also be interpreted as a nominal sentence: *susaṃdṛ́śaḥ suprátīkasya sudyútaḥ* 'The splendour(s) (or light-rays) of 'the one with a beautiful face' are pleasing ('good to look at')'. Having been completely freed from the preconceptions of the predecessors, the only obstacle to the interpretation of the last two lines is *bhā́tvakṣasaḥ*. I removed that obstacle in the simplest (but not simplistic!) possible way: *bhā́tvakṣas* = *bhā́-* 'light' + *tvakṣas-* 'maker' ('somebody who makes something with his hands', e.g., 'a carpenter'), from *tvakṣ-* (*takṣ-*) 'to create, produce' (Avestan *ϑβaχš-*); *bhā́tvakṣasaḥ ati*: 'beyond the light-makers' (or: carpenters of light, i.e., the stars);

aktúr ná ... agnéḥ: 'as [if] the anointment of Agni'; *ásasantaḥ*: 'not-sleeping (i.e., awakened by the incitements of Agni)'; *ajárāḥ*: 'unageing' (without the incitements of Agni, time [= creation] is not yet in the making). So the translation is:

> His rays are his ceaseless incitements: the splendour of the one with a beautiful face is good to look at. Beyond the light-makers – as the anointment of Agni – the not-sleeping, unageing streams begin to move. (1.143.3)

Dīrghatamas' New Vision of Agni

'Sun and its rays' means the culmination of the creative process. On the other hand, Agni's incitements begin the process of creation. Without the incitements of Agni, the time (creation) is not yet in the making. The Sun with its rays is a kind of a final cause, but it is better to say that Dīrghatamas' imagery is one of the first expressions of the Vedic idea of re-creation. Agni creates the Sun and the Sun re-creates Agni.

Later on the images of Vedic poets followed the path of Dīrghatamas vision and his insight helped them to formulate their answer to the mysteries of creation. Cf. ṚV 10.72.4: Dakṣa → Aditi and Aditi → Dakṣa, ṚV 10.90.5: Puruṣa → Virāj and Virāj → Puruṣa, ṚV 10.121.7 & 9: *ā́pas* → *garbha* and *garbha* → *ā́pas*. The first three *brāhmaṇa*s in the *agnicayana* section of the *Śatapatha-brāhmaṇa* are the culmination of this new insight into mutual creation: ŚB 6.1.1–3: Prajāpati → Agni and Agni → Prajāpati. The analysis of this development will be discussed in another paper (see also Fórizs 2005).

Analysis of ṚV 1.143.7

The above solution is based on my understanding of *ak-ra-*, adj. 'anointed', m. 'someone who is anointed' (cf. *vip-ra-* 'inspired'; *gṛ́dh-ra-* 'greedy') and the understanding of the hymn as a whole. My translation of verse 7 corroborates that of verse 3:

> Having been kindled, it (i.e., our heart) reaches (*ṛñjate*) your Agni, whose face shines with ghee (or: your ghee-faced Agni), as a (good) friend in (or: under) the yoke of *Ṛta*; the anointed one (*akró*) in the [sacrificial] assemblies (*vidátheṣu*), the kindling one (= Agni) stretches out (or: sustains, maintains, *yaṃsate*) our bright-colored vision. (1.143.7)

To give an idea of the divergences and serious problems with other renderings, it suffices to quote Geldner and Elizarenkova:

> Eurem Agni, dem Schmalzgesicht, der auf der Deichsel des rechten Werkes sitzt, läßt der Anzündende den Vortritt wie einem verbündeten Freund. Entflammt bei den Opfern leuchtend möge er (wie) ein Elefant*(?) unser lichtfarbenes Gedicht emporheben.
>
> *Oder nach Ludwig: (Wie) eine Säule entflammt bei den Opfern leuchtend, möge er emportragen. (Geldner 1951: 201–202)

> К вашему Агни с ликом, (обмазанным) жиром, сидящему на дышле закона, (Жрец,) зажигающий (его,) направляется как к другу. Зажженный, сверкающий на местах жертвенных раздач, (этот) боевой конь (?). Пусть понесет вверх нашу светлоокрашенную поэтическую мысль! (Elizarenkova 1989: 182)

Translation of ṚV 1.143.2

> He (who is) being begotten in the highest heaven, Agni revealed himself to *Mātariśvan*. By the inspiration (*krátvā*), by the greatness/majesty (*majmánā*) of the [one who] kindled [himself, his] radiance/flame (*śocíḥ*) glittered on Heaven and Earth. (1.143.2.)

Analysis of ṚV 1.143.4

yám eriré bhṛ́gavo: 'The possessor/knower of all (or: the all-possessor/all-knower) whom the *Bhṛ́gus* (have) obtained'; *ā+ir-* can mean not only 'to set in motion, set to work' (Oldenberg), 'spornen' (Geldner), 'to strengthen' (Elizarenkova), but also 'to procure, obtain'. All these choices are acceptable with more or less equal probability.

nā́bhā pṛthivyā́ bhúvanasya majmánā: '(who is) on the navel of the earth, and of the world, with/in (all his) majesty/might/greatness (*majmánā*, instr.)'. Grammatically not only the instrumental, but also *majmánā* used as an indeclinable adverb is acceptable (cf. Geldner's solution: 'in den Nabel der Erde[16], der Welt insgesamt eingesetzt haben'), but taking into account the occurrence of *majmánā* in verse 2, the first choice is preferable.

agníṃ tám: It is a concrete thing that is referred to here, the fire that can be grasped with one's hands and then carried. But if this is the case, then a vessel is also required for carrying the fire. This carrying of fire is accompanied with the utterance of praises (*gīrbhír*). *ā́+hi-* can mean 'to stir up' (Oldenberg) or 'spornen' (Geldner), but it is more likely that here it means 'to convey, bring, carry' or 'подгонять' (Elizarenkova: 'Этого Агни подгони к своему дому хвалебными песнями'). *yá éko vásvo váruṇo ná rā́jati*: That (sacrificial) fire (*agni*) is, on the other hand, (mysteriously) identical with Agni (Apāṃ Napāt and even the *iṣṭi*, altar, see further on), (that Agni) who – like Varuṇa (the lord) of the Vasus – is the (only) One who rules. A possible connotation here is 'the One (lord) who – like Varuṇa (the lord) of the Vasus – rules (over everything)'. So this Agni is not only the Fire of the Vasus, but also the Fire of all of us, like Agni Vaiśvānara. However, Vaiśvānara is not found in the Dīrghatamas cycle: the word occurs only in two hymns of the first Maṇḍala, four times in ṚV 1.59, a *triṣṭubh* hymn of Nodhas (of the Gotama family)[17] and four times in ṚV 1.98, another *triṣṭubh* hymn of Kutsa (Aṅgiras family). It is also important to note that Agni Vaiśvānara does not occur in the hymns of the Gṛtsamada clan (Book 2) at all; in fact, this is the only book of the Ṛgveda where Agni Vaiśvānara is not found. This requires an explanation all the more because he is found already in the oldest strata of the Ṛgveda, in Book 6, where three entire hymns (two *triṣṭubh*s and a *jagatī*) laud him: 6.7 (7x), 6.8 (6x), 6.9 (2x). Note also that the status of Agni Vaiśvānara is unique in these hymns. No individual god is named except him, and when all the

[16] Cf. Geldner's note quoted above (n. 4), equating the navel of the earth with the Fire altar.

[17] *Jaiminīyabrāhmaṇa* 1.147 tells about a Nodhas, the son of Kakṣīvat.

gods are named (in 6.9.7) we hear: *víśve devā́ anamasyan bhiyānā́s tuvā́m agne támasi tasthivā́ṃsam | vaiśvānaré avatu ūtáye no ámartiyo avatu ūtáye naḥ.* In the Maṇḍala of the Atri clan, Agni Vaiśvānara occurs in 5.27 (2x), 5.51 and 5.60. I am going to discuss Agni Vaiśvānara and the Bharadvāja clan on another occasion.

Taking into account all the above considerations, my translation is as follows:

> Whom the Bhṛgus [have] obtained, the possessor/knower of all [who is] on the navel of the earth and of the world with all his majesty/might, carry that fire with thy prayers to [your] own house, [that Agni] who – like Varuṇa, [the lord] of the Vasus – is the [only] One who rules.(1.143.4)

Previous Translations of ṚV 1.143.8

The first part is straightforward: 'O Agni (Sun, cf. verse 1ab), attentive with your attentive, kind and powerful guardians (i.e., the stars, cf. verse 3), preserve us.' The second part is a challenge, but there is hope of a great victory.

Oldenberg translates:

> Preserve us, O Agni, never failing with thy never-failing, kind and mighty guardians; protect our people all around with those undeceived, undismayed, never slumbering (guardians), O thou our wish! (Oldenberg 1897: 158))

Renou's solution is similar to Oldenberg's: 'ô (dieu qui es l'objet de notre) recherche' (Renou 1964: 35). Both of them interpret *iṣṭe* as a vocative. The problem with their interpretation is that they could not provide the word of which *iṣṭe* is the vocative.

Elizarenkova rightly criticizes Renou (and Oldenberg whom she does not refer to) for his solution. It seems to her 'несколько натянутым'. In fact this is not only a forced solution (as Elizarenkova calls it), but also a wrong one. In her own interpretation, Elizarenkova follows a different path that closely resembles that of Geldner:

> Schirme uns, o Agni, unablässig mit deinen unablässigen, freundlichen, wirksamen Schirmern; mit den unbetörten, nie zerstreuten, lieben(?), die die Augen nie schließen, beschirne unsere Kinder! (Geldner 1951: 202).

Cf. also Geldner's note on 8c:

> *iṣṭé* (Pp. *iṣṭe*) mit Abfall der Endung für *iṣṭébhiḥ*, ebenso in der Parallele 6, 8, 7. Man müßte sonst *iṣṭe* als Vok. von *iṣṭi* = Gegenstand des Wunsches, Liebling (wie später *kāma*) fassen.

Elizarenkova translates 8cd as follows:

> С не допускающими обмана, нерассеянными, желанными, не смыкающими глаз (защитниками) защити со всех сторон наше потомство! (Elizarenkova 1989: 182)

adding a note on 8c:

> Последняя форма рассматривается как усеченная вместо *iṣṭebhiḥ* наряду с другими формами (Elizarenkova 1989: 633).

As we can see, they interpret *iṣṭe* as a short (i.e., cut-off) form of *iṣṭebhiḥ*. Elizarenkova's solution also abuses grammar and is unconvincing for this reason as well. Again, all these scholars are almost there, but there is something still missing, and none of them could provide a decisive solution.

My Solution of ṚV 1.143.8

The crucial point is the analysis of *iṣṭe*. We have to find a solution that does not abuse grammar nor vocabulary. Formally, *iṣṭe* is the sg. voc. of an *i*-stem. Our job is to find a stem that fits the context best. To derive it via a past passive participle either from the root *yaj-* 'to sacrifice' or from the root *iṣ-* 'to desire', is not only a forced but also a false solution. The problem is that no Ṛgvedic word easily fits our case without abusing grammar or vocabulary or both. When a word notoriously resists all attacks of researchers (as has been the case with *iṣṭe* since the beginning of Vedic scholarship), one has to try a different approach. First of all, one has to enlarge the horizon and look at the problem from a different perspective. This is what I have essentially done in my completely independent and new solution. Nevertheless, it is worth noting that the problem of *iṣṭe* has not been taken too seriously by the majority of scholars; definitely not as seriously as the problem deserves. The core of the problem is the fact that 1.143.8c seems to be the only occurrence of this difficult word in the Ṛgveda. Consequently, our success will finally depend on our understanding of the context and the complex imagery of the hymn as well as the consistency of our analysis. In fact, the situation is not that bad; rather, it is promising, because the word in question occurs in the hymn of a great poet with clear vision and poetical insight and unity of thought. Let us analyse the structure of the poem.

The beginning (Verses 1–2):

Agni, son of strength	Begotten in the highest Heaven	radiance/flame glittered on Heaven (Sun)
Apāṃ Napāt, the beloved *hotā*	He has sat down on the Earth	radiance/flame glittered on Earth (altar)

The middle:

a) Cosmic level (especially verse 3): Streams (not sleeping, unageing) begin to move by the incitement of Agni (Sun). On the other hand, the Sun corresponds to the completion of the process of creation.

b) The level of the ritual (especially verse 4): Carry that fire with thy prayers to (your) own house. (1) That fire is the possessor/knower of all, the (only) One who rules (over everything); (2) whom the *Bhṛgus* (have) obtained; (3) it is on the navel of the earth and of the world (*nā́bhā pṛthivyā́ bhúvanasya*), a likely reference to some form of an altar (I am going to discuss this issue later).

c) Microcosmic (personal/inside the heart) level: Would Agni be fond of our hymn? Would He – the Vasu together with the

Vasus – fulfil our desire? Will He, the inciter/inspirer, stir our visions that they may be successful? I praise Him whose face is bright, with this vision/prayer (of mine)[18]

The end:

First of all, note that there is a clear parallelism between the first and the last verse: 1ab is related to 8ab and 1cd to 8cd. Now let us start our rendering with the neighbouring words of *iṣṭi*. *á-dabdhebhir*: the usual rendering of *á-dabdha-* is 'undeceived', but I prefer 'unimpaired, intact, unbroken, unharmed', from the root *dabh-* 'to harm'; *á-dṛpita-*, usual solution: 'uninfatuated' from the root *dṛp-* 'to rave', but 'uninflamed' from the root *dṛp-* 'to light, kindle, inflame' (*Dhātupāṭha* 39.14) is at least as acceptable as the previous meaning; *á-nimiṣadbhiḥ*, from *á-nimiṣá-*, mfn. 'unwinking' from *ni+miṣ-* 'to shut the eyelids, wink, fall asleep'. *nimiṣá-*, mfn. 'winking' is applied also to the stars, therefore *á-nimiṣá-* qualifies something that corresponds not to the stars, not to the heavenly guardians (and the Sun), but to their earthly counterpart, something connected with the (sacrificial) fire/altar (and/or the altar/fire itself).

1ab: I bring forward a stronger and newer vision (praise) to Agni, a hymn of Vāc to the son of strength;

1cd: Apāṃ Napāt, the beloved *hotā*, who together with the Vasus has sat down on the Earth observing the appointed time.

8ab: O Agni (cf. verse 1ab), attentive with your attentive, kind and powerful guardians (i.e., the stars), preserve us;

8cd: O *Iṣṭi* (?, but cf. 1cd), with your unimpaired, uninflamed, unwinking [something, not known yet] (however, cf. 8ab), protect our children!

---

18 One can see from this short summary that the hymn intertwines the three main levels of Ṛgvedic sacerdotal poetry. A later masterpiece of the same poet which uses this technique is the great Riddle hymn (1.164). See Brown 1967, Fórizs 1995, and especially Houben 2000.

Let us summarize our findings:

8ab

Agni:	attentive, kind and powerful guardians	Heaven
	belonging to or parts of Heaven (the stars)	Sun

8cd

iṣṭi	unimpaired, uninflamed, unwinking guardians	(the navel of the) *Earth*
can be identified with Apāṃ Napāt	belonging to or parts of *iṣṭi* (requires further analysis of the etymology and meaning of *iṣṭi-*)	can be identified with *iṣṭi*

We have arrived at the following situation: *Iṣṭi* can be identified with (a form of) Apāṃ Napāt (that sat down on the Earth). It is also clear from the context that the use of the vocative of this still 'unknown' word is legitimate. The use of the vocative together with the connotations of the neighbouring words is consistent with the assumption that the primary meaning of *iṣṭi-* is not an abstract notion, but some real thing. It is a new word on its own right.

On the other hand, the earlier expression *nā́bhā pṛthivyā́ bhúvanasya* together with a clear reference to the sacrifice and a form of an altar in 164.34ab and 35ab (in the same Dīrghatamas cycle of hymns) – *pṛchā́mi tvā páram ántam pṛthivyā́ḥ pṛchā́mi yátra bhúvanasya nā́bhiḥ* (34ab) *iyáṃ védiḥ páro ántaḥ pṛthivyā́ ayáṃ yajñó bhúvanasya nā́bhiḥ* (35ab) – makes it probable (or even reasonable) that this new word (that represents the visible earthly form of Apāṃ Napāt, the Child of the Waters) refers to a special form of an altar (or, at least, can be identified with it). We could arrive at these conclusions without preliminary assumptions about the semantic field of the word *iṣṭi-* or the knowledge of its etymology.

Etymology of the Word *iṣṭi-*

We have reached a point where the etymological analysis of the word is necessary. I would like to emphasize that there is no known Ṛgvedic word that fits in well with our previous analysis. There exists a possibly related word in Vedic, but it occurs only in the early Yajurveda: *íṣṭakā-* 'brick'. It denotes almost exclusively the sacred bricks of the *agnicayana* ritual. Converse (1974: 83–85) suggested two possible Tamil candidates as its etymology: *cengal* (*cennu* + *kal/gal*) and *cuṭakal/suṭakal* (*cuṭa/suṭa* + *kal*). On account of Emeneau's critique of Converse's proposal, Staal (1983: I, 131–132) turned to other possibilities and offered the Avestan *ištiia-* and Old Persian *ištiš* as a starting point. Witzel (1995: 103) not only accepted this, but also enlarged the horizon significantly by arguing – on the basis of the slightly different Vedic and Iranian (Avestan and Old Persian) forms – that 'the origin as a loan word from some unknown pre-Aryan culture should be considered'. He also made a proposal for this pre-Aryan language: that of the Bactria-Margiana Archaeological Complex (BMAC) alias the 'Oxus culture' of Bronze Age (ca. 2500–1500 BCE).

Since that time a considerable amount of work has been done on the BMAC language (Witzel 1999; Lubotsky 2001). An important innovation was the use of Common Tocharian as a 'control language'. Archaeological evidence shows not only contacts between Xinjiang and the BMAC, but also the direction of transfer of both material and non-material culture: Proto-Tocharians borrowed among other things the usage of mud bricks, and the widespread use of ephedra, especially in burial ceremonies. On the other hand, it is reasonable to assume that Common Tocharian and Indo-Iranian borrowed independently from the BMAC language. On these grounds Witzel suggested a BMAC origin for the words denoting 'brick' (Witzel 1995: 103; 1999: 342, n. 26) and reconstructed by him as ***išt-* (Witzel 2001: 63, 74). Pinault (2002) could even show that BMAC **išt(i)-* had been integrated into the inflection of *i*-stems in Common Tocharian: **išt(i)-* 'clay, mud brick', Toch. B *iścem* 'clay', **iścake* (*iṣcake* in St. Petersburg bilingual manuscript) 'a kind of clay', from a paradigm Toch. B **iśce*, acc. sg. **iśc*, Toch. A **iśäc*, borrowed into Old Turkic (Uighur) *išič*, *äšič* 'cooking pot'. Indo-Iranian: Old Persian *išti-*, Middle Persian *xišt* 'brick', Late Avestan *ištiia-* 'brick', *zəmōištiuua-* 'brick of clay', Vedic *íṣṭakā-* fem. 'brick', *iṣṭikā-*, etc. (Pinault 2006)

Now we are in a position to give a preliminary translation of verse 8:

> O Agni (cf. verse 1ab), attentive with your attentive, kind and powerful guardians (i.e. the stars), preserve us; O *Iṣṭi* [brick altar], with your unimpaired, uninflamed, unwinking (guardians) [bricks], protect our children! (1.143.8.)

We have come to the conclusion that it cannot be excluded that before the innovation of Vedic *íṣṭakā-*, *iṣṭikā-*, an earlier form *iṣṭi-* also found its way to the Ṛgveda, or – more precisely – to a singular hymn of a great western poet, who praised an equally singular form of fire, Apāṃ Napāt, the Child of the Waters (identified with *iṣṭi*) as well as a widely known one, Agni, in the same hymn. The intertwining imagery of the hymn gave Agni (and Apāṃ Napāt and *iṣṭi*) such a unique cosmological significance that was unparalleled in the contemporary sacerdotal poetry.

I hope that my analysis of ṚV 1.143 – along with the corroborating evidence of the Apāṃ Napāt *sūkta* of the Gṛtsamada clan (ṚV 2.35) – will reopen an old debate and some scholars may even reconsider the possibility of tracing the construction of a brick altar in the Ṛgveda. As for me, I am confident that I have found strong indirect evidence for the presence of brick in the Ṛgveda. Remarkably enough, it turned out that the most important obstacle that confused the evidence was the brick-altar itself. In other words, we have not seen the bricks for the altar.

TRANSLATION OF ṚV 1.143

prá távyasīṃ návyasīṃ dhītím agnáye vācó matíṃ sáhasaḥ sūnáve bhare | *apā́ṃ nápād yó vásubhiḥ sahá priyó hótā pṛthivyā́ṃ ní ásīdad ṛtvíyaḥ* || 1 ||

1. I bring forward a stronger and newer vision (praise) to Agni, a hymn of Vāc to thẹ son of strength; [he is] Apāṃ Napāt, the beloved *hotā*, who together with the Vasus has sat down on the Earth observing the appointed time.

sá jā́yamānaḥ paramé víomani āvír agnír abhavan mātaríśvane | *asyá krátvā samidhānásya majmánā prá dyā́vā śocíḥ pṛthivī́ arocayat* || 2 ||

2. [He who is] being begotten in the highest heaven, Agni revealed himself to Mātaríśvan. By the inspiration, by the majesty of the [one who] kindled [himself], radiance/flame glittered on Heaven and Earth.

asyá tveṣā́ ajárā asyá bhānávaḥ susaṃdṛ́śaḥ suprátīkasya sudyútaḥ | *bhā́tvakṣaso áti aktúr ná síndhavo agné rejante ásasanto ajárāḥ* || 3 ||

3. His rays are his ceaseless incitements; the splendour of the one with a beautiful face is good to look at. Beyond the light-makers – as the anointment of Agni – the unsleeping, unageing streams begin to move.

yám eriré bhṛ́gavo viśvávedasaṃ nā́bhā pṛthivyā́ bhúvanasya majmánā | *agníṃ táṃ gīrbhír hinuhi svá ā́ dáme yá éko vásvo váruṇo ná rā́jati* || 4 ||

4. Whom the Bhṛgus (have) obtained, the possessor/knower of all, [who is] on the navel of the earth and of the world in [all his] majesty; carry that fire with thy prayers to [your] own house, [that Agni] who – like Varuṇa [the lord] of the Vasus – is the [only] One who rules.

ná yó várāya marútām iva svanáḥ séneva sṛṣṭā́ diviyā́ yáthāśániḥ I *agnír jámbhais tigitaír atti bhárvati yodhó ná śátrūn sá vánā ní ṛñjate* II 5 II

5. He who is unstoppable like the roar of the Maruts, like an arrow that is sent forward, like the thunderbolt of heaven, Agni eats with his sharp jaws, he chews, he throws down the forests as a warrior throws down his foes.

kuvín no agnír ucáthasya vī́r ásad vásuṣ kuvíd vásubhiḥ kā́mam āvárat I *codáḥ kuvít tutujyā́t sātáye dhíyaḥ śúcipratīkaṃ tám ayā́ dhiyā́ gṛṇe* II 6 II

6. Would Agni be fond of our hymn? Would He – the Vasu together with the Vasus – fulfil our desire? Will He, the inciter/inspirer, stir our visions that they may be successful? I praise Him whose face is bright, with this vision/prayer [of mine].

ghṛtápratīkaṃ va ṛtásya dhūrṣádam agním mitrám ná samidhāná ṛñjate I *índhāno akró vidátheṣu dī́diyac chukrávarṇām úd u no yaṃsate dhíyam* II 7 II

7. Being kindled it reaches your Agni, whose face shines with ghee, as a [good] friend under the yoke of *Ṛta*; the anointed in the [sacrificial] assemblies, the kindling one (Agni) stretches out / sustains our bright-colored vision.

áprayuchann áprayuchadbhir agne śivébhir naḥ pāyúbhiḥ pāhi śagmaíḥ I *ádabdhebhir ádṛpitebhir iṣṭe ánimiṣadbhiḥ pári pāhi no jā́ḥ* II 8 II

8. O Agni (Sun), attentive with your attentive, kind and powerful guardians (i.e., the stars), preserve us; O *Iṣṭi* (Altar/Apāṃ Napāt), with your unimpaired, uninflamed, unwinking [guardians], protect our children!

REFERENCES

BÖHTLINGK, Otto & Rudolf ROTH 1852. *Sanskrit-Wörterbuch*, I. St. Petersburg: Kaiserliche Akademie der Wissenschaften.

BROWN, W. Norman 1967. Agni, Sun, Sacrifice, and Vāc: A sacerdotal ode by Dīrghatamas (Rig Veda 1.164). *JAOS* 88: 199–218.

CONVERSE, H. S. 1974 The agnicayana rite: Indigenous origins? *History of Religions* 14.2: 81–95.

EGGELING, Julius 1897. *The Śatapatha-Brāhmaṇa according to the Text of the Mādhyandina School Translated*, IV. (Sacred Books of the East, 43.) Oxford: Clarendon Press.

ELIZARENKOVA, T. Ya. 1989. *Rigveda – Mandaly 1–4*. Moskva: Nauka.

FINDLY, Ellison Banks 1979. The 'Child of the Waters': A revaluation of Vedic Apāṃ Napāt. *Numen* 26: 164–184.

FÓRIZS, László 1995. *Rigveda – Teremteshimnuszok* [Ṛgveda – Hymns of Creation, in Hungarian]. Budapest: Farkas Lőrinc Imre K.

—— 2005. Hosszú, mély sötétség (Dírghatamasz és Whitehead). In: Ella Csikós & Gábor Karsai (eds.), *Folyamat és kaland*: 290–313. Veszprém: Veszprémi Humán Tudományokért Kiadó.

GELDNER, Karl Friedrich 1951. *Der Rig-Veda, aus dem Sanskrit ins Deutsche übersetzt und mit einem laufenden Kommentar versehen*, I. (HOS, 33.) Cambridge, Mass.: Harvard University Press.

GELDNER, Karl & Adolf KAEGI 1875. *Siebenzig Lieder des Rigveda übersetzt.* Mit Beiträgen von R. Roth. Tübingen: H. Laupp.

GRASSMANN, Hermann 1876. *Rig-Veda übersetzt und mit kritischen und erläuternden Anmerkungen versehen*, I. Leipzig: F. A. Brockhaus.

HILLEBRANDT, Alfred 1980. *Vedic Mythology*, I–II. Translated from the original German [of the 2nd edition, 1927–29] by Sreeramula Rajeswara Sarma. Delhi: Motilal Banarsidass.

HOUBEN, Jan E. M. 2000. The ritual pragmatics of a Vedic hymn: The "Riddle Hymn" and the Pravargya ritual. *JAOS* 120.4: 499–536.

LUBOTSKY, Alexander 2001. The Indo-Iranian substratum. In: Christian Carpelan, Asko Parpola & Petteri Koskikallio (eds.), *Early Contacts between Uralic and Indo-European: Linguistic and Archeological Considerations* (Mémoires de la Société Finno-Ougrienne, 242): 301–317. Helsinki: Suomalais-Ugrilainen Seura.

LUDWIG, Alfred 1876–88. *Der Rigveda, oder Die heiligen Hymnen der Brāhmaṇa zum ersten Male vollständig ins Deutsche übersetzt mit Commentar und Einleitung*, I–VI. Prag: F. Tempsky.

MACDONELL, A. A. 1916. *A Vedic Grammar for Students*. London: Oxford University Press.

MAYRHOFER, Manfred 1992–2001. *Etymologisches Wörterbuch des Altindoarischen* I–III. (Indogermanische Bibliothek, Reihe 2: Wörterbücher.) Heidelberg: Universitätsverlag Carl Winter.

MYLIUS, Klaus 1978. *Älteste indische Dichtung und Prosa: Vedische Hymnen, Legenden, Zauberlieder, philosophische und ritualistische Lehren.* Leipzig: Reclam.

NOOTEN, Barend A. van & Gary B. HOLLAND (eds.) 1994. *Rig Veda: A Metrically Restored Text with an Introduction and Notes.* (HOS, 50.) Cambridge, Mass: Department of Sanskrit and Indian Studies, Harvard University.

O'FLAHERTY, Wendy Doniger 1981. *The Rig Veda: An Anthology. One Hundred and Eight Hymns, Selected, Translated and Annotated.* (The Penguin Classics.) Harmondsworth: Penguin Books.

OLDENBERG, Hermann 1897. *Vedic Hymns*, II: *Hymns to Agni (Maṇḍalas 1–5).* (Sacred Books of the East, 46.) Oxford: Clarendon Press.

—— 1988. *The Religion of the Veda.* Translated into English [from the first German edition of 1894] by Shridhar B. Shrotri. Delhi: Motilal Banarsidass.

PARPOLA, Asko 1988. The coming of the Aryans to Iran and India and the cultural and ethnic identity of the Dāsas. *Studia Orientalia* 64: 195–302.

—— 2005. The Nāsatyas, the chariot and Proto-Aryan religion. *Journal of Indological Studies* 16–17 (2004–2005): 1–63.

PETERSON, Peter 1888. *Hymns from the Ṛigveda, Edited with Sāyaṇa's Commentary, Notes, and a Translation.* (Bombay Sanskrit Series, 36.) Bombay: Government Central Book Depot.

PINAULT, Georges-Jean 2002. Tokh. B *kᵤccañe*, A *kᵤcim* et skr. tokharika. *Indo-Iranian Journal* 45.4: 311–345.

—— 2006. Further links between the Indo-Iranian substratum and the BMAC language. In: Bertil Tikkanen & Heinrich Hettrich (eds.), *Themes and Tasks in Old and Middle Indo-Aryan Linguistics* (Papers of the 12th World Sanskrit Conference, 5):167–196.

RAU, Wilhelm 1976. The meaning of *pur* in Vedic literature. (Abhandlungen der Marburger Gelehrten Gesellschaft, 1973.1.) München: Wilhelm Fink Verlag.

RENOU, Louis 1964. *Études védiques et pāṇinéennes*, XII. (Publications de l'Institut de Civilisation Indienne, Série in-8°, 20.) Paris: Institut de Civilisation Indienne de l'Université de Paris.

—— 1965. *Études védiques et pāṇinéennes*, XIV. (Publications de l'Institut de Civilisation Indienne, Série in-8°, 23.) Paris: Institut de Civilisation Indienne de l'Université de Paris.

STAAL, Frits (ed.) 1983. *Agni: The Vedic Ritual of the Fire Altar*, I–II. Berkeley: Asian Humanities Press.

WITZEL, Michael 1995. Early Indian history: Linguistic and textual parameters. In: G. Erdosy (ed.), *The Indo-Aryans of Ancient South Asia. Language, Material Culture and Ethnicity*: 85–125. Berlin: Walter De Gruyter.

—— 1999. Aryan and non-Aryan names in Vedic India. Data for the linguistic situation, c. 1900–500 B.C. In: Johannes Bronkhorst & Madhav M. Deshpande (eds.), *Aryan and Non-Aryan in South Asia. Evidence, Interpretation and Ideology* (HOS, Opera Minora 3): 337–404. Cambridge, Mass.: Department of Sanskrit and Indian Studies, Harvard University.

—— 2001. Autochthonous Aryans? The evidence from Old Indian and Iranian texts. *Electronic Journal of Vedic Studies* 7.3: 1–93.

Manuscripts of the Jaiminīya Sāmaveda Traced and Photographed in 2002–2006

MASATO FUJII & ASKO PARPOLA

INTRODUCTION

Within the thematic panel 'Fieldwork on Vedic manuscripts, recitation and ritual traditions' organized by the two of us in the Vedic section of the 12th World Sanskrit Conference, we presented a paper entitled 'Documenting the Present Jaiminīya Traditions and Manuscripts: An Interim Report'. The following was its abstract:

> The rare Jaiminīya school of Sāmaveda has been preserved only in South India, in the states of Tamil Nadu and Kerala. We have been documenting the oral, ritualistic and genealogical traditions as well as the manuscripts of this schools in the field since 1971. In recent years our research has been sponsored by the Japan Society for the Promotion of Science. This paper will give a brief survey of the present state of documentation and research.

The paper was subsequently enlarged and published with the title 'The Jaiminīya Sāmaveda Traditions and Manuscripts in South India' by Masato Fujii; it appeared in 2012 in the proceedings of an international symposium on 'Manuscript culture in South India' (Fujii 2012).

After the 12th World Sanskrit Conference we have continued our work with the sponsorship of the Japan Society for the Promotion of Science (Project no. 17320015). The present paper lists the results of our field research on the present Jaiminīya traditions and manuscripts, conducted by us from 2002 to 2006. Most of the listed manuscripts belong to Jaiminīya families or individuals living in Tamil Nadu and Kerala. Some of the documented manuscripts were deposited, donated or sold to libraries by their original owners, whose names unfortunately have not always been recorded in the library catalogues or registers. We have been interested to document the total content of the manuscript libraries of Jaiminīya Brahman houses and have therefore included also their non-Sāmavedic holdings, though normally these have not been photographed. In the libraries, we have occasionally photographed or listed also rare Sāmavedic texts belonging to schools other than Jaiminīya.

We would like to express our gratitude to the Japan Society for the Promotion of Science for its financial support, to Śrī Muṭṭattukkāṭṭu N. Nārāyaṇan Nampūtiri for his assistance during our field work in Kerala, Tamil Nadu, and Karnataka, and to all the people and libraries owning the manuscripts for permitting us to document them.

The material is presented in the following order:

1. Manuscripts of Tamil Jaiminīya Sāmavedins

1.1. T. N. Makarabhūṣaṇam (Tōkūr)
1.2. Kiṭāmaṅkalam
1.3. K. Kaṇṇaṉ (Kalpākkam/Teṉtiruppērai)
1.4. Aḻakiyapāṇṭiyapuram
1.4. Neṭumpiḷḷi Sāmavedic Manuscripts

2. Manuscripts of Nampūtiri Jaiminīya Sāmavedins

2.1. Muṭṭattukāṭṭu Māmaṇṇŭ Mana
2.2. Nellikkāṭṭu Māmaṇṇŭ Mana
3.3. Perumaṅṅāṭŭ Mana
3.4. Mūttiriṅṅōṭŭ Mana
3.5. Kāṇippayyūr Mana

3. Manuscripts in Libraries

3.1. Manuscript Library of the Department of Malayalam, University of Calicut

3.2. The Oriental Research Institute and Manuscripts Library, University of Kerala, Trivandrum

3.3. The Adyar Library and Research Centre, Chennai

3.4. The Saraswathi Mahal Library, Thanjavur

3.5. The Oriental Institute, Baroda

3.6. Lal Chand Research Library, DAV College, Chandigarh

3.7. The Punjab University Library, Lahore

3.8. Melkote

3.9. The Rashtriya Sanskrit Vidyapeetha Manuscripts Library, Tirupati

As an interim report, the present list provides the following information about the manuscripts:

Titles

The titles and/or indications of content in the list are provisional, as all manuscripts could not be identified exactly or with certainty or exhaustively (many manuscripts contain additional leaves with minor works left unidentified). We have reproduced the titles or identifications given on wooden covers or on palm-leaf labels, though we have studied ourselves many manuscripts to identify them.

Measurements

The first two figures of the measurements tell in centimeters the length and width of the manuscript, and they have usually been taken from the wooden boards of the manuscript. The third figure gives the thickness of leaves between the covers (i.e. the wooden covers have not been included in this measure). Sometimes a manuscript contains leaves of different sizes, in which case different measures are given.

Photography

Photography was done with optical cameras by Asko Parpola (AP) and Muṭṭattukkāṭṭu N. Nārāyaṇan Nampūtiri (NN) and with a digital camera by Masato Fujii (MF) in 2002, and with digital cameras by all the three in 2003–2006. The photographer and the date of photography is indicated as the last item. Some earlier photography is occasionally mentioned in addition.

1. MANUSCRIPTS OF THE TAMIL JAIMINĪYA SĀMAVEDA

For the Jaiminīyas and their Sāmaveda traditions in Tamil Nadu, see Raghavan 1957: 55–57; A. Parpola 1973: 22–23; Howard 1977: 154–199; Fujii 2012: 101–106.

1.1. T. N. Makarabhūṣaṇam (Tōkūr)

T. N. Makarabhūṣaṇam is a leading *purohita* (chaplain) for the Tamil Jaiminīya. He is the present principal of the recitation school (*pāṭhaśālā*) of the Jaiminīya Sāmaveda at Tōkūr (Thogur) in Tañcāvūr (Thanjavur) District. The *pāṭhaśālā* was established by his teacher, the late T. Rājagōpāla Aiyaṅgār (Staal 1975: 170; A. Parpola 1973: 6; Howard 1977: 163; Fujii 2012: 102f.).

(1) Jaiminīya-Uttaragāna with musical notation. 44.2 x 4.4 x 11.7. AP & NN & MF 10.2.2004.

(2) Jaiminīyaprakṛtigāna (Grāmageya + Āraṇa). 39.5 x 4 x 9.5. NN 16.2.2006.

(3) Pūrva-Ārcika. 39 x 3 x 3.2. MF 17.2.2006.

(4) Aparakriyās. 38 x 3 x 3.7. NN 17.2.2006.

(5) T. Rājagopāla Aiyaṅgār's notebooks:

(5.1) Dhāraṇalakṣaṇa. NN 17.2.2006.

(5.2) Jaiminīya Sāmaveda Aparaprayoga. AP 17.2.2006.

(5.3) Jaiminīya Sāmaveda Gṛhya texts. AP 17.2.2006.

(5.4) Jaiminīya Sāmaveda marriage rituals. AP 17.2.2006.

(5.5) Jaiminīya Uttarārcika + Keṅa-Upaniṣad. AP 17.2.2006.

(5.6) Jaiminīyasāmagānam (< palm leaves 1–92). AP 16.2.2006.
(5.7) Jaiminīyagṛhyasūtra Bhavatrātabhāṣya, pūrvabhāga. AP 16.2.2006.
(5.8) Jyotiṣāṃ pañcaviṃśati. AP 16.2.2006.
(5.9) Jyotiṣāṃ pañcaviṃśati + Jaiminīyaśrautasūtra (Agniṣṭomasūtra) + Agniṣṭomasāmāni. AP 16.2.2006.
(5.10) Śrīnivāsa's commentary on Jaiminīyagṛhyasūtra. AP 16.2.2006.
(5.11) Ūham (< palm leaves 91–160). MF 17.2.2006.
(5.12) Ūṣāṇi. AP 17.2.2006.

1.2. Kiṭāmaṅkalam

Kiṭāmaṅkalam (Kidamangalam) is a small village in the Nākappaṭṭiṉam (Nagapattinam) District near Kāraikkāl (Karaikal), where four Jaiminīya *purohitas* are living (Fujii 2012: 102; cf. Howard 1977: 154, n. 1.)

(1) Jaiminīyasāmaveda. 38 x 3.5 x 2.2. MF 15.2.2006.
(2) Jaiminīyasāmaveda. 39.4 x 3.2 x 1.4; 30.8 x 3.0 x 0.2. AP 15.2.2006.
(3) Jaiminīyasāmaveda. 27 x 3.4 x 0.2. NN 15.2.2006.
(4) Jaiminīyasāmaveda. 28.3 x 2.8 x 0.8. NN 15.2.2006.
(5) Notebook. AP 15.2.2006.
(6) Notebook. MF 15.2.2006.

1.3. K. Kaṇṇaṉ (Kalpākkam/Teṉtiruppērai)

K. Kaṇṇaṉ, a Jaiminīya engineer living in Kalpākkam near Chennai, officiates as a *purohita* for Teṉtiruppērai, his native Jaiminīya village near Āḻvār Tirunakari (Alvar Tirunagari), formerly in Tirunelvēli District, now in Tūttukkuṭi (Tuticorin) District. (Fujii 2012: 103; cf. Howard 1987: 163f.) Due to lack of time Kaṇṇan's paper manuscripts were not measured.

(1) Pūrva-ārcika & Uttara-ārcika (complete). MF 19.1.2004.
(2) Cilavā sāma ēṭu (manuscripts of some sāmans). MF 19.1.2004.

(3) Āraṇam & Āgneyam. MF 19.1.2004.
(4) Pūrvaprayoga with Sūtra. MF 19.1.2004.
(5) Aparaprayoga. MF 19.1.2004.
(6) Aparaprayoga. MF 19.1.2004.
(7) (a) Jaiminīyagṛhyasūtra (Sūtra-text only); (b) Nakṣatramālika; (c) Āraṇam (some sāmans only). MF 19.1.2004.
(8) A big notebook written by Śrī Veṅkaṭācala Aiyaṅgār of Teṉtiruppērai, containing Pūrvaprayoga & Aparaprayoga. AP 19.1.2004.
(9) Many notebooks written by Śrī Veṅkaṭācala Aiyaṅgār:
   (9.1) A bundle of manuscripts dealing with Pūrva- and Aparaprayogas. AP 19.1.2004.
   (9.2) A notebook with miscellaneous contents: Aṅkurārpaṇakrama, Nāndikrama, Puṃsavana, Sīmānta, Sthālīpāka, etc. AP 19.1.2004.
   (9.3) A notebook dealing with Darpasaṃskāram, Uttappanāgnisandhānam, etc. AP 19.1.2004.
   (9.4) A collection of mostly loose leaves with various contents. AP 19.1.2004.
   (9.5) A hard-covered notebook beginning with Āraṇasāmans, then Pūrvārcika, Kena-Upaniṣad, Nārāyaṇa-Upaniṣad, Nakṣatras, etc. AP 19.1.2004.
   (9.6–13) Eight 'less important' (not thoroughly studied!) notebooks. AP 19.1.2004.
   (9.14) Kaṇṇan's copy of A. Rangasvāmi Aiyaṅgār's Jaiminīyaprayogavivaraṇam. AP 19.1.2004.
(10) Prayogamantras + Kena-Upaniṣad & Nārāyaṇa-Upaniṣad. AP 19.1.2004.
(11) [Jaiminīya]Pūrvaprayoga. AP 24.1.2004.
(12) Śrāddhaprayoga. AP 19.1.2004.
(13) Pūrvaprayoga (Jātakarma to Sīmanta). AP 19.1.2004.
(14) Pūrvaprayoga. AP 19.1.2004.
(15) Jaiminīyapūrvaprayoga with Sūtra. AP 23.1.2004.

1.4. Aḻakiyapāṇṭipuram

There are Jaiminīya families in Aḻakiyapāṇṭipuram and Pūtapāṇṭi, neighbouring villages north of Nākarkōvil (Nagercoil) (Fujii 2012: 104).

(1) A short text of Jaiminīyagāna with musical notation, the plain text of the first book of the Jaiminīyaśrautasūtra and a portion of the Jaiminīya-Ārcika. AP 10.3.2002; MF 10.3.2002.
(2) Jaiminīyaprakṛtigāna (Grāmageya + Āraṇa). 37.5 x 4.9 x 4.8. MF 16.2.2006.

1.5. Neṭumppiḷḷi Sāmavedic Manuscripts

Neṭumpiḷḷi Mana, one of the two main Vādhūla houses in Iriññālakkuṭa (Irinjalakuda), Kerala, keeps several Tamil Jaiminīya Sāmavedic manuscripts found in Padmanābha Svāmi Temple in Tiruvanantapuraṃ, for which male members of Neṭumpiḷḷi Mana have been serving as the chief priest (*tantrin*) (Fujii 2012: 104 and n. 21 for the possible relationship of the manuscripts with Aḻakiyapāṇṭipuram).

(1) Jaiminīyagrāmageyagāna. 35.5 x 5.0 x 2.8. MF 19.2.2003.
(2) Jaiminīya-Ārcika. 36.0 x 4.5 x 1.9. MF 20.2.2003.
(3) Pūrva-Ṛk; Āraṇyaka-Ṛk; Uttara-Ṛk; Jaiminīyaśrautasūtra (agniṣṭoma); sāmans of agniṣṭoma & atirātra; Āgneyam & Aindram of Jaiminīyagrāmageyagāna. 36.7 x 4.7 x 3.6. AP 20.2.2003.
(4) Jaiminīya-Ārcika (incomplete). 23.3 x 5.0 x 2.1. MF 20.2.2003.
(5) Jaiminīyagrāmageyagāna. 35.5 x 5.4 x 3.8. MF 20.2.2003.

2. MANUSCRIPTS OF NAMPŪTIRI JAIMINĪYA SĀMAVEDINS

Among the Nampūtiri (Nambudiri) Brahmins, Malayāḷam-speaking native Brahmins in Kerala, all the Sāmavedins are Jaiminīyas. At present there are twenty Jaiminīya houses (or twenty-one houses if Kāmpram Mana is included). Here 'house' refers to a Nampūtiri patrilineal descent group as well as to its abode; the Malayāḷam word used by the Nampūtiris is *mana*, while other castes use the word *illam*. A large number of manuscripts is found in the three teacher houses of the Nampūtiri Jaiminīyas, namely Muṭṭattukāṭṭŭ Māmaṇṇŭ Mana, Nellikkāṭṭŭ Māmaṇṇŭ Mana and Perumaṅṅāṭṭŭ Mana, all three in the village of Pāññāḷ (Panjal) in Tṛśśūr (Trichur) District, as well as in the Mūttiriṅṅōṭŭ Mana of Maṇṇēṅṅōṭŭ village, Pālakkāṭŭ (Palakkad, Palghat) District. (Staal 1961: 86; A. Parpola 1984: 432–435 or 6–9; Fujii 2012: 106–108)

2.1. Muṭṭattukāṭṭŭ Māmaṇṇŭ Mana

This is the house of the late Śrī MM. S. Iṭṭi Ravi Nampūtiri (1904–1989), a great master of the Nampūtiri Jaiminīya Sāmaveda (see Staal 1983: I, xxiii; II, 762–763; M. Parpola 2000: 163–167; A. Parpola 2011: 262–263; Fujii 2012: 110). The manuscripts there have several different numbers written on them. Iṭṭi Ravi Nampūtiri (FIGURE 1) has made at least two lists of these manuscripts, the older one (I) comprising 45 items, the newer (II) 44; different numbers have been given by him on the palm-leaf labels on first leaves of the manuscripts (in both cases written with ink). The numbers of these lists will be mentioned below with the prefixes I and II in parentheses. Some manuscripts (mainly the largest ones) had titles and numbers written on their wooden covers with pencil in January 2004 by Mr. Shaji of the Oriental Research Institute and Manuscripts Library, Trivandrum. These numbers will be mentioned prefixed with S.

FIGURE 1.
Muṭṭattukkāṭṭil Māmaṇṇu S. Iṭṭi Ravi Nampūtiri (1904–1989) examining his ancestral palm-leaf manuscripts in 1971. (Photo: Asko Parpola).

We have taken as the basis of our inventory the numbers (prefixed here with P) written on most of the manuscripts with red oil colour or painted in white or gold on the wooden covers by Asko Parpola in his inventory in January 1987. By 2004 many of the manuscripts had lost their labels with numbers and titles completely due to their consumption by insects (even within one year, after 2003). As the copy of the 1987 list left in the house could not be found, we used only those original P numbers that were known for certain, leaving gaps for those that could not be identified and assigned new P numbers P107–P132 to the manuscripts that in 2004 were without P numbers. In the list below, whenever possible, these new numbers have been correlated with the missing old P items (marked with *).

(P1 = I.16?, II.33?) Smārtaprāyaścittam; Āśaucadīpika. 28.8 x 4.3 x 7.3. NN 28.1.2004.
(P2*) Yāgakriyakaḷ.
(P3 = I.35, II.17) Parāśarasmṛtivyākhyānaṃ mādhavīyam. 35.5 x 4.3 x 5.2.
(P4) Bhāratam, Virāṭaparvvan. 33 x 4 x 7.2.
(P5 = I.34, II.19) Yājñavalkyasmṛti. 26.5 x 4.4 x 5.5
(P6* = P117) Tuḷasīmāhātmyam.
(P7 = I.41) Muhūrttapadavi. 30.2 x 3.3 x 6.5.
(P8 = I.15, II.23) Tamprākkaḷuṭe bhāṣa jyotiṣam. 18.4 x 3.7 x 4.7.
(P9 = I.31, II.9) Parāśarasmṛtivyākhyānam & Puruṣasūkta-vyākhyānam. 32.5 x 4.4 x 6.5.
(P10 = I.26, II.2) Agniyuṭe taittirīyam (bhāṣa). 35.6 x 4.5 x 3.6. NN 30.1.2004.
(P11 = I.44) Śrautaprāyaścittam. 32.2 x 4.2 x 3.8. MF 23.2.2003.
(P12 = I.27, II.41) Yāgaṃ taittirīyaṃ / yāgakriyakaḷ (bhāṣa). 6 x 5 x 4.3. MF 29.1.2004.
(P13 = I.38, II.25) Siddhāntakaumudi. 35 x 4.5 x 4.5.
(P14 = II.3, S16) Naiṣadhaṃ vyākhyānasahitam. 35.4 x 3.9 x 4.5.
(P15 = I.5, II.15) Sarvānukramaṇika (Vedam vaka). Not found in 2004.
(P16*) Smārttakriyakaḷ.
(P17 = I.29, II.18) Bhāṭṭadīpika of Śrīkhaṇḍadeva. 30 x 4.8 x 2.3.
(P18 = I.37, II.26) Devīmāhātmyam. 15 x 4.2 x 1.8.
(P19 = II.44) Jyotiṣam (parahitam) 9.5 x 3.4 x 2.5.
(P20 = I.18, II.6) Āśaucacintāmaṇi. 23.5 x 4 x 4.9. NN 29.1.2004.
(P21 = marked 49) Muhūrttapadavivyākhya. 24 x 4.4 x 4.3.
(P22*) Saṃskṛtattil cila padyaṅṅaḷ.
(P23 = I.8, II.28) Yāgattinṭe Sāmaccaṭaṅṅū (I.8), Yāgakriya (Sāmam) (II.28): Kutirakkuṟuśśi; Kūṣmāṇḍi; etc. 27.1 x 4.2 x 2.4. AP 1987, 2003; MF & AP 26 & 31.1.2004.
(P24 = I.30) Manusmṛti. 25 x 4.4 x 4.
(P25 = I.2, II.12) Upaniṣattukaḷ. 16.4 x 4.5 x 2.6; 17.7 x 4 x 5.5.
(P26*) Kumārasaṃbhavaṃ.

(P27 = I.22, II.7) [Viṣṇu]Sahasranāmam. 16.5 x 3.7 x 0.8.
(P28* = P127) Mahābhāratam.
(P29 = II.22) Āśaucam. 25.7 x 4 x 1.3. MF 26.1.2004.
(P30) Bhavatrātīyaṃ on Jaiminīyaśrautasūtra (last part).
35.5 x 4.5 x 5. MF 26.1.2004.
(P31*) Tantravuṃ ācāravuṃ.
(P32 = I.25) Bhavatrātīyaṃ on Jaiminīyaśrautasūtra.
35.5 x 4.6 x 5.6. NN 21–23.2.2003.
(P33) (Bhavatrāta's Jaiminīya)Gṛhya(sūtra)vṛtti. 31.4 x 4 x 4.
AP 1987; AP 30.1.2004.
(P33bis = I.32) (Bhavatrāta's Jaiminīya)Gṛhya(sūtra)vṛtti.
31.1 x 4.3 x 4.6. AP 1987; AP 21–22.2.2003.
(P34 = I.20, II.10) Tantram vaka. 18.5 x 3.7 x 3.6.
NN 28–29.1.2004.
(P35 = I.16?, II.33?) Smārttaprāyaścittam. 23.6 x 4 x 4.
MF 29–30.1.2004.
(P36 = I.14, II.24) Muktāvali Dinakari; Kāsikāvṛtti. 24.1 x 4 x 2.4.
(P37*) Vaidikadaivaṅṅaḷe pratipātikkunnatŭ.
(P38*) Pūjātantraṃ.
(P39* = P116) Devīmāhātmyam.
(P40 = II.28) Yāgakriya: Two śrautaprayogas in Malayāḷam.
9.2 x 3.3 x 2.8. NN 30.1.2004.
(P41* = I.12 = P114) (Bhagavad)Gīta.
(P42 = I.40) Tarkkasamgrahavuṃ Manusmṛtiyuṃ vyākhyānattōṭu
kūṭiyatŭ. 25.1 x 4.3 x 7.8.
(P43 = I.11, II.4) Śāṅkarasmṛti. 24 x 4.2 x 2.7. MF 28.1.2004.
(P44*) Āyurvedaṃ.
(P45 = I.10, II.5) Agnihotraṃ caṭaṅṅŭ mutalāyita. 26.5 x 4.1 x 5.3.
MF 22.2.2003.
(P46) Muhūrttapadavi. 23.5 x 3.4 x 5.3.
(P47*) Gṛhya(sūtraṃ).
(P48 = II.30) Naiṣadhakāvyam (with commentary, incomplete).
30.7 x 4.4 x 1.
(P49* = P112) Smṛti.

(P50 = I.19, II.27) Vaiśākhamāhātmyam. 29.7 x 4.5 x 2.1.
(P51* = P115) Devīstotravuṃ gītayum.
(P52 = II.21) Smārttaprāyaścittam. 32.5 x 4.7 x 5.5. AP 29.1.2004.
(P53 = I.43, II.43) Śrīnivāsa's Vyākhyāna on Jaiminīyagṛhyasūtra & Sannyāsaccaṭaṅṅū. 25.8 x 3.9 x 2.9. AP 23.2.2003; 30.1.2004.
(P54* = P119) Jyotiṣam (kāladīpikam).
(P55*) Bhānavam (vyākhyānam).
(P56 = I.21, II.34) Mīmāṃsākaustubham (Khaṇḍadevanṯe vyākhyānattōtu kūṭiyatū). 35.6 x 4.3 x 7.2.
(P57 = I.24, II.11) Siddhāntakaumudī. 34.6 x 4.2 x 4.
(P58*) Kāśikāvṛtti.
(P59* = II.39 = P124) Siddhāntacandrika vyākhyānam.
(P60*) Ācāram.
(P61* = P110?) Brāhmaṇam.
(P62*) Dhātupratyayavācikā.
(P63 = II.1) Vyākaraṇam: Rūpāvatāram. 35.2 x 4.5 x 3.8. MF 28.1.2004.
(P64 = I.36, II.35) Tarkkam: Muktāvali Dinākariyōṭu kūṭi. 24.3 x 3.9 x 2.4 .
(P65 = I.13) Tarkkasaṃgrahaṃ dīpikayum. 18 x 4.2 x 2.
(P66 = I.3, II.20) Vyākaraṇam: Rūpāvatāram. 35 x 4.9 x 2. MF 25.1.2004.
(P67 = I.17, II.16) (Siddhānta)Kaumudi uttaraṃ bhāgam. 24 x 4.4 x 4.4.
(P68* = I.4, II.14) (Jaiminīya)Gṛhyasūtravuṃ kriyākramavum. Not found in 2004.
(P69 = I.40) Ceṟumukkil vacca smārttaprāyaścittam (bhāṣa). 26.9 x 4.2 x 5. MF 22.2.2003.
(P70* = P120) Rāmāyaṇam (campū).
(P71 = I.7, II.29) Bhāṣāśaucavum maṯṯum 18 x 3 x 1.7. MF 1.2.2004.
(P72 = I.33, II.8) Dvādaśyārādhana; Gaṇapatihoma. 19.6 x 2.3 x 1.2.

(P73 = I.6, 50) Vaidyaṃ vaka. 18.5 x 3.3 x 7.6.

(P74* = II.37 = P118) Muktāvali Dinakari.

(P75* = P109) Sāmasmārttaccaṭaṅṅŭ.

(P76* = I.1 = P103) Jaiminīya-Upaniṣadbrāhmaṇam.

(P77* = P104) Bhavatrāta's commentary on Jaiminīyaśrautasūtra I.

(P101) Jaiminīyabrāhmaṇa. 43.5 x 4.8 x 4.2. MF 1997; 31.1.2004.

(P102) Jaiminīyabrāhmaṇa. 43 x 4.5 x 1.8. MF 1997; 31.1.2004.

(P103 = P76*) Jaiminīya-Upaniṣad[brāhmaṇa]. 19 x 3.3 x 3.8. MF 21.2.2003.

(P104 = P77*) Bhavatrāta on Jaiminīyaśrautasūtra I (agniṣṭoma-sūtra). 37.7 x 4.3 x 3. AP 26.1.2004.

(P105 = I.28, 47) Yāgattinṯe caṭaṅṅŭ; Agnikku sāmaccaṭaṅṅŭ. 18 x 3.6 x 3.2. AP 1.2.2004.

(P106) Aptoryāmattinṯe sāmaccaṭaṅṅŭ. 17 x 3.2 x 2. AP 31.1.2004.

(P107) Bhavatrāta on Jaiminīyagṛhyasūtra. 34 x 4.7 x 4.5. AP 28.1.2004.

(P108) Text related to Jaiminīyagṛhyasūtra; bhāṣa (Malayāḷam text) on āśauca?; Śrīsūktabhāṣya 34.6 x 3.4 x 2. MF 1.2.2004.

(P109 = P75*) Sāmasmārtacaṭaṅṅŭ & related texts. 25.3 x 4.5 x 5.4. AP 31.1.2004.

(P110 = P61*?) Caturdaśaka, adhyāyas 1–2 (Śāṅkhāyana-Āraṇyaka 1–2). 11.8 x 4.4 x 1.3. MF 30.1.2004.

(P111) Rudrasūktattinṯe vyākhyānam; alaṃkāraśāstra? 26.5 x 2.5/3.2 (8 fol.); 25.5 x 4 (13 fol.).

(P112 = P49*) Manusmṛti. 34.7 x 5.3 x 2.

(P113) Commentary on a Smṛti? 31.2 x 3.5 x 2.

(P114 = marked 12 = P41*) Bhagavadgītā. 19.8 x 3.9 x 2.4.

(P115 = P51*) Devīmāhātmyam?; Bhagavadgītā. 24.2 x 4.3 x 3.

(P116 = marked 56 = P39*) Devīmāhātmyam. 8.5 x 2.2 x 2.1.

(P117 = P6*) Rudrākṣa- & Tulasīmāhātmyam (from Skanda-purāṇa). 8.5 x 2.2 x 2.1.

(P118 = P74*) Muktāvali Dinakari. 24 x 3.9 x 5.5.

(P119 = P54*) Jyotiṣam: Kāladīpika. 24.5 x 4 x 3.8.

(P120 = P70*) A poem connected with Rāma. 29 x 3 x 2.3.

(P121) Kirātārjunīyam. 27 x 5 x 2.2.
(P122 = S3) Śiśupālavadha. 28 x 3.9 x 4.7.
(P123 = S3bis) Vyākaraṇam. 40.5 x 4.5 x 4.7.
(P124 = S10 = P59*) Siddhāntakaumudīvyākhyānam. 50.6 x 5 x 5.
(P125 = S9) Vaidyanāthadīkṣitīyam āhnikam. 53 x 5.3 x 3.
(P126 = S13) Rāmāyaṇam: Sundarakāṇḍam. 47.5 x 5.7 x 2.
(P127 = S14 = P28*) Bhāratam. 41.5 x 4.2 x 4.
(P128 = S7) Bhāratam: Virāṭaparvan, vyākhyā. 48.8 x 5.2 x 3.6.
(P129 = S15) Bhāgavatam; Bhāratam. 52 x 4.5 x 1.9.
(P130 = S8) Bhāgavatam. 47 x 4.9 x 4.6.
(P131 = S5) Bhāgavatam. 58.4 x 5.5 x 5.1.
(P132) Bhāgavatam. 56.6 x 5 x 5.1.

2.2. Nellikkāṭṭŭ Māmaṇṇŭ Mana

Muṭṭattukkāṭṭu and Nellikkāṭṭu Māmaṇṇu Manas are said to have split from a single Māmaṇṇu Mana more than ten generations ago. The late N. Nīlakaṇṭhan Akkitirippāṭu (1905–1997), another great master of Jaiminīya Sāmaveda, has handed the sāman chanting to his sons. Like its neighbour, Nellikkāṭṭu Māmaṇṇu Mana has many palm-leaf manuscripts. The three-digit numbers mentioned in the second place are the ones we previously assigned to, and marked on the manuscripts.

(1 = 034) Vyākaraṇasūtram [by Pāṇini]. 19.5 x 2.7 x 2.8.
(2 = 035) Vārarucavākya (Jyotiṣa). 24 x 4.3 x 3.6.
(3 = 037) Kāṇādasiddhāntacandrikā (Tarka). 21 x 3.2 x 2.7.
(4 = 042) Āśaucadīpaka. 19 x 3.8 x 3.
(5 = 030) An Āyurveda text in Malayāḷam. 17 x 4 x 2.
(6 = 027) Vālmīkipraśna (Jyotiṣa). 15 x 4 x 2.2.
(7 = 038) Muktāvalī (Tarka). 20.8 x 3.8 x 4.
(8 = 062) Nāgānandam [by Harṣa] (drama). Old and broken. 32.5 x 4.8 x 6.
(9 = 020) A text on Tarka. 20 x 4.2 x 3.
(10 = 067) Āśaucadīpa in Malayāḷam. 23.7 x 3.7 x 2.2.
(11 = 039) Mahiṣamaṅgala-āśaucam. 24 x 4.4 x 2.7.

(12 = 016) A text on Mantravāda in Malayāḷam. 41.5 x 4.5 x 1.7. AP 2.3.2002.

(13 = 033) Śākuntalam [by Kālidāsa] (drama). 21.6 x 2.1 x 3.

(14 = 075) A kiḷippāṭṭŭ type text on Bhāratam, in Malayāḷam. 29.2 x 4.3 x 3.2.

(15 = 014) Bhāgavatam. 34.3 x 4.3 x 4.2.

(16 = 006) Śabdakaustubham. 29.6 x 4.8 x 5.3.

(17 = 079) Tantric and Gṛhya texts; mythical history of Kerala, all in Malayāḷam. Old. 29.6 x 3 x 2. AP 1990.

(18 = 001) Agniyuṭe bhāṣa (in Malayāḷam). 183 folia. 25.7 x 4.2 x 6. NN 1.3.2002.

(19 = 032) Āśaucam. 12 x 3.3 x 2.

(20 = 050) Vālmīkirāmāyaṇam. 33 x 5.5 x 3.4.

(21 = 017) Śekharavyākhyā Śāṅkarī. 38 x 4.5 x 2.7.

(22 = 072) Adhyātmarāmāyaṇam by Eḻuttacchan (in Malayāḷam). 29.5 x 4.2 x 1.8.

(23 = 049) Bhāgavatam. 53.5 x 5.3 x 4.8.

(24 = 070) Āśaucam (in Malayāḷam). 24 x 3 x 2.3.

(25 = 052) A text on Nyāya. 33 x 4.5 x 2.8.

(26 = 021) Pradyumnābhyudaya by Ravivarman (drama) and Śāṅkarabhāṣya. Old. 37 x 3.8 x 2.

(27 = 053) Bhāgavatam. 30 x 4.4 x 3.2.

(28 = 029) Devīmāhātmyam. 16 x 4.7 x 2.7.

(29 = 010) Vālmīkirāmāyaṇam. 33 x 5.5 x 5.

(30 = 064) Sāmasmārttacaṭaṅṅŭ & pulayuṭe ślokam. 18.8 x 4 x 5. AP 1985; AP 3.3.2002.

(31 = 054) Ādhānam. 23 x 3 x 5.6. MF 26.2.2002.

(32 = 028) Sadpīṭhapūjāvidhi (Tantra). 14.2 x 3.2 x 3.6.

(33 = 058) Śrautaprāyaścitta. 24.2 x 4.3 x 5. MF 1.3.2002.

(34 = 065) Bhagavadgītā. 17.8 x 3 x 3.

(35 = 051) Campūrāmāyaṇam. Very old. 21.5 x 3.7 x 3.

(36 = 015) Bhāṭṭadīpikā by Khaṇḍadeva. 35.4 x 4.5 x 2.8.

(37 = 066) Nārāyaṇīyam by Nārāyaṇabhaṭṭa of Mēlputtūr (in Malayāḷam). 21 x 4.8 x 2.8.

(38 = 005) Bhāgavatam. 23 x 5.7 x 6.
(39 = 044) A work on iṣṭi in Malayāḷam. 17.4 x 3.6 x 1.8. MF 26.2.2002.
(40 = 011) Śrautakriyās, Pakaḻiyam (= Āśvalāyana) (in Malayāḷam). 27.6 x 4.3 x 3.8. MF 1.3.2002.
(41 = 019) Pakaḻiyam (= Āśvalāyana) Kārikā. Old. 32.5 x 3.5 x 3.5. AP & NN 1.3.2002.
(42 = 061) Hṛgvidhānam (sic). Very old. 29.5 x 4 x 2.1. AP 2.3.2002.
(43 = 076) Unidentified Sāmavedic Śrauta texts. Very old. 27 x 4 x 3. AP 1990; MF 3.3.2002.
(44 = 078) Sāmacaṭaṅṅu of Yāgam and Agni (in Malayāḷam). 25 x 4.3 x 4.4. AP & MF 1.3.2002.
(45 = 012) Yāgattinṟe bhāṣa (in Malayāḷam). 38.7 x 4.2 x 4.3. NN 2.3.2002.
(46 = 025) A commentary on Muktāvalī (Tarka). 32.6 x 4.5 x 4.3.
(47 = 073) Gītāṭīkā Subodhinī by Śrīdhara. 27 x 4.4 x 4.8.
(48 = 009) Siddhāntakaumudī, uttarārdha. 35.8 x 4.3 x 5.
(49 = 013) Mahābhāṣya by Patañjali. 35.5 x 5 x 4.
(50 = 060) Tantrasamuccaya. 33.5 x 5 x 3.6.
(51 = 022) Kṛṣṇagātha (in Malayāḷam). 26.5 x 5 x 5.8.
(52 = 059) Nayatattvasaṃgraha (Mīmāṃsā). 29 x 3.5 x 5.3.
(53 = 047) Śrautasmārttaprāyaścitta. Old. 35.4 x 5 x 4.8. MF 2.3.2002.
(54 = 003) Smārttacaṭaṅṅu Pakaḻiyam (= Āśvalāyana). 35.7 x 5 x 2.7.
(55 = 004) (a) Nāradaśikṣā. 17.7 x 3.6 x 3. NN 2.3.2002.
(b) Vaidikasvaraprakaraṇa. 94 +7 folia. 20.5 x 2.5 x 4. AP 3.3.2002.
(56 = 055) Paribhāṣenduśekharavyākhyā. 35 x 4.8 x 4.2.
(57 = 071) Ādhānagrantham. 17.9 x 3.5 x 1.9. NN 26.2.2002.
(58 = 031) Keraḷāvakāśakrama (in Malayāḷam). 18.2 x 3.7 x 4.2.
(59) Sāmasmārttacaṭaṅṅu & pulayuṭe ślokāḥ. 18.4 x 4 x 5.7. AP 2–3.3.2002.

(60 = 068) Smārttakriya (in Malayāḷam). 23 x 5.5 x 6.1. AP 26.2.2002.
(61 = 018) Siddhāntakaumudī, pūrvārdha. 35.6 x 4.3 x 4.7.
(62 = 036) Kauṣītakaṃ caṭaṅṅū. 23.6 x 4 x 3.6.
(63 = 043) Jaiminīya-Upaniṣad[brāhmaṇa]. 16.6 x 4 x 3.7. MF 1985; NN 26.2.2002.
(64 = 040) Jaiminīya-Upaniṣad[brāhmaṇa]. 23.5 x 4 x 3.2. MF 1990; 17.2.2003.
(65 = 077) Jaiminīyabrāhmaṇa (Ekāha 2.83–234). Old. 76 folia. 31.5 x 4 x 3.5. MF 1995.
(66 = 007) Jaiminīyabrāhmaṇa (1.271–2.154). 132 folia. 33 x 4.5 x 3.9. MF 1995; NN 17–18.2.2003.
(67 = 023) Mañjūṣavyākhyaṃ. 36 x 4.8 x 2.8.
(68 = 026) Sāmacaṭaṅṅū of Yāgam. 15 x 3.4 x 3.9. AP 26.2.2002.
(69 = 045) Sāmattinṯe prastāvam. 12.2 x 3.7 x 2.1. AP & MF 26.2.2002.
(70 = 024) Jaiminīyabrāhmaṇam (1.1–270). 108 folia. 38.8 x 4.6 x 3.5. MF 1995; 18.2.2003.
(71 = 041) Kauṣītakaṃ bhāṣa on Yāgam (in Malayāḷam). 16.7 x 4.2 x 2.3. NN 26.2.2002.
(72 = 008) Jaiminīyabrāhmaṇam (2.154–3.386). 213 folia. 42.5 x 4.9 x 6.7. MF 1995; NN 19.2.2003.
(73 = 069) Śrautaprāyaścitta. 23.6 x 3.7 x 3. AP 1.3.2002.
(74 = 057) Unidentified Sāmavedic ritual texts. Old. 36.8 x 3.5 x 1.3. AP 1990; MF 3.3.2002.
(75 = 056) Jaiminīyabrāhmaṇa (Ahīna, 2.235–333). Old. 28.7 x 2 x 3.3. MF 2–3.3.2002.
(76 = 074) Ādhānakalpa (on Yāgam). 26.4 x 3 x 1.7. NN 2.3.2002.
(77 = 048) Jaiminiyaśrautasūtravṛtti by Bhavatrāta. Old and broken. 53 x 5.5 x 5.5. AP 1983; 1985.
(78 = 046) Agnihotraṃ veḷi (in Malayāḷam) & punarādhānam (in Malayāḷam). 14 folia, no boards. 27.3 x 3 x 1.4. AP 26.2.2002.
(79) Śaiva stotras, including Dakṣiṇāmūrtipañjaram, on 1st page only. 27 x 4.5 x 1.

(80) Empty leaves, excepting initial salutations. 32.8 x 4.5 x 0.7.
(81) Pretaśuddhi (only a few inscribed leaves, rest empty). 33 x 4.7 x 1.
(82) A list of saṃbhāras for Atirātraṃ. 6 folia. 38 x 2.8 x 0.7. AP 2.3.2002.
(83) Empty leaves. 34.7 x 4.6 x 0.7.
(84) Empty leaves. 36.7 x 4.6 x 0.4.
(85) Empty leaves. 38.7 x 4.2 x 0.5.
(86) Empty leaves. 36 x 5 x 0.3.
(87) Empty leaves. 39 x 4.2 x 2.5.
(88) A Nyāya or Tarka text in Sanskrit with several uninked pages, several empty leaves at the end. 36 x 5 x 2.
(89) Letters in Malayāḷam on the management of the Narasiṃha temple belonging to the Vaṭakañcēri Mana. 39 x 3.5 x 1.
(90) A Jyotiṣa text, perhaps Vālmīkipraśna. Bamboo covers. 17.8 x 3.2 x 1.
(91 = 002) Śrautakriyās in Malayāḷam. 23.8 x 4.2 x 6. NN 1.3.2002.

2.3. Perumaṅṅāṭŭ Mana

As one of the three teacher houses, this house has kept many manuscripts. We painted the numbers with white paint on the wooden boards or (in the absence of such boards) on the manuscripts while examining them.

(1) Bhāgavatam. 25.5 x 3.9 x 5.3.
(2) Paribhāṣenduśekhara. Date given in the colophon. 33 x 4.5 x 3.8.
(3) Jaiminīya-Upaniṣad[brāhmaṇa]. 23.5 x 4.8 x 4. MF 1985; 1990.
(4) Sāmasmārttacaṭaṅṅŭ. 30 x 4.9 x 4.2. MF 5.3.2002.
(5) Jātakādeśamārgam. 18 x 4.3 x 1.8.
(6) Śrautacaṭaṅṅŭ. 24 x 3.6 x 6. MF 4.3.2002.
(7) Bhāratam? 41.5 x 5 x 4.
(8) Chāndogya-Upaniṣad (in Grantha script). 37.5 x 4.2 x 2.3. NN 4.3.2002.

(9) Dīkṣitahariviracite prauḍhamanoramāvyākhyāne laghuśabdaratne subantaṃ samāptim agamat (Vyākaraṇa). 29.8 x 4.5 x 5.8.
(10) Prakriyāsarvasvam. 38.5 x 4.8 x 4.4 &.
(11) Ceṟuśśēribhāratam (in Malayāḷam). 35.5 x 4.5 x 6.
(12) Putrakāma-iṣṭi. 28 x 4.5 x 3.7. AP 4.3.2002.
(13) Śrīkṛṣṇavilāsam (in Malayāḷam). 13 x 1.8 x 3.1.
(14) Harilīlā by Vopadeva. 18.8 x 3.5 x 3.7.
(15) Bhagavadgītā. 17.7 x 3.5 x 3.
(16) Aṣṭādhyāyī by Pāṇini & the commentary by Śāntanavācārya. 26.7 x 3.5 x 2.7.
(17) [Jaiminīya]gṛhyagatamantravṛtti. 27 x 3.5 x 3. AP earlier; 5.3.2002.
(18) Jaiminīyagṛhyasūtra-Ṭīkā by Śrīnivāsa (in Malayāḷam script). 4 x 4 x 2.3. AP 1985; NN 5.3.2002.
(19) Śrautacaṭaṅṅū. Old. 23.5 x 4 x 1. MF 4.3.2002.
(20) Sāmavyākhyānam by Sāyaṇa (in Malayāḷam script). 21.2 x 4.5 x 5.2. The beginning photographed, the rest uninked and left unphotographed. NN 5.3.2002.
(21) Anubhavapañcaratnam (in Sanskrit). 17.7 x 3 x 3.6.
(22) Prayogasāra. 31.7 x 3.6 x 2.2.
(23) Bhagavadgītāṭīkā Subodhinī by Śrīdharasvāmin. 24 x 3.5 x 5.
(24) Kārttikamāhātmyam of Pādmapurāṇa. 23.5 x 3.3 x 3.
(25) Tamprākkaḷ uṇṭākkiya muhūrttabhāṣāvyākhyānam (in Malayāḷam). 21.2 x 4.3 x 4.
(26) Pārāśaradharmaśāstra (with Malayāḷam commentary?). 12 x 3.8 x 4.
(27) A commentary on some Kāvya work (in Sanskrit). 22 x 4 x 3.3.
(28) Tattvabodhinī (Vyākaraṇa) (in Sanskrit). 41.1 x 4.6 x 6.2.
(29) Some Tantric text (in Sanskrit). Old. 25 x 4 x 3.
(30) Vālmīkirāmāyaṇam. 53.5 x 4.8 x 8.
(31) Sāmasmārttacaṭaṅṅū. Old and worm-eaten. 24.5 x 3.2 x 4.3. MF 4.3.2002.
(32) Some Tantric work on yantras (in Sanskrit). 42 x 4.4 x 3.3.

(33) Bhāgavatam (5th skandha). 29.3 x 4.2 x 3.7.
(34) Rāmāyaṇam (and other poems?). 28.5 x 4.5 x 4.2.
(35) A commentary on some text on Kṛṣṇa (in Sanskrit). 29.8 x 3 x 7. (Cf. no. 39.)
(36) Jaiminīyagṛhyasūtravṛtti by Bhavatrāta. 24 x 5 x 6.2. AP 1985; 4.3.2002.
(37) [Jaiminīya]gṛhyaprayogaratnamālā. 26.5 x 3.2 x 2.5. AP 1985; 5.3.2002.
(38) Vijñāneśvarīyam on Yājñavalkyasmṛti. 44.4 x 5 x 5.3.
(39) A commentary on some work on Kṛṣṇa (in Sanskrit). 33 x 4.7 x 1.5. (Cf. no. 35.)
(40) Brahmānanda (and possibly some other Vedānta texts). 25.4 x 3.8 x 4.2.
(41) Siddhāntamuktāvalīgūḍhārtha. 32.5 x 4 x 4.7.
(42) Paribhāṣenduśekhara. 21.2 x 3.5 x 5.
(43) Ādhānam (in Malayāḷam). 17.7 x 3 x 3.7. NN 5.3.2002.
(44) Bhagavadgītā (1–16 only). 14.9 x 3.2 x 3.7.
(45) Smārttaprāyaścittam (latter portion). 24 x 4 x 2.6. NN 4.3.2002.
(46) Two works on poetics, Alaṃkāraśāstra. (a) 30 x 4.2 x 1.5. (b) 33 x 4 x 3.1.
(47) A text on Jyotiṣa. 24 x 4 x 4.8.
(48) Darśapūrṇṇamāsan tuṭaṅṅuvān caṭaṅṅū (only a few leaves, the rest empty). 23.8 x 4 x 1.5. MF 7.3.2002.
(49) A kośa? (in Sanskrit). 18 x 4.5 x 1.
(50) An extensive text on Kṛṣṇa (in Malayāḷam). 40.3 x 5.3 x 8.
(51) A manual on Tantric worship (in Malayāḷam). Old. 20 x 3.3 x 1.1. MF 5.3.2002.
(52) Raghuvaṃśavyākhyānaṃ, padadīpika (2 manuscripts). (a) 33 x 4 x 0.3. (b) 31 x 4.1 x 0.9.
(53) Bhāṣyaratnaprabhā by Govindānandabhagavat (in 4 adhyāyas). 27 x 4.3 x 4.6.
(54) Bhāgavatam. 31.2 x 5.2 x 5.

(55) A text dealing with both Rāmāyaṇa and Mahābhārata (in Sanskrit). 18.2 x 4 x 6.8.
(56) A text on philosophy, perhaps Nyāya (in Sanskrit). 41.5 x 5 x 1.
(57) Numbered verses (in Sanskrit). 12 x 2.4 x 2.5.
(58) A manual on Tantric ritual (in Malayāḷam). 50 x 4.5 x 0.7.
(59) Vedāntasāra. 13 x 3.4 x 1.8.
(60) Sahasranāmavyākhyānam. 13.4 x 2.4 x 3.
(61) Some Purāṇic? text including Santānagopālam. 9 x 3.8 x 3.5.
(62) A commentary on an epic or Purāṇic text (in Sanskrit). 30 x 4.5 x 0.7.
(63) Rūpāvatāra [by Dharmakīrti] (Vyākaraṇa). 36.5 x 4.5 x 3.
(64) A commentary on some philosophical text (in Sanskrit). 41.5 x 4.5 x 7.
(65) Ātmabodhaprakaraṇa with its ṭīkā (Vedānta). 18 x 4 x 4.5.
(66) Jaiminīyaśrautasūtra (plain text of the first book). 23.5 x 3.5 x 4.2. AP earlier; 7.3.2002.
(67) [Jaiminīya]Gṛhyakarmakriyākrama (and other texts). 26.5 x 4.7 x 3. AP earlier; MF 7.3.2002.
(68) Aparakriyās and prāyaścittas. 24 x 4 x 4. NN 7.3.2002.
(69) Devīmāhātmyam. 12 x 3.5 x 3.8.
(70) Govindacaritam. 16.2 x 3 x 1.4.
(71) Two Tantric texts, incomplete. 24 x 4.5 x 1.2.
(72) Vedāntasūtram. 41.5 x 5 x 0.1.
(73) A commentary on the 5th skandha [of Bhāgavatam] by Śrīdharasvāmin. 41.5 x 5 x 6.
(74) 9 stray leaves and empty leaves. Different sizes, 23.2 x 4.2 and less x 1.7.

2.4. Mūttiriṅṅōṭŭ Mana

This is one of the houses which are thought to be descended from Bhavatrāta, the famous commentator on the Śrautasūtra and Gṛhyasūtra of the Jaiminīya school, whose grandfather came from the Cōḷa kingdom of Ṭamil Nadu to Kerala, around the seventh century

CE (Raghavan 1957: 50; A. Parpola 1967: 185ff.; 1984: 432, 435, 445–446; 1986: 83, 85; 2011: 341; Fujii 2012: 101–102, 108). Most of the manuscripts belonging to this house have been deposited in the Kāṇippayyūr Mana, where a large number of manuscripts have been gathered from Nambudiri houses for preservation. We could not trace any manuscript of the Jaiminīya-brāhmaṇa among the manuscripts in the Mūttiriṅṅōṭŭ Mana nor in the Kāṇippayyūr Mana, in spite of Sreekrishna Sarma's statement in his letter to W. Rau in 1972:

> I am told that there is a copy of JB in the Baroda Oriental Institute, which is most probably of [sic, W.R.] the copy of a palm-leaf which I could not trace out but believed to be in the collections of a Namudiri [sic, W.R.], Mūttirangode, in Kerala. It is believed that this family produced the famous Bhavatrāta some centuries ago (Rau 1988: 25).

Manuscripts now kept in Mūttiriṅṅōṭŭ Mana:

(1) Jaiminīya-Upaniṣad[Brāhmaṇa]. 24 x 4 x 4.1. MF 1985; 22.1.2004.
(2) Bhavatrāta on Jaiminīyagṛhyasūtra. 26.5 x 4.2 x 4.3. AP 1985; AP & MF 22.1.2004.
(3) Jaiminīyaśrautaprayoga. 27.5 x 4.2 x 2.7. NN 22.1.2004.
(4) Bhāgavatam. 24.5 x 4.4 x 6.3.
(5) Rāmāyaṇam (part). Old. 32.5 x 4.2 x 2.5.
(6) Bhagavadgītāṭīkā. 23.7 x 4.3 x 4.1.

Manuscripts deposited in Kāṇippayyūr Mana. (' ' = title in the reception list)

(7 = K1) 'Vaidikam'. Prāyaścittacaṭaṅṅŭ. 35.8 x 4.6 x 4.5. NN 27.1.2004.
(8 = K2) 'Mahābhāratam'.
(9 = K3) 'Caṭaṅṅŭ'. Smārtacaṭaṅṅŭ & Jaiminīyagṛhyasūtra. [no. 17] 22.5 x 3.8 x 5.8. AP 24.1.2004.
(10 = K4) 'Ācārasaṃgraham'. 21.7 x 4.2 x 2.6.
(11 = K5) 'Āśaucam'. 34.2 x 4.9 x 2.8.

(12 = K6) 'Śaivasiddhānta(mīmāṃsa)'. Old. 40.5 x 4.8 x 3.3.
(13 = K7) 'Nyāyasiddhāntamaṇḍari'. 36 x 5 x 2.8.
(14 = K8) 'Rāmāyaṇam Sundarakāṇḍham'. 45 x 5.4 x 5.2.
(15 = K9) 'Bhāgavatam vyākhyānam'. 23.5 x 4.6 x 3.3.
(16 = K10) 'Citradīpavyākhyānam'. [no. 27.] 32.8 x 4 x 2.3.
(17 = K11) 'Bhāratam'. 44.7 x 4.6 x 4.
(18 = K12) 'Vedāntam'. 26.1 x 2.5 x 3.8.
(19 = K13) 'Śaktipūja'. Old. 41.4 x 4.1 x 3.9. AP & MF & NN 27.1.2004.
(20 = K14) 'Daśamam'. 45.2 x 5.2 x 2.3.
(21 = K15) 'Tarkkam'.
(22 = K16) 'Brahmaprāyaścittam'. 23.5 x 4.1 x 1.8.
(23 = K17) 'Kaumudi'. 32.6 x 4.2 x 3.
(24 = K18) 'Bhaviṣyat Purāṇam'.
(25 = K19) 'Nyāyasiddhāntamaṇḍari'. 35.8 x 4.5 x 5.8.
(26 = K20) 'Vedāntam'. 25.2 x 4.3 x 7.5.
(27 = K21) 'Jyotiṣam (mādhavīyam)'. [no. 44]. 18 x 3.8 x 3.5.
(28 = K22) 'Vedāntam'. [no. 35]. 18 x 4 x 3.5.
(29 = K23) 'Bhāratam'. 50.4 x 4.5 x 5.5.
(30 = K24) 'Bhāratam kiḷippāṭṭŭ'.
(31 = K25) 'Santānagopālam bhāṣa'. [no. 66 or 99]. 18 x 4.4 x 0.6.
(32 = K26) 'Śāṃkari'. 25.3 x 4.2 x 3.1.
(33 = K27) 'Keraḷotpatti'. 14.2 x 3.3 x 4.6. MF 23.1.2004.
(34 = K28) 'Devīmāhātmyam'. 27.5 x 4.2 x 2.6.
(35 = K29) 'Kaumudi'. 35.7 x 4.6 x 5.1.
(36 = K30) 'Tṛptidīpanyāyam'. 42 x 5 x 2.5.
(37 = K31) 'Dharmmaśāstram'.
(38 = K32) 'Kuvalayānandam'. 36.4 x 4.5 x 3.2.
(39 = K33) 'Daśamam'. Bhāgavataṃ daśamakhaṇḍam. 37.5 x 4.5 x 4.5.
(40 = K34) 'Tarkkamuktāvalivyākhyānam'. 34.3 x 4.6 x 5.
(41 = K35) 'Yudhiṣṭhiravijayam kāvyam'.
(42 = K36) 'Mahābhāratam'.
(43 = K37) 'Amarakōśam vyākhyānam'. 34.3 x 5 x 2.

(44 = K38) 'Bhāgavatam'. 34.5 x 5.1 x 3.4.
(45 = K39) 'Vyākaraṇam'. 23.8 x 3.9 x 5.5.
(46 ≐ K40) 'Haricaritam'. &
(47 = K41) 'Paribhāṣenduśekharam'. 44.6 x 4.5 x 5.
(Not in the list:)
(48 = K42) Jaiminīya caṭaṅṅŭ (in Malayāḷam). 29.5 x 5 x 3. NN 23.1.2004.
(49 = K43) Bhāgavatam. 29.8 x 3.9 x 3.6.
(50 = K44) Mīmāṃsā ? 12.2 x 2.5 x 1.5. MF 24.1.2004.
(51 = K45) Rāmāyaṇam Yuddhakāṇḍam. 45 x 5 x 4.8.
(52 = K46) Vākyārttham. Old. 47.3 x 5.5 x 3.3.
(53 = K47) Vedāntagrantham. 27.6 x 4 x 4.
(54 = K48) Bahvṛcaprāyaścittam. 23.6 x 4.2 x 1.7. MF 24.1.2004.

1.5. Kāṇippayyūr Mana

For the manuscripts from the Mūttiriṅṅōṭŭ Mana (K1 to K48), see above.

(K49) From Muppāṭṭu Mana: Taittirīyabrāhmaṇa (from TB 1.7.10.6 to: odanam udbrabate). AP 27.1.2004.
(K50) From Ōkki Mana: Brāhmaṇam Prāyaścittam. NN 24.1.2004.
(K51) Brāhmaṇam Pūrvam (AB 1.1.1–5.16.23). MF 24.1.2004.
(K52) From Perumpiḷḷi Mana: Śāṅkarasmṛtigrantham. MF 27.1.2004.

3. MANUSCRIPTS IN LIBRARIES

3.1. Manuscript Library of the Department of Malayalam, University of Calicut

(1) 2013 from Koraṭṭikkara Mana: Agniṣṭomaccaṭaṅṅŭ etc. AP 24.2.2003.
(2) 2014 from Koraṭṭikkara Mana: Jaiminīya-Upaniṣad-[brāhmaṇa]. MF 24.2.2003.
(3) 3967. Yajurvedapadam. Uttarārdham. NN 24.2.2003.
(4) 3971. Yajurvedaśākhā. MF & NN 24.2.2003.

3.2. The Oriental Research Institute and Manuscripts Library, University of Kerala, Trivandrum

Alphabetical Index of Sanskrit Manuscripts: Kunjan Pillai 1957–65; Bhaskaran 1984; Bhaskaran & Visweswari Amma 1986–88; Visalakshy & Girija 1995–2000.

(1) 8161. Jaiminīyasāmagānam (āgneyam only). 38.8 x 3.9 x 0.4 & 33.3 x 3.3 x 0.8. AP 4.2.2004.
(2) 8162. Atirātrasāma jaiminīyam. NN 4.2.2004.
(3) 8163. Jaiminīyasāmagānam. 39.5 x 3 x 1.8. AP 5.2.2004.
(4) 8165. Jaiminīyasāmagānam (Prakṛti). 46.8 x 3.2 x 2.8. AP 6.2.2004; NN 6.2.2004.
(5) 8166. Agniṣṭomasāma jaiminīyam; Jaiminīyaśrautasūtra [I]. 33.3 x 3.3 x 1.9. AP 4.2.2004.
(6) 8167. Jaiminīyasāmasaṃhitā. 34 x 3.9 x 4.4. NN 4–5.2.2004.
(7) 11783. Jaiminigṛhyaprayogakārikā. 28.7 x 4.3 x 2. AP 4–5.2.2004.
(8) 11784. Śrautādhānakriyākrama. 37.5 x 4.6 x 0.7. NN 5.2.2004.
(9) 11785. Śrīnivāsa's Ādhānapūrvakāgniṣṭomaprayoga. 23 x 4 x 2.3. AP 5.2.2004.
(10) 11797A. Upagranthasūtram. 25 x 15.4 x 0.8. NN 5.2.2004.
(11) 11800. Kalpānupadasūtra. 24.5 x 15.4 x 0.3. AP 5.2.2004.
(12) 11802. Taṇḍālakṣaṇam. 21 x 8.7 x 0.3. AP 5.2.2004.
(13) 13097E. Jaiminīya-Upaniṣad[brāhmaṇa]. 34.3 x 4.7 x 0.1. MF 6.2.2004.
(14) 23015. Jaiminīya-Upaniṣad[brāhmaṇa]. 14.3 x 3.7 x 4.7. MF 5.2.2004.
(15) 23030. Gṛhyamantravṛtti. 19.4 x 3.8 x 2.3. AP 5.2.2004.
(16) 23040. From Pakarāvūr Mana: Smārttaṃ Sāmacaṭaṅṅŭ. 23.5 x 5.4 x 4.3. AP 5–6.2.2004.
(17) 23044. From Pakarāvūr Mana: Yāgattinṯe Sāmacaṭaṅṅŭ. 23.5 x 4.4 x 3.2. NN 5.2.2004.
(18) 23045. From Pakarāvūr Mana: Iṣṭiyuṭe Caṭaṅṅŭ. 16 x 4.4 x 1.6. NN 5.2.2004.

(19) 23046. From Pakarāvūr Mana: Ādhānādyagniparyantam. 17.3 x 2.2 x 3. NN 6.2.2004.
(20) C826. Jaiminīyagṛhyamantravṛtti. 24.3 x 4 x 3.2. AP 5.2.2004.
(21) L308. Jaiminīya-Upaniṣad[brāhmaṇa]. 25.2 x 4.8 x 3.7. MF 4–5.2.04.
(22) L321. Bhavatrāta on Jaiminīyaśrautasūtra. 55.5 x 4.8 x 5.6. MF & NN & AP 3.2.2004.
(23) L1247. Jaiminīya-Upaniṣad[brāhmaṇa]. 30 x 5 x 2.8. MF 5.2.2004.
(24) T577. Jaiminīyagṛhyamantravṛtti (a transcript of C826). AP 5.2.2004.

3.3. The Adyar Library and Research Centre, Chennai

For a catalogue of the Vedic manuscripts, see Sarma 1942.

(1) 75583. Jaiminīyaśrautasūtravṛtti by Bhavatrāta. 56 x 5.4 x 6.1. MF & NN 12.2.2004.
(2) 75584 (34D10). Jaiminīyagṛhyasūtravṛtti by Bhavatrāta. Fol. 1–107. 36 x 4.8 x 3.7. AP 12.2.2004.
(3) 75585 (34D11). Jaiminīyagṛhyasūtravṛtti by Bhavatrāta. Fol. 108–146. 22.3 x 3.3 x 1.5. AP 12.2.2004.

3.4. The Saraswathi Mahal Library, Thanjavur

Catalogues of the manuscript holdings: Burnell 1880 and Subrahmaṇya Sastri 1928–34.

(1) Burnell 9102 = D 1969. Kalpabrāhmaṇam. 118 palm leaves in grantha script. AP 1971; 17.2.2006.
(2) Burnell 9117 A = D 2623. Sāmaprayogavṛtti by Candraśekhara Bhaṭṭārya. 160 palm leaves in grantha script. 41 x 3.2 x 8. AP 1971; NN & MF 17.2.2006.
(3) Burnell 9117 B = D 2045. Pratihārasūtrabhāṣya. 14 palm leaves in grantha script. 41 x 3.2 x 8. MF 17.2.2006.

(4) Burnell 2517 = D 1967. Upagranthasūtra. 30 paper leaves in nāgarī script. 27 x 11.5 (injured). AP 18.2.2006.

3.5. The Oriental Institute, Baroda

Manuscript catalogues: Nambiyar Śiromaṇi 1942–50; Shrigondekar 1925; Ramaswami Śāstrī Śiromaṇi 1942. All manuscripts photographed are palm leaves in the grantha script unless otherwise mentioned. Items included in the list, which we had no time to photograph ourselves, were ordered and afterwards photographed by the Oriental Institute = OIB.

(1) 92. Gāyatravidhāna with commentary (no beginning). Nāgarī, paper. Fol. 9–13. OIB.
(2) 2446 A. Gītikalpam by Rāmaśukla. Nāgarī, paper. Fol. 2–7 (leaf 1 missing). OIB.
(3) 2535. Upagranthasūtra (4 prapathakas). Nāgarī, paper. Fol. 1–32. OIB.
(4) 4081. Kalpapañjikā (Sāmaveda, beginning and end missing). Nāgarī, paper. 90 folia. OIB.
(5) 5882. Vāmanakārikā on Khādiragṛhyasūtra. Nāgarī, paper. 84 folia. OIB.
(6) 6383 B. Garuḍacayanagānaprakāra, fol. 26–27. OIB.
(7) 6383 C. Gaṇeśakārikā (incomplete), fol. 28–31. OIB.
(8) 6383 D. Jyotiraptoryāmaprayoga (audgātra), fol. 32–36. OIB.
(9) 6784 B. Sāmaparibhāṣā, fol. 95–105. OIB.
(10) 7409. Mātrālakṣaṇa. Nāgarī, paper. 4 folia. OIB.
(11) 7840. Śrīnivāsa's commentary on Jaiminīyagṛhyasūtra 1.1–2.5 (injured, 3 leaves missing in the middle). 124 folia. OIB.
(12) 9798. Jaiminīya gṛhya texts: A. Karmapradīpa; B. Pitṛmedhasāra (incomplete), fol. 17–20; C. Vainateyakārikā/Prayogasāra on Jaiminīyagṛhyasūtra, fol. 21–27; D. Jaiminīyagṛhyasūtra 1.1–2.2, fol. 28–42. 43 x 4.2 x 3. AP 22.11.2006.
(13) 9800: A. Jaiminīyaśrautasūtra (agniṣṭoma), fol. 1–14; B. prāyaścittakārikā; C. Trikāṇḍī. 30 x 3.2 x 7. AP 21.11.2006.

(14) 9801 B. Prāyaścittaprayoga with Kalpakārikā. 9 folia. OIB.

(15) 9805 D. Gāyatravidhāna. 3 folia. OIB.

(16) 9851. Jaiminīyabrāhmaṇa: A. Mahābrāhmaṇa, fol. 1–65; B. Dvādaśāha, fol. 66–133; C. Mahāvrata, fol. 134–160; D. Ekāha, fol. 161–184; E. Ahīna, fol. 185–202; F. Satra, fol. 202–209. 45 x 5.5 x 8. MF 21.11.2006.

(17) 9852 A. Śrinivāsa's commentary Subodhinī on Jaiminīyagṛhyasūtra, fol. 1–45. OIB. [Not photographed: Karmavipākamahārṇava 1–3, 12 folia.]

(18) 9855: A. Jaiminīyagṛhyasūtra, fol. 1–24; B. Prayogasāra on Jaiminīyagṛhyasūtra, fol. 25–49; C. Śrāddhaprayoga (Sāmaveda), 87 folia. 18.6 x 4.3 x 4.9. AP 22.11.2006.

(19) 9856. Jaiminīyasaṁhitā: A. Gāna, fol. 1–200 (fol. 60–66 missing); B. Ārcika, fol. 201–236. AP 21.11.2006.

(20) 9857: A. Prayogaratnamālā (Pañcāgnikārikā) of Sarvakratu on Jaiminīyagṛhyasūtra, fol. 1–26; B. Siddhāntamālākārikā of Bhavatrāta on Jaiminīyagṛhyasūtra, fol. 27–37; C. Prayogasāra on Jaiminīyagṛhyasūtra, fol. 38–67; D. Prayogakārikā of Sabhāpati on Jaiminīyagṛhyasūtra, fol. 68–77 (incomplete at end); E. Prayogakārikā on Jaiminīyagṛhyasūtra, fol. 78–82. 45 x 4 x 4.8 (injured). AP 22.11.2006.

(21) 9859. Śrīnivāsa Adhvarin's Sarvānukramaṇī (from darśapūrṇamāsa to iṣṭiprāyaścitta, said to follow Āpastamba). 42 folia (injured). OIB.

(22) 9860: A. Vainateyakārikā on Jaiminīyaśrautasūtra, 12 folia; B. Sannyāsavidhi, 2 folia. 41.5 x 2.8 x 1.2. AP 22.11.2006.

(23) 9863: A. Jaiminīya-Ārṣeyabrāhmaṇa, 17 folia; B. Jaiminīya-Upaniṣadbrāhmaṇa, 86 folia. 42 x 3.8 x 6.5 (injured). MF 21.11.2006.

(24) 9864. Dhāraṇalakṣaṇa of Sabhāpati. 67 folia (beginning and end missing). 47 x 4 x 3.5 (injured). AP 22.11.2006.

(25) 9865; A. Prayogasāra on Jaiminīyagṛhyasūtra, fol. 1–6a; B. Prayogamālā of Śrīnivāsa on Jaiminīyagṛhyasūtra (incomplete), fol. 6a–9; C. student's writing exercise

including verses from the beginning of Bhavatrāta's Jaiminīyaśrautasūtravṛtti (bad handwriting, repeated on the other side), fol. 10; D. Āyuṣyahomaprayoga, fol. 11; E. Vivāhāgnyupagataprāyaścitta, fol. 12; F. Jaiminīyagṛhyasūtra (beginning missing), fol. 13–23. 47 x 4 x 1.2 (injured). AP 22.11.2006.

(26) 9867. Ādhānāgniṣṭomasāma. 21 folia. 40.7 x 3.8 x 1.2. AP 22.11.2006.

(27) 9868. Kratudīpikā by Kuraṅgarāja (a prayoga on Jaiminīyaśrautasūtra), fol. 1–29. 40.8 (fol. 1–22) / 36.1 (fol. 23–29) x 3.6 x 1.6. AP 22.11.2006.

(28) 9869. Jaiminīyagāna: A. Prakṛti, fol. 1–165; B. Ūha, first 14 folia. 41 x 23.6 x 4.4. MF 22.11.2006.

(29) 9870. Audgātrādi (incomplete). 26 folia. AP 22.11.2006.

(30) 9903 D. Upagranthasūtra (1.1–3.7). 19 folia. 32.2 x 3.3 x 1. AP 22.11.2006.

(31) 9910. Upagranthavyākhyā by Śrīnivāsa (1.6–2.4). 55 folia. OIB.

(32) 9911: B. Anustotrasūtra, fol. 1–5; C. Kalpānupadasūtra, 17 folia. 25.5 x 3.9 x 1.4 (= B+C). AP 21.11.2006.

(33) 9915: A. Nidānasūtra (almost complete), fol. 1–82; B. Naiga, 17 folia. OIB.

(34) 9916 C. Gāyatravidhāna with commentary. 9 folia. OIB.

(35) 10880. Jaiminīyaprakṛtigāna, fol. 1–90. 48 x 5 x 2.8. MF 22.11.2006.

(36) 10881 A. Jaiminīyaśrautasūtra (agniṣṭoma), fol. 1–17. 18.5 x 4.3 x 0.4. AP 21.11.2006.

(37) 10881 B. Jaiminīyaśrautasūtraprayoga by Śrīnivāsa, fol. 18–66 (sic). 18.4 x 4.4 x 1.5. AP 21.11.2006.

(38) 10881 C. Jaiminīya-Upaniṣadbrāhmaṇa, fol. 50 (sic) – 123. 18.8 x 4.4 x 2. MF 22.11.2006.

(39) 10885. Dhāraṇalakṣaṇa of Sabhāpati (6 parvans), fol. 1–53. 45.5 x 4 x 3 (injured). MF 22.11.2006.

(40) 11985. Mātrālakṣaṇa with commentary. Nāgarī, paper. 12 folia. OIB.

(41) 13472 A. Jaiminīyagṛhyasūtra, fol. 1–43. Palm leaves in Telugu script. OIB. [13472 B. Pravargyaprayoga. 24 palm leaves in grantha script. Not photographed.]

(42) 13752. Śāṅkarasmṛti, fol. 1–100. OIB.

3.6. Lal Chand Research Library, DAV College, Chandigarh

Catalogue of manuscripts: http://www.davchd.com/assets/files/downloads/10.pdf.

(1) 4362. Śāṭyāyanagṛhyasūtra. 6 pages. Nāgarī, paper. 32 x 21. AP 25.11.2006.

(2) 5786. Jaiminīyasaṃhitā (Prakṛtigāna). 152 folia. 43 x 4.5 x 10. AP 25.11.2006.

(3) 5791. Jaiminīyasaṃhitā (Gāna, damaged and incomplete). 122 folia. 44 x 4 x 6.5. MF 25.11.2006.

(4) 6357. Anustotrasūtra. 9 pages. Nāgarī, paper. 11 x 26. AP 25.11.2006.

3.7. The Punjab University Library, Lahore

On his state visit to Finland in 2004, President Pervez Musharraf invited AP to witness the opening of the National Museum of Ethnography in Islamabad and to visit other Pakistani institutions of his choice. This enabled AP to document Sāmavedic manuscripts kept at the Lahore University Library during two days. As the *Catalogue of the Sanskrit Manuscripts in the Panjab University Library* does not give the shelf marks, these had to be searched first with the help of the card catalogue. With the good and effective cooperation of the library staff, most manuscripts were located and found to be in good condition. Then the manuscripts were analyzed for their actual contents, and a selection for photography was made. All remaining time was used to photograph as many manuscripts as possible, but as can be seen from the list below, a number of important manuscripts had to be left to wait later photography.

(1) 7217. Jaiminisaṃhitā Ṛkbhāṣya by Bhavatrāta. 48 x 4.8 x 1. AP 16.8.2004.

(2) 7223. Three texts of Jaiminīya Sāmaveda: 1. Dhāraṇalakṣaṇa by Sabhāpati; 2. Svaraprakāśa by Śrīnivāsa Dīkṣita; 3. Saṃhitābrāhmaṇakhaṇḍasaṃkhyā. 41 x 4 x 0.5. Photographed twice. AP 16 & 17.8.2004.

(3) 7217. Jaiminisaṃhitā Ṛkbhāṣya by Bhavatrāta (fragment). 45 x 4 x 0.7. AP 16.8.2004.

(4) 7224. Four texts of Jaiminīya Sāmaveda: 1. Ūhapaurvāparyabheda; 2. Uttara-Ṛkkārikā; 3. Ādhānasomasāmakrama Īśvaraśāstrīśrautakārikā; 4. Agnyādhānasāma. 44 x 4 x 2.8. AP 16.8.2004.

(5) 7225. Two texts of Jaiminīya Sāmaveda: 1. Śrautasūtra (agniṣṭoma, complete); 2. Agniṣṭomātirātrasāma. 42 x 4 x 1.8. AP 16.8.2004.

(6) 7226. Two texts of Jaiminīya Sāmaveda: 1. Śrautasūtra (agniṣṭoma, complete); 2. Gṛhyasūtrabhāṣya by Śrīnivāsa. 34 x 4.5 x 3.8. Uninked manuscript. AP 16.8.2004.

(7) 8016. Three texts of Jaiminīya Sāmaveda: 1. Ūhalakṣaṇakārikā; 2. Agnyādhānasāmakārikā; 3. Ādhānasomakārikā. 41.5 x 3.5 x 2. AP 17.8.2004.

(8) 8013. Two texts of Jaiminīya Sāmaveda: 1. Jaiminīyagṛhyasūtra Śrāddhapaṭalabhāṣya by Bhavatrāta (?); 2. Jaiminīyagṛhyasūtra Śrāddhapaṭalabhāṣya by Śrīnivāsa Nārāyaṇaputra. 31 x 4 x 5. AP 17.8.2004.

(9) 8015. Five texts of Jaiminīya Sāmaveda: 1. Sāmans of Udakaśānti, etc; 2. Jaiminiśrautasūtra (agniṣṭoma); 3. Jaiminigṛhyasūtra; 4. Gṛhyakārikā Vainateya; 5. Aparaprayoga. 24 x 5 x 3.5. AP 17.8.2004.

(10) 7142. Sāmalakṣaṇam (Jaiminiśākhā). 36 x 3 x 3.4. Only fol. 1–42 & 76–97 photographed. AP 17.8.2004.

(11) 7222. Three texts of Jaiminīya Sāmaveda: 1. Prakṛti-Ṛk, fol. 1–27; 2. Ārṣeyabrāhmaṇa, fol. 28–38 (only this text

photographed); 3. Uttara-Ṛk, fol. 39–72. 36 x 5 x 2.7. Dated 931 ME = 1764 CE. AP 17.8.2004.

(12) 7765. Vāmanakārikā on GGS of Chandogaśākhā. 40 x 4 x 4. (Only the first three and last three leaves of this thick uninked manuscript photographed.) AP 17.8.2004.

(13) 7233. Jaiminiśākhīyānām ūrdhvadehaprayoga by Īśvaraśāstrī (Gṛhya). 39 x 4 x 1.3. AP 17.8.2004.

(14) 7234. Four Gṛhya texts of Jaiminīya Sāmaveda: 1. Prayogacandrikā by Śrīnivāsaśiṣya; 2. Upanayana; 3. Vivāha; 4. Udakaśānti. 39 x 3.5 x 1.6. AP 17.8.2004.

(15) 8011. Three Sāmavedic Gṛhya texts: 1. Rāṇāyanisūtra on Vṛṣotsarga; 2. Jaiminivṛṣotsargaprayoga; 3. Jaiminiśākhā Ūrdhvadehaprayoga. 41 x 3.5 x 3. AP 17.8.2004.

(16) 7140. Jaiminīyagṛhyasūtra with Śrīnivāsa's commentary.

(17) 7139. Jaiminiśākhā Sāmasaṃhitā (Pūrvagāna), dated 1737 CE, 132 folia, in excellent condition, altogether 1523 sāmans: 1. Āgneyaṃ parva, 182 sāmans; 2. Aindraṃ parva, 641 sāmans; 3. Pāvamānaṃ parva, 404 sāmans; 4. Āraṇam, 291 sāmans.

(18) 8010. Jaiminiśākhā Sāmasaṃhitā (Prakṛti, 1523 sāmans), dated 1822 CE (R.A. Sastri): 1. Āraṇaṃ sāma; 2. Saṃhitāsāma.

(19) 8009. Sāmaveda Jaiminisaṃhitā: Pāvamānasāma, 391 sāmans.

(20) 7218. Jaiminisaṃhitā: Aindram parva.

(21) 7219. Jaiminisaṃhitā: Āraṇam, dated 1763 CE.

(22) 7220. Jaiminiśākhā: Āgneyam & aindraṃ parva. Old manuscript.

(23) 7221. Jaiminiśākhā Pūrva-Ṛk & Uttara-Ṛk with Vedalakṣaṇa, dated 1030 ME = 1852 CE. Text small and badly visible, but the pages are whole and broad.

(24) 7229. Jaiminīyagṛhyasūtrabhāṣya by Śrīnivāsa.

(25) 7232. Jaiminīyagṛhyasūtrabhāṣya by Śrīnivāsa. Old and injured manuscript.

3.8. Melkote, Karnataka

Jaiminīyas belonging to the Śrīvaiṣṇavas fled Śaiva prosecution with Rāmānuja to Melkote in Karnataka. A small Jaiminīya Sāmaveda community survives in Melkote today. On the history of Melkote, see Apte et al. 1998.

3.8.1. Notebooks written by Śrī S. R(āmasvāmi) Śrīnivāsa Ayyaṅgār

(1) Notebook in Kannaḍa script on Jaiminīya sāmans sung in Melkote. 41 written pages. 18 x 12 x 1.3. AP 21.2.2006.
(2) Notebook in Kannaḍa script on Jaiminīya Sandhyāvandanam and Upākarmaprayoga. NN 22.2.2006.
(3) Notebook (dated 11.9.1967) in Kannaḍa script on Aṅkurārpaṇam and Vivāhaprayoga. NN 22.2.2006.

3.8.2. Academy of Sanskrit Research, Melkote

http://vedavid.org./ASR.

(1) 1182. Sāmaveda Upākarmaprayoga. Grantha and nandināgarī scripts on palm leaves. 16.5 x 5.7 x 0.8. NN 22.2.2006.
(2) 1450. Sāmavedalakṣaṇagrantha (incomplete). Nandināgarī script on 50 palm leaves. 33 x 4.7 x 1.6. MF 22.2.2006.
(3) 5160. Sāmaveda Upākarma. Telugu script on palm leaves. 47.2 x 3.8 x 1.8. NN 22.2.2006.

3.8.3. The Government Sanskrit College, Melkote

(1) 453. Sāmaveda. Grantha script on palm leaves. 43.5 x 3.5 x 5.6. MF & NN 22.2.2006.
(2) Sāmavedasūtram & Prāyaścittavidhi. Uninked grantha script on palm leaves. 32 x 3.5 x 4. AP 22.2.2006. Begins: *śrī oṃ te rāmānujamahādeśikāya namaḥ* | *śubham astu* | *nirvighnam astu* | *ābhi tvā śūra nonumo vā* | *svayoni* | *catvāri rathantarāṇi* || ... | *idānīṃ vinnitaṃ sāmnām āraṇyānāṃ yathākramaṃ* | ...

3.9. The Rashtriya Sanskrit Vidyapeetha Manuscripts Library, Tirupati

The following nine manuscripts recorded in the alphabetical index of Govindan (2003), which we obtained in 2008, are yet to be photographed. The first four-digit number is the serial number of Govindan's index, the second is the manuscript stock number. These manuscripts may have their origin in the Koṭuntirappuḷḷi village of Palghat District, Kerala, as the Jaiminīya people there have told us that a person from Tirupati had come and collected their manuscripts.

(1) 1050/1772. Jaiminīyabrāhmaṇa (complete). Devanāgarī script, 203 paper leaves, 17 lines per page. Good condition.

(2) 1051/1771. Jaiminīyabrāhmaṇa (complete [sic]). Devanāgarī script, 27 paper leaves, 17 lines per page. Good condition.

(3) 1054/1775. Jaiminīya-Ārṣeyabrāhmaṇa (complete). Devanāgarī script, 19 paper leaves, 23 lines per page. Good condition.

(4) 1055/1773. Jaiminīya-Upaniṣadbrāhmaṇa (incomplete). Devanāgarī script, 29 paper leaves, 30 lines per page. Good condition.

(5) 1056/1676. Jaiminīya-Upaniṣadbrāhmaṇa (complete). Grantha script, 59 paper leaves, 53 lines per page. Good condition.

(6) 1057/1776. Jaiminīya-Upaniṣadbrāhmaṇa (incomplete). Devanāgarī script, 19 paper leaves, 24 lines per page. Good condition.

(7) 1058/1774. Jaiminīya-Upaniṣadbrāhmaṇa (incomplete). Devanāgarī script, 6 paper leaves, 17 lines per page. Good condition.

(8) 1222/1769. Talavakarabrāhmaṇe Upaniṣadbrāhmaṇam (complete). Devanāgarī script, 176 paper leaves, 15 lines per page. Good condition.

(9) 367/1770. Ārṣeyabrāhmaṇa (complete). Devanāgarī script, 27 paper leaves, 15 lines per page. Good condition.

REFERENCES

APTE, Prabhakar P. et al. 1998. *Melukote through the Ages*. Melukote: Academy of Sanskrit Research.

BHASKARAN, T. 1984. *Alphabetical Index of Sanskrit Manuscripts in the Oriental Research Institute and Manuscripts Library, Trivandrum*, III: *Ya to Sa*. (Trivandrum Sanskrit Series, 254.) Trivandrum: The Oriental Research Institute and Manuscripts Library, University of Kerala.

BHASKARAN, T. & K. VISWESWARI AMMA 1986–88. *Alphabetical index of Sanskrit manuscripts in the Oriental Research Institute and Manuscripts Library, Trivandrum* IV–V: *Sa-Ha & Supplementary: A to Ta*. Trivandrum Sanskrit Series 256 & 259. Trivandrum: The Oriental Research Institute and Manuscripts Library, University of Kerala.

BURNELL, A. C. 1880. *A Classified Index to the Sanskrit Mss. in the Palace at Tanjore, Prepared for the Madras Government*. London: Trübner & Co.

Catalogue of the Sanskrit Manuscripts in the Panjab University Library I–II. Lahore: University of the Panjab, 1932–41.

FUJII, M. 2012. The Jaiminīya Sāmaveda traditions and manuscripts in South India. In: Saraju Rath (ed.), *Aspects of Manuscript Culture in South India*: 99–118. Leiden: Brill.

GOVINDAN, K. E. (ed.) 2003. *An Alphabetical Index of Sanskrit Manuscripts in the Rashtriya Sanskrit Vidyapeetha Manuscripts Library, Tirupati*. Tirupati: Rashtriya Samskrta Vidyapitham.

HOWARD, W. 1977. *Sāmavedic Chant*. New Haven: Yale University Press.

—— 1987. The body of the bodiess Gāyatra. *Indo-Iranian Journal* 30: 161–173.

KUNJAN PILLAI, Suranad 1957–65. *Alphabetical Index of the Sanskrit Manuscripts in the University Manuscripts Library, Trivandrum*, I–II: *A to Ṇa & Ta to Ma*. (Trivandrum Sanskrit Series, 186 & 215.) Trivandrum: University Manuscripts Library, University of Kerala.

Lal Chand Research Library, DAV College, Chandigarh, Catalogue of Manuscripts (http://www.davchd.com/assets/files/downloads/10.pdf).

NAMBIYAR ŚIROMANI, Raghavan 1942–50. *An Alphabetical List of Manuscripts in the Oriental Institute, Baroda*, I–II. (Gaekwad's Oriental Series, 97 & 114.) Baroda: Oriental Institute.

PARPOLA, A. 1967. On the Jaiminīyaśrautasūtra and its annexes. *Orientalia Suecana* 16: 181–214.

—— 1973. *The Literature and Study of the Jaiminīya Sāmaveda in Retrospect and Prospect*. (Studia Orientalia 43.6.) Helsinki: The Finnish Oriental Society.

—— 1984. On the Jaiminīya and Vādhūla traditions of South India and the Pāṇḍu/Pāṇḍava problem. *Studia Orientalia* 55: 429–468 (3–42).

—— 2011. Codification of Vedic domestic ritual in Kerala: *Pārvaṇa-sthālīpāka* – the model of rites with fire-offerings – in *Jaiminīya-Gṛhyasūtra* 1,1–4 and in the Malayāḷam manual of the Sāmaveda Nampūtiri Brahmins of Kerala, the *Sāma-Smārtta-Caṭaṅṅü*. In *Travaux de Symposium International: Le Livre. La Roumanie. L'Europe. Troisième édition, 20 à 24 September 2010*, III: La troisième section: Études euro- et afro-asiatiques: 261–354. Bucarest: Éditeur Bibliothèque de Bucarest. (http://www.bibliotecametropolitana.ro/Uploads/Simpozionul%20 International Cartea Romania Europa III V3 mic.pdf).

PARPOLA, M. 2000. *Kerala Brahmins in Transition: A Study of a Nampūtiri Family*. (Studia Orientalia, 91.) Helsinki: The Finnish Oriental Society.

RAGHAVAN, V. 1957. Present position of Vedic chanting and its future. *Bulletin of the Institute of Traditional Cultures, Madras University*: 48–69.

RAMASWAMI ŚĀSTRI ŚIROMAṆI, K. S. 1942. *A Descriptive Catalogue of Manuscripts at the Oriental Institute, Baroda*, II: *Śrauta Sūtras and Prayogas*. (Gaekwad Oriental Series, 96.) Baroda: Oriental Institute.

RAU, W. 1988. Die Handschriften des Jaiminīya-Brāhmaṇa. In: Peter Kosta (ed.), *Studia Indogermanica et Slavica: Festgabe für Werner Thomas zum 65. Geburtstag*. (Specimena Philologiae Slavicae 26): 21–35. München: Verlag Otto Sagner.

SARMA, K. Madhava Krishna 1942. *Descriptive Catalogue of Sanskrit Manuscripts in the Adyar Library*, I: *Vedic*. Supervised by C. Kunhan Raja. (Adyar Library Series, 35.) Madras: The Adyar Library.

SHRIGONDEKAR, Gajanan K. 1925. *A Descriptive Catalogue of Manuscripts in the Central Library of Baroda*, I: *Veda, Vedalakṣaṇa, and Upaniṣads*. (Gaekwad Oriental Series, 27.) Baroda: Central Library.

STAAL, J. F. 1975. Some Vedic survivals: Report on research done in India Dec. 1970 – March 1971. *Journal of the Ganganatha Jha Kendriya Sanskrit Vidyapeetha* 31: 167–180.

—— (ed.) 1983. *Agni: The Vedic ritual of the Fire Altar*, I-II. Berkeley: Asian Humanities Press.

S[UBRAHMANYA] SASTRI, P. P. 1928–34. *A Descriptive Catalogue of the Sanskrit Manuscripts in the Tanjore Mahārāja Serfoji's Sarasvatī Mahal Library, Tanjore*. I–XIX. Srirangam: Sri Vani Vilas Press.

VISALAKSHY, P. & R. GIRIJA 1995–2000. *Alphabetical Index of Sanskrit Manuscripts in the Oriental Research Institute and Manuscripts Library, Trivandrum*, VI–VII: *Supplementary Da to Ra & Ra to Ha*. (Trivandrum Sanskrit Series, 264 & 266.) Trivandrum: The Oriental Research Institute and Manuscripts Library, University of Kerala.

The Khilas and Upakhilas of the Ṛgveda according to the *Yāmalāṣṭakatantre Khila-Upaniṣad*

CEZARY GALEWICZ

A text purposely imitating another text is not an uncommon phenomenon in the history of Indian religions. We have multiple examples of such textual mimicry in the various Gītās, and in the miraculous recoveries of supposedly lost chapters of well-known scriptures, such as the *Bhāgavatamāhātmya* that claims to be a part of the *Padmapurāṇa*.[1] In this presentation we are confronted with a textual intrusion into a relatively recent Āśvalāyana Ṛgveda compendium known as the *Ṛgvedadaśagrantha* or *Ṛgvedīyadaśagrantha* (ṚDG). This compendium is nowadays current in Konkan and Maharashtra, among others by Āśvalāyana Ṛgvedins of Gokarṇa.[2] We might perhaps speak here of an extension of a textual corpus of canonical status through the addition of a new text to this closed collection apparently having established authority. The title gives the apocryphal addition a supposedly Tantric appearance.

The ṚDG collection as a whole deserves a few remarks of its own. Contrary to what its very name suggests, it appears to contain more than ten different books. However, there seems to be a living tradition to cope with this discrepancy: several texts are grouped

[1] See Christof 2001: 73.

[2] I happened to come across a loose-leaf edition of the RDG published by the Ghaisasa Veda Pāṭha Śālā and printed by Vasanta Press in Pune in 1986.

together so as to match the number ten, leaving aside the rest. According to one of its contemporary users, the ten granthas comprise the following works: 1) the *Ṛgvedasaṃhitā*, 2) the *Aitareya-brāhmaṇa*, 3) the *Aitareya-Āraṇyaka* and the *Aitareya-Upaniṣad*, 4) the *Āśvalāyanagṛhyasūtra*, 5) *Śikṣā*, 6) *Kalpa*, 7) *Vyākaraṇa*, 8) *Chandas*, 9) *Jyotiṣa*, 10) *Nirukta* (*Nighaṇṭu*).[3]

Everything looks fine but for the fact that several texts actually contained in the collection are said not to belong to it, namely, a group of 32 short texts packed under the heading of *Ṛksaṃhitā-sthapariśiṣṭa* [*Viṣayānukramaṇikā*], the *Ṛgvidhāna* and, finally, a text calling itself the *Yāmalāṣṭakatantre Khila-Upaniṣad* (YATKU). The last-mentioned text is not listed in the attached *anukramaṇikā* at all. Its full title is given as *yāmalāṣṭakatantre khilopaniṣanmantrasaṃhitāsvarūpaṃ* and the colophon at the end adds that the text is the 13th chapter (*paṭala*) of such a seemingly Tantric work. We are told that the work in question appears in a fragmentary manner only, at the very end of the ṚDG.

The text in question is very short, covering only two leaflets. For the most part it is an enumeration of would-be Vedic Khilas and Upaniṣads. It has the structure of a dialogue between Pārvatī and Śiva, where the former asks the latter to reveal her the most important part of the Veda in the form of Khilas and Upakhilas as well as Mahopaniṣads and other collections of mantras, all of them said by her to form the essence, or the most excellent part, of the Veda (*vedānāṃ sarabhūta*). As the text reads, Lord Śiva, filled with compassion, fulfils her request and declares the required names, giving the reasons for each choice. The names are formulated as inner qualities of those texts that help to dispel the darkness of ignorance and lead to *mukti*. Some of the enumerated texts, however, look a bit strange for the Āśvalāyana Ṛgveda. So does the very title of the text in question. The word *khila* suggests that the text pretends to be an appendix to a canonical collection, comparable to the *Ṛgvedakhila* (ṚVKh) or the Khilas to other

[3] Personal communication of Somayaji Nana Kale of Maharashtra.

Vedic Saṃhitās which are, by the way, also enumerated in the text in question. The name of the YATKU resembles also the term *khilakāṇḍa* used in Yajurvedic tradition of the closing books of the *Maitrāyaṇīsaṃhitā* and the *Kāṭhakasaṃhitā*, of *Vājasaneyisaṃhitā* 26–35[4] and of the *Bṛhadāraṇyaka-Upaniṣad*. Perhaps these are the associations that the title is supposed to bring to mind in order to justify the appearance of this text at the end of a Ṛgvedic compendium. On the other hand, the colophon declares the YATKU to be the 13th chapter (*paṭala*) of the Upaniṣad, thus suggesting that the term *khila* refers here to the defective, incomplete nature of the Upaniṣad itself.

It seems characteristic that Pārvatī seeks instruction from Lord Śiva by explicitly demanding the names of Khilas, Upakhilas, Mahopaniṣads and Mantrasaṃhitās put in one row and said to represent the essence of the Veda and to have the power of *sakalārthada* or fulfilling all desires. Śiva tells a short story of Vedavyāsa who, while working on Vedic Saṃhitās, at a certain moment found out that they could not contain any more mantras. As a result, the remaining mantras came to be called Khilas and Upakhilas. This explanation suggests that the Khilas essentially have the same status as the mantras that actually form the Saṃhitās proper.

The texts solemnly declared by Śiva as Khilas and Upakhilas of the Ṛgveda are nine in number: *Vālakhilya*, *Rājanya*, *Lakṣmīsūkta*, *Gāruḍa*, *Svāstika*, *Bhautika*, *Bhauma*, *Āyuṣya* and *Grāha*; and the Upakhilas four in number: *Paiśāca*, *Rātrikāṇḍa*, *Traiveṇya* and *Svāpna*.

While the names *Vālakhilya*[5] and *Lakṣmīsūkta*[6] are among those usually enumerated as *khailikasūktāni* of the *Rgvedasaṃhitā*, the remaining ones are not so easy to be identified and they escape the

---

[4] See Gonda 1975: 330.

[5] Cf. Scheftelowitz 1906: 2, 3, 10, 11, 35–45. Cf. also Kapadia 1960; Aithal 1969; Renou 1947: 20–25.

[6] Actually ṚVKh 2.6 is called Śrīsūkta; cf. Scheftelowitz 1906: 3–4, 72–79.

help rendered by the Khila research of Scheftelowitz (1906). For the lack of direct references we can only suggest here that these names reflect a purposeful insertion of new textual units into the ṚDG.

Perhaps one of the reasons for this assumed textual intrusion into the ṚDG may once have been a need to include, under the headings Khila and Upakhila, a certain amount of minor mantric texts used in daily practice by Citpavan brahmins acting in the domains of healing, exorcism, magic or divination. While for the Gokarṇa Āśvalāyana Ṛgvedis, who are the contemporary users of the ṚDG, this could look a bit unorthodox, we must remember their close connection with the Śaiva cult of the nearby Mahābaleśvara temple as well as their *kuladevatā* Vedapuruṣa and other not so orthodox elements of their daily customs including special reverence towards the book form of the Veda styled as 'Bhagavān Veda' which is treated almost as a sacred object. Not without meaning is the fact that the same group of Citpavan brahmins has been using the ṚDG collection that comprises also the *Ṛgvidhāna*, a text teaching magical uses of Ṛgvedic mantras.

Keeping in mind this, and the fact that the YATKU comes after the *Ṛgvidhāna* at the end of the ṚDG collection, one can assume that it introduces magical rites and mantra texts of Atharvanic or Tantric type. Under this assumption we propose tentative identifications for some of the headings in this text.

Thus the second item of the Khila group, *Rājanya*, might refer to mantras said to help the king execute his power, and possibly to *khila* hymns of the *Kuntāpa* group[7] as well.

The fourth item, *Gāruḍa*, could refer to a collection of mantras used to counteract the effects of poison, in particular the hymn ṚVKh 2.1, in which mention is made of *garuḷa*.[8] In Tantric literature,

[7] On the *Kuntāpa* hymns, see Bloomfield 1899: 96–101; Scheftelowitz 1906: 1–2, 155–167.

[8] On ṚVKh 2.1, see Scheftelowitz 1906: 69–70.

> the most effective rites against poison invoke the mythical bird Garuḍa, the enemy of snakes ... The whole Garuḍa Up[aniṣad] ... is 'simply a charm for the prevention of snakebite.' (Goudriaan 1978: 348)[9]

There is also a text with the title *Gāruḍatantra*.[10]

The fifth Khila, *Svāstika*, might refer to ṚVKh 2.4, which begins with the word *svastyayanam*. These two verses are added after Ṛgveda 5.51, the last five verses of which often use the word *svasti* and are therefore referred to in *Ṛgvidhāna* 1.3.5 as *svastimatyaḥ*.[11] All of them might be characterized as mantras for well-being or spells for good luck.

The sixth Khila, *Bhautika*, seems to have something to do with demoniac spirits called *bhūtas*; it could refer to a collection of mantras effecting expulsion of such demons or guarding against them. An enumeration of the traditional realms of knowledge to be studied and remembered also by a brahmin in *Chāndogya-Upaniṣad* 7 includes *bhūtavidyā*.

The seventh Khila, *Bhauma*, seems to refer to a set of mantras used in order to protect or increase one's land-dominion (the term is met with in Kauṭilya's *Arthaśāstra* referring to the king's land possessions). The very same name occurs in *Kauśikasūtra* 5.2.16, where it refers to a set of mantras to be recited in *japa* form.

The name of the eighth Khila, *Āyuṣya*, sounds as if it referred to the domain of healing practices, perhaps to mantra-texts said to be preservative of life and embodying vital power – such texts are meant when the word is used in the *Atharvavedapariśiṣṭas*[12] and in the *Ṛgvidhāna* as well[13]; but it could also be a *prātika* of ṚVKh 4.6 that begins with this word[14] and is actually attested as the *prātīka* of that Khila in *Bṛhaddevatā* 8.45.

---

[9] Cf. also Goudriaan 1978: 92 and 199.

[10] Cf. Goudriaan 1978: 258.

[11] See Gonda 1951: 45.

[12] See Gonda 1951: 107, n. 4.

[13] Cf. *Ṛgvidhāna* 1.11.2, 20.5; 2.2.5; 4.9.1.

[14] On ṚVKh 4.6 beginning with *āyuṣyaṃ varcasyaṃ*, see Scheftelowitz 1906: 117–118.

Grāha, listed here as the ninth Khila, perhaps indicates mantras against 'seizing diseases' or against any agent, ailment or substance that can 'seize' or maliciously 'grasp'. In *Mahābhārata* 3.219.24–58, malicious *grahas* or 'Grabbers, Seizers' emerge from Skanda's body to afflict young children.

Coming now to the short list of Upakhilas we meet *Paiśāca*: this title suggests mantras against demoniac beings or mantras used in connection with the *paiśāca* type of marriage.

The *Rātrikāṇḍa* given as the second Upakhila is perhaps the same as the Rātrisūkta in ṚVKh 4.2.[15] However, the title here suggests rather a group of mantras and therefore we should opt rather for mantras used to protect one at night.[16]

The name *Traiveṇya* given here as the third Upakhila suggests some connection with the confluence of the three holy rivers and the goddess said to preside over it, as well as certain yoga practices concerned with the triple inner energy channels *(nāḍī)* of the human body meeting in one particular place.

The fourth and last Upakhila named *Svāpna* could be associated with ṚVKh 2.14 and refer to mantras used with a view to protect one at sleep or to obtain auspicious predicatory dreams.[17]

The above identifications being only conjectural, one could ask whether any confirmation could be found in the title of the YATKU, and the tradition to which this text might have initially belonged. The title literally points to a Tantric tradition of the Yāmala type. The Yāmalas form a class of Tantra works usually taken to be of Śākta character and rather little-known today.

The YATKU claims to be a part of the *Yāmalāṣṭakatantra*. It is rather difficult to locate or to trace a work of this title within the multiple classifications offered by different Tantric traditions.

---

[15] See Scheftelowitz 1906: 110–112.

[16] Cf. Ṛgveda 10.127; *Atharvaveda* (Śaunaka) 19.47–49.

[17] On ṚVKh 2.14, see Scheftelowitz 1906: 86–87.

According to one enumeration,[18] as many as 64 Bhairava Āgamas of the Śākta tradition are said to exist, all classed under the category of *aṣṭaka*, in eight groups. The second group is called Yāmalāṣṭaka and comprises: *Brahma*, *Viṣṇu*, *Rudra*, *Ātharvan*, *Ruru*, *Vetāla*, *Indra* and *Svacchanda Āgamas*. A similar list is said[19] to be given in the *Śrīkaṇṭhīsaṃhitā*[20] which however has only seven out of the eight *aṣṭakas* stating the eighth one to be lost. In this enumeration, too, the Yāmalāṣṭaka is the second one. No mention, however, is made anywhere of an independent work called *Yāmalāṣṭakatantra*, nor of any Upaniṣad belonging to it. Perhaps we have here an example of 'an artificial locus of attribution'. What, then, could be the reason for referring to a tradition of Yāmalas that are not so authoritative even among Tantra followers, not to mention Hindus in general? Hindus tend to consider Yāmala priests as non-*pakka* brahmins, and the Yāmala scriptures (like those known by the names *Uvaccan* and *Pāraśava*) are thought to be used by non-brahmin temple priests of South India. Perhaps this might have something to do with the peculiar status of the group of brahmins among whom the collection of *Daśagrantha* remains at least in theoretical use, namely that of the above-mentioned Citpavan brahmins.

Some Vaidikas of Maharashtra who possess the ṚDG book remember that both the *Ṛgvidhāna* and the YATKU used to be contained in the *vedaparāyaṇa*, being 'recited just once'. Nowadays their *vedaparāyaṇa* is restricted to recitation of the *Ṛgvedasaṃhitā* only, both the *Ṛgvidhāna* and the YATKU being left aside. Though the YATKU has thus fallen out of use, certain formulae of

---

[18] See Bhattacharya 1982: 66–67. Unfortunately, Bhattacharya does not provide us with any source for this classification.

[19] Personal communication of Somayaji Nana Kale, one of the present-day users of the ṚDG text.

[20] Cf. Hanneder 1998 where the appendix contains a fragment of the text of *Śrīkaṇṭhī*.

the *Ṛgvidhāna* are still used in the present day *prayoga* practices of the ṚDG users.[21]

Another aspect of the ṚDG collection is that almost every separate text or passage commences with a homage to the Vedapuruṣa. This deity represents the embodiment of the holy scripture. His images decorate the walls of the Joglekar Gurukula house in Gokarṇa and are proudly pointed at when asked about the deity presiding over the family. Sāyaṇa mentions Vedapuruṣa as the deity who is to preside over the stanza commencing the first hymn of the *Ṛgvedasaṃhitā*.

Provisionally, then, the following hypothesis to explain the appearance of the YATKU at the end of a canonical collection may be proposed on general grounds. A text of seemingly Tantric origin was at one point of time attached to the collection because it needed Vedic authority. In other words, Ṛgveda priests using the *Ṛgvidhāna* had in their possession some Khila texts, for which they sought Tantric authorisation in their competition with Atharvanic priests. Including them within the ṚDG collection may have been thought to supply them with additional authority.

Instead of a final conclusion I would rather like to deliberate on the capacity of the old concept of Khila to be used as a means of transgressing the boundaries of canonical scriptures. It could serve well in introducing new religious ideas or cults which at a certain historical moment had to be elevated to a higher status. I have suggested that it was used for this purpose by a group of Ṛgvedic brahmins who must have competed for authority and social status in a changing socio-religious context. By including new texts into a closed body of authoritative works they laid claim to scriptural authority for works that were important for them on doctrinal or ritual grounds. Although the exact circumstances of this inclusion escape us, we may assume that the book was guarded by people who could decide about its extension. The *Bhāgavatamāhātmya* was made into another Purāṇa in order to gain for it access to

---

[21] Personal communication of Nana Kale.

the fold of the *Bhāgavatapurāṇa*. But the YATKU exemplifies a double claim: it is said to be both the closing chapter of a Ṛgvedic collection and part of a supposedly lost Tantra work.[22] By means of its very title, the YATKU pretends to form the essence of both of these scriptural collections to which it seeks access. This is yet another example of the interrelations between Vedic and Tantric textual traditions whose contemporary history must be further investigated through research focusing on the social identity of the communities guarding their respective scriptures and their integrity. Seemingly excluding one another, *vaidika* and *tāntrika* textual traditions could, perhaps more often than we are usually prone to admit, live under one roof: to quote Alexis Sanderson,

> one could be 'internally a Kaula, externally a Śaiva [a worshipper of Svacchandabhairava in the Kashmirian context] while remaining Vedic in one's social practice' (Sanderson 1986: 205).

REFERENCES

AITHAL, K. Parameswara 1969. ṚV Khila-s and the Sūtra-s of Āśvalāyana. *Adyar Library Bulletin* 33: 182–194.

BHATTACHARYYA, N. N. 1982. *History of the Tantric Religion. A Historical, Ritualistic and Philosophical Study*. New Delhi: Manohar.

BLOOMFIELD, Maurice 1899. *The Atharva-Veda and the Gopatha-Brāhmaṇa*. (Grundriss der indo-arischen Philologie und Altertumskunde, II.1.B.) Strassburg: Karl J. Trübner.

CHRISTOF, Martin 2001. The legitimation of textual authority in the *Bhāgavatapurāṇa*. In: V. Dalmia, A. Malinar & M. Christof (eds.), *Charisma and Canon. Essays of the Religious History of the Indian Subcontinent*: 62–76. New Delhi: OUP.

GONDA, Jan (trans.) 1951. *The Ṛgvidhāna. English Translation with an Introduction and Notes*. Utrecht: N.V. A. Oosthoek's Uitgevers Mij.

—— 1975. *Vedic Literature. Saṃhitās and Brāhmaṇas*. (A History of Indian Literature, 1.1.) Wiesbaden: Otto Harrassowitz.

---

[22] A copy of a manuscript entitled *Yāmalāṣṭakatantra* has recently been located by the author in one of the manuscript libraries in South India. Its evaluation, however, has to await for another occasion.

GOUDRIAAN, Teun 1978. *Māyā Divine and Human. A Study of Magic and Its Religious Foundations in Sanskrit Texts, with Particular Attention to a Fragment on Viṣṇu's Māyā Preserved in Bali.* Delhi: MLBD.

HANNEDER, Jürgen 1998. *Abhinavagupta's Philosophy of Revelation. An Edition and Annotated Translation of Mālinīślokavārttika I, 1–399.* (Gonda Oriental Series, 14.) Groningen: Egbert Forsten.

KAPADIA, B. H. 1960. The relation of the khilāni with the Ṛksaṃhitā and their position in Indian literature. *Journal of the University of Bombay*, N.S. 29: 19–38.

ṚDG = *Ṛgvedadaśagrantha*. Ed. by Ghaisasa Veda Pāṭha Śālā. Pune: Vasanta Press, 1986.

RENOU, Louis 1947. *Les écoles védiques et la formation du Veda.* (Cahiers de la Société Asiatique, 9.) Paris: Imprimerie Nationale.

SANDERSON, Alexis 1986. Purity and power among the Brahmans of Kashmir. In: M. Carrithers, S. Collins & S. Lukes (eds.), *The Category of Person: Anthropology, Philosophy, History*: 190–216. Cambridge: Cambridge University Press.

SCHEFTELOWITZ, Isidor (ed.) 1906. *Die Apokryphen des Ṛgveda (Khilāni)* (Indische Forschungen, 1.) Breslau: Verlag M. und H. Marcus.

Organizational Levels in Vedic Ritual: The Problem of the Meaning of the Nihnavana Rite

JAN E. M. HOUBEN

In memory of Frits Staal (1930–2012)

1.1. Just as strings of by themselves meaningless phonemes may have a capacity for linguistic meaning, like that ritual may be meaningless from one perspective and meaningful from another. In language we have a good idea of types of meaning which are to be expected at different organizational levels. Words are generally regarded as meaningful units, and so are sentençes and syntagmas, but also many morphemes. Phonemes are distinctive but not independently meaningful, unless they happen to coincide with a morpheme or word. The meaningfulness of sentences is generally thought of as being derived from the meaning of the constituent words, but some theories want to have it the other way round and state that the meaning of the word is derived from the meaning of the sentence or utterance.[1]

In Vedic ritual, however, we still have hardly any idea what kind of organizational levels and functional units there are in

---

[1] In accordance with Schmitter 1987: 205, 'word' and 'sentence' may be seen as linguistic universals, even though all attempts to define these two notions satisfactorily for all languages of the world have till now remained unsatisfactory. Cf. Houben 1995 for further references to studies on word and sentence as units in language, and for a discussion of Bhartṛhari's view on these two.

between the most basic acts and utterances, and the complex performance as a whole of for instance the Agniṣṭoma. A large ritual will hence appear as an amorphous mass of acts. In his arguments for seeing ritual as meaningless, Frits Staal (1989: 186f.) used the example of the Nihnavana rite, which is a small element in the Agniṣṭoma and in other, more complex *soma* sacrifices. According to Staal the Nihnavana is an entirely meaningless act.[2] It can be demonstrated that its meaninglessness results from strictly isolating it from its context. A different presentation of this rite – making use of recent videoregistrations of a *soma* sacrifice – and some basic background information on Vedic ritual which every performer may be expected to be familiar with (also known to Staal, 1989: 116) show that performers must have generally experienced it as clearly significant.[3] On the basis of this demonstration it is argued that different organizational levels are to be distinguished in Vedic ritual, and that meaningfulness or meaninglessness of an element in the ritual is not an ontological problem but a matter of seeing that element at an appropriate level in relation with other elements of the same level. This finding suits a general theory of

---

[2] His direct claim is that it is *transmitted* 'without meaning' and even 'without language' (Staal 1989: xv); in the larger context of his argument the reference to the Nihnavana (e.g. pp. 186f.) should demonstrate that with regard to ritual (and music) the question 'what does it mean?' does not make sense (p. 182). A few years earlier, Staal (1983: 359) referred to a study of Brough (1950) which, on the basis of Brāhmaṇa discussions of the Nihnavana rite, does presuppose that the term and the rite Nihnavana have a certain meaning (see also below). At that time Staal wrote: 'The priests understand this rite as a salutation (*namaskāra*) of earth (*bhūmi*), though originally it might have expressed the "hiding" of the movement in the inauspicious southern direction' (Staal 1983: 359). Apparently, Staal had at this moment not yet arrived at the thesis of meaninglessness of ritual. (Meaninglessness appears again differently in Staal's 2008 synthesis on Vedic ritual: here it is mainly the meaninglessness of ritual speech, i.e., mantras, that is emphasized.)

[3] The slides, pictures and videoclip that support the argument and that formed the basis of the audiovisual presentation at the World Sanskrit Conference in Helsinki, will in due course be made available on the Vimeo channel 'Vedic Ritual' (vimeo.com/channels/990046). Houben 2010a and 2010b continue the exploration of Vedic ritual from the perspective of its meaningful structure and morphology.

ritual structure and ritual meaning as propounded recently by Rappaport (1999). It will further be shown that two distinct interpretations proposed in ancient Brāhmaṇa passages dealing with the Nihnavana imply two different structural positions of the Nihnavana in the Agniṣṭoma, whereas a consistent application of Staal's meaninglessness to the Nihnavana and neighbouring ritual episodes would lead to an amorphous Agniṣṭoma consisting of a mass of basically unrelated episodes.

1.2. After Hubert and Mauss studied the nature and function of sacrifice at the end of the nineteenth century (Hubert & Mauss 1899), Frits Staal was the first scholar who made an extensive study of Vedic ritual and formulated on that basis a comprehensive theory of ritual. For theoretical reflections on Vedic ritual we may hence take Staal's theory of ritual as a starting point. The first presentation of the theory appeared in the article 'The Meaninglessness of ritual' (1979); its elaborated form in *Rules without Meaning* (1989). Both publications refer back to the performance of an Agnicayana in Kerala in 1975, which was described in detail in the two volumes of *Agni* (1983). In his work Staal has demonstrated the crucial importance of fieldwork and the registration of performances for an adequate analysis and study of Vedic ritual. I will here make use of some results of these methods in my discussion of a specific problem in the analysis of Vedic ritual; my discussion also involves a sketch of a theory of Vedic ritual which can take into account both ritual form *and* dimensions of ritual meaning.

According to Staal (1989: 131), 'Ritual is pure activity, without meaning or goal.' Moreover, he states,

> [t]o say that ritual is for its own sake is to say that it is meaningless, without function, aim or goal, or also that it constitutes its own aim or goal (Staal 1989: 131–132).

Staal argues that participants, ritual authorities and scholars can verbalize the meaning of such rituals only in a very unsatisfactory manner or in mutually contradictory ways.

> In the development of our concepts and theories of ritual it is only a small step from 'changing meaning' to: 'no intrinsic meaning' and 'structural meaning', and from there to: 'no meaning' (Staal 1989: 134).

In other words, Staal's theory wants to look exclusively at the ritual form and to completely neglect dimensions of ritual meaning.

1.3. Even if it turns out to be impossible to verbalize satisfactorily the 'meaning' of a complex ritual performance as a whole, elements and details may be indisputably 'significant' in some sense. So much is admitted by Staal:

> It might be more proper and fruitful to ask specific questions about the meaning of particular rites. Some such questions do receive specific answers, on which participants and scholars agree. The Yajamāna must keep his hands closed 'like a child in the womb of its mother, ready to be reborn'. The fire altar has the shape of a bird because fire, as well as Soma, were fetched from heaven by a bird. The priests do not go south if they can help it for the southern direction is inauspicious. (Staal 1989: 116)

Apparently, Staal's denial of meaning concerns the meanings attributed to the units of some level – that is, large complex rituals as a whole – while units of a lower level or lower order are in some cases accepted to have generally acknowledged 'meanings'. Other ritual details he presents as an example of his main thesis of the meaninglessness of ritual. There are first of all Vedic utterances: here Staal quickly passes over the *praiṣa*s and their undeniable pragmatic meanings in order to emphasize the meaninglessness of the *stobha*s (chanted insertions) in Sāmavedic chant (Staal 1989: 199–208). Apart from these, his main example of a meaningless ritual detail or meaningless sub-ritual is the so-called Nihnava rite or *nihnavanam* at the *soma* sacrifice.

2.1. Staal describes the Nihnava as follows:

> This mysterious rite is performed twice daily, in the morning and afternoon, during several consecutive days. The ritual patron and several of his priests place their hands on a bundle of grass, which lies to the west of the altar. The position of the hands is different in the two surviving traditions ... (follow details on the placing of the hands). (Staal 1989: xv)

Elsewhere, the reader is informed how a performer of Vedic ritual learned the Nihnava from his father. Remarkable about 'this case of ritual transmission', according to Staal, is that 'it disregards not only meaning, but does not even use language' (Staal 1989: 187).

If we regard the rejection of meaning as the negative side of Staal's theoretical approach, there is also a positive side to it, viz., the study of ritual forms on their own terms. However, is it possible to study the ritual forms properly and satisfactorily without any consideration to meanings attributed to them? This may have been Staal's ideal, in accordance with a now largely abandoned trend in twentieth-century linguistics to approach language without any reference to meaning. In such an approach, the relation between the complete rituals – which according to Staal are entirely meaningless – and the units of lower organizational levels which may occasionally be meaningful remains unclear. The very determination of basic units remains unfounded if meaning is consistently neglected. As Lawson and McCauley observed, Staal does not give us a motivated account of what his 'ritual sequence' is a sequence of (Lawson & McCauley 1990: 59).

2.2. Let us return to the Nihnavana, and let us accept for the moment that the detail about the placing of the hands is 'meaningless' (or is transmitted without reference to its meaning). Even then, the Nihnavana as a whole can hardly be so regarded.

The rite has, to begin with, a name. It is true that translators of ritual texts have often rendered this name, *nihnava* or *nihnavana*, in a vague or too general way.[4] But dictionaries do record and illustrate a quite specific meaning for the verb *ni-hnu* and derived nouns such as *nihnava, nihnavana* and *nihnuti*;[5] the verb may be translated as 'to deny', 'to disavow', 'dissimulate';[6] or it may be variously paraphrased as:

– to distract the attention from a wrong act by means of nice words or gestures;
– to hide a big crime with a small nice act;
– to beat about the bush.

It is probably not necessary to illustrate the concept with examples from current world politics. The name *nihnava* or *nihnavanam* thus says something about the meaning or expected function of this rite. Second, its sense is explained in the *Śatapathabrāhmaṇa* (ŚB 3.4.3.19–21) and elsewhere: because the participants in the sacrifice had to turn their back to the fires and go southwards in the immediately preceding rite, they now disavow this undesirable but contextually necessary act by pronouncing a prayer to heaven and earth while placing their hands in a certain position near the ground. The *Taittirīyasaṁhitā* (TS 6.2.2.6) speaks of 'falling away from this world' rather than turning the back to the fires and going

---

[4] Eggeling, for instance, in his translation of the *Śatapathabrāhmaṇa*, translates *nihnuvate* as 'to make amends'. Caland translates *atha nihnuvate* (ĀpŚS 11.1.12) as 'Dann halten sie Abbitte'. Brough 1950 arrives at the following meaning for the verb *ni-hnu*: 'to conceal one's actions from a person, so as to avoid arousing his anger.'

[5] Cf. Monier-Williams' dictionary, s.v.

[6] Staal's paraphrase of *nihnava* as 'hiding rite' is misleading, as it could suggest that the bundle of grass is hidden in this act. It would correspond to Haug's interpretation and translation ('concealment'; Haug 1863: 58), which was justly criticized by Weber in *Indische Studien* 9: 'Und obschon Haug hinzufügt: the concealment is done in the manner expressed in the translation as I myself witnessed it, so verhält sich die Sache, den Ritualtexten nach, denn doch erheblich anders, als er angiebt. [... :] (bei der vormittagigen upasad) legen sie (die Priester) ihre Hände, die rechte aufwärts gerichtet, auf den prastara nieder – bei der nachmittägigen die linke aufwärts – , und entziehen sich (durch diesen demüthigen namaskāra allen üblen Folgen dessen, dass sie vorher nach Süden gegangen sind ...).' (Weber 1865: 221)

south as the problem that is to be taken care of, but the end result and the necessity for going through the Nihnavana are the same. Third, the accompanying prayer is a very general formulation consisting of a request for wealth and a respectful greeting to Heaven and Earth. As such it suits and supports the meaning and function attributed to it in the *Śatapathabrāhmaṇa* and *Taittirīyasaṁhitā*.

Staal himself mentioned earlier that the inauspicious nature of the southern direction was a detail on which participants and scholars will agree (Staal 1989: 116, cited above). Hence, finally, the 'disavowal' with the prayer and gesture make sense, and even if the young ritualist in Staal's example is not told so explicitly, he may very well understand it by himself from the structure of the ritual, just as any scholar may do who is willing to open his eyes for it. As we will see, however, this is not the only nor necessarily the most original meaning attributed to the Nihnavana.

3.1. So far I briefly demonstrated the meaning and function of the Nihnava by means of abbreviated references to the relevant mantra, prescriptions and Brāhmaṇical explanations. My demonstration remains in conflict with the statements of Staal who was familiar with the performance and the textual sources but presented the Nihnava as a meaningless rite. To get a more solid establishment of its place, meaning and function we will need a brief visual demonstration of a performance of the Nihnava in its immediate context. This will not only illustrate the meaning of the Nihnava; it will also show that the Nihnava will indeed appear as meaningless if considered in utter isolation, but that it appears with meaningful dimensions when it is linked with the ritual actions in which it is embedded. In other words, the performance and its analysis will illustrate both Staal's position and my counterposition. Eventually, this means that Staal succeeded in perceiving 'meaninglessness' at the level of the ritual element called Nihnava by rigorously isolating it from its context – which, it is true, is a bewilderingly complex context as can also be seen in the visual representation. Staal was aware of some of the discussions on the Nihnava in the *soma* sacrifice as he cites in his 1983 descriptive study of the Agnicayana the discussion of *ni-hnu* and the *nihnava* (Staal 1983: 359) by Brough which itself refers to previous discussions, for instance the one by Weber in his review of Haug's translation of the *Aitareya-brāhmaṇa* (Weber 1865). These discussions have helpful contributions to make to the understanding of the Nihnava but they remain somewhat in the air without a clear illustration of the basic acts involved. Although their expositions are not always clear, it seems that Weber, Caland and Brough did acquire an acceptable understanding of the orientations and directions of the various relevant rites. However, they had no clear idea of the central gesture in the Nihnavana. This was for the first time recorded by Frits Staal. But his information needs supplementation and is open to a quite different evaluation. Since directions and locations play a role in the relevant ritual prescriptions, the mantra and the Brāhmaṇic explanations, we start with a plan of the sacrificial area where the acts take place (*Plan 1*). It concerns the Tānūnaptra rite, which precedes the Nihnavana. The Tānūnaptra establishes a contract between the priests and the sacrificer. It takes place at the *vedi* altar which is located between the three fires.

Next (see *Plan 2*), the Āpyāyana or rite of 'making the *soma* swell' takes place at the so-called 'king's throne' next to the *āhavanīya* or offering fire. Each priest and the sacrificer move from the place north of the *vedi*, via the front of the *āhavanīya* fire to the 'king's throne' where they sprinkle hot water on the *soma* stalks and pronounce an accompanying mantra. Finally (*Plan 3*), the priests and the sacrificer walk behind the fires back to the *vedi* to do the Nihnavana.

The Āpyāyana and Nihnavana are further performed after each Pravargya and Upasad, before the Subrahmaṇyā invocation. The videoclip (of the corresponding audiovisual presentation) shows the first Āpyāyana and Nihnavana including the Tānūnaptra which precedes both. The registration concerns the performance of the

Atyagniṣṭoma at Nana Kale Veda Ashram in Barsi Maharashtra, 19–24 February 2001, with Shri Dikṣit Vijaya N. Manerikar and Saubhāgyavatī (Mrs.) Vedavatī Manerikar as *yajamāna* and *patnī*, Dīkṣit Raghunath N. Kale as *hotṛ*, Shri Sunil C. Limaye as *adhvaryu*, Shri Caitanya N. Kale as *udgātṛ*, and Shri Prasad D. Mone as *brahman*.

If we apply Staal's approach consistently to the Nihnavana, it would have neither meaning nor any function that would go beyond its own performance; hence it would have no relation with preceding and following ritual episodes, except for accidental contingency. The same would apply to other episodes, and we would have a series of unrelated episodes, and even each individual episode would be an adventitious grouping of smaller acts.

The situation is different if we accept the meaning and function attributed to the Nihnavana in the *Śatapathabrāhmaṇa* and the *Taittirīyasaṁhitā*. The Nihnavana then acquires a very specific relation with the neighbouring rites. To be more precise, since it disavows the undesirable but unavoidable act of turning the back to the fires and going south, it is exclusively dependent on the preceding Āpyāyana rite. It is an appendix to the Āpyāyana rite, where it was necessary to do these inauspicious acts. It has nothing to do with the rites that follow, for instance the Subrahmaṇyā invocation. Nor does it have any contribution to make to the receiving and installing of the *soma* which is the major theme of the surrounding ritual episodes. Thus, if we do take into account meaning and function, we perceive that the units have specific relations and form a specific structure which would be absent if meaning were consistently neglected. Here we see, therefore, that there is a structure of relationships which are absent if meaning is neglected (see *Diagrams 1* and *2*).

Since authoritative interpretative texts such as the *Śatapathabrāhmaṇa* and the *Taittirīyasaṁhitā* attribute to the Nihnavana the interpretation of a 'disavowal' after having gone into an inauspicious direction (south or away from this world), we may infer that generations of learned ritualists of these traditions accepted these as the canonical meaning of the rite, which, moreover, suits the context and the accompanying mantra. We can thus accept the performative reality of this interpretation for an important part of the performers. The Brāhmaṇa passages reflect, and on account of their status prescriptively encourage, an interpretation that was actually current among generations of performers of the rite.

3.2. This need not mean that it is the only or necessarily the most original meaning attributed to the Nihnavana. In the *Maitrāyaṇīsaṁhitā* we first find a passage which is very similar to the relevant passage in the *Taittirīyasaṁhitā*. Next, the *Maitrāyaṇīsaṁhitā* (MS 3.8.2, 94.3) gives an alternative explanation according to which the 'disavowal' would not concern a wrong or inauspicious act that has already taken place – viz., going south or away from this world – but a wrong act that is still to take place, viz., the killing or pressing of the *soma*.

We note that Nihnavanas in other ritual contexts, discussed for instance by Brough, are also frequently before the wrong or inauspicious act concerned. According to the mentioned *Maitrāyaṇīsaṁhitā* interpretation, the priests would ask Heaven and Earth for their forgiveness even before they commit the terrible crime of killing King Soma. This interpretation suits the mantra as well as the name Nihnavana no less than the first interpretation. It has, however, consequences for the structure of the complex ritual. This structure becomes quite different, because the Nihnavana is now directly, on its own accord, related to one of the main actions of the *soma* ritual. With this interpretation the Nihnavana is directly linked to the action of pressing or, if you like, 'killing' the *soma* stalks in order to extract their juice. The structure may then be represented as follows (*Diagram 3*).

It is to be noted that by itself it is very well possible to have a Nihnavana which is entirely secondary to another subsidiary act and is not directly related to one of the main actions in the ritual.

Such a Nihnavana is found in several of the ritual episodes mentioned by Brough (1950: 77). But in the second *Maitrāyaṇīya-saṁhitā* interpretation the Nihnavana would directly concern the central action in the *soma* sacrifice, viz., the pressing or 'killing' of the *soma*. We also note that episodes which functionally go together need not always occur together: they may be separated by episodes which have an entirely different function. For instance, after their consecration the sacrificer and his wife consume the *vrata* food, and this continues on the days which are concerned with the reception and installation of the *soma*. A parallel in language would be a verbal phrase split up by a noun phrase. Similarly, the Nihnavana would be part of an action, the pressing, which properly speaking has not yet begun.

4.1. Just as we may look at words as units and turn next our attention to morphemes within that word, we may now, after our general study of the Nihnava and its meaning and context, turn our attention to a central ritual morpheme within this episode, namely the gesture that accompanies the mantra that expresses obeisance to Heaven and Earth. Just as people need not be aware of the history and diachronic semantic associations of a morpheme that forms part of a word they use, the performers of the Nihnavana need not be aware of the background of the accompanying gesture, but it may still have significant links with gestures of other contexts, and of other times and cultures.

We have another look at the gesture that accompanies the Nihnavana. We see that the palm of the right hand is directed upwards, holding the bundle, and that the left hand is placed on top of it (see *Picture 1*). Staal recorded a different gesture in the 1975 performance in Kerala. He notes that his performers follow one of two available traditions, viz. the one of the Kauṣītakins, who adhere to the *Śāṅkhāyanaśrautasūtra*.[7] The other tradition is, according to

[7] Incidentally, the Kauṣītakins consider the Śāṅkhāyana a *sūtra* authored by a certain Suyajña, cf. Sreekrishna Sarma in Staal 1983, II: 161f.

Staal, the Taittirīya tradition. The gesture recorded by me is different from both ways mentioned by Staal. In the 1975 performance the Kauṣītaki tradition was followed where they place

in the morning:	first the left hand palm down, then the right hand on left hand with palm up (*Picture 2*);
in the evening:	first the left hand palm up, then the right hand on the left hand with palm down (*Picture 3*) (Staal 1983: 359)

The other tradition, according to Staal, is that of the Taittirīyas who have

in the morning:	the left hand palm up and right hand with palm down on left hand (as evening gesture in Kauṣītaki tradition (*Picture 3*);
in the evening:	right hand palm up, left hand with palm down on the right hand (*Picture 4*).

It turns out, however, that the gesture attributed by Staal to the Taittirīyas suits the *Baudhāyanaśrautasūtra* only, not the other Sūtras of the Taittirīya tradition. Other Taittirīya Sūtras such as the *Āpastambaśrautasūtra* which was followed in the performance recorded by me in Barsi, Maharashtra, have prescriptions which are largely equivalent with those in the Ṛgvedic Śāṅkhāyana which was authoritative for the priests in the 1975 performance in Kerala. Moreover, the performers in Barsi would have remained in full accord with their *Āpastambaśrautasūtra* if they would have done the gesture in the same way as the priests in the 1975 performance in Kerala. But they do it in quite a different way. Surprisingly, this quite different way also perfectly suits the strict wording of the *Āpastambaśrautasūtra*, though it would go a bit uneasily with Śāṅkhāyana where the latter prescribes explicitly to place the hands on top of the *prastara* bundle of grass. The Barsi performers take the bundle in their hand. This way of performing the Nihnava has, to my knowledge, not yet been recorded. It is very well possible that the Barsi performers derived their practice from the instruction of the renowned ritualist Viśvanath Śrauti from Nellur, Andhra Pradesh, who passed away in 1997.

The Āpastamba practice recorded by me would be the inverse of the practice which Staal attributed to the Taittirīyakas but which in fact suits only the prescriptions of Baudhāyana who seems to be entirely isolated among the Śrautasūtras of all the Vedas. All other Śrautasūtras have prescriptions which are more or less parallel to those of Śāṅkhāyana. On the other hand, Baudhāyana's prescriptions taken literally would allow the taking into the hand of the *prastara* bundle which seems excluded in Śāṅkhāyana but which is the practice recorded by me and which Āpastamba does not exclude.

4.2. There are now different ways of dealing with the gesture and its variations in prescriptions and in practices. For Staal the variations and the silent way of transmitting the specific gesture of one's school point to meaninglessness. Caland understood and translated the gesture as prescribed in the *Āpastambaśrautasūtra* in accordance with the practice recorded by me, except that the *prastara* is not taken in the hand (Caland on ĀpŚS 11.1.12).

Caland gave more details than provided in the relevant *sūtra* and may hence have followed additional directions found in a Prayoga text used by him. As for the interpretation of the gesture, he suggested that the right hand represents the earth and the left hand heaven. This interpretation was referred to with approval by Gonda in his study of the function of grasses when he states without further justification that

> the position of the hands 'symbolizes' the relation between heaven and earth which are being invoked (Gonda 1985: 213).

It makes much more sense, however, to see in the gesture a full gesture of obeisance, which is also what the accompanying mantra expresses. The main deviation from the normal gesture of *namaskāra* or *añjali*[8] would be the position near the ground. The mainte-

[8] Cf. Liebert 1976, s.v., where the two are not properly distinguished.

nance of more or less arbitrary distinctions in the execution of the gesture (palm up / palm down, left/right hand below) may be a marker of group identity.[9] The explicit mention in the Śrautasūtras of the *uttāna* position of one of the hands links the gesture, both as recorded by me and as recorded by Staal, with an ancient gesture of respectful greeting which need not always have been exactly identical with the modern *namaskāra* of the joined hands. One may here compare also the expression *uttā́nahasto namasā́* in the Ṛgveda (6.16.46),[10] and the expression *nəmaŋhā ustāna.zastō* in the Avesta (Yasna 28.1).[11]

As for the holding of the grass instead of placing the hands on it, as other Śrautasūtras explicitly prescribe, if it is not an innovation – but I do not see a reason for this – it must derive from a Maharashtrian, Andhra or Tamil Nadu practice. It reminds us of the function of holding grass or fresh and soft branches as a gesture of appeasement, for which Walter Burkert pointed to parallels in Avestan and Vedic cultures with the ancient Greek *hiketêría* (olive branch in ceremonial supplication) and *stibás* (bed of grass).[12] In that case it would suit the second Maitrāyaṇī explication which would make the Nihnavana a request for mercy *before* the 'crime' of killing the *soma* is performed.

5. I am not intent on reaching a final solution regarding these diachronic links which suggest different histories and different values for the gesture under discussion. What should be emphasized is that these considerations concern the ritual at an entirely different organizational order than the considerations on the function and

[9] Cf. Derrida 1986 on more or less arbitrary – seemingly insignificant – distinctions in the pronunciation of sibilants as very significant identity markers.

[10] Cf. also *Vājasaneyisaṁhitā* 18.75ab: *vayáṁ te adyá rarimā́ hí kā́mam uttānáhastā námasopasádya*; ŚB 14.1.3.24: *átha dakṣiṇatá uttānéna pāṇínā níhnute | víśvābhyo mā nāṣṭrā́bhyas pāhī́ti.*

[11] For an interpretation of Celtic worship where the priest's hands may be said to be *uttāna* see Squire 1979, plate opp. p. 42.

[12] Burkert 1979, in chapter 'The persistence of ritual', p. 44 and notes.

context of the Nihnavana as a whole. The dimensions of meaning are quite different on different levels and may be perceived as absent if we search for a certain type of meaning on a wrong level. We have seen that Staal's definition of ritual as pure action intentionally neglects the meaning dimension. In the light of our findings a different definition of ritual may be proposed which allows the study of both the ritual form and its capacity for dimensions of meaning. A definition which, like the one by Staal, emphasizes the formal structure of ritual has been proposed by Rappaport (1999) who did not study Vedic ritual but the rituals of a people, the Maring, in New Guinea. Rappaport's definition is:

> ritual is 'the performance of more or less invariant sequences of formal acts and utterances not entirely encoded by the performers' (Rappaport 1999: 24).

Here it is the word 'encoded' that points to 'something that is encoded', i.e., the dimension of meaning. The observational fact of 'changing and varying meanings' of rituals inspired Rappaport not to reject 'meaning' but to develop an expanded theory of meaning that takes into account some crucial distinctions such as, self-referential vs. canonical message; symbolic, iconic, indexical meaning. Rappaport's definition and elaboration suggest a promising approach in the study of Vedic ritual. To Rappaport's model we may add on the basis of our investigations that at least in Vedic ritual we have to recognize that dimensions of meaning are different on different organizational levels in order to avoid a number of unnecessary misunderstandings.

6. I would like to conclude with some prospects:

- A strict analysis of the ritual form and its organizational structure provides the basis for strict comparisons between rituals as well as for reconstructions of cultural developments which in some cases may go back to the Indo-Iranian period and earlier.

- The analysis of dimensions of meaning is indispensable for the study of a ritual's organizational structure.
- It will enable us to place ritual in a context of social, linguistic and political practice.
- Vedic fieldwork – to use the term introduced by Kashikar (Staal 1989: 149) and to highlight the link of my presentation with the theme of the panel – has provided, and promises to provide, crucial contributions to the study of ritual form and meaning.
- Frits Staal (1930–2012), to whom I dedicate this study, has for several years defended the 'meaninglessness of ritual', evidently in an attempt to focus the attention on the formal side of ritual which is open to morphological analysis or, as Staal argued, syntactic study (but with significant differences to normal human language). In his presentation this should contribute to the scientific study of Vedic ritual and of ritual in general, which in turn contributes to a new perspective on 'sciences' in Europe and Asia (Staal 1990; 1993; 2006; 2008). Although the posited 'meaninglessness' cannot be defended in a strict sense (this article and Houben 2010a and 2010b) it has opened up new vistas in the scientific exploration of ritual.

REFERENCES

BROUGH, John 1950. The meaning of nihnu in the Brāhmaṇas. In: Vishva Bandhu (ed.), *Siddhabhāratī or Rosary of Indology. Presenting 108 Original Papers on Indological Subjects in Honour of the 60th Birthday of Dr. Siddheshwar Varma*, I: 126–130. Hoshiarpur: V.V.R. Institute P. and P. organisation. [Also in: John Brough, *Collected Papers*. Edited by Minoru Hara & J. C. Wright: 74–78. London: School of Oriental and African Studies, University of London.]

BURKERT, Walter 1979. *Structure and History in Greek Mythology and Ritual.* Berkeley: University of California Press.

DERRIDA, Jacques 1986. *Schibboleth. pour Paul Celan.* Paris: Editions Galilee.

GONDA, Jan 1985. *The Ritual Functions and Significance of Grasses in the Religion of the Veda.* (KNAW Verhandelingen Letterkunde, Nieuwe Reeks, deel 132.) Amsterdam: North-Holland Publishing Company.

HAUG, Martin. 1863. *The Aitareya Brahmanam of the Rigveda Containing the Earliest Speculations of the Brahmans on the Meaning of the Sacrificial Prayers and on the Origin, Performance, and Sense of the Rites of the Vedic Religion. Edited, translated and explained*, I–II. London: Trübner.

HOUBEN, J. E. M. 1991. *The Pravargya Brāhmaṇa of the Taittirīya Āraṇyaka*. Delhi: MLBD.

—— 1995. Bhartṛhari on the primary unit of language: Bhartṛhari's perspectivism (2). In: Klaus D. Dutz & Kjell-Ake Forsgren (eds.), *History and Rationality. The Skövde Papers in the Historiography of Linguistic*: 29–62. Münster: Nodus Publikationen.

—— 2010a. Formal structure and self-referential loops in Vedic ritual. In: A. Michaels & A. Mishra (eds.), *Ritual Dynamics and the Science of Ritual*, I: *Grammar and Morphology of Ritual*: 29–63. Wiesbaden: Harrassowitz.

—— 2010b. The Sviṣṭakṛt: Formal structure and self-reference in Vedic ritual. *Lucrările simpozionului internaţional: Cartea. România. Europa. Ediţia a II-a – 20–24 septembrie 2009* (sous la dir. de A. Berciu, R. Pop et J. Rotaru): 596–621. Bucharest : Editura Biblioteca Bucureştilor.

—— forthcoming. Yājñavalkya's accent and the bhāṣika: On the language of the Śatapathabrāhmaṇa and its context. *Proceedings of the Fourth International Vedic Workshop, Texas, May 24–27, 2007.*

HUBERT, Henri & Marcel MAUSS 1899. Essai sur la nature et la fonction du sacrifice. *L'année sociologique* 2: 29–138.

LAWSON, E. Thomas & Robert N. MCCAULEY 1990. *Rethinking Religion*. Cambridge: Cambridge University Press.

LIEBERT, Gösta. 1976. *Iconographic Dictionary of Indian Religions. Hinduism, Buddhism, Jainism*. Leiden: E.J. Brill.

RAPPAPORT, Roy A. 1999. *Ritual and Religion in the Making of Humanity*. Cambridge: Cambridge University Press.

SCHMITTER, Peter 1987. *Das sprachliche Zeichen. Studien zur Zeichen- und Bedeutungstheorie in der griechischen Antike sowie im 19. und 20. Jahrhundert*. Münster: Institut für Allgemeine Sprachwissenschaft.

SQUIRE, Charles 1979. *Celtic Myth & Legend, Poetry and Romance*. New York: Bell Publishing Company. [Reprint of the 1910 edition, London: Gresham Pub. Co.; First published in 1905 under the title *The Mythology of the British Islands*.]

STAAL, Frits 1979. The meaninglessness of ritual. *Numen* 26: 2–22.

—— 1983 (in collaboration with C. V. Somayajipad and Itti Ravi Nambudiri). *Agni: The Vedic Ritual of the Fire Altar*, I–II. Berkeley: Asian Humanities Press. [First Indian edition: Delhi: MLBD, 2001.]

—— 1989. *Rules without Meaning. Ritual, Mantras and the Human Sciences.* New York: Peter Lang.

—— 1990. *Jouer avec le feu. Pratique et théorie du rituel védique.* Paris: Collège de France, Institut de Civilisation Indienne.

—— 1993. *Concepts of Science in Europe and Asia.* Leiden: International Institute for Asian Studies.

—— 2006. Artificial languages across sciences and civilisations. *Journal of Indian Philosophy* 34: 89–101.

—— 2008. *Discovering the Vedas. Origins, Mantras, Rituals, Insights.* New Delhi: Penguin Books.

WEBER, Albrecht 1865. Über Haug's Aitareya-Brāhmaṇa. *Indische Studien* 9: 177–380. [a. aus der Bombay Native Opinion (pp. 177–196); b. aus der Saturday-Review (pp. 196–209); c. vom Herausgeber (pp. 210–380).]

APPENDIX 1:

Texts and partial translations

(Editions used: as in Houben 1991: xi–xii, supplemented by relevant passages of *Śrautakośa*, Pune: Vaidika Saṁśodhana Maṇḍala, 1970–)

A. Brāhmaṇa passages interpreting the Nihnavana rite

ŚB 3.4.3.19, 21
(for accentuation cf. discussion in Houben, forthcoming)

átha prastaré níhnuvate | *uttaratá-upacāro vái yajñó 'thaitád*
dakṣíṇevānvítyā́pyāyayanty agnír vái yajñás
tád yajñám pṛṣṭhatáḥ kurvanti tán mithyā́ kurvanti devébhya āvṛ́ścyante
yajñó vái prastarás
tád yajñáṁ púnar ā́rabhante
tásyo haiṣā́ prā́yaścittis
tátho haiṣām etán ná mithyā́kṛtaṁ bhávati
ná devébhya ā́vṛścyante
tásmāt prastaré níhnuvate
...
té níhnuvate | *éṣṭā rā́yaḥ prèṣé bhágāya ṛtáṁ ṛtavādíbhya íti*
satyáṁ satyavādíbhya íty evàitád āha
námo dyā́vāpṛthivī́bhyām íti tád ābhyāṁ dyā́vāpṛthivī́bhyāṁ níhnuvate yáyor
idáṁ sárvam ádhy [*ádhi*]

TS 6.2.2.6

prá vā́ eté 'smā́l lokā́c cyavante yé sómam āpyāyáyanty
antarikṣadevatyò hí sóma ā́pyāyita
éṣṭā rā́yaḥ préṣé bhágāyéty āha
dyā́vāpṛthivī́bhyām evá namaskṛ́tyāsmín loké práti tiṣṭhanti

MS 3.8.2 (93.18ff.)

yánti vā́ etè 'smā́l lokā́d yé sómam āpyāyáyitum udásthuḥ
párāñco hí yántīśvarā́ḥ prámetor
yád ā́héṣṭā rā́yā éṣṭā vāmā́ni préṣé bhágāyéti
ténāsmā́l lokā́n náiti ténāsmíṁl loké dhṛtā́[*-táḥ*]

MS 94.3

anáyor vā́ eṣá gárbha ābhyā́m eṣá ā́vṛścate yáḥ sómaṁ hanti
yád ā́ha námo divé námaḥ pṛthivyā́ íty
ābhyā́m evá námo 'kar

AB 1.26

dyāvāpṛthivyor vā eṣa garbho yat somo rājā
tad yad eṣṭā rāya eṣṭā vāmāni preṣe bhagāya
ṛtam ṛtavādibhyo namo dive
namaḥ pṛthivyā iti prastare nihnuvate,
dyāvāpṛthivībhyām eva tan namaskurvanty
atho ene vardhayanty eva vardhayanty eva.

B. Actions and recitations of the Adhvaryu and his helpers according to TS 1.2.10–11 and ĀpŚS 11.1.2ff.

TĀNŪNAPTRAM

ĀpŚS 11.1.2

anādhṛṣṭam asīti yajamānasaptadaśā ṛtvijas tānūnaptraṁ samavamṛśanti

TS 1.2.10g

ánādhṛṣṭam asy anādhṛṣyáṁ devā́nām ójo 'bhiśastipā anabhiśastenyám
'Thou art unapproached, the unapproachable might of the gods, guarding from imprecations, impervious to imprecations.' (Trans. Keith)

SOMASYĀPYĀYANAM

ĀpŚS 11.1.8

agnīn madanty āpā3 iti pṛcchati
He (the Adhvaryu) asks: 'Agnīdh, are the waters boiling?'

ĀpŚS 11.1.9

madanti devīr amṛtā ṛtāvṛdha ity agnīdhraḥ pratyāha
The Agnīdh answers: 'The (waters who are) immortal goddesses thriving in truthfulness are boiling.'

ĀpŚS 11.1.10

tābhir ehīti sampreṣyati
He summons: 'Come here with them.'

ĀpŚS 11.1.11

madantīr upaspṛśya tānūnaptriṇo visrasya rājānaṁ sahiraṇyaiḥ pāṇibhir āpyāyayanty aṁśur-aṁśus te deva somāpyāyatām iti

TS 1.2.11ab

aṁśúr-aṁśus te deva somā́pyāyatām índrāyaikadhanavída
ā́ túbhyam índraḥ pyāyatām ā́ tvám índrāya pyāyasva-
ā́ pyāyaya sákhīnt sanyā́ medháyā svastí te deva soma sutyā́m aśīya
'Let every shoot of yours, o Soma, swell, for Indra who acquires a unique portion of wealth; Indra must swell for you, do you swell for Indra; make (us, your) friends swell with a reward and with intelligence; happily, o Soma, may I attain your pressing.'

NIHNAVANAM

ĀpŚS 11.1.12

atha nihnuvate | *dakṣiṇe vedyante prastaraṁ nidhāya dakṣiṇān pāṇīn uttānān kṛtvā savyān nīca eṣṭā rāyaḥ preṣe bhagāyeti*

Then they disavow | Then they distract the attention from their inauspicious act | Then they perform the Nihnavana rite: Having placed down the *prastara* bundle (of grass) in the southern part of the *vedi* altar, having made their right hands stretched (with palm) up, the left downwards, (they recite):

TS 1.2.11c

éṣṭā rā́yaḥ préṣé bhágāyartaṁ ṛtavādíbhyo námo divé námaḥ pṛthivyái
'Wished hither are riches, exceedingly, for food, for well-being, (and wished is) the divine order for those promulgating the divine order; obeisance to heaven, obeisance to the earth.'

[ĀpŚS 11.4.2
savyottānais tu sāyaṁ nihnavaḥ]

C. Other Śrautasūtras on the Nihnavana of the *soma* sacrifice:

(ṚV) Śāṅkhāyana 5.9.5

upaspṛśya dakṣiṇottānān pāṇīn prastare nidhāya nihnuvate savyottānān aparāhṇe eṣṭā rāyaḥ preṣe bhagāya ṛtam ṛtavādibhyo namo dyāvāpṛthivībhyām iti.

(ṚV) Āśvalāyana 4.5.7

spṛṣṭvodakaṁ nihnavante [sic] *prastare pāṇīn nidhāyottānān dakṣiṇānı savyān nīca eṣṭā rāya eṣṭā vāmāni preṣe bhagāya*
ṛtam ṛtavādibhyo namo dive namaḥ pṛthivyā iti.

ĀśvŚS 4.8.10–11:

[aparāhṇe]
viparyāso yājyānuvākyānāṁ pāṇyoś ca nihnava ity upasadaḥ.

(YV/Taittirīya)
Baudhāyana 6.19[178.7f.]:

taṁ dakṣiṇārdhe vedyai nidhāya tasmin dakṣiṇottariṇo nihnuvata eṣṭā rāyaḥ preṣe bhagāyartam ṛtavādibhyo namo dive namaḥ pṛthivyā iti.

Baudhāyana 6.21[181.4ff.]:

[athāparāhne ... etāvad eva nānā]
savyottariṇo nihnuvate.

(YV/Taittirīya)
Bhāradvāja 12.1.10

*dakṣiṇe vedyante prastare *nihnuvate dakṣiṇān uttānān pāṇīn kṛtvā savyān nīcaḥ eṣṭā rāyaḥ preṣe bhagāya iti*

Bhāradvāja 12.3.20

*upasadaṁ hutvā tathaiva rājānam āpyāyayanti tathā *nihnuvate*

Bhāradvāja 12.4.4

*[etāvan nānā ... sāyam ...] savyān uttānān pāṇīn kṛtvā *nihnuvate dakṣiṇān nīcaḥ*

(YV/Maitrāyaṇī)
Mānava 2.2.1.13

prastare pāṇīn nidhāya nihnuvate nīcaḥ savyān uttānān dakṣiṇān – nīco dakṣiṇān uttānān savyān āparāhṇikyām – eṣṭā rāyā eṣṭā vāmānīti japanti

(YV/Vājasaneyi)
Kātyāyana 8.2.8

pratyetya prastare nihnuvata uttānahastā dakṣiṇottānā vā-eṣṭā rāya iti

(SV) Lāṭyāyana 5.6.9

kāśamaye prastare nihnuvīran dakṣiṇān uttānān pāṇīn kṛtvā savyān nīca eṣṭā rāya eṣṭā vāmāni preṣe bhagāyartam ṛtavādibhyo namo dive namaḥ pṛthivyā iti [= Drāhyāyaṇa 14.2.6; *Dhanvin's comm. on this: nihnavo namaskāraḥ | kṛte hi namaskāro puruṣasya doṣaś chādito bhavatīti | tadupāyatvān nihnava ity ucyate*]

(AV) Vaitānasūtra 13.24

punar upaspṛśyottānahastāḥ prastare nihnuvata eṣṭā rāya eṣṭā vāmāni preṣe bhagāya ṛtam ṛtavādibhyo namo dive namaḥ pṛthivyā iti

APPENDIX 2:

Plans

PLAN 1.
The Tānūnaptra establishes a contract between the priests and the sacrificer. It takes place at the vedi altar which is located between the three fires.

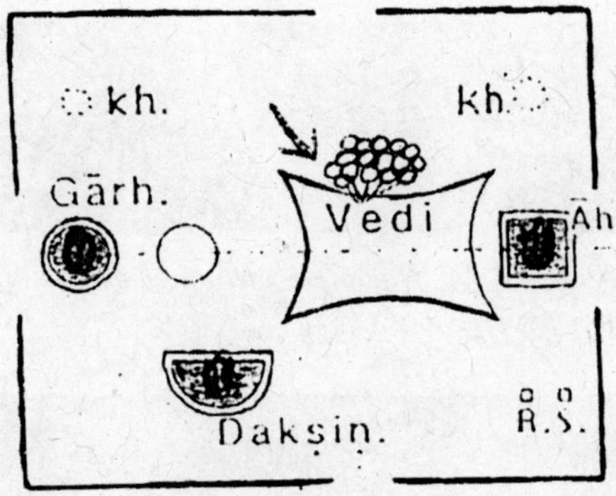

PLAN 2.
The Āpyāyana, 'making the soma swell', takes place at the 'king's throne' next to the āhavanīya or offering fire

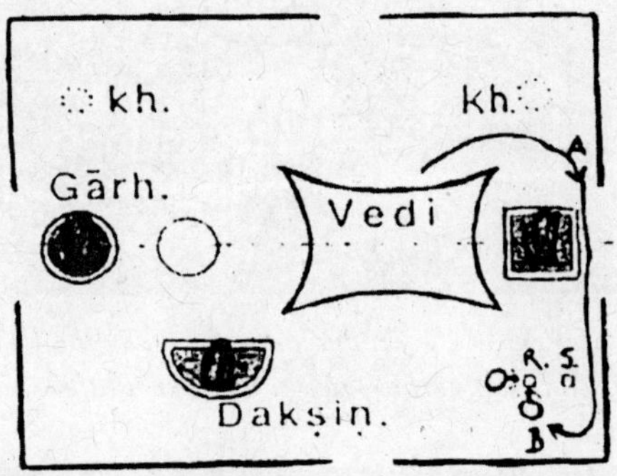

PLAN 3.
The priests and the sacrificer walk behind the fires back to the vedi to do the Nihnavana.

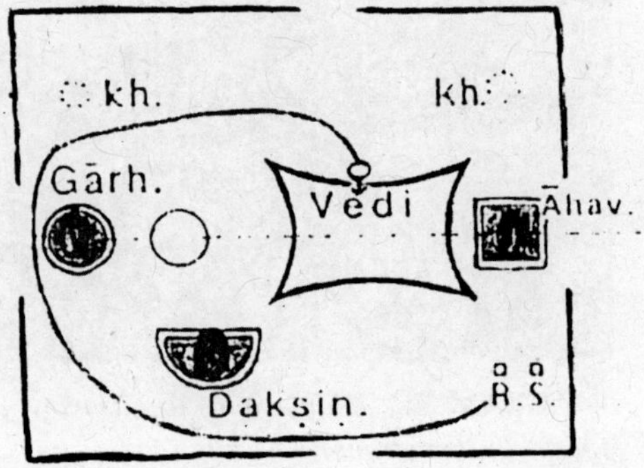

APPENDIX 3:

Diagrams

DIAGRAM 1. *Complete meaninglessness: ritual consists of utterly disconnected elements..*

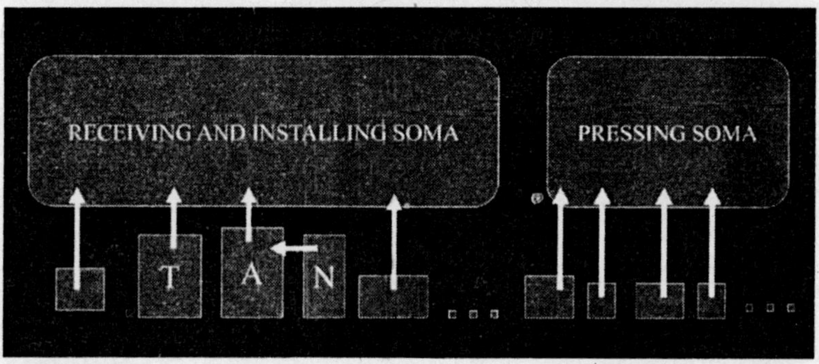

DIAGRAM 2 *Nihnavana to disavow a necessary but unfavourable (possibly dangerous) act in the immediately preceding episode.*

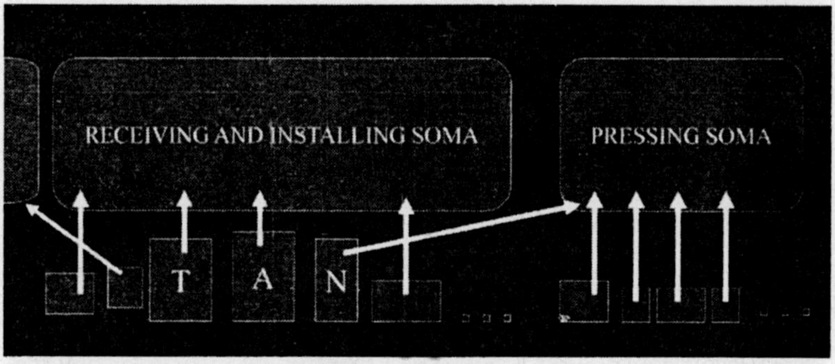

DIAGRAM 3. *Nihnavana to disavow a necessary but unfavorable (possibly dangerous) act in the following episode (of the subsequent part of the main action).*

APPENDIX 4:

Pictures

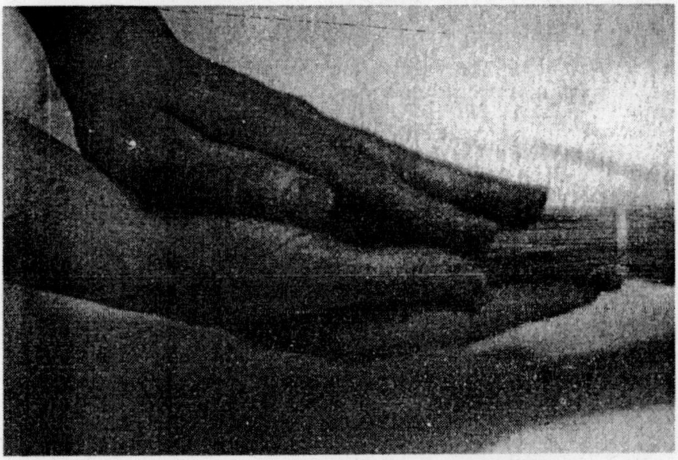

PICTURE 1. *Palm of the right-hand directed upwards, holding the bundle, left hand placed on top.*

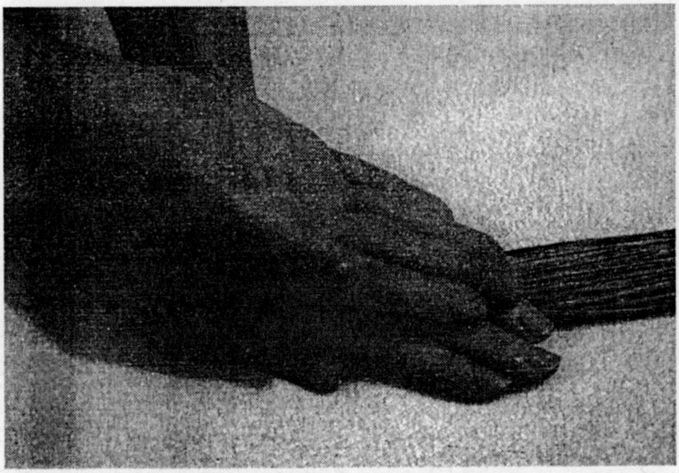

PICTURE 2. *First the left hand palm down, then the right hand on left hand with palm up.*

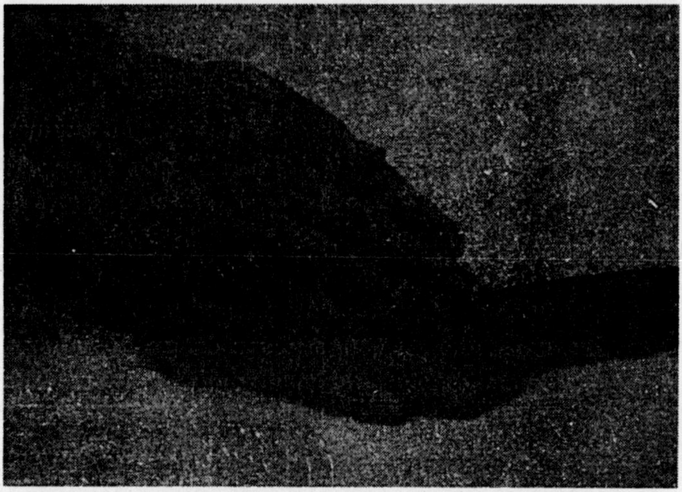

PICTURE 3. *First the left hand palm up, then the right hand on the left hand with palm down.*

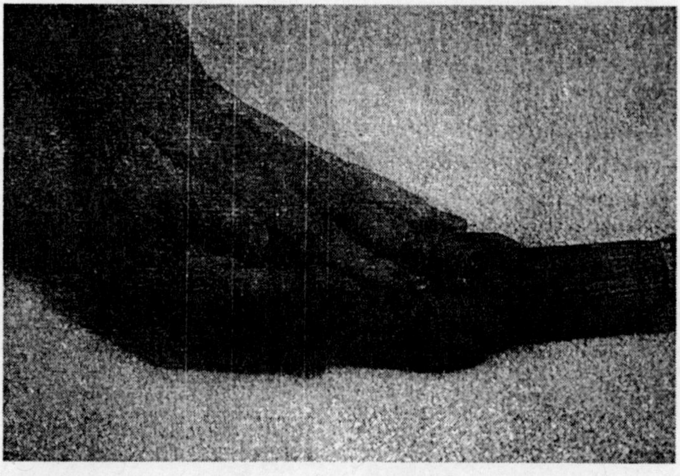

PICTURE 4. *Right hand palm up, left hand with palm down on the right hand.*

Ritual Texts and Performances: Reinvention of a *vaidika* Tradition

UTE HÜSKEN

In 1992 K. K. A. Venkatachari wrote in reference to rituals performed by Indian Hindu immigrants in the U.S.A.:

> Rituals are powerful mechanisms for the preservation and adaptation of religious traditions. Both written prescriptions for the observance and the practice of rituals are important in the process of transmission. ... (Venkatachari 1992: 177)

– in space as well as in time, I would like to add.

Rituals are, in fact, powerful mechanisms not only for the preservation but also for what one might call the 're-invention' of certain traditions. To my knowledge, Eric Hobsbawm (1983) was the first to hint explicitly at the fact that many seemingly age-old traditions actually have been 'invented' only recently. Although his considerations regarding the nature of 'invented traditions' are based on developments of the last 200 years alone, starting from the industrial revolution, they are nevertheless stimulating in a wider context. He characterizes 'invented traditions' as 'responses to novel situations which take the form of reference to old situations' (Hobsbawm 1983: 2) and concludes that they are attempts to structure parts of social life as unchanging and invariant, in order to compensate for the constant change of the 'modern world'. However, in reference to Indian ritual traditions I would suggest not to draw an artificial clear-cut boundary between 'invented' and 'original' traditions, but to allow for floating transitions, which I would like to label 'reinvented' or 'transformed' traditions.[1] Moreover, in the present paper I argue that each and every tradition, even those which have a very long traceable history, could only survive up to the present day exactly because they are flexible enough to constantly adapt to the changing context:[2] tradition is always (re-)invented tradition.

In the narrower context of Hindu traditions in many cases reference to 'the Veda' is of utmost importance.[3] In this paper on 'the reinvention of a *vaidika* tradition' I will first introduce the relevant ritual tradition, the Vaikhānasas with their literature, and then show how the mediaeval and modern Vaikhānasas refer to their 'being Vedic', their *vaidikatva*. Next I will deal in more detail with one of those *vaidika* features, namely with the *saṃskāra*s (life-cycle rituals), which constitute the connecting link between the Vaikhānasas as a Vedic 'branch' (*śākhā*) and the Vaikhānasas as a caste of Brahmin temple priests. Concentrating on the *saṃskāra*s, I will then show how, after the 12th century, the Vaikhānasas adapted to the demands of the socio-religious context, which was mainly moulded by the devotees, who belong to the religious grouping called Śrīvaiṣṇavas. It will be demonstrated how the Vaikhānasas adapted to central Śrīvaiṣṇava concepts on the practical, theological and soteriological levels, but at the same time managed to retain as distinctive feature their *vaidikatva*, by the subordination of the ritual elements taken from the Pāñcarātra

---

[1] An anonymous reviewer on Hobsbawm's book remarks: '... all traditions are in fact invented in one way or another, and they become traditions because, at least at the time of their inception, they serve strongly felt political, social, [religious, U.H.], cultural or even economic needs'. (http://www. socialsciences-web.com/The Invention of Tradition 0521437733.html).

[2] Hobsbawm (1983: 2) rightly points out that the claim that 'things are like that from time immemorial' expresses not historical facts but a balance of forces at a given time.

[3] Here I follow B. K. Smith who proposes that Hinduism is the religion of those people who create, continue and reshape traditions while referring to the authority of 'the Veda' as legitimizing force (Smith 1989: 13–14).

initiation and adapted to their own concept of hereditary priesthood. Ritual modification here is fundamentally interdigitated with the maintenance of tradition.

THE VAIKHĀNASAS AS TEMPLE PRIESTS AND THEIR TEXTUAL TRADITION

The contemporary Vaikhānasas are members of a Brahmin caste in South India. They are one of two major groups performing rituals in South Indian Viṣṇu temples,[4] mainly in the coastal regions of Tamil Nadu and Andhra Pradesh and in Karnataka.[5] As temple priests the Vaikhānasas contribute greatly to the picture of South Indian 'temple Hinduism' presented to the national and international public since they perform for example the rituals in the famous Veṅkaṭeśvara temple in Tirumalai (Andhra Pradesh), which claims to be the most important pilgrimage centre in India. The yearly festival *brahmotsava* there attracts thousands of pilgrims from all over India and is telecasted live. Moreover, the temple elaborately presents itself in the internet.[6]

However, although the Vaikhānasas' profession as temple priests points to an *āgamika* or *tāntrika* ritual tradition, the Vaikhānasas themselves insist on being purely *vaidika*.[7] Being *vaidika* in

---

4 The other group are the Pāñcarātrins. It seems that from the 12th century onwards the Vaikhānasas and Pāñcarātrins vied for patronage from the side of the (Srī)Vaiṣṇava devotees. The two ritual traditions are mutually exclusive: a temple can follow either the Vaikhānasa or the Pāñcarātra mode of worship. Change of ritual tradition is considered a serious transgression in the ritual texts of both traditions (for the Pāñcarātrins, see *Aniruddhasaṃhitā* 29.16 and *Īśvarasaṃhitā* 19.458; for the Vaikhānasa Saṃhitās, see *Khilādhikāra* 41.1–2 and *Yajñādhikāra* 51.1–2).

5 See Colas 1984: 343f.

6 See, for example, http://www.tirumala.org/.

7 See *Ānandasaṃhitā* 2.87, 3.28, 8.21; *Khilādhikāra* 41.8; *Kriyādhikāra* 1.17, etc. From some interviews I conducted with Pāñcarātra temple priests in Kāñcīpuram in 2003 it became apparent that the contemporary Pāñcarātrins do not claim to be *vaidika* but insist on following a *tāntrika* tradition.

this context usually is understood as being based exclusively on the Veda.

The *Vaikhānasaśrautasūtra* and the *Vaikhānasasmārtasūtra* are the oldest surviving texts of this tradition. They are considered to be of utmost importance and are taken as the main authority for the Vaikhānasa ritual tradition. The *Vaikhānasagṛhyasūtra* is in fact followed in practice to date: the life-cycle rituals, the *saṃskāra*s enlisted therein are till this day allegedly performed 'as laid down in the Vaikhānasa Sūtras'.[8] Moreover, these life-cycle rituals are the crucial factor making the Vaikhānasas eligible to perform rituals in Viṣṇu temples (see below).

These Vaikhānasa Sūtras date back to the third or fourth centuries AD and belong to the Taittirīya branch of the Black Yajurveda.[9] These oldest Vaikhānasa texts, which are of 'Vedic' origin, do not contain any reference to the Vaikhānasas' profession as temple priests. However, the *Vaikhānasasmārtasūtra* insofar differs from most of the other Sūtra texts as it in fact shows a strong Vaiṣṇava influence. Moreover, therein the first insinuations of an image cult are discernible. Yet, this image cult, as described in the *Vaikhānasasmārtasūtra*, most probably is not a public temple cult, but mainly refers to the domestic worship of Viṣṇu as Nārāyaṇa.[10]

The next literary genre of the Vaikhānasa tradition is constituted by the so-called Saṃhitās, which mainly deal with the ritual in Viṣṇu temples.[11] They are authored by a group of four *ṛṣi*s, pupils of Vikhanas, the mythical founder of the Vaikhānasa school. In these texts each and every aspect of temple rituals are dealt with, from the ritual preparation of the site for temple construction to the

---

[8] See, for example, *Ānandasaṃhitā* 4.73, 9.2, 11.13, 13.37; *Daśavidhahetunirūpaṇa* 2.5–9, 14.24–15.1, 25.6–7; see also Hüsken 2004.

[9] See Caland 1926; for the dating of the Sūtras, see Bloch 1896; Caland 1926; and Keith 1927.

[10] For the diverse textual references to an image cult in the *Vaikhānasasmārtasūtra* and an analysis of these passages, see Colas 1996: 22–26.

[11] The standard work on this literary genre is Colas 1996.

making of the images and their installation, including the necessary requisites and the establishment of the ritual fires in the temple. Moreover, much space is devoted to the description of daily rituals to be performed in the Vaikhānasa temples. The dates of origin of these Vaikhānasa Saṃhitās are according to Colas (1996: 94–97) the 9th to 14th centuries AD. The Sūtras and the Saṃhitās together are considered the authoritative text corpus of the Vaikhānasas.

THE VAIKHĀNASAS' *VAIDIKA* FEATURES

Since the contemporary hereditary occupation of the Vaikhānasas is the performance of temple rituals,[12] the question arises as to what exactly makes the Vaikhānasas *vaidika*. Within the Sūtra or Saṃhitā literature of the Vaikhānasas the concept of *vaidikatva* is not explicitly defined. Only since Śrīnivāsa Dīkṣita's commentary on the *Vaikhānasagṛhyasūtra* we find explicit references to those texts which are supposed to represent the *vaidika* tradition according to the Vaikhānasas.[13] Śrīnivāsa Dīkṣita mainly refers to 'Śruti, Smṛti, Itihāsa and Purāṇa' as authoritative sources and legitimizes this wide concept of Veda with a well-known verse from the *Mahābhārata* (1.1.204)[14] which implies that 'the Veda' (here evidently referring to the three Vedic Saṃhitās) can only be understood with the help of Itihāsas and Purāṇas which are consequently therefore also 'Vedic' in character.

It is evident from the discussions in Śrīnivāsa Dīkṣita's text and the subsequent Vaikhānasa literature that the Vaikhānasas' *vaidikatva* was used as a tool to establish their superiority over other ritual traditions. In that process some concrete interrelated features of the

---

[12] Another traditional occupation of the Vaikhānasas is that of an Āyurvedic doctor (Colas 1984: 345).

[13] Hüsken 2009 provides detailed references on Śrīnivāsa Dīkṣita's text *Daśavidhahetunirūpaṇa* and on some post-Saṃhitā developments within the Vaikhānasa tradition.

[14] This verse is quoted in *Daśavidhahetunirūpaṇa* 3.18–19. On this verse and its reference to the Veda, see also Smith 1989: 25.

Vaikhānasa tradition are referred to in order to establish their *vaidikatva*, the last of which I deal with in more detail in the present paper.

The first *vaidika* feature of the Vaikhānasas is the exclusive use of Sanskrit in religious contexts: even in the 21st century Vaikhānasa texts are compiled in Sanskrit, and the language used during rituals inevitably is Sanskrit and no local contemporary language such as Tamil or Telugu.[15]

Second, the *mantras* used in the rituals are all without exception *vaidika*. Naturally here again the question arises as to what texts are referred to as 'Veda'.[16]

Third, the Vaikhānasa Sūtras are part of the Vedic corpus and are as such considered the only authority by the Vaikhānasas. However, this claim is extended also to the Vaikhānasa Saṃhitās, since these texts have also been proclaimed by Vikhanas and have then been written down in an abridged form by the four *ṛṣis*. Therefore, this entire corpus has 'Vedic' authority.[17]

Fourth, it is of utmost importance that a Vaikhānasa is endowed with the *saṃskāras* as given in the *Vaikhānasasmārtasūtra*: the performance of these Vedic *saṃskāras* is considered a necessary precondition for the qualification to serve as a priest in South Indian Viṣṇu temples of the Vaikhānasa tradition.[18]

All these features refer to ritual. Therefore one can justifiably say that in this context the identity of the Vaikhānasas as against

---

[15] From the middle of the 20th century onwards some Sanskrit ritual texts with translations into Tamil or Telugu were published (see Hüsken 2001: 172, n. 14). These passages in vernacular languages, however, only serve as explanations and are not recited during the performance of rituals.

[16] This question is extensively dealt with in a passage of the *Daśavidhahetunirūpaṇa* (94.5–21).

[17] See *Daśavidhahetunirūpaṇa* 2.5–9.

[18] *vaikhānasena sūtreṇa niṣekādikriyānvit[a]*. This half-verse frequently appears in the Saṃhitās. See for example *Ānandasaṃhitā* 4.73ab; *Yajñādhikāra* 51.2cd; *Khilādhikāra* 1.38cd, etc. Evidently the concept of 'Veda' here can be understood with B. K. Smith as a mixture of some models of reference to the Veda, namely 'to be on par with the Veda', 'derivation from the Veda', and 'being in accordance with the Veda' (Smith 1989: 20–29).

other traditions is negotiated via ritual.[19] The Vaikhānasa *saṃskāras* thus have two opposed but interrelated aims:

1) They give evidence of the *vaidikatva* of the Vaikhānasas insofar as they are listed and described in the Vaikhānasa Sūtras, and
2) being endowed with these *saṃskāras* constitutes the indispensable precondition for the performance of rituals in Vaikhānasa temples. Here the Vaikhānasas are characterized by *vaidikatva*, in contradistinction to other traditions, which are *tāntrika* in character.

Thus two ostensibly unconnected patterns are linked by a causal connection: the reference to the Veda, in which temple ritual is unknown, is the decisive factor legitimizing the Vaikhānasas' performance of temple rituals.

I want to show on the following pages that the concrete performance of the *saṃskāras* changed together with their superimposed 'meaning' on the theological and soteriological levels within the stable 'frame concept' of being Vedic, the *vaidikatva*. This concept is referred to on diverse levels of performance and interpretation. In this way the *vaidikatva* transcends and encompasses any other element which enriched and added to the Vaikhānasa tradition.

THE RITUAL CONSTRUCTION OF *ADHIKĀRA* IN TEXT AND PERFOMANCE

It will be argued here that the 'construction of the ritual body of a Vaikhānasa' is framed by the reference to the Vaikhānasa's *vaidikatva.* On the textual level the 'ritual competence' of the Vaikhānasas is constructed by means of the performance of the *saṃskāras*.

---

[19] This seems to be a vivid confirmation of Hobsbawm's definition of 'invention of tradition' as referring 'to a set of practices which is rule-governed and ritual or symbolic in nature' (Hobsbawm 1983: 1). Hobsbawm emphasizes repetition as a major feature of rituals. According to him rituals are therefore powerful means to 'invent' traditions, since repetition automatically implies continuity with the past (Hobsbawm 1983: 1–2).

The first prenatal *saṃskāra* called *niṣeka* here stands for the whole set of 18 *saṃskāras* as listed in the *Vaikhānasagṛhyasūtra*. The concrete formula which refers to the Vaikhānasa *saṃskāras* in the Saṃhitās reads: 'endowed with the rituals beginning with the *niṣeka* as laid down in the Vaikhānasa Sūtras'. In the Saṃhitās this phrase is used as a synonym for (potential) Vaikhānasa temple priests. However, as I showed elsewhere, the information there as to how and when the *niṣeka* is performed is very vague. Although up to the present day the view is maintained that the *niṣeka* is the first *saṃskāra* for a Vaikhānasa, this does not necessarily have any impact on the actual ritual practice, since nowadays the *niṣeka* is rarely performed. Here the reference to the ritual frame remains intact, whereas the frame itself is virtually nonexistent.[20] In fact, in the course of time the prenatal *viṣṇubalisaṃskāra,* instead of the *niṣeka*, became constituent of Vaikhānasa identity – especially with regard to the qualification (*adhikāra*) to perform temple rituals. This development, however, did not have any impact on the 'formal' definition of a Vaikhānasa as 'endowed with the Vaikhānasa *saṃskāras* beginning with the *niṣeka*.'

On the basis of the Vaikhānasa ritual texts (commentaries, Prayoga texts and the Saṃhitā literature) it can be shown that the meaning, function, interpretation and performance of the prenatal *viṣṇubalisaṃskāra* were subject to considerable changes due to transformations of society which evidently weakened established structural patterns.[21] The concrete context of this change was the emerging necessity to map out a Vaikhānasa identity, which had to be different from the competing ritual school, the Pāñcarātrins, who seem to have been favoured by the Śrīvaiṣṇava devotees. At least from the time of Rāmānuja onwards[22] (12th century) the Vaikhānasas had to compete with the Pāñcarātra tradition for the

[20] For details, see Hüsken 2005.

[21] For detailed references, see Hüsken 2009.

[22] See Jagannathan 1994, especially p. 90.

elegibility to perform rituals in South Indian Viṣṇu temples. In this dispute the question was discussed whether

- one is a temple priest by birth, as is the case for the Vaikhānasas whose prenatal *viṣṇubalisaṃskāra* makes them eligible to perform the rituals,
- or whether one becomes a temple priest through an initiation, as is the case for the Pāñcarātrins, they undergo an initiation called *pañcasaṃskāra*, in which the shoulders are branded with heated metal seals bearing the symbols of disk and conch.

ADAPTATION IN THE RITUAL TEXTS

The detailed investigation of diverse Vaikhānasa ritual handbooks clearly proves that on the textual level the 'branding element' of the *pañcasaṃskāra* was incorporated into the *viṣṇubalisaṃskāra*.[23] It is still absent in the *Vaikhānasasmārtasūtra*, according to which the *viṣṇubali* – in brief – mainly consists of the invocation of Puruṣa (*puruṣāvāhana*), ghee and milk-rice offerings into the sacrificial fire, the invocation of twelve forms of Viṣṇu, the recitation of two *mantra* series (the *Vaiṣṇavasūkta* and the *Viṣṇusūkta*), and the subsequent feeding of the remaining milk-rice to the pregnant woman.[24]

However, already in some of the Vaikhānasa Saṃhitās the 'branding' element from the *pañcasaṃskāra* was incorporated into the ritual performance of the *viṣṇubali*: at the end of the milk-rice offering, the father of the unborn child (*yajamāna*) recites the *saṃkalpa* for the so-called *garbhacakrasaṃskāra*, worships the domestic Viṣṇu image, offers worship to two metal symbols of disc and conch, heats them in the sacrificial fire and dips them into the remaining milk-rice. Only then he feeds his wife with it. These elements of the *viṣṇubali* ritual are not given in the *Vaikhānasa-*

---

[23] For details, see Hüsken 2009.

[24] See *Vaikhānasasmārtsūtra* 3.13.

gṛhyasūtra but are introduced by the later Saṃhitās and commentaries.[25]

This change in the performance of the ritual accompanies a change of super-imposed meaning, as can be seen from the statements on the intended result of the ritual: while the *Vaikhānasagṛhyasūtra* and the early commentaries conceive the *viṣṇubali* as a means of protection of the unborn child, subsequent developments turned it into the *saṃskāra* authorizing a Vaikhānasa to perform temple rituals. The change of the intended result of the ritual reflects the social and clerical changes, in the course of which Vaikhānasas often lost their temple assignment to the Pāñcarātrins, whose reputation received a boost through the efforts of Rāmānuja and his successors.[26]

THE INCORPORATION OF THE 'CONCEPT OF INITIATION' ON THE THEOLOGICAL LEVEL

The theological foundation of this development is given in the *Purātantra*, one of the so far unpublished Vaikhānasa Saṃhitās. There it is stated that the Vaikhānasas are born as Vaiṣṇavas, since Nārāyaṇa himself applies his emblems disc and conch on them while they are still in the mother's womb during the *viṣṇubali-saṃskāra*.[27] The *Ānandasaṃhitā* (8.3) points out that the *viṣṇubali* is the branding of the Vaikhānasas with disc and conch.[28] Since this *saṃskāra* is performed before birth, the Vaikhānasas are called *garbhavaiṣṇavas*. Therefore, the *viṣṇubali* is the Vaikhānasa equivalent of the initiation which comprises branding of the body, the *pañcasaṃskāra*, but is superior because it is 1) performed by Viṣṇu himself, and 2) because the Vaikhānasas are already initiated at the time of their birth.

---

[25] See *Ānandasaṃhitā* 10 and *Tātparyacintāmaṇi* 434.1–435.15.

[26] On the close connection between ritual handbooks and practice, see Colas 2004.

[27] See *Purātantra* as quoted in *Daśavidhahetunirūpaṇa* 26.19–24.

[28] See *Ānandasaṃhitā* 4.50.

The theological reinterpretation of the *viṣṇubali* evidently accompanied fundamental changes in the soteriological interpretation of the ritual itself. While the *pañcasaṃskāra* came to be identified or equated with the Śrīvaiṣṇava concept of 'taking refuge to Viṣṇu-Nārāyaṇa' (*śaraṇāgati/prapatti*), the *viṣṇubali* fulfilled this function for the Vaikhānasas. This reinterpretation is again carried out by Śrīnivāsa Dīkṣita in his commentary on the *Vaikhānasasmārtasūtra*. There he explicitly equates the *viṣṇubali* with this concept taken from the Śrīvaiṣṇava milieu, the 'taking refuge to Viṣṇu-Nārāyaṇa' (*śaraṇāgati/prapatti*). However, he distinguishes a superior *vaidikaprapatti* from an inferior *tāntrikaprapatti*. According to him, the *vaidikaprapatti* is the invocation of Puruṣa and so on (*puruṣāvāhana*), which is in accordance with the Veda and which begins with the *praṇava* (*oṃ*). This definition clearly refers to the *puruṣāvāhana* which is to be performed in the beginning of the *viṣṇubali* (see *Vaikhānasasmārtasūtra* 3.13). That way Śrīnivāsa Dīkṣita identifies the *vaidikaprapatti* with the prenatal *viṣṇubalisaṃskāra* on the level of ritual performance. Furthermore, he states that the *vaidikaprapatti* implies that the devotee constantly is aware of the fact that Viṣṇu is the cause of all being, is the protector of the whole world and encompasses all beings: the devotee sees himself as a part (*śesa*) of the God (*śeṣin*). Thus the *vaidikaprapatti*, as Śrīnivāsa Dīkṣita sees it, is not only enacted through the ritual *viṣṇubali*, but is also a permanent attitude, which exists in a Vaikhānasa from the *viṣṇubali* onwards. The inferior *tāntrikaprapatti*, on the other hand, on the level of ritual performance is identified with the act of branding the shoulders in the course of the *pañcasaṃskāra*. This ritual is explicitly prohibited for the Vaikhānasas by Śrīnivāsa Dīkṣita.[29]

Śrīnivāsa Dīkṣita's explicit distinction between a superior *vaidikaprapatti* (the *viṣṇubali*) and an inferior *tāntrikaprapatti* (the *pañcasaṃskāra*) thus constitutes the integration of the soteri-

[29] See *Daśavidhahetunirūpaṇa* 104.15–106.2.

ological Vaiṣṇava concept of *prapatti*, and at the same time establishes a separation line with regard to other Vaiṣṇava groups. The incorporation implies that the Vaikhānasas adapted to the Śrīvaiṣṇava concept that marking a person with disc and conch is a necessary precondition to be considered a true Vaiṣṇava. However, in contradistinction to, for example, the Pāñcarātrins, the Vaikhānasas receive this mark already before birth, during the *viṣṇubali*, whereas other Vaiṣṇavas are not branded before the *upanayana*.

This whole process is no arbitrary religious debate but the outcome of the confrontation of two fundamentally different concepts: the *vaidikatva* in the case of the Vaikhānasas refers to hereditary priesthood whereas the *pañcasaṃskāra* refers to priesthood through initiation, which is not necessarily linked to a hereditary transmission of the profession. Through the prenatal *viṣṇubali-saṃskāra* the socio-ritual demarcation as family is emphasized: religious identity is linked with lineage and marriage alliances. In the context of Indian caste system these boundaries are virtually unsurmountable. Moreover, since this identity is not constituted out of free will and choice, it is perceived as objective and 'natural'. Initiation – as in the case of the *pañcasaṃskāra* – on the other hand implies much more permeable and flexible boundaries, since not prenatal determination but 'free will' and conscious decision are involved. Through the integration of the branding element into the *viṣṇubali* ritual the Vaikhānasas linked hereditary priesthood and initiation and at the same time subordinated the elements derived from initiation to the hereditary elements. In both cases the *adhikāra* is effected via ritual.[30] For the Vaikhānasas, initiation is laid into the hands of Viṣṇu himself and is brought forward to a

[30] As B. K. Smith points out, everybody is born 'incomplete', but the potential to overcome the defects are not the same for everybody: 'Humans, then, are the result of both their inborn potential and their realization of it, and these two components come in unequal portions. Intrinsic, inherent potential and the actualization of that potential through a personal record of ritual performance combine to create distinctions in the competence (*adhikāra*) of particular individuals.' (Smith 1989: 83)

time before birth. Thus the hereditary element retains its prominence and encompasses the element relating to initiation.

That way the Vaikhānasas managed to adapt to competing groups and to the demands from the side of the devotees, but at the same time secured the continuity, conceptual superiority and exclusiveness of their own tradition. Moreover, since thus the Vaikhānasas' performance of temple rituals is explicitly sanctioned by the Veda (i.e., through the *viṣṇubali*), their authority can in no way be disputed. This interpretation of 'the Veda' prescribes the worship of Nārāyaṇa 'for oneself' (*ātmārtha*) as well as 'for others' (*parārtha*): some Vaikhānasa Saṃhitās state very explicitly that Viṣṇu himself not only ordered the Vaikhānasas to perform his worship, but also allowed them to 'live on his goods'.[31] Furthermore, it is frequently emphasized that all people who perform Viṣṇu's worship without having undergone the Vaikhānasa *saṃskāra*s, are *devalaka*s – a pejorative term for temple priests.[32]

CONCLUSION

In the present example, the label *vaidika* serves as an affirmation that nothing has changed from time immemorial. Within this frame, adaptations and changes are possible and accepted.[33] As we could see, the concrete performance and the 'superimposed meaning' of the prenatal Vedic *viṣṇubalisaṃskāra*, which visibly creates the *vaidika* Vaikhānasa identity, changed to a considerable degree in the course of time. However, this change did in no way effect the 'frame concept' of being *vaidika*.

---

[31] E.g. *Ānandasaṃhitā* 4.87.

[32] See *Daśavidhahetunirūpaṇa* 38.4–15.

[33] The ritual in this context evidently functions as a marker of boundaries between religious groups and thus contributes to collective group identity of the respective ritual tradition. At the same time rituals also have an integrative dimension: they encompass members of a certain group and create solidarity and identity within this group. Rituals thus can be seen as a strategy of mutual assurance of religious identity.

This framing takes place on diverse levels:

- 'Labelling' the Vaikhānasas as *vaidika* describes them as 'being endowed with the *saṃskāra*s which start with the *niṣeka*' – irrespective of the fact that nowadays the *niṣeka* is rarely performed.
- Moreover, on the level of ritual performance, 'new' elements are added within the framework of the 'traditional' *vaidika* performance; thereby the adherence to the *vaidika* frame guarantees the *vaidikatva* of the performance, irrespective of the soteriological and theological interpretation of the added elements.
- On plane of the theological and soteriological interpretation of the ritual, certain crucial elements gain a 'new' or so far unmentioned meaning and importance.

The permanent process of reinvention of tradition in order to stabilize it is enacted within a *vaidika* 'frame' which is constantly referred to. In this way, innovation can be blinded out and becomes acceptable. 'Traditional tradition' is constantly replaced by 'innovative tradition', which in turn very soon becomes 'traditional tradition' itself. I explicitly want to assure the reader that it is not at all my intention to call into question the Vaikhānasas' or any other group's claim on being *vaidika*. Rather I wanted to show how tradition constantly reconstitutes and redefines itself in order to survive. K. K. A. Venkatachari puts it into the following words:

> Times of ... change provide impetus for adaptation of rituals because such adaptation preserves the vitality of ritual in new ... settings and functions to preserve the tradition at the time it is being transformed (Venkatachari 1992: 178).
>
> It is not a new process that should be attacked as dangerous; indeed, it is essential to the vitality of any religion (Venkatachari 1992: 190).[34]

---

[34] I would like to thank the Deutsche Forschungsgemeinschaft for not only sponsoring the research for my Habilitations-project on the life-cycle rituals of the Vaikhānasas (2000–2002), on which this article is based, but also for financing my research and my visit to Helsinki for the WSC in July 2003 as a research

REFERENCES

Ānandasaṃhitā, śrīvaikhānasabhagavacchāstre bhagavanmarīcimaharṣiproktā. Ed. by R. Pārthasārathi (with the Sanskrit commentary *Ānandasaṃhitā-vyākhyā* and a Telugu commentary of the editor), I–IV. (Vaikhānasagranthamālā, kusuma 12.) Īgāvāripālem: Vaikhānasavidyānilaya, 1924–25 [reprint: Tirupati: Tirumala Tirupati Devasthānam, 1998].

Aniruddhasaṃhitā: *Anirudha Samhitā. One of Divyasamhitā in Pāñcarātra*. Ed. by A. Srinivasa Ayyamgar. Mysore: A. Srinivasa Ayyamgar, 1956.

BLOCH, Theodor 1896. *Über das Gṛhyasūtra und Dharmasūtra des Vaikhānasa*. Leipzig: G. Kreysing.

CALAND, Willem 1926. *Over het Vaikhānasasūtra*. (Mededeelingen der koninklijke Akademie van Wetenschappen, Afdeeling Letterkunde, Deel 61, Serie A, No. 8). Amsterdam: Koninklijke Nederlandse Akademie van Wetenschappen.

COLAS, Gérard 1984. Presentation et analyse de la Marīcisaṃhitā. *JA* 272: 343–368.

—— 1996. *Viṣṇu, ses images et ses feux. Les métamorphoses du dieu chez les vaikhānasa*. (École française d'Extrême-Orient, Monographies, 182.) Paris: Presses de l'École française d'Extrême-Orient.

—— 2005. Rites among Vaikhānasas and related matters: Some methodological issues. In: J. Gengnagel, U. Hüsken & S. Raman (eds.), *Words and Deeds. Hindu and Buddhist Rituals in South Asia*. (Ethno-Indology: Heidelberg Studies in South Asian Rituals, 1): 23-44. Wiesbaden: Harrassowitz Verlag.

Daśavidhahetunirūpaṇa of Śrīnivāsa Dīkṣita. In: R. Pārthasārathi Bhaṭṭācārya (ed.), *Śrīvaikhānasagṛhyasūtram with the Commentary Śrīvaikhānasa-sūtratātparyacintāmaṇi by Śrīnivāsa Dīkṣita* (2 vols.): 1–122. Tirupati: Tirumala Tirupati Devasthānam, 1967.

HOBSBAWM, Eric 1983. Introduction: Inventing traditions. In: Eric Hobsbawm & Terence Ranger (eds.), *The Invention of Tradition*: 1–14. Cambridge: Cambridge University Press.

HÜSKEN, Ute 2001. Die Vaikhānasas: Tempelpriester im südindischen Viṣṇuismus. In: S. Wild & H. Schild (eds.), *Akten des 27. Deutschen Orientalistentages. Norm und Abweichung* (Kultur, Recht und Politik in muslimischen Gesellschaften, 1): 169–179. Würzburg: Ergon.

---

fellow of the Sonderforschungsbereich Ritualdynamik (SFB 619) in Heidelberg, which provides the stimulating intellectual background for my project on South Indian ritual traditions and which very much influenced the theoretical approach of the present paper.

—— 2004. Vermittlung von ritueller Kompetenz und Wandel der Rituale in einer hinduistischen Tradition. In: D. Harth & G. J. Schenk (eds.), *Ritualdynamik: Kulturübergreifende Studien zur Theorie und Geschichte rituellen Handelns*: 382–403. Heidelberg: Synchron Verlag.

—— 2005. Saṃskāras in theory and practice: A South Indian case. In: J. Gengnagel, U. Hüsken & S. Raman (eds.), *Words and Deeds. Hindu and Buddhist Rituals in South Asia.* (Ethno-Indology: Heidelberg Studies in South Asian Rituals, 1): 153–198. Wiesbaden: Harrassowitz Verlag.

—— 2009. Viṣṇu's children: Prenatal life-cycle rituals in South India. Translated from German by Will Sweetman. With a DVD by Ute Hüsken & Manfred Krüger. (Ethno-Indology: Heidelberg studies in South Asian rituals, 9.) Wiesbaden: Harrassowitz Verlag.

Īśvarasaṃhitā, prativādibhayaṃkarānantācāryais saṃśodhitā. (Śāstramuktāvaḷi, 45). Kāñcī: Kāṃcī Sudarśana, 1923.

JAGANNATHAN, Sarojini 1994. *Impact of Śrī Rāmānujācārya on Temple Worship.* Delhi: Nag Publishers.

KEITH, Arthur Berriedale 1927. Review of Caland's *Over het Vaikhānasasūtra. Bulletin of the School of Oriental Studies* 4: 623–624.

Khilādhikāra (Bhṛgusaṃhitā). Ed. by Roṃ. Bh. Pārthasārathi Bhaṭṭācārya. Tirupati: Tirumala Tirupati Devasthānam, 1961 (reprint: 1997).

Kriyādhikāra, vaikhānasīya (Bhṛgusaṃhitā). Ed. by C. Anna Rao. (Śrī Veṅkaṭeśvara Oriental Series, 40.) Tirupati: Śrī Veṅkaṭeśvara Oriental Institute, 1953.

Parāśarasaṃhitā: *Parāśara Saṃhitā* (with Sanskrit text & Tamil translation). Transliteration from the Telugu to Devanagari by Thirukannapuram Satakopachar Swami; translation from Sanskrit to Tamil by E. S. V. Narasimhachariar Swami. (Sri Pancharatra Agama Samrakshana Trust Publication Series. 1.) Srirangam: Sri Pancharatra Agama Samrakshana Trust, 2000.

SMITH, Brian K. 1989. *Reflections on Resemblance, Ritual and Religion.* New York: OUP.

Tātparyacintāmaṇi of Śrīnivāsa Dīkṣita: *Śrīvaikhānasagṛhyasūtram with the Commentary Śrīvaikhānasasūtratātparyacintāmaṇi by Śrīnivāsa Dīkṣita*, I–II. Ed. by R. Pārthasārathi Bhaṭṭācārya. Tirupati: Tirumala Tirupati Devasthānam, 1967.

VENKATACHARI, K. K. A. 1992. Transmission and transformation of rituals. In: Raymond Brady Williams (ed.), *A Sacred Thread. Modern Transmission of Hindu Traditions in India and Abroad*: 177–190. Chambersburg, PA: Anima.

Yajñādhikāra (*Bhṛgusaṃhitā*). Ed. by D. Raṅgācārya. (Vaikhānasagranthamālā, Kusuma 19.) Īgāvāripāḷem: Vaikhānasavidyānilaya, 1931.

The Hymns of Apālā and Ghoṣā: Production of Gender Self-identity

GABRIELA NIK. ILIEVA

Unfortunately, archaeological evidence does not provide much information about what it entailed to be a woman in ancient India, the main question of this paper. The Ṛgveda (ca. 1300–900 BCE), that most ancient Indo-European monument of religious poetry, mostly describes men's experience and participation in public, religious, administrative, and economic life. The present study focuses on three prayer-songs of this collection, the only ones among the 1028 hymns that explicitly and exclusively stage women's voices. Through an empirically based discussion of gender, my aim is to show how the female characters, who are represented as addressing gods, construct their gender identity. The analysis does not address any pre-specified problems nor does it presuppose any concepts on a priori grounds, nor is gender considered a pre-established category, simply because our socio-cultural knowledge about this epoch is limited. The study strictly attends to those aspects, which are evoked in the poems, and gender is approached as a dynamic process, in which the female voices articulate their self-identity by using the Vedic language. Specifically, the paper's objective is to examine their lexico-grammatical rhetorical choices and the contextual setting they bring about. Thus, I intend to reveal how the female speakers formulate who they are, what their current situation is, and what they want from the gods. I then compare my findings with what we know about men.

INTRODUCTION

Several works in the fields of philology, anthropology and religious studies have focused on women in ancient India.[1] They have discussed the exclusion of women from public affairs and their restricted value vis-à-vis fertility and sexuality. Yet, they have rarely conducted their research exclusively on the Ṛgveda, and because they have included the later commentary literature, the chronological frame of their studies has changed into that of the classical period, which is described as different from the early Vedic society. On the other hand, Indian Vedicists[2] have done research only on the Ṛgveda. Interestingly, they have projected a high degree of excitement and pride in their claims that the Ṛgveda, ca. 1300–900 BCE, gives a picture of the early Vedic society that is fairly egalitarian, in that men and women enjoyed very similar rights and opportunities in the public and sacrificial spheres of socially constructed experience. Unfortunately, archeological records do not provide evidence in material culture to support or oppose any of the claims mentioned above. The originality of the present paper stems from its application of culturally contexted gender-based discourse and pragmatic approach to a text that has not been analyzed in this way previously. Thus, the paper represents an attempt to further contribute to the ongoing discussion about men and women in early Vedic India.[3]

Gender is explored here as a gradual accomplishment through language use, not as an established construct, simply because there is not enough comprehensive linguistic and extra-linguistic data to substantiate claims about what gender must have entailed during this remote historical period. The so-called 'doing/performing gender' approach is essential on account of its understanding that in conversation people gradually present themselves as certain gen-

---

[1] Dange 1971; O'Flaherty 1980; Leslie 1991; Jamison 1996; S. Goldman 2000.

[2] Shastri 1954; Altekar 1956; Sharma 1987; Chadially 1988.

[3] For best descriptions see Thapar 1990; Erdosy 1995; Witzel 1997.

dered beings as well as produce and reproduce any asymmetry of their mutual relationship.[4] The context of the hymns is scrutinized as a dynamic temporally unfolding process through which social contexts are actively constructed by the participants.[5] The approach deployed here is one of the 'culturally-contexted' variety.[6] Most especially in cases of obscurity and ambiguity when the use of local idiom and metaphor in reproducing these gendered positions is decoded, the discussion will need to be particularly informed by a historical and philological knowledge of the culture, in which it was created.[7] Thus, certain aspects of the present study relate to critical discourse analysis, which tries to explain discourse structures that reproduce or challenge relations of power and dominance in society.[8] The present study has also been informed by the methodological framework of pragmatics in its employment of the 'inductive methods' in a 'rigorously empirical approach'.[9]

Thus, I hope to discover what gendered beings are formulated by the female voices staged in the selected poems by examining how they present their identity through use of the ancient language, Vedic Sanskrit. We have to keep in mind that we deal with very limited resources in this study. We have to be aware that the female figures act typically in a ritualistic setting of praying to the gods and that the conventionally established form and content of the genre also posit restrictions on what they express. In addition, the hymns inevitably contain biases of the poets, based on their social status, occupation, experience, family background, gender, age, etc. This is important to state in the beginning because it prepares the grounds for certain expectations regarding the results of the analy-

---

4 Cameron 1997; Coates 1998; Uchida 1998.

5 Schegloff 1991; Peräkylä 1997; Heritage 1997; Sacks 1992; Goodwin 2000.

6 Wetherell 1998.

7 Moerman 1988; Sacks 1992.

8 van Dijk 1997.

9 Levinson 1983: 286.

sis: what the gendered beings reveal in the songs will be relatively similar and not multifaceted and diverse.

THE DATA

Among the vast number of laudatory songs in the Ṛgveda, there are only four hymns, those by Ghoṣā (10.39 and 10.40), Apālā (8.91) and Viśvavārā (5.28), in which a female voice directly addresses the gods with a wish. These prayers are discourse events with two participants, the composer, who is the sole speaker, and the god, who is addressed in the song. Song 5.28 I will not deal with here, since there is no consensus on whether this is indeed the case.[10] Most importantly, the tradition, the *anukramaṇī*, ascribes them to female composers. Their names are mentioned as examples of the

---

[10] I should mention that although the *anukramaṇī* identifies the *ṛṣi* of 5.28 as Viśvavārā, belonging to the *gotra* of Atri, there are no explicit references to men or women in Viśvavārā's hymn and there is not enough information to claim that there is a female character in it or even that a female voice is expressed in it. *Viśvavārā* is actually an adjective, which means 'possessing all choice things' or 'containing all good things', 'bestowing all treasures'. It is mentioned only once in the second verse of the first stanza in the following way: 'The ghee-ladle, possessing all choice things, goes forth (east) refreshing the gods with reverence, with a libation' (5.28.1cd: *éti prā́cī viśvávārā námobhir devā́m̐ ī́ḷānā havíṣā ghṛtā́cī*). Evidently, *viśvávārā* seems to be a feminine singular adjective in the nominative form agreeing and defining the noun 'ghee-laddle' (*ghṛtā́cī*), which is also feminine singular in nominative case. This is not an exceptional occurrence and function. There are other instances where we find the same adjective in the feminine form, such as 1.123.12a and 5.80.3d, where *viśvávārā* agrees with Dawn (*úṣas*), and 3.4.3a, where 3.4.3a *viśvávārā* characterizes splendor (*dī́dhitir*). Based on the syntactic and morphological structure here, *viśvávārā* cannot be a personal name, because if it is so, a female with this name is the agent of *éti* ('goes') and then the function of the noun 'ghee-ladle' (*ghṛtā́cī*) will not be understandable, because it also is in the nominative case, but there is no other finite form for it to be the subject of. It cannot have an adjectival function, because it is not a bahuvrīhi formation, since the accent has not changed its place from its determinative[10]. In addition, it is not unusual for *ghṛtā́cī* to be the subject in the verse, for example in 3.6.1cd 'ghee-laddle' (*ghṛtā́cī*) similarly 'goes' (*eti*) and is 'to the east' (*prā́cī*) or in 6.63.4b it 'moves forward' (*prá ... eti*) and is characterized by epithets, such as 'favorable' (*rātír*) and 'glowing' (*jūrṇínī*). Therefore, we do not have enough linguistic data to claim that a female agency is expressed in this verse.

freedom and independence women enjoyed in terms of participation in sacrifice, composition of poetry, invocation of the gods, choosing a husband, etc. that contemporary Indian society needs to be inspired by for change. Their names are found in students' textbooks, in book dedication notes, etc. These songs have been the subject of a number of commentaries in the later Sanskrit literature and have received relatively consistent interpretations of their meaning, which supports the degree of confidence with which I will make claims.

One essential question arises at this point – whether these female voices are authentic, which is what the tradition claims,[11] or whether male authors express them. To answer this question it would be helpful if the research literature had a list of stylistic features, which are cross-cultural markers of femininity. Unfortunately, at present too little research has been done on this empirical matter and no firm conclusions could be drawn. Thus, only speculations about the authorship issue are possible and they could be made in two main directions. The first one is from a socio-historical perspective.

Vedic Sanskrit has become the official public language of the sacrificial institution, which is mostly a male domain. It should be emphasized that it is not the language spoken at home, where, actually, a variety of vernaculars are spoken. Women are engaged in sectors of social life that are different from those of men. Hence, women are linguistically prepared for their involvement in life differently from men. Therefore, an expectation builds that women are trained and in control of a different language, dialect or vernacular, as well as style and genre.[12] In support of this, in the classical

---

[11] See for more details Deshpande 1988.

[12] This is supported, on the one hand, by research showing that colloquial forms of speech are used by the wives and the gods in the Ṛgveda (Hoffmann 1975: II, 581), and on the other, that nowadays women most often speak dialects and not clear Hindi or English in many areas of Northern India, also that they tend to redefine gender, kinship and identity and challenge tradition through their songs and stories (Raheja & Gold 1994).

dramas for example, Sanskrit is the language of gods, brahmans, sages, kings, and other men of higher status and, exceptionally, of only a handful of women. Generally, Prakrits are assigned to male characters from lower social strata, and it is a Prakrit, namely Śaurasenī, that female characters speak no matter what their particular social status is. Also, when we look at the history of women's literary involvement in India, it is only after Sanskrit lost its total dominance due to ideological and philosophical changes that favorable conditions developed for women's writing in the vernaculars in non-traditional forms.[13] For this reason, since there are no indications for such favorable ideological conditions to promote women's writing at a later period, the supposition that women were involved in the composition of hymns does not seem a very likely one. Furthermore, researchers of the texts have not noticed any language-based stylistic incongruities at the morphological, lexical and syntactic levels[14] in the songs that are under scrutiny here, compared to the rest of the hymns, in order to offer women's authorship as an explanation. It is even possible to assume that these prayers were a part of a larger collection of women's compositions that were eventually lost; this, however, is a statement that stumbles over the fact that there are no references to such a body of songs in the compositions and the commentary literature that has come down to us.

The second direction of speculation goes the opposite way. In the early male dominated Vedic society, there is a dominant mode of expression. It is the only one that gets heard publicly and it is a male privilege. The right to exercise this privilege requires extensive training from one generation to another in order for members of the brahman class to gain access to the symbolic tools and themes with which to create hymns. Women, who wish to commu-

---

[13] A prominent example is the Buddhist nuns' compositions in Pali (Tharu & Lalita 1993).

[14] The language-based stylistic features of the Vedic hymns have been described in detail by Renou (1928; 1939; 1955), Gonda (1959), Witzel (1989) and Elizarenkova (1995).

nicate and to be heard, would have to be members of this class, would have to go through a rigorous training and would have to adopt the dominant mode. In order to express themselves, they would have to produce discourse within the conventional mainstream, rather than generate new modes independently. The question whether in such circumstances these poetesses are actually able to express what they really want to say still remains unanswered for two main reasons. On the one hand, ancient Aryan men established an order of values and were the arbiters of social conventions, which are reflected in the hymns. On the other hand, both the form and the content of Vedic songs are strictly conventionalized, which diminishes the chance of deviations from the mainstream to express personal views. In other words, it might not be conceivable to seek evidence for female gender markers in what they say or how they say it. Nevertheless, this is one possible explanation as to why among the 1028 songs in the Ṛgveda, one can find hymns that the tradition ascribes to female authors: Ghoṣā (10.39 and 10.40), Apālā (8.91) and Viśvavārā (5.28).

ANALYSIS

There is one obvious and common feature of these hymns, namely, that female speakers directly invoke gods and that these are primary gods of the Vedic pantheon – the Aśvins in Ghoṣā's songs, Indra in Apālā's and Agni in Viśvavārā's hymn. It is insightful to examine what identity the female voices project through their self-representation and through their wishes, which are directly related to them.

Apālā

In a narrative verse in the beginning of 8.91 the poet/poetess describes Apālā:

> A maiden going down to the water found on the road a Soma plant. Carrying it home she said, 'I will press it for you Indra, I will press it for you Mighty One.' (*kanyā̀ vā́r avāyatī́ sómam ápi srutā́vidat | ástam bhárantȳ abravīd índrāya sunavai tvā śakrā́ya sunavai tvā*).

The Soma plant is the one from which the drink of immortality for the gods used to be extracted. The female character expresses her intention to press out Soma. Post factum, we understand in verse 2 that this act must have taken place, because Apālā invites Indra to drink what has been pressed out with her teeth, 'accompanied by grain, having gruel, and accompanied by cake and praise' (8.91.2cd: *imáṃ jámbhasutam piba dhānā́vantaṃ karambhíṇam apūpávantam ukthínam*). Later on, in 3ab, she reveals that she is one of those who do not desire to know Soma, and who yet do not not understand him (8.91.3ab: *ā́ caná tvā cikitsāmó 'dhi caná tvā némasi* |). Then, in 3cd, she urges the Soma: 'Slowly, very slowly, o Soma, flow around for Indra'[15] (8.91.3cd: *śánair iva śanakáír ivéndrāyendo pári srava* ||). In the next two stanzas it becomes clear that she is speaking specifically as a woman concerned about her general welfare, as she says in 4ab: 'Certainly, he will be able, he will do it, he will make us more excellent' (8.91.4ab: *kuvíc chákat kuvít kárat kuvín no vásyasas kárat* |). This verse represents a typical rhetorical strategy based on the Vedic belief that what is being emphatically said would become true by the power of the speech act. She continues in 4cd: 'Certainly, we who are hostile to husbands,[16] we shall go and unite with Indra' (8.91.4cd: *kuvít patidvíṣo yatī́r índreṇa saṃgámāmahai* ||).

---

[15] Typically, the process is described as loud and noisy as the drink roars flowing down in many streams (e.g. 4.58.7; 9.74.6; 10.94.1, 5, etc.).

[16] One cannot translate with Geldner (1951: II, 414) the compound *patidvíṣ-* as '*vom Gatten gehaßt*' because all compounds where the root noun *dvíṣ-* is the second member have an active meaning and the first member denotes the object: 8.20.24d *asacadviṣaḥ* 'persecuting non worshippers or not persecuting worshippers', 8.45.23c, 8.64.1c, 3.30.17d, 5.42.9d, 6.22.8d, 6.52.2d, 10.36.9c, 10.125.6b *brahmadvíṣo* 'hostile to sacred knowledge', 1.39.10c *ṛṣidvíṣe* 'hostile to *ṛṣis*, 7.66.13b *anṛtadvíṣaḥ* 'persecuting untruth', etc. A past participle of a transitive verb would have a passive meaning.

The most intriguing aspect of Apālā's prayer is her unusual request, which she formulates next in 5:

> These three places, O Indra, cause them to sprout! My daddy's head and seed field, and this here under my belly. (8.91.5: *imā́ni trī́ṇi viṣṭápā tā́nīndra ví rohaya | śíras tatásyorvárām ā́d idám ma úpodáre*).

Thus, at the end of the prayer she includes her father and his fields along with the wish about herself. She reinstates the same request in stanza 6, by clarifying how exactly it relates to her body:

> This field of ours and this body of mine, and also my daddy's head, make all these hairy. (8.91.6: *asaú ca yā́ na urvárā́d imā́ṃ tanvàm máma | átho tatásya yác chíraḥ sárvā tā́ romaśā́ kṛdhi*).

It becomes obvious that the hymn is a spell for pubic hair in the womb area. The final narrative stanza 7 testifies about the success of the prayer:

> In the hole of the chariot, in the hole of the cart, in the hole of the yoke, o you possessor of hundred powers,[17] having cleansed Apālā three times, o Indra, you gave her a sun-skin.[18] (8.91.7: *khé ráthasya khé 'nasaḥ khé yugásya śatakrato | apālā́m indra trís pūtvy ákṛṇoḥ sū́ryatvacam ||*)

To summarize, she describes in vague terms that she is experiencing some kind of trouble with men/husbands and most probably this is due to either certain skin disorder or to the fact that she has not reached reproductive maturity yet. The latter problem I find more convincing. I have in mind that a spell for signs of biological ripeness in the context of finding a husband has relevance to far greater number of women (and indirectly men), for whom it might be performed, and that this would be a sound reason for the inclusion and preservation of this hymn in the Vedic collection. It is

---

17 *śatákratu-* is a common epithet of Indra used to address him as the possessor of hundred powers.

18 This stanza reveals most clearly that the hymn is a magic spell about puberty.

less likely that this is a spell against some rare skin disease, which would be too specific and have relevance to few people.

Furthermore, we need to point out that according to what Apālā shares in her prayer, she indirectly identifies herself as the daughter of some farmer, who has fields with crops. It seems that she is not married, as she was referred to in the poet's first line in the beginning as a 'maiden'. Also, it is important that she identifies herself as one who performs a ritual and makes an offering to Indra herself in order to ask him for help.

Let me share now a few observations at this point. I would like to address first some of the grammatical-rhetorical choices made by the speaker. Apālā expresses her intention to extract Soma by using the verb 'to press out' (√*su*) in the middle voice first person singular in the subjunctive mode (*sunavai* in 8.91.1çd). Later on, she uses active voice in the first person plural form when she says that she does not desire to know Soma, yet, she does not not understand him (*cikitsāmó* and *némasi* in 8.91.3ab). Then, she wants to go and unite with Indra and again she uses the middle voice in the first person plural (*saṃgámāmahai* in 8.91.4d). In pragmatic terms, she hedges behind a modal middle form in the first person singular, which is far less imposing than an active indicative statement. Also, she redressed her speech with the first person plural form of the verbs, as if speaking on behalf or from the point of view of other women who are in a similar situation and have some troubles with husbands/men.

There is one more interesting observation to be made in terms of the lexical choices and their pragmatic function. What stands out here is that she calls Indra with an uncharacteristically diminutive epithet 'little man' (in 8.91.2a *vīrakó*),[19] which is not the way the sages refer to the king of the gods, the supreme warrior, thunderer, conqueror, and which is in contrast with the way the narrator calls him at the end – 'possessor of hundred powers'. It seems that by

---

[19] I disagree with the most famous commentator Sāyaṇa, who explains *vīraka-* as *vīra-* 'hero'.

using such an endearing epithet, she establishes in this way some kind of non-threatening intimacy. In addition, she introduces her father by using an endearing term 'daddy' (*tatá*), as if to show her attachment and love to him. Thus, a little child-like identity is put forward as an apparent technique of negotiation with the god and of hedging her demand, which is ultimately for her own benefit. There are numerous instances in the rest of the hymns, where the composers refer to their relationship with the gods as one between a father and a son, but they never project such a child-like identity.

Furthermore, let me address the concern voiced by the young woman. It is obviously about her outer appearance and her biological attributes. Her wish is for biological maturity for reproduction, emphasized by the focus on the area 'under the belly' (*úpodáre*), which seems to be an intimate issue. However, even though she expresses a wish for her own sake, which clearly is the core of the song, she expresses it in both statements in the second place (in 8.91.5 and 8.91.6). Her father's head and seed fields, which need to sprout, are in the first place. If we read only these two statements, where she specifically articulates her request, it will sound as if her father's benefit is the goal of the hymn. Yet, the rest of the hymn's content is not related to her father at all, since she mentions that she has some problems with men and that she expects Indra to make her more excellent. In addition, as we understand from the narrator's verses at the end, the outcome of the prayer is not related to her father either, but to her body and skin.

I should like to note here that father references in Ṛgvedic hymns are very common. Usually in a prayer the poet pays respect to his forefathers with the hope that he will attain their status. Father references are sometimes used to illustrate how the gods will guide the mortal sages: the gods are compared with fathers who give instructions to their sons. However, the father figure in this particular song appears to be almost out of context. A question can be raised here: what is the reason why she talks about herself in reference to her father in this way? Most certainly, this is a conscientious and delicate attempt to make the prayer sound less female specific and thus her ritual speech performance to be allowed to take place so that it can be heard by the gods.

My final observation is about the sacrificial aspect of the hymn. The young woman portrays herself obviously as being involved in some kind of Soma ritual. Apālā mentions in the beginning that she will press Soma for Indra and afterwards she refers to what has already been pressed by her teeth. The sacrificial act is presented in very vague terms, because it does not have a description per se, as it usually does in a great number of hymns. In terms of grammatical-rhetorical choices, the noun 'maiden' is singular, meaning that she is alone, represented as heading towards 'water' and coming back 'home'; this does not place her in an official ritualistic environment, as we would expect vis-à-vis the Soma ritual. Later, she invites the juice to flow 'slowly' for the god.

However, the learned reader knows that the Soma ritual is a solemn highly structured ceremony, which takes place in an official public setting, which is performed by especially trained priests for wealthy patrons, and where the drink is extracted by pressing the plant between grinding stones, described as loud and noisy process as the drink roars gushing down in many rapid streams (4.58.7; 9.74.6; 10.94.1, 5, etc.). Obviously, there are striking differences between what Apālā does and what we encounter in the rest of hymns. Several questions rise from this incongruity. Is it possible that 8.91 has the only reference in the Vedas to a ritual that did not gain popularity[20] and for this reason we don't find explanations about it in the commentary literature? Is it possible that this is a type of metaphor that was well known, although this is the only occurrence in the hymns, and that its meaning was gradually lost, since the commentators never explained it? Or maybe wishes were ranked and matched with the volume of the Soma drink and her request needed only a little bit of it?

[20] For a more comprehensive discussion of Apālā's story, see Schmidt 1987: 1–29.

The most plausible assumption for the incongruity is this: as a female, Apālā has not undergone any formal training and therefore is not allowed to perform the official Soma sacrifice. For this reason, the Soma pressing ritual is performed in a different, non-traditional way in a private rather than public setting. Yet, I agree with Stephanie Jamison[21] that Apālā seems to know very well what is required to be done and includes all the needed ingredients in the offering to Indra, by accurately listing them in 2cd ('accompanied by grain, having gruel, and accompanied by cake and praise'; *imáṃ jámbhasutam piba dhānā́vantaṃ karambhíṇam apūpávantam ukthínam.*)

Ghoṣā

Ghoṣā's songs are more elaborate from the point of view of invocation. There is a redundancy of address forms and enumeration of the god's attributes and conquests, which makes them a little obscure. However, I find several verses very helpful with regard to my attempt to reveal her self-identity and her situation. After a careful examination of the text we find in 10.39.3a the following statement: 'you become the lord of the maiden growing old at home' (10.39.3a: *amājúraś cid bhavatho yuvám bhágo*). It is an indirect self-referential description in the third person, which brings up the age issue.

In another verse, 10.39.6ab, she reveals herself:

> I am the one who calls you, o Aśvins, listen to me. As the parents (teach) the son, instruct me. I am without friends, knowledge, relative by blood, and intelligence. Protect me from this shame.[22] (10.39.6: *iyáṃ vām ahve śṛṇutám me aśvinā putrā́yeva pitárā máhyaṃ śikṣatam* । *ánāpir ájñā asajātyā́matiḥ purā́ tásyā abhíśaster áva spṛtam* ॥)

Ghoṣā describes herself as a female with no friends, no knowledge, no relatives and no intelligence (10.39.6c: *ánāpır ájñā asajātyā́ma-*

---

[21] Stephanie Jamison, personal comment.

[22] *abhíśasti-* seems to have a sense of ill-fame.

tiḥ) and therefore she appeals that the gods treat her like a child who needs instruction. Apparently, she is fatherless and brotherless and cannot receive any assistance from a male member of her family in the search for a husband. The most direct piece of information about her is found in the second hymn, 10.40.5ab, where she states:

> Ghoṣā, the king's daughter, revering you, o Aśvins, has spoken, 'Now I am asking you, o Men!' (10.40.5ab: *yuvā́ṃ ha ghóṣā páry aśvinā yatī́ rā́jña ūce duhitā́ pṛché vāṃ narā*).

Ghoṣā gradually discloses her wishes in the two hymns. First, she defines her demand in general terms in 10.39.2c: 'May you make honorable fortune for us, o Aśvins' (*yaśásam bhāgáṃ kṛṇutaṃ no aśvinā*). Later on, in 10.39.11bcd, she specifies what she means by 'honorable fortune' (*yaśásam bhāgáṃ*) in less broad terms:

> He does not reach any anxiety, no sin and fear reach the person whom you make to possess a foremost chariot together with a wife (10.39.11bcd: *nā́ṃho aśnoti duritáṃ nákir bhayám* | *yám ... puroratháṃ kṛṇutháḥ pátnyā sahá* ||).

She not only wishes to find a husband, but she also asks the gods to protect him as well, and even she elucidates in what respects this protection should be.

It is interesting that in her sophisticated request in 10.39 Ghoṣā does not explicitly state the wish to find a husband. She is a little less vague about this in the next hymn, 10.40.5cd, where she asks the gods: 'Be with me day and night! Do what you can for a possessor of a horse and a chariot, and for a horse.' (10.40.5cd: *bhūtám me áhna utá bhūtam aktávé 'śvāvate rathíṇe śaktam árvate* ||). Again, she omits the word 'husband', but she makes clear what the husband's major attributes are in her view. Further, in 10.40.7cd, she elaborates that she seeks happiness with their assistance (10.40.7cd: *yuvór ahám ávasā sumnám ā́ cake*). Slowly, in 10.40.11bcd, she adds in additional dimensions to what she has in mind:

> Speak nicely that a youth indeed dwells in the young woman's womb. May we enter the house of the semen-giving bull who loves (the cow), o Aśvins. This we wish. (10.40.11: ... *sú prá vocata yúvā ha yád yuvatyā́ḥ kṣéti yóniṣu* | *priyósriyasya vṛṣabhásya retíno gṛhā́m gamemāśvinā tád uśmasi* ||).

Later on, she recycles this wish in 10.40.12d: 'May we as the beloved ones enter the house of Aryaman' (10.40.12cd: ... *patī priyā́ aryamṇó dúryām̐ aśīmahi*) and 'Bestow wealth full of hero-sons for the eloquent one' (10.40.13ab: ... *ā́ dhattáṃ rayíṃ sahávīraṃ vacasyáve*), which is the sage composing and chanting the verses.

In other words, Ghoṣā is the daughter of a king, she is a *kṣatriya* woman. Although she is a woman of a very high rank, she reveals her identity as non-authoritative. She shares that she is getting old, that she has no intelligence, no friends and no male relatives around to protect her. It is as if she is searching for an indisputable excuse as to why she is bothering the gods with these invocations and she presents her reason to do so in a very smart and witty way. Her own depiction makes her character seem quite weak and in a devastating need of support. She intentionally instigates a sense of desperation and urgency, which presumably could ultimately help in getting her voice heard. She uses a popular simile in 10.39.6b: 'As the parents (teach) the son, instruct me' (*putrā́yeva pitárā máhyaṃ śikṣatam*), a request found elsewhere. In this way, she skillfully avoids to identify herself explicitly as a 'daughter' or a 'maiden' or a 'woman' that the gods are expected to teach, in order to stay within the norms.

Interestingly, Ghoṣā's actual request is not so much for her own sake, than it is for her future suitor's benefit. First, she formulates her wish as 'fortune' (*bhāgáṃ* in 10.39.2c).[23] This word is intriguing, because across the hymns of the Ṛgveda it exhibits a semantic split based on the gender of the person to whom it relates. In other words, it has different gender-based dimensions. I have translated *bhāgáṃ* as 'good fortune', but this translation does not

[23] For further discussion of 'marital felicity', see McGee 1991: 71–87.

reflect the fact that the word has a strictly family and household connotation. When related to women, it seems to refer to a good rich loving man and to having offspring, and when related to men, 'wealth'.[24] Ghoṣā also specifies 'honorable fortune' (*yaśásam bhāgám*), which means that he should have the attributes of a noble, rich and brave man. It is worth noting here, that Ghoṣā's request is to have 'wealth', but not as implying 'riches', 'cattle', 'land', which is what we find in the prayers of men: for her it specifically means to have 'hero-sons' (*rayíṃ sahávīram* in 10.40.13b). First, she asks the gods, obviously, for male children, who, as we know, are important for the continuation of the male's lineage and second, in her mind they will become heroes on the battlefield, which is important for her husband's reputation outside of the house.

In a way this brings in a different non-personal dimension to the wish. It seems that she purposefully avoids burdening the gods with her individual female concerns and demands. It is as if the presence of a male figure in the prayer is an unavoidable condition. Instantaneously, an analogy can be made with Apālā's strategies to cleverly and resourcefully navigate her discourse in such a way that would cause minimum resistance most probably both from other sages and the gods.

---

[24] The noun *saúbhaga-* and the adjective *subhága-* are also instructive. In the wedding hymn the use of *subhága-* is accompanied by 'having good sons', *suputrā́* in a very clear family related context, as in 10.85.25c (*suputrā́ subhágā́sati*), in 10.85.45b (*suputrā́ṃ subhágāṃ kṛṇu*) and 10.85.33c (*saúbhāgyam asyai*). We find also in 10.86.11 that Indrāṇī́ is considered the most fortunate among women because her husband will never die from old age (*indrāṇī́m āsú nā́riṣu subhágām ahám aśravam* | *nahy àsyā aparáṃ caná jarásā márate pátir* ...) and 10.39.2c the female character asks the gods to make honorable fortune for her (*yaśásam bhāgáṃ kṛṇutaṃ no*), which based on the content of the hymn depends on her finding a husband. On the other hand, in more than 90 cases when referring to men the noun seems to mean 'prosperity', 'wealth' and the adjective 'prosperous', 'fortunate', on the basis of the lexical and contextual environment in which they are employed, defined by 'wealth' (1.34.5 *rayím*), 'protection' (1.34.6 *śármaṇi*), etc.

CONCLUSIONS

To conclude, first of all, the female self-identity formulated in these prayers is filled with vulnerability and misfortune, because both the speakers, Apālā and Ghoṣā, characterize themselves as women in crisis on account of their being non-wives and non-mothers. Even further, it seems that their voices intentionally express a sense of low self-esteem and even emergency and, most importantly, they present their grave situation as somehow solvable inevitably in relation to a male figure and/or offspring. They do not seem to search for opportunities to remain independent of men or ask for opportunities available for them to get engaged in other spheres of social life, as men do in the rest of the songs.

In addition, in these monologues both speakers tactically reveal their kin-identity by relating themselves to a male family member, father (in the case of both female speakers) or suitor (in the case of Ghoṣā). Neither of the women expresses wishes wholly pertaining to their own independent benefit; they do not ask for protection, health and long life, beauty and riches for themselves. They express elaborate requests for the sake of a male family member: Apālā makes wishes for her father's head and fields, and Ghoṣā for her future husband's prosperity. The female characters, thus, convey a belief that this automatically will contribute to their own fortune as well. In this way, it seems that they project themselves as a helping vehicle for the male's welfare and place themselves in an auxiliary and marginal position.

Furthermore, out of a total of 1028 hymns, female voices as the main speakers in the event are expressed in only three hymns (again, Viśvavārā's hymn does not provide clear evidence for this) and in all of them the situation is very similar. Obviously, the two speakers are aware of certain conventions. Since women were involved in the domestic sphere, their requests were confined within the domestic realm. Yet, it was not considered an important subject for the poet's and the god's attention; this has become clear from the topic selection throughout the hymns. It is the man's welfare and his activities in the public and the ritual sphere that are conventional topics, because they are relevant to sacrifice and gods.

In any case, it is very possible that it was highly unacceptable for a woman to disturb the gods with prayers exclusively related to herself. Therefore, Apālā's and Ghoṣā's characters are laudable, because they exhibited extreme astuteness, perceptiveness and intuition and were able to find a productive approach to put forward their wishes in the realm of public discourse. However, this further attests to the limitations in the scope of their gender identities. It offers further evidence about the restrictions vis-à-vis the prescriptions for social involvement of women encoded in the hymns: this was limited to the domestic, family and reproduction domains derived from their biological attributes.

REFERENCES

ALTEKAR, A. S. 1956. *The Position of Women in Hindu Civilization: From Prehistoric Times to the Present Day.* 2nd edition. Delhi: MLBD.

CAMERON, D. 1997. Theoretical debates in feminist linguistics: Questions of sex and gender. In: R. Wodak (ed.), *Gender and Discourse*: 21–36. London: Sage Publications.

CHADIALLY, R. 1988. *Women and Indian Society.* New Delhi.

COATES, J. 1998. 'Thank God I'm a woman': The construction of differing femininities. In: D. Cameron (ed.), *The Feminist Critique of Language. A Reader*: 295–320. 2nd edition. London: Routledge.

DANGE, S. A. 1971. *Vedic Concept of "Field" and the Divine Fructification.* Bombay: University of Bombay.

DESHPANDE, Uma 1988. Some Ṛgvedic poetesses: A study. *Bharatiya Vidya* 48.1: 14–29.

DIJK, T. A. van (ed.) 1997. *Discourse as Social Interaction.* (Discourse Studies: A Multidisciplinary Introduction, 2.) London: Sage Publications.

ELIZARENKOVA, T. J. 1995. *Language and Style of the Vedic Ṛṣis.* Albany: State University of New York Press.

ERDOSY, George (ed.) 1995. *The Indo-Aryans of Ancient South Asia: Language, Material Culture and Ethnicity.* Berlin: Walter de Gruyter.

GELDNER, K. F. (trans.) 1951. *Der Rig-Veda*, I–III. (HOS, 33–35.) Cambridge, Mass.: Harvard University Press.

GOLDMAN, S. J. Sutherland 2000. Speaking gender: Vāc and the Vedic construction of the feminine. In: J. Leslie & M. McGee (eds.), *Invented Identities. The Interplay of Gender, Religion and Politics in India*: 57–83. New Delhi: OUP.

GONDA, J. 1959. *Epithets in the* Rigveda. (Disputationes Rheno-Traiectinae, 4.) 's-Gravenhage: Mouton.

GOODWIN, C. 2000. Action and embodiment within situated human interaction. *Journal of Pragmatics* 32: 1489–1522.

HERITAGE, J. 1997. Conversation analysis in institutional talk: Analysing data. In: D. Silverman (ed.), *Qualitative Research. Theory, Method, and Practice*: 161–182. London: Sage Publications.

HOFFMANN, K. 1975. *Aufsätze zur Indoiranistik*, herausgegeben von J. Narten, I–II. Wiesbaden: Dr. Ludwig Reichert Verlag.

JAMISON, S. 1996. *Sacrificed Wife / Sacrificer's Wife. Women, Ritual and Hospitality in Ancient India*. New York: OUP.

LESLIE, J. (ed.) 1991. *Roles and Rituals for Hindu Women*. Rutherford: Fairleigh Dickinson University Press.

LEVINSON, S. 1983. *Pragmatics*. Cambridge: Cambridge University Press.

MCGEE, M. 1991. Desired fruits: motive and intention in the votive rites of Hindu women. In: J. Leslie (ed.), *Roles and Rituals for Hindu Women*: 71–87. Rutherford: Fairleigh Dickinson University Press.

MOERMAN, M. 1988. *Talking Culture: Ethnography and Conversational Analysis*. Philadelphia: University of Pennsylvania Press.

NOOTEN, B. van & G. HOLLAND 1994. *Ṛgveda: A Metrically Restored Text*. (HOS, 50.) Cambridge, Mass.: Department of Sanskrit and Indian Studies, Harvard University.

O'FLAHERTY, W. D. 1980. *Women, Androgynes, and Other Mythical Beasts*. Chicago: The University of Chicago Press.

PERÄKYLÄ, A. 1997. Reliability and validity in research based on transcripts. In: D. Silverman (ed.), *Qualitative Research. Theory, Method, and Practice*: 201–220. London: Sage Publications.

RAHEJA, G. & A. G. GOLD 1994. *Listen to the Heron's Words. Reimagining Gender and Kinship in North India*. Delhi: OUP.

RENOU, L. 1928. Les formes dites d'injonctif dans le Ṛgveda. In: *Étrennes de linguistique offertes par quelques amis à Émile Benveniste*: 63–80. Paris: Paul Geuthner.

—— 1939. L'ambiguïté du vocabulaire du Ṛgveda. *JA* 231: 161–235.

—— 1955. Le problème de l'ellipse dans le Ṛgveda. In: *Études védiques et pāṇiniennes*, I: 29–43. Paris: Institut de Civilisation Indienne de l'Université de Paris.

SACKS, H. 1992. *Lectures on Conversation*, I-II. Edited by Gail Jefferson. Oxford: Basil Blackwell.

SCHEGLOFF, E. A. 1991. Reflections on talk and social structure. In: D. Boden & D. H. Zimmerman (eds), *Talk and Social Structure: Studies in Ethnomethodology and Conversation Analysis*: 44–70. Cambridge: Polity Press.

SHARMA, T. 1987. *Women in Ancient India*. New Delhi: ESS Publications.

SHASTRI, S. R. 1954. *Women in the Vedic Age*. Bombay: Bharatiya Vidya Bhavan.

SCHMIDT, H.-P. 1987. *Some Women's Rites and Rights in the Veda*. Pune: Bhandarkar Oriental Research Institute.

THAPAR, R. 1990. *From Lineage to State*. Delhi: OUP.

THARU, S. & K. Lalita (eds.) 1993. *Women Writing in India. 600 BC to the Present*, I. Delhi: OUP.

UCHIDA, A. 1992. When 'difference' is 'dominance': a critique of the 'anti-power-based' cultural approach to sex differences. *Language and Society* 21: 547–558.

WETHERELL, M. 1998. Positioning and interpretative repertoires: conversation analysis and post-structuralism in dialogue. *Discourse and Society* 9: 431–456.

WITZEL, M. 1989. Tracing the Vedic dialects. In: C. Caillat (ed.), *Dialectes dans les Littératures Indo-Aryennes*: 97–264. Paris: Institute de Civilisation Indienne.

—— 1997. The development of the Vedic canon and its schools: the social and political milieu. In: M. Witzel (ed.), *Inside the Texts, Beyond the Texts*. (HOS, Opera Minora, 2): 257–345. Cambridge, Mass.: Department of Sanskrit and Indian Studies, Harvard University.

Of Animals and (Wo)men: Traditional Philology and New Paradigms for Studying the Past

STEPHANIE W. JAMISON

I am deeply honored to be addressing the Plenary Session of the Twelfth World Sanskrit Conference, and I extend my thanks to the Organizing Committee for this invitation. Asko Parpola, while generously leaving the topic of this talk entirely up to me, suggested gently that I try to give some account of why 'Sanskrit studies continue being important and even relevant in our modern world' – a charge that on first thought left me somewhere between speechless and desperate. I'm afraid I've never given any thought to being either important or relevant, as the titles of my published works amply demonstrate, but have simply self-indulgently pursued whatever struck my fancy and my intellect as engaging – and such topics abound in our very absorbing field. But on second thought – which came a good deal after the first one, I must confess – I decided I, and more important our field, was up to the challenge. And on the third one, the foolhardy thought – that there are few disciplines more important and relevant. Well, to qualify that egregious statement, Sanskrit studies are unlikely to end hunger as we know it or produce a cure for cancer, though they probably have as good a shot as any at bringing peace to the world. (Learning Sanskrit grammar leads to patience and a certain detachment.) But if, as I believe, intelligent management of the Present and the

Future requires us not only to understand and learn from the Past in a general way, but not to condescend to it, but to be intimately anchored to it and the people inhabiting it, to their essential humanity and to the intricate texture of their lives and thoughts, then the discipline of Indology, and traditional philology in general, has an essential role in this enterprise. With the proliferation of new models and paradigms for studying the past, our field must serve as the balance and the testing ground for these models at the very least, and more ambitiously should allow new models to be generated from our own old methods.

Before I continue preaching in this vein, let me start with an example, not from my own work, but from one of my heroes, in whose *paraṃparā* I am proud to be, namely Paul Thieme, in many ways the Indologist's Indologist of the last century – both for his philological precision and for the boldness (sometimes overboldness) of his hypotheses. I choose this particular case (Thieme 1954) because it exemplifies, on the one hand, several of the features that outsiders find most off-putting and fussy about philology: it concerns a single word, in fact a word found only once in all of Sanskrit literature and learning; Thieme's analysis of it depends on historical linguistics, on the application of nineteenth century Neogrammarian sound laws – and the linguistic component of philology often defeats even many philologists. And, for good measure, there's a little *vyākaraṇa* (traditional Sanskrit grammar) involved, and *vyākaraṇa* is not for the faint of heart, even in Indology. It is also incredibly cute, in my opinion; elegantly brief (it takes up less than a half-page, seventeen lines including the title, in Thieme's *Kleine Schriften*; and gives us access to some knowledge about the daily conduct of life in very ancient India for which we have no other information.

The word is *akhkhalī-kṛtyā*, found only in the *Ṛgveda*, our most ancient text in Sanskrit, in verse 3 of the famous 'Frog Hymn', ṚV 7.103. For those of you unfamiliar with it, this hymn depicts, on the surface, the delight of frogs at the arrival of the monsoon and their joyous behavior in the teeming rain, as they croak, hop about, and greet each other (or, as it turns out, engage in frantic sex). The frogs are compared with brahmins, and the hymn can be read on several levels – the possibility of this multi-level reading was much enhanced by Thieme's brief note. (For further analysis of the hymn see Jamison 1991–92.) Early in this ten-verse hymn the frogs are 'making' (*kṛtya*) '*akhkhalī*'. Now it doesn't take a trained philologist to recognize this as imitative of a froggy sound, taking its place with Aristophanes' '*brekekekex koax koax*' in Greek, and the vastly less literary American English 'ribbit'. (In fact, this trio used to serve as my examples for the relative arbitrariness even of onomatopoeia when I used to teach historical linguistics.)

But Thieme pointed out that the expression could also be lexically meaningful, if we run it backwards through the sound laws that derive Middle Indo-Aryan from Old Indo-Aryan (i.e., Sanskrit) and if we recognize this form grammatically as the first attested so-called '*cvi*-construction', in which the final short *a* of a noun stem is replaced by long *ī* in certain verbal compositions. Perform these linguistic manipulations and – presto, chango – from *akhkhalī* we arrive at the underlying word *akṣara-* 'syllable' (with only a slight adjustment of the expected consonant cluster ***kkh** to *khkh* [otherwise not a permitted sequence in Sanskrit or MIA] to make it sound froggier). What the frogs are doing is 'making syllables' – the expression is a pun that works not only on the froggy level but on the brahminical one. And what is happening on the brahminical level? The verse in translation reads

> 3. When it has rained on them, who are desiring, thirsting, when the rainy season has come, saying '*akhkhala*' / repeating syllables *like a son to a father*, one goes up close to another, who is speaking.

Two verses later:

> 5. When one of them speaks the speech of the other, like a pupil that of his teacher, every section is as if in unison ...

From these two short quotations we learn as much as we are likely to about pedagogical methods in the earliest Vedic period – the frogs croaking in antiphonal chorus are compared to students *repeating syllables by rote* after and in imitation of their father (and/or) teacher, a method still followed in traditional Vedic education today (as described, e.g., by Edwin Gerow in his recent 2002 presidential address to the American Oriental Society [Gerow 2002]). And this information about ancient Indian education depends on the correct (and, in my view, inspired) interpretation of a single word, with the application of very technical tools from the toolkit of traditional philology.

* * *

Let me leave the particular for a moment and return to my general rant. Sanskrit studies or, put more generally, traditional philology, textual studies broadly construed, have been rather battered ideologically in recent decades, as new approaches to historical study have arisen and new areas of interest have opened up. The emphasis has shifted in many ways to areas marginal or invisible to traditional historical study – disempowered social groups, women, minorities, daily life, and so forth – using materials marginal to traditional historiography. Political and military history – the Great Man / Great Deed approach – has yielded, however reluctantly, to social history. The Subaltern has Spoken, and the general view is that he doesn't speak Sanskrit. Traditional Indology has suffered from guilt-by-association with the 'colonialist' or 'orientalist' enterprises of yore. Philology had its golden age, or its coming of age, in many ways in the nineteenth century, whose dead white males we are meant to repudiate and many of whose interactions with India we certainly all deplore. Moreover, texts, it is felt, 'privilege' the dominant paradigm, reflect only the elite, and cannot be used to probe the margins. Some years ago I was told by some feminist scholars that it was simply impossible to do scholarship on women depending only on texts. I think I and others have proved them wrong (see, e.g., Jamison 1996).

In fact, I would maintain that texts are far more multi-valent, flexible, and multiply useful than such attitudes allow for. They can as easily *subvert* as *assert* the dominant paradigm; they can be made to reveal information about apparently invisible social groups and topics. In fact, they are the best such sources for the ancient world: the art historical and archaeological records are far less yielding, especially for our geographical area and for much of our time period.

Now I would first like to point out that for better or worse the Great Man / Great Deed approach to history was never easy to practice for pre-Muslim India anyway, hampered as we are by the lack of the types of texts and monuments ordinarily used to construct such histories (in, for example, the ancient Near East or Greece): annals and chronicles, governmental documents like treaties and proclamations, detailed bureaucratic records for city or state, inventories, censuses, and so forth. Though I am not trying to resurrect the hoary and misleading cliché that 'India has no sense of history', I think we can agree that ancient India has not transmitted to us the raw material for official or political history – and indeed, on the most straightforward level, offers us very little even securely datable, which is a prerequisite for much political history. In the past this situation was something apologetically to lament; perhaps now in the new climate of historical writing we can proudly claim always to have been ahead of the curve. In any case, because of the dearth of hard information, historical writing on India has always had to make extensive and creative use of 'soft' sources such as literary and religious texts, private inscriptions, and so forth.

And extracting historical information from such sources has always required close reading and ingenious interpretation of limited and partial data, in other words, philological methods. In fact I would not only claim that these methods are value-neutral, that is, they can be used to investigate any type of question, not simply the questions that interested the devisers of these methods. But I would also claim that they are ideally suited for the new paradigms and interests of contemporary historians – the marginal, the disempowered, and so on. Since we do not have direct and straightforward records pertaining to such social groups and such questions, we must make the texts tell us things they don't know they're saying. The best way to do this is to tap into the intricate web of associations offered us by the language of the texts – close attention to the semantic nexus of words and grammatical constructions. Close attention to *language* in all its uses can be a powerful tool in such studies because it can give us access to levels of expression that are not the overt intent of a text. All words have a complex nexus of associations, of primary and secondary meanings, of habitual collocations available to the speakers of the language and the inhabitants of the culture it expresses. By careful attention to the original language of a text, we can gain at least partial access to this associational nexus and begin to see the conceptual links between apparently separate notions that are particular to the culture.

Let me give a brief Sanskrit example, from some older work of mine (Jamison 1991, Part II 'Svarbhānu and the Wounded Sun'). There is a Vedic myth, rather rarely told, about the darkened sun, which the gods and mortals cooperate to save. Three times they remove darkness from the sun. A simple synopsis gives you no clue as to what this is about: the 'removal of darkness' is a rather nebulous concept. But once we note that one of the words applied to darkness is also used of the removal of the amnion at birth, the plot line becomes clear. The myth is interpretable as an enactment of birth (or rebirth), using the technical vocabulary of the obstetrical sphere. Comparing the several versions of this myth with other mythic and symbolic depictions of birth gives us a window on how the ancient Indians conceptualized gestation and birth and how they set about the practical details of delivery. All of which turns out to be a good deal more detailed and accurate than my knowledge of the same. The point is – we don't have to hope (vainly) for the preservation of an obstetrics manual from 1000 BC, nor need we bemoan the fact that the lore of the midwife, being woman's knowledge, was excluded from the preserved tradition. We can find this knowledge, or some of it, lurking behind the words of another discourse entirely.

Questions about women in ancient India have preoccupied me off and on for some years, and the challenge is always that it must be done at second-hand (at the very least). We have no direct channel to women's experience, no texts that we can be sure reflect a real unmediated woman's voice – like the letters and diaries that have recently enriched the account of women's history in many other eras and societies. If I may use a linguistic model, the writing of women's history in ancient India may be best likened to writing a grammar of a language. Like linguists we are attempting to construct, from partial, misleading, and often biased data, the conceptual system, like the system of grammatical rules, that defines women's experience in ancient India. We cannot hope to attain to the real, felt experience of any particular woman or women, to their actual utterances, as it were, but we can aim to extract from the scattered, indirect, often tainted data available to us in texts an underlying set of structures into which their lived experience would fit and from which it would be generated.

Recently I've been investigating how women are depicted in the early dharma or legal texts, first the prose *sūtra*s growing out of the late Vedic *śākhā*s, then the versified *śāstra*s, particularly the famous Laws of Manu or *Mānavadharmaśāstra*, to see if there is any change in the legal attitude towards women in this tumultuous period of Indian history – roughly the second two thirds of the first millennium BC (Jamison, 2006). It's an interesting little problem in part because the actual provisions of the laws change very little from text to text, often simply copied verbatim or converted into *śloka* meter with minimal adjustments, so any changes in attitude can be discerned only very indirectly. It's interesting in another way, too, because the texts belong to a particularly narrow and restricted sphere, the normative prescriptions of conservative brahminical orthodoxy. Are changes and disruptions in the larger social fabric reflected at all in this deliberately sequestered corpus? I think we can trace some changes of attitude in these texts, just below the surface, signalled by a few changes in wording, some alterations in sentence structure. And I also think these changes in attitude are in part reverberations from social changes outside the brahminical sphere, which, as it were, set up sympathetic vibrations (or unsympathetic ones) in the dharmic texts. (Before I go on, though, I should admit that some of my conclusions have aroused some controversy when I have presented them elsewhere.)

I see several major trends in the portrayal of women in the progression of dharma texts. First and most important – for the other differences arise from this, I think – is a growing tendency to attribute agency, especially mental agency, to women. By this I do *not* mean that they are necessarily granted freedom to act independently, rather that there is growing recognition in the dharma texts that women have the capacity and often the desire to act independently. This is not always welcome news, and it generates various reactions.

One of these is an attempt to control and rein in this capacity – the famous 'guarding' of women that is so insisted upon by Manu. Another is reflected in the moralizing view of women found in the later dharma texts, dichotomizing the sex into virtuous wives worthy of honor and scheming, sex-crazed hussies. I will claim that the rise of overt misogyny is in part closely tied to the first tendency, the recognition of women as potential agents.

What is the evidence for these claims? – Not very much, I must admit. As it turns out, the best place to look for independent action on the part of women comes from their bad behavior, and how this behavior is characterized and punished. Bad behavior is primarily sexual behavior outside of marriage, which, not surprisingly, is forbidden in all the texts in question. But what changes, ever so subtly in these texts, is how the participation of the woman in adulterous relationships is characterized. In the earliest Dharmasūtra (*Āpastambha*) the provisions are entirely phrased in terms of the man; the participation of the woman, willing or unwilling, goes unnoted. In the later *sūtra*s, *Baudhāyana* and *Vasiṣtha*, the typology of adultery becomes richer, with imaginatively conceived punishments, partly framed in terms of the woman. In *Vasiṣṭha* the first set of provisions concerns men (of various lower *varṇa*s) 'approaching' a Brahmin woman. Though the man is the subject of the verb, the woman the object, both are punished, publicly. The woman in each case is shaved, smeared with ghee, and led naked along the highway on a donkey, whose color is determined by the *varṇa* of her lover, e.g., a black one when he is a *śūdra*. These scenarios are followed by a series in which the woman is the subject, and most strikingly this begins with a wife who is unfaithful to her husband *only in her mind*: VDS 21.6 *manasā bhartur aticāre* ... I find this passage particularly significant because it attributes to the woman *mental agency*, motivation, intellectual autonomy. It does not require overt action to make her guilty of transgression. Note that the shift in attitude that I see here is signalled by a syntactic fact: the woman is the grammatical subject. The increasing autonomy of the woman in the *Manusmṛti* is signalled by a different kind of linguistic means, this time lexical: whether the woman is 'willing' (*sakāmā*) or 'unwilling' (*akāmā*), a category even further developed in the *Arthaśāstra*, for all sorts of sexual offenses. Mental agency is simply an accepted fact about women in this latter text, and those who exercise this agency in prohibited behavior are duly punished, while those who mentally resisted deserve the protection of the law – and we see this, primarily, in the constant repetition of this pair of adjectives: *sakāmā* 'willing' / *akāmā* 'unwilling'.

Now, the official recognition that women are capable of acting and thinking on their own cannot have been entirely comfortable or welcome (even though, privately and domestically, it can't have been much of a novelty), so that it is not surprising that hand-in-hand with the growing textual representation of women's agency *in practice* comes the nervous assertion of the *principle* that they lack independence. The famous and widespread doctrine of (*a*)*svātantryam* '(lack of) independence' for women becomes more and more prominent in the dharma texts, best exemplified by the oft-repeated verse:

> Her father guards (her) in childhood; her husband guards (her) in youth; And her son in old age. A woman does not deserve independence. (VDS 5.3; MDŚ 9.3; cf. also 9.2, 5.148, etc.)

Thus we are confronted with something of a paradox – that the more woman is textually endowed with agency the more her capacity for independence is denied. A paradox indeed, but perhaps a psychologically understandable one. An autonomous woman is a threatening woman, and denial may be the best defense. It is also in Manu that the notion of 'guarding' women, already present in *Āpastambha*, becomes a major theme. Perhaps what is most striking about the treatment of guarding in Manu, as compared to the earlier mentions of it, is the virulence of the verbal justification for guarding women. The practical reason for it, fear that another man will impregnate one's wife, was dealt with in a single participial phrase (*bibhyantaḥ pararetasaḥ*) in *Āpastambha* and subsequent texts (ĀpDS 2.13.6, BDS 2.3.34 [sim. 2.4.2], cf. VDS 17.9). But Manu begins his section on the laws concerning husbands and wives with verse upon verse (9.2–21, with occasional eruptions later) detailing the vicious and sensual tendencies of women and the consequent necessity to keep them as closely guarded as possible. Again it is a verbal cue that alerts us, this time the harping upon the root *rakṣ-* 'guard', which occurs seventeen times in verses 3–16 of Book 9.

What is astonishing about this outpouring is that the legal provision is the same one we encountered already in *Āpastambha* and throughout the Dharmasūtras; it has simply been invested with an emotional punch that is not there (or at least not overt) in the *sūtra*s. The 'law' hasn't changed, but the sentiment it evokes seems to have – or at least has achieved textual expression for the first time in the dharmic tradition. To keep hammering my lesson home, a mere summary or paraphrase of the various dharma texts on this issue would miss the change in attitude entirely, since 'guarding' is present from the beginning. It is only a thorough engagement with the texts, the minutiae of the texts including the smallest grammatical and lexical details, that reveals the emerging differences.

What has caused this apparent stiffening of attitude towards women? Of course, one thing may be the nature of the text itself: Manu has broader aims than the Dharmasūtras; gratuitous moralizing has little place in the *sūtra*s. And we have already identified another major motivation in my view – the gradual realization that women have both mental agency and the capacity to act, and the apprehension and hostility that realization evoked. But there is at least one other possible contributor, namely the rise of a threatening new female type, the unmarried religious woman. In the Brāhmaṇic late Vedic form of 'Hinduism' reflected in the dharma texts we have been examining, there is only one model for virtue and religious devotion in women, that of the dutiful wife. No separate path of religious devotion, renunciation, asceticism, or good works was available for her. However, outside of brahmin orthodoxy there had arisen a model of the lone ascetic woman, namely in the 'heterodox sects' (for us, read Buddhism and Jainism) which had recently instituted orders of nuns. That women might live together, apart from men, and move about freely while pursuing a religious vocation must have been shocking enough to brahmin sensibilities; that the vocation was not that of brahmin dharmic orthodoxy must have made it even more threatening. And I contend that part of the impetus for the intensely misogynist sentiments in Manu comes from the challenge posed by this new female type, the independent *and* religiously unorthodox woman. The growing anxieties about women's agency which we have identified in these texts are crystallized in this rather alien figure.

Some time ago I referred to the reflection of these women in dharma texts as 'reverberations' or 'sympathetic vibrations'. By this I mean that they are barely represented there directly; rather we must infer their effects by some passing provisions concerning them and, indirectly, from their impact on the attitudes towards brahmin women depicted there. In Manu ascetic women are several times mentioned as undeserving of normal dharmic niceties – denied funeral libations and protection from sexual harassment. This view of ascetic women is supported by the richer materials in a text somewhat akin to Manu in chronology and subject matter, the *Arthaśāstra*, where ascetic women inhabit the raffish world of shady dealings and are often employed as secret agents or agents provocateuses, encouraging illicit sexual behavior in others. Their indirect impact on the stiffening of attitudes towards women in Manu I have already argued for. I would like to point out here, as an aside, that if my reconstruction is correct, we have *no direct* evidence of the effect that the existence of these Buddhist nuns exerted on their brahminical sisters; we can only infer it from disturbances in the brahminical texts, just as certain astronomical bodies are posited only because of the effect they exert on the motion of directly perceptible ones. In philology even negatives have their place.

* * *

I would like to end by returning, very briefly, to animals, whom I love – as subjects of research – even more than women. And I would like to examine another negative, a textual absence, and what conclusions we can draw from it (Jamison, 2009). We will also return to an earlier era, the Vedic period, and our two earliest Sanskrit texts, the *Ṛgveda* and the *Atharvaveda*. I noticed a few years ago a surprising fact – or rather the absence of a fact. There is a remarkable dearth of wild animals in the *Ṛgveda*. Now this is not because the poets were indifferent to animals in general; the text abounds with domestic animals, especially livestock – horses, cows, sheep, goats. These real animals are embodied, animate wealth, the most desirable prizes in battle and competitions and in compensation for poetic production; their poetic counterparts are probably the most common source for similes and metaphors in the text, and participate in the mythology, in close association with major divinities. It is hardly possible to read a Ṛgvedic verse without stumbling up against some animal or other – but, notably, seldom a wild one. This absence is immediately made up for in subsequent texts. The second oldest text in Sanskrit, the *Atharvaveda*, abounds in wild beasts, and Middle Vedic ritual makes extensive use of them. The treatments of that elaborate royal ritual, the *aśvamedha* or horse sacrifice, enumerate a remarkable list of animals, both domestic and wild, dedicated to particular deities, the wild ones to be released without being sacrificed at the end of the ritual.

This remarkable shift between the *Ṛgveda* and later Vedic texts is not because (or only because) the Vedic people began encountering new fauna as they moved southward. Indeed several of the words for wild beasts missing or rare in the *Ṛgveda* are inherited words. Rather, if I may sum up and over-simplify a complex argument, the shift is an *indirect marker* of an important socio-political change. Wild animals, especially fierce and powerful ones like lions, are associated with the *royal* realm back into Indo-European times, associated with *kṣatriya*s and *rājan*s to put it in Sanskrit terms. But the *Ṛgveda* is a text that reflects priestly, brahminical sensibilities; the regal sphere is certainly represented, but the balance of power is more equal, with the poet-sages controlling the production of the texts. The consolidation of royal power and the subordination of priests and poets to this power is already evident in the *Atharvaveda*, as has been discussed by others, using more direct data. The representation of animals in the texts is simply another support for these views.

There is one striking exception to the dearth of wild animals in the *Ṛgveda*, the devilish hymn 10.28, which in its inner core contains a number of wild beasts who figure in a series of the most fleeting hints of animal fables, such as 'The fox has crept up on the lion facing (him); the jackal sprang on the boar from out of the (under)brush. ... The hare swallowed the razor facing him' (verses 4, 9). These sketches remind us powerfully of the beast fables of later Indic literature, probably the most enduring and widely distributed product of Indic literature, spread through the world in the myriad versions and adaptations of the *Pañcatantra* on the one hand, and dispersed through the greater Buddhist realm in the Jātaka tales. But there is nothing like them elsewhere in Vedic. Why do we find this faint hint of them in just this place, this challenging hymn, ṚV 10.28?

The answer again lies in close reading of the text. The animal sketches are embedded in something identified (well, hinted at) as the instruction of the great god Indra to a callow, simple mortal. Let us recall the actual function of the *Pañcatantra* and its various offshoots. The stories in these texts are not meant simply to entertain and amuse: the texts containing them count as *nītiśāstra*, textbooks in proper conduct, especially political conduct. They are 'Mirrors of Princes' – remember the ill-regulated princelings who listen to the *Pañcatantra* or the *Hitopadeśa* in their frame stories. What I think we see in ṚV 10.28 is the first instantiation of this pedagogical practice. If this reading of the hymn's general scenario is correct, then we must assume already for the Ṛgvedic period not only the existence of a body of story literature, of animal fables, but also (more interestingly) a fairly organized functional role for this literature in an instructional setting, conforming to the same model that we find quite a bit later in Indic literature in general. The teaching method then went underground for several thousand years, unreflected in the texts though (I would suggest) still regular in practice. Why are they not found in Vedic? Because the Vedic texts are essentially instructional manuals for brahmins, not *kṣatriyas*.

* * *

I began this talk with a pedagogical example – the frogs imitating brahmin schooling – and ended with one as well – fables as princes' instruction. We are all students here – and my point, in this defense and celebration of philology, is that we could do worse than learn from the beasts – remembering that each syllable uttered by the frogs, each detail, is as important to our understanding of this rich culture as the 'big picture', the whole story lurking behind the tagline of a beast fable.

REFERENCES

GEROW, Edwin 2002. Primary education in Sanskrit: Methods and goals. *JAOS* 122.4. 661–690.

JAMISON, Stephanie W. 1991. *The Ravenous Hyenas and the Wounded Sun: Myth and Ritual in Ancient India.* Ithaca, N.Y.: Cornell University Press

—— 1991–92. Natural history notes on the Rigvedic 'Frog' hymn. *Annals of the Bhandarkar Oriental Research Institute* 72–73: 137–144.

—— 1996. *Sacrificer's Wife / Sacrificed Wife: Women, Ritual, and Hospitality in Ancient India.* New York: Oxford University Press.

—— 2006. Women 'between the Empires' and 'between the Lines'. In: Patrick Olivelle (ed.), *Between the Empires: Society in India 300 BCE to 400 CE*: 191–214. Oxford: Oxford University Press.

—— 2009. The function of animals in the Rig Veda, RV X.28, and the origins of story literature in India. In: Nalini Balbir & Georges-Jean Pinault (eds.), *Penser, dire et représenter l'animal dans le monde indien* (Bibliothèque de l'École des Hautes Études, Sciences historiques et philologiques, 345): 197–218. Paris: Librairie Honoré Champion.

THIEME, Paul. 1954. akhkhalīkṛtyā, *Zeitschrift für vergleichende Sprachforschung (KZ)* 71: 109. [Reprinted in: Renate Söhnen-Thieme (ed.), Paul Thieme, *Kleine Schriften*, II (Glasenapp-Stiftung, 5, II): 138. Stuttgart: Franz Steiner Verlag, 1995.]

Etymologies in the Brāhmaṇas and the Ṛgveda: A Case Study of 'Fire's Precedence'

JOANNA JUREWICZ

I would like to begin my analysis by quoting two passages of the *Śatapathabrāhmaṇa* (with Eggeling's translation). They contain an etymology of the name *agní-*, explained to be a derivative of *ágri-*, which, in turn, is said to mean 'one who is the first':

> (1) *tád vā́ enaṃ etád ágre devā́nām ajanayata* | *tásmād agnír agrír ha vái nā́maitád yád agnír íti sá jātáḥ pū́rvaḥ préyāya yo vái pū́rva ety ágra et·ti vái tám āhuḥ sò evā̀syāgnítā* | (ŚB 2.2.4.2, ed. Weber 1855: 151)
>
> He thus generated him first (*agre*) of the gods; and therefore (he is called) Agni, for *agni* (they say) is the same as *agri.* He, being generated, went forth as the first (*pūrva*); for him who goes first, they say that he goes at the head (*agre*). Such, then, is the origin and nature of that Agni. (Eggeling 1882: II, 323.)

> (2) *átha yo gárbho 'ntarāsīt* | *sò 'grír asṛjyata sá yád asya sárvasyā́gram ásṛjyata tásmād agrír agrír ha vái tám agnír íty ā́cakṣate parókṣaṃ parókṣakāmā hí devā́ḥ* (ŚB 6.1.1.11, ed. Weber 1855: 500)
>
> Now the embryo which was inside was created as the foremost (*agri*): inasmuch as it was created foremost (*agram*) of this All, therefore (it is called) Agri: Agri, indeed, is he whom they mystically call Agni; for the gods love mystic. (Eggeling 1894: III, 146.)

According to Jan Gonda, the composers of the Brāhmaṇas created etymologies because they wanted to explain the world and have power over it.[1] I would like to focus on the first of these two functions of the etymologies singled out by Gonda and explore it more thoroughly. Etymologies can be seen as part of an overall attempt to build a conceptual system and terminology that aim at organizing knowledge about the world, in both theoretical and pragmatic terms, and at organizing a language to express this knowledge. In this system, the etymologies should be treated as definitions that name the constitutive features of an entity – those features without which it would not be what it is. In other words, they define the essence of an entity.

I use the word 'definition' in a general sense, without distinguishing – as is done in European logic – between nominal and real definitions.[2] The etymologies have features belonging to both of these last-mentioned categories: they explain words as well as the world. Explaining words, they explain the origin of their lexical form and their semantics. The semantics of a word can be stratified into two levels: the level of meanings and the level of concepts. I assume that a meaning is a mental representation of a collection of features of things referred to by words. A concept is a complex mental representation that can be expressed in many words.[3] We can say, then, that the etymologies of *agní-* explain the concept of fire, the meaning of the word *agní-*, the lexical roots of this word, and the real fire that it denotes. In the present paper, I will be mostly concerned with the concept of fire as defined in the etymologies of the ŚB.

The formation process of a conceptual system expressed by definitions requires an ability to abstract and to generalize. Abstraction is a strategy that allows one to omit details of a thing in its

---

[1] Gonda 1975: 377. See also Gonda 1955–56.

[2] Ajdukiewicz 1965: 62ff.; Blackburn 1997: 77–78.

[3] In ŚB 6.1.3 fire is given eight names: Rudra, Śarva, Paśupati, Ugra, Aśani, Bhavān, Mahān Deva, Īśāna, Kumāra. These names do not grasp its essence in full. At the same time, however, these names are not mentioned at random. They refer to different aspects of the Brāhmaṇic concept of fire.

conceptual representation. Generalization is a strategy that allows one to create a concept of a thing, characterized by a very wide semantic range. The definition of fire given in the etymologies omits all particular features of fire, focuses on the one of its precedence, and names it as its essence (*agnítā-*).[4] In this way, the abstract meaning of the word *agní-* is created. It is a general meaning that denotes all possible fires. Its general character can be also seen in the fact that the idea of precedence expressed by the word *agní-* lays the foundation for many specific aspects of the concept of fire in the ŚB and for its association with concepts connected with other gods.[5]

I accept the main assumption of cognitive linguistics according to which our ability of abstract and general thinking stems from experience and is determined by it.[6] Conceptual metonymy and metaphor are the main strategies that allow us to use the concept of our direct experience in philosophical thinking.[7]

According to Lakoff, each metaphor has a source domain, a target domain and a source-to-target mapping.[8] The source domain is a concept or an image, which lends its categories to conceive

---

[4] As I have shown elsewhere (Jurewicz 2003b), the Brāhmaṇas, which see the essence of things as realized in action, usually define things dynamically rather than statically, as is commonly the case in the traditional European philosophy. I use the expression 'precedence' for the sake of convenience, although instead of 'fire's precedence' one should speak of fire as 'he who precedes'.

[5] Precedence of fire is the basis for the concept of fire as the messenger of gods (since the messenger goes always first, ŚB 1.4.1.34); as the root and progenitor of deities (since in order to give birth to the deities fire must appear before them, ŚB 2.5.1.8); as speech, the head of deities, the mouth of gods and eater (ŚB 3.2.2.13, 6.1.2.28, 3.7.4.10, 7.1.2.4, 10.6.2.2), see below, section 2. Precedence can be the basis for the fire's association with other gods, because precedence is a feature of other gods already in the ṚV (see especially ṚV 10.103.8cd). Apart from the precedence of fire, the ṚV most often mentions the precedence of Indra, e.g. ṚV 1.54.3, 1.129.9, 8.17.9, 10.152.2.

[6] See Lakoff & Johnson 1980; Lakoff 1987; Lakoff & Johnson 1999; Radden 1992.

[7] Lakoff 1993: 205, 209ff.; Lakoff 1999.

[8] Lakoff 1987: 288. See also Lakoff & Johnson 1980.

another concept, i.e., the target domain.[9] The source-to-target mapping is crucial for understanding how people think, because it shows how the source domain is transformed in order to express the target domain in particular metaphors. In the present paper, I will focus on images evoked by the source domain, which influence the way of thinking about the target domain.[10] I will use the term 'formative event' to denote experience which is the base for the source domain.

Conceptual metonymy is a strategy that allows one to replace the concept of one thing with the concept of another thing, which both form a whole or which are closely connected with each other (e.g., they can be connected by the part-whole relation, or by causal relation).[11] Unlike metaphor, the metonymic mapping occurs within a single conceptual domain.[12]

Conceptual metonymy and metaphor are based on experience and on cultural models (i.e., common beliefs about the world shared by a community).[13] They manifest themselves in language and its particular expressions.[14] According to cognitive linguistics, there is

---

[9] For example, there is a common metaphor TIME IS MONEY which allows us to conceive time in terms of money (Lakoff & Johnson 1980: 7–9).

[10] This influence is called motivation in cognitive linguistics. It is reconstructed in the analysis of denoted and connoted meanings, which takes into account conceptual strategies used in building cognitive models (image-schemas, propositions, metonymy and metaphor, Lakoff 1987: 68). For motivation see also Lakoff 1987: 107–109, 346, 417–418, 438.

[11] For example, there is a metonymy HEAD FOR A PERSON which replaces the person with his/her head (Lakoff & Johnson 1980: 37).

[12] Lakoff 1987: 288.

[13] Cultural models are 'presupposed, taken-for-granted models of the world that are widely shared ... by the members of a society and that play an enormous role in their understanding of that world and their behaviour in it' (Holland & Quinn 1987: 4).

[14] The linguistic expression 'The flat tire *cost* me an hour' reveals the conceptual metaphor TIME IS MONEY, which allows us to conceive an abstract notion of time in terms of money (Lakoff & Johnson 1980: 8). The linguistic expression 'We need some *good heads*' reveals the conceptual metonymy HEAD FOR A PERSON (Lakoff & Johnson 1980: 36).

a tight connection between the thought and the language.[15] When we analyze the language and when we get to know mental strategies characteristic of human thinking, we can understand – at least to some extent – what and how people who speak in this language think.

It is well known that the Brāhmaṇas are commentaries to the Ṛgveda and other Vedas. I would like to show how deeply, how consciously, and how consistently the Brāhmaṇic thought referred to the ṚV. As an example, I will use the etymology of the name *agní-* quoted at the beginning of my paper. I do not think that these etymologies are very convincing when we refer only to the ŚB. They explain the name of fire as deriving from its concept of an entity that is first, but it is interesting to ask: why is fire first? The answer lies in the Ṛgvedic concept of fire to which the ŚB refers. If we refer to the ṚV, we will see the rational motivation of the Brāhmaṇic etymology.

Both etymologies refer to creation as the formative event for the concept of the precedence of fire. Both claim that it was created first, before all other entities, and this is the reason for its name. This is the most general and abstract sense of being the first.

The first etymology (ŚB 2.2.4.2) is more detailed. According to it, precedence constitutes the essence of fire, *agnítā-*, which makes that fire is fire. As has been already argued, it is the abstract meaning of the word *agní-* that denotes fire not as something that shines, smokes, burns and throws ashes,[16] but as something that comes in first. This etymology also shows empirical motivation for that abstract meaning. In its explanation, it refers to common experience 'for him who goes first, they say that he goes at the head' (*agre*).

---

[15] As Lakoff puts it: 'Language is made meaningful because it is directly tied to meaningful thought and depends upon the nature of thought. ... Language and thought are meaningful because they are motivated by our functioning as part of reality.' (Lakoff 1987: 291–292.)

[16] These are essential features of fire according to ŚB 6.2.1.5 (see Jurewicz 2003b).

Thus, it evokes the image of someone who goes at the head of a group.

In my opinion, this very image brings us back to the ṚV. It evokes the Ṛgvedic images of fire and thus it leads us to the Ṛgvedic concept of fire. At the same time, it refers to the Ṛgvedic use of the word *ágra-* to express the concept of fire. So association with the ṚV takes place on the conceptual, imaginary, and lexical levels.

The very concept of fire as an entity characterized by precedence comes from the ṚV. This concept of fire is expressed in the ṚV both in the images of fire and in the use of specific lexemes. My analysis of several lexemes will enable us to reconstruct the concept of fire and fire-related images.[17]

Before I begin my analysis, I have to add that the ṚV used the same conceptual strategies as the ŚB. As we will see, the concept of fire's precedence is built with the aid of conceptual metonymy and metaphor that use various images and that refer to various concepts. At the same time, we will see that the images are consciously chosen and derive from the experience characteristic of the Aryans, related to producing fire, raising cattle, expansion and ritual chariot races.

1. *ágra-*

Let us begin with a term used in the Brāhmaṇic etymologies, i.e., *ágra-*. In the context of descriptions of fire, the word is most frequently used to build the metaphoric image of fire at the head of dawns (*ágre uṣásām*):

> *indhé rā́jā sám aryó námobhir yásya prátīkam ā́hutaṃ ghṛténa* |
> *náro havyébhir īḷate sabā́dha ā́gnír ágra uṣásām aśoci* || (ṚV 7.8.1)

[17] I will not analyze the role of fire in the appearance of rain, in the preparation of the Soma draught, and the metaphysical concept of fire, because it would go beyond the scope of this paper. I have dealt with these topics in my book (Jurewicz 2001a). I will just limit myself to saying that the precedence of fire is built also in these concepts.

> The favourable king whose face is decked with clarified butter is kindled with homage. Men eagerly call him with oblations. Agni has shone forth at the head of dawns.[18]

Since cows in the ṚV are a conventional metaphor for dawns and since fire is often presented as a cowherd or a bull, it seems almost inevitable that this stanza evokes the image a herd of cows, following their cowherd or their leading bull.[19] This metaphoric image expresses fire's precedence in the morning.

To understand this image fully, we have to refer further to the Ṛgvedic experience and beliefs. Firstly, fire was produced before dawn appeared in the sky. Secondly, according to the ṚV. fire is identical with the rising sun, which brings the brightness of the dawn to the dark sky.[20] So we can see that the concept of fire's precedence is built on the basis of *what* people did in the morning and *how* they understood that. In other words, it is built on the basis of experience and of the cultural model regarding the nature of sunrise.[21]

The plural form of the word *uṣás-* allows us to expand the range of fire's precedence. We can interpret it as referring not only to the beginning of one day but also to the beginning of all the days throughout the year. The same meaning can be evoked by the metaphoric image of fire at the head of days (*ágre áhnām*):

---

[18] See also ṚV 7.9.3, 10.1.1, 10.8.4, 10.45.5.

[19] For cows as a metaphor for dawns, see Srinivasan 1979: 117ff. For Agni as a shepherd (*gopā́-*), see, e.g., ṚV 1.1.8, 3.15.2; for Agni as a bull (*vṛṣabhá-*, *vṛ́ṣan-*), see, e.g. ṚV 1.128.3, 3.27.13, 14, 15.

[20] These two actions (producing fire and sunrise) were not understood as taking place separately on earth and in the sky. There was a crucial link between them expressed in the idea that it was just the same fire enkindled in the morning which rose up in the sky in its solar form. For the identification of fire with the sun, see Macdonell 1897: 93; Oldenberg 1988: 63–64.

[21] Producing fire in the morning can be both a ritual and a secular activity, and although the ṚV is mostly concerned with the ritual action, I think both are implied in these descriptions. On the other hand, probably only the ritual act could have been conceived as having cosmic results like sunrise. Fire's precedence in the ritual is expressed with the use of *ágra-* in the image of fire being at the head of sacrifice (*ágre yajñásya*) in ṚV 7.15.5.

jániṣṭa hí jényo ágre áhnāṃ hitó hitéṣv aruṣó vánesu | (ṚV 5.1.5ab)

The noble One was born at the head of the days, red, laid in the well-laid fuel.[22]

This is a variant of the metaphoric image of the fire which burns at the head of dawns. The link between these two images is metonymy, which allows identifying the dawn, or the beginning of the day, with the whole day. At the same time, the image of fire at the head of days more explicitly denotes the first day of the year that consists of many days.

There is another, even more abstract, aspect of fire's precedence – its being first in the creative act. This aspect is implied in the idea of fire coming first in the year, because – as Kuiper has shown – the beginning of the year was viewed as the moment when creation began.[23]

The image of a herd of cows led by a cowherd or a leading bull evoked in the description of fire at the head of dawns highlights the dynamic character of fire's precedence. It includes the movement forward (implied by the source domain of the herd going forward on ground) and upward (implied by the source domain of the sun going up in the sky).[24] The movement upward is also implied in the following stanza:

dvimātā́ hótā vidátheṣu samrā́ḷ ánv ágraṃ cárati kṣéti budhnáḥ |
(ṚV 3.55.7ab)

Child of two mothers – priest in the assemblies – the monarch goes along the summit, his bottom is still.

The stanza describes burning fire; *ágra-* denotes the place where the top of its flames constantly moves up, while the bottom of fire

---

[22] See also ṚV 5.1.4.

[23] Kuiper 1960: 225. Such a concept of fire's precedence is confirmed by the Ṛgvedic descriptions which present the morning as being caused by the fire and which express the creation of the world; see, e.g., ṚV 6.7.6, 10.88.2–3.

[24] These two movements are within the semantic range of the word *ágra-* (see Jurewicz 2003a).

is still. In fact, while denoting this place, the word *ágra-* denotes the top of the flames. But not only the earthly fire is meant here. The term *samrā́j-* evokes the idea of the solar form of fire.[25] In this context, *ágra-* denotes the highest point in the sky reached by the flames of fire in the form of the rising sun. Its immovable bottom is the earth called the bottom of the great space in the ṚV.[26] The whole image implies movement upward.

This short analysis of the usage of the word *ágra-* shows that fire in the ṚV was conceived of as the entity which is first to appear in the morning, in the year and in creation.[27] Its precedence covers the movement forward and upward.

Now I will briefly analyze some other words used in the ṚV to denote fire's precedence. I focus only on the most important aspects of their usage.

2. *purás*

Let us begin with the word *purás*. It is often used to express fire's precedence understood in terms of the place in front of the speaker:

> *préddho agne dīdihi puró nó 'jasrayā sūrmyā̀ yaviṣṭha* | (ṚV 7.1.3)
>
> Shine before us, O Agni, well-kindled with your unextinguishable pillar of flame, O you, the youngest one.[28]

---

[25] For the solar meaning of the king, see Auboyer 1949: 74ff.

[26] The smoke and flames of fire are described in the ṚV as reaching the sky, see ṚV 6.2.6, 7.16.3, 10.45.7. For fire reaching the summit of the sky, see ṚV 1.58.2, 3.2.12, 7.2.1. For the earth as the bottom of the great space on which fire is produced, see ṚV 4.1.11.

[27] In the general meaning *ágra-* is used to denote precedence of fire enkindled in the morning without evoking the image of group following it (ṚV 10.69.1). In one stanza a compound with *ágra-* is used (*agrayā́van-* – 'going at the head') to denote general precedence of fire and to highlight its dynamism (ṚV 10.70.2ab). In one place *agriyá-* is used (ṚV 6.16.48) to denote general precedence of fire in the morning.

[28] See also ṚV 1.170.4.

It is the verbal root *dhā-* that is most frequently used to denote the production fire in connection with the adverb *purás*:

> *bṛhád váyo hí bhānáve 'rcā devā́yāgnáye* |
> *yám mitrám̐ ná práśastibhir mártāso dadhiré puráḥ* || (ṚV 5.16.1)
>
> I want to sing [about his] great power to the flame – to the god Agni whom men have placed in front like Mitra with their eulogies.[29]

These descriptions express the production of fire, evoking the image of placing fire before people.

The use of *purás* enriches the concept of fire's precedence with fire's relation to the human being, whom fire also precedes.[30] In addition, in these descriptions, the image of a group following fire is evoked, this group consisting of human beings.[31] The collective subject of these descriptions allows expanding their semantic range: it activates the general meanings of the mankind and of the first cosmogenetic creation of fire.[32]

In one stanza, *purás* is used to express the structure of fire:

> *kṛṣṇám̐ ta éma rúśataḥ puró bhā́ś cariṣṇv àrcír vápuṣām íd ékam* |
> (ṚV 4.7.9ab)
>
> Black is the path of you who are bright: light is at the front – a moving flame. It is one of your wonders.

The stanza presents fire, which goes forward, burning the earth and leaving a dark trail. At the same time, it goes upward with its

---

[29] See also ṚV 3.2.5, 6.10.1, 8.44.3, 10.140.6.

[30] Cognitive linguists show that human cognition reflected in language is deeply anthropocentric (especially the way how the world is categorized and evaluated), see Maćkiewicz 1999: 53; Tokarski 1988: 51–52; 1990: 133–134: 1991: 51.

[31] The dynamic character of fire's precedence in this context is clearly expressed also in ṚV 10.20.5.

[32] *purás* does not often directly express fire's temporal precedence. In one stanza (ṚV 6.15.7), the expression *purá adhvaré* is used, comparable to the expression *ágre yajñásya*; in another stanza (ṚV 4.15.4), *purás* expresses fire's general temporal precedence.

moving flames. *purás* denotes the front and the upper part of fire that is bright and moving.

If we compare this usage of *purás* with the usage of *ágra-* in ṚV 3.55.7ab quoted above, we see that their ranges overlap. At the same time, their usage in these specific contexts highlights different movements: *ágra-* the movement upward, *purás* the movement forward.

I would like to pay some more attention to these two stanzas. Both present fire as a fiery entity whose front and upper parts move and are bright, while the back and lower parts are still and dark.[33] Fire conceived in this way is a radial category, common for everyday thinking. This is a category that is internally differentiated into groups of more and less representative members.[34] The centre of the Ṛgvedic category of fire is constituted by the flames, which represent better fire than its base.[35] This central part is denoted by the words *ágra-* and *purás*. Denoting the best representative part of fire, they also denote its preceding part. We can say that they denote the essential part of fire, or even – its very essence.

In my opinion, the radial concept of fire, whose essence is precedence, is the basis for later identifications of fire with the head and its parts.[36] Fire in the ṚV was conceived anthropomorph-

---

[33] Thus both descriptions present fire as an internally contradictory entity consisting of opposing aspects: in ṚV 3.55.7, its upper part moves and lower part is stable; in ṚV 4.7.9ab its front and upper part moves and is bright, while its back and lower part is dark and probably does not move, although the way in the ṚV is also presented as moving (e.g. ṚV 7.75.1, see Elizarenkova 1999: 72ff.).

[34] For example the category of bird is a radial category: people usually think that a sparrow is a better representative of the bird than an ostrich (Lakoff 1987: 83, 91ff.).

[35] In the same way fire is conceived in the expression *prācā́jihva-* ('with tongue directed forwards', ṚV 1.140.3), which builds the image of fire the center of which is its tongue directed forwards. Actually, if someone asked us to draw fire, most probably we would draw its flames, that is, the part which is denoted by *purás/ágra-*.

[36] In the ṚV, fire is called 'head of the sky' (*mūrdhā́ divó, divó mūrdhán*), see ṚV 1.59.2, 6.7.1, 8.44.16. In the ŚB, fire is identified with speech: ŚB

ically and its front and upper parts denoted by *ágra-* and *purás* evoke the image of the head. The main conceptual strategy operating here is metonymy. It operates both on the level of images and concepts. On the level of images, it takes the head for the whole body. On the level of concepts, it takes the most representative part of a thing, i.e., its essence (precedence) for the whole thing (fire).

The radial concept of fire with precedence as its essence is also the reason for the identification of fire with human beings. This identification is reflected in some linguistic expressions in the ṚV, i.e., in the name *áṅgiras-* used to denote both human beings and fire.[37] In this case, the image of fire conceived anthropomorphically with its most representative part expressed in the image of the head overlaps with the image of human beings following fire. The image of the body corresponds to human beings, whereas the head corresponds to fire. Conceptual metonymy reinforces this identity: it allows taking the most representative part of the category (expressed in the image of the head, i.e., fire) for the whole category (expressed in the image of the body, i.e., the human beings). Thus the idea of their identity is implied.

3. COMPOUNDS WITH *purás*

3.1. The First Group

Now I will analyze the group of compounds with *purás*. I divide the compounds with *purás* into two groups: the first group highlights the dynamic character of fire's precedence, the second group presents it more statically.

The first group consists of the following compounds: *puraetár-*, *purogavá-*, *purogā́-* and *puroyā́van-*.[38] I quote two stanzas to show the context of these compounds:

3.2.2.13, 6.1.2.28; with head: ŚB 3.7.4.10; with mouth: ŚB 7.1.2.4; with eater: ŚB 10.6.2.2.

[37] E.g., ṚV 1.1.6, 1.31.1, 1.62.2, 1.71.2.

[38] *purogavá-*: ṚV 10.85.8; *purogā́-*: ṚV 10.124.1 and 1.188.11. The latter stanza describes Agni who goes at the head of gods. This description is very

éhy agna ihá hótā ní ṣīdā́dabdhaḥ sú puraetā́ bhavā na I (ṚV 1.76.2ab)

Come hither, Agni, sit down as a priest, be truly our leader not to be deceived.

tám marjayanta sukrátum puroyā́vānam ājíṣu I
svéṣu kṣáyeṣu vājínam II (ṚV 8.84.8)

They polish him who has good intention – the leader in the races – who conquers the prize for his settlements.

These descriptions present fire in a way similar to those that use *purás*. Fire's precedence is determined in relation to human beings: it is expressed in the image of fire that is in front of them. The descriptions strongly highlight the dynamic character of fire's precedence: both fire and the people who follow it move.

Both stanzas refer to producing fire in ritual. The first one expresses it literally, the second metaphorically, using the verb *mṛj-*, 'to rub, to polish, to clean, to adorn', to denote this act. The experiential domain of this metaphor is 'combing the horse's back'.[39] The image of a horse is here evoked by the noun *vājín-*, which in this stanza denotes fire, but also means 'steed'.

But in this stanza producing fire is not the formative event for the concept of fire's precedence. Here this concept is built on the basis of another experience connected with horses. The stanza mentions races and winning the prize, thus referring to chariot races. Since *ā́ji-* and *vā́ja-* are also used in the context of war,[40] we

---

close to the etymology of the ŚB, which also describes fire as being at the head of gods. The difference lies in the words used to denote fire's precedence: *purás* in the ṚV, *ágra-* in the ŚB.

[39] Grintser 1998: 58–59; Jurewicz 2001b: 181–183.

[40] Elizarenkova 1987. Sparreboom (1985: 14) observes: 'The oldest texts feature the chariot mainly as an instrument of conquering or raiding expeditions, warfare and chariot races. Unfortunately, the Ṛgvedic evidence on this point is more than once ambivalent, because its terminology often does not allow one to make a sharp distinction between a ceremonial race, for which the technical term is *ājí* and a raid or conquering expedition or another kind of warlike encounter, because frequently only general terms are used.' Here I use the term 'expansion' in order to denote also all kinds of warlike activities with the use of chariot,

can assume that the stanza refers not only to ritual races but also to events that took place during the Aryan expansion. The ṚV presents images of fire in the context of expansion. Fire finds the way for the Aryans, destroys their enemies and enclosures hiding riches.[41] Already Malamoud (1996: 198) has shown the importance of the expansive experience for the formation of the concept of fire's precedence (see also Heesterman 1983). I think that expansion is the main event that provides the basis for the dynamic image of fire that *goes* at the head of a group.

The following stanza containing a compound with *purás* allows us to see other aspects that build up the concept of fire's precedence on the basis of expansive events:

> *ádābhyaḥ puraetā́ viśā́m agnír mā́nuṣīṇām* |
> *tū́rṇī ráthaḥ sádā návaḥ* || (ṚV 3.11.5)
>
> Agni – the leader of tribes not to be deceived – a chariot overcoming [obstacles] and ever new.

The identification of fire with chariot is crucial here. It has a double role: it evokes the concept of expansion and at the same time builds the concept of fire's precedence in the expansive march. For the Ṛgvedic poets often expressed the wish that their chariot was in front of them, and they denoted the desired place of the chariot using the words *purás* or *purástāt*. In the stanza quoted below, the chariot is qualified with the compound *puroyā́van-*:

---

because I would presume that the experience of real war preceded its ritual expression.

[41] Fire destroys enemies; see Blair 1961: 47, 81ff.; Kaelber 1979: 192–193. Fire destroys enclosures made of rock: ṚV 8.60.16, 10.45.6. In ṚV 10.80.5 fire is presented as the main factor allowing one to move in march. See also Jurewicz 2001a: 120–128. If we activate the spatial meaning of *ágra-* in ṚV 1.31.5, we will get the image of fire which is in front of the community and which wants to overcome enemies. ṚV 1.41.3 expresses the idea of killing enemies who are in front with use of the word *purás* (although here it is not fire who kills them).

asmā́kam indra duṣṭáram puroyā́vānam ājíṣu |
sayā́vānaṃ dháne-dhane vājayántam avā rátham || (ṚV 5.35.7)

O Indra, protect our chariot – the leader in the races – difficult to overpass – which goes together in every fight – which conquers the prize.[42]

The chariot in the ṚV is an entity for which precedence is a desirable – or even normative – state. So identification of fire with the chariot is an important conceptual factor building fire's precedence.[43]

3.2. The Second Group

The second group of compounds with *purás* expresses fire's precedence more statically. It consists of two compounds: *puraḥsád-* which occurs once (ṚV 1.73.3) and *puróhita-*, used in the ṚV mostly to denote the fire.[44] My analysis shows the rational motivation of this word. Its conceptual source is the concept of fire's precedence. Its image source is the image of fire in front of people. Its lexical source is the verbal root *dhā-* used to express the production of fire together with the adverb *purás*.

We could say that *puróhita-* is the term denoting fire, which expresses its precedence on the most general level. It is not coincidental that the very first verse of the ṚV is

agním īḷe puróhitaṃ yajñásya devám ṛtvíjam |
hótāraṃ ratnadhā́tamam || (ṚV 1.1.1.)

I invoke Agni – the *puróhita-* – the god – the priest of sacrifice – the *hótar-* who yields treasures the best.

---

[42] See also ṚV 1.102.9, 6.75.6, 8.80.4, 10.39.11, 10.133.1

[43] Many sub-events of the Aryan expansion in the ṚV are metaphors for cosmogony. All the descriptions of fire quoted above imply the meaning of the first triumphant march of fire that creates the world for the Aryans, see Jurewicz 2001a.

[44] E.g., ṚV 1.1.1 (quoted below), 1.44.10, 1.94.6, 3.11.1, 8.27.1, 9.66.20.

Thus the concept of fire is 'placed before' the whole ṚV, i.e., at its beginning. Fire's precedence also incorporates its precedence in relation to the ṚV itself, as the text that describes the Aryan world of thought and culture. In my opinion, in this way the Ṛgvedic poets gave their audiences a hint how to understand the ṚV. They should listen to the ṚV having placed fire in front of them, also on the conceptual level, as the most important concept of the text.[45]

4. *pū́rva-*, *pūrvyá-* AND *prathamá-*

To denote the concept of fire's precedence the ṚV also uses the words *pū́rva-*, *pūrvyá-* and *prathamá-*. The formative experience to which the stanzas using these words refer is the production of fire, less often the expansion. Many stanzas merely state fire's precedence without enabling us to reconstruct how the concept is built.

Pū́rva- is not so often used to denote fire as *pūrvyá-* and *prathamá-*. It occurs a few times in a ritual context. In two cases it denotes fire's temporal precedence (fire is enkindled first and it sacrifices before human priests).[46] In ṚV 10.53.1, *pū́rva-* denotes fire's general precedence. There are two stanzas which seem to form a dialogue about fire's precedence: ṚV 3.17.5 mentions a *hótar-* who is before fire, who sacrifices better than fire and whose activity is the model for the activity of fire, ṚV 5.3.5 says that there is no such *hótar-* who would be before fire. In one place (ṚV 10.87.7), *pū́rva-* denotes fire's precedence in killing demons.

Pūrvyá- is much more often used to denote fire's precedence. It is used to express that fire is kindled first, that fire is the first *hótar-* and the first guest.[47] Fire is called the first among sacrifices

---

[45] The later usage of *puróhita-* to denote a priest is rooted in the Ṛgvedic identification of fire with people who follow it and who are the *ṛ́ṣis* – the poets, the seers and the priests at the same time. In the tenth *maṇḍala* of the ṚV Vasiṣṭha is called *puróhita-*. Agni is called *vásiṣṭha-* in ṚV 2.9.1, 7.1.8.

[46] ṚV 2.3.3, 10.69.4.

[47] Fire is kindled first: ṚV 3.14.3, 3.23.3. Fire is the first *hótar-* and the first guest: ṚV 1.94.6, 5.8.2, 8.23.7, 8.75.1.

(*yajñéṣu pūrvyáḥ*) and the first shining sign of the sacrifice (*yajñásya ketúḥ pūrvyáḥ*).[48] In one stanza (ṚV 1.74.2), *pūrvyá-* is used to denote fire's precedence in fight. In many stanzas, *pūrvyá-* denotes fire's general precedence.[49]

Prathamá- is very often used to denote fire as the first priest and poet (*hótar-*, *áṅgiras-*, *ṛ́ṣi-*)[50]. It is first who is worthy of sacrifice (ṚV 8.23.18). Parallel to *pūrvyá-*, *prathamá-* appears in the expression *yajñásya ketúḥ prathamáḥ.*[51] In one stanza (ṚV 8.23.22), *prathamá-* expresses fire's precedence generally. There are also two other terms expressing its precedence in the sense of being born first: *purājā́-* and *prathamajā́-*.[52]

5. CONCLUSIONS

We can see that in the ṚV, precedence is an essential feature of the concept of fire. It is built on the basis of the experience of producing fire, the sunrise, and expansion as well as on the basis of cultural models. The precedence is static and dynamic, spatial and temporal, horizontal and vertical. The main image used to express fire's precedence is the image of a group of beings (dawns, days, cows, humans) following fire. Fire's precedence fire is expressed in the ṚV with several words which themselves express precedence in all its aspects (*ágra-*, *purás* and its compounds, *pū́rva-*, *pūrvyá-* and *prathamá-*).[53]

Since fire is identified with the rising sun in the cultural model, we can include in the concept of fire's precedence the idea of east, understood as a place, as a movement eastward, and as a moment of time. This idea finds its basis also in another event that is forma-

---

[48] Fire is the first among sacrifices: ṚV 8.23.22, 8.39.8, 8.60.2, 8.102.10. Fire is the first shining sign of the sacrifice: 3.11.3.

[49] E.g., ṚV 3.1.20, 5.15.1, 6.14.1, 8.7.36, 8.31.14, 8.39.3.

[50] E.g., ṚV 1.31.1,2, 3.4.3, 6.9.4, 10.88.4.

[51] ṚV 3.29.5, 10.122.4.

[52] *prathamajā́-*: 10.5.7; *purājā́-*: 10.5.5.

[53] See Jurewicz 2003a.

tive for fire's precedence, namely, expansion, the idea of which, as Malamoud has shown, includes the idea of movement forward and eastward.[54] The idea of east, incorporated in the concept of fire's precedence, finds its lexical expression in the usage of *purás* and *purástāt* in the ṚV, which denote the place where the dawn and the sun go.[55] Also *pū́rva-* is used to denote the eastern part of the sky.[56]

The etymologies in the ŚB refer to this concept of fire. The links on the conceptual, imagerial and lexical levels are evident. The concept of precedence is preserved and included in the definition of fire. But the precedence is narrowed to spatial and horizontal precedence. Temporal precedence is conceived in terms of spatial precedence. The idea of east is totally lost.

To explain the precedence, the ŚB uses the Ṛgvedic image of fire at the head of a group. Among the different words expressing fire's precedence, the ŚB chooses the word *ágra-* which is closest to *agní-* phonetically and which in the Brāhmaṇas expresses cosmogonic primordiality.[57]

---

[54] See Malamoud 1996: 198. Malamoud refers to ŚB 1.4.1.10–17 which clearly shows that the expansion was led eastward (*prāñc-*). This passage also expresses the predominant role of fire in the expansion which made the earth cultivable after fire had burnt it. See also Heesterman 1983.

[55] *purás*: ṚV 10.171.4, 5.82.8, 7.62.2; *purástāt*, the dawn: ṚV 1.123.10, 4.51.1, 2, 8, 5.80.4, 7.67.2, 7.78.3; the sun: 1.191.8, 10.139.1. *purástāt* is once used to express fire's precedence in the image of fire which goes in front (ṚV 3.27.7). Since *purástāt* is very often used to denote the place where the dawn and the sun are, the meaning of east can also be evoked in this stanza which in that case describes not only fire which burns in front of people, but also fire which burns on the eastern side of the altar (as ritual fire) and on the eastern part of the sky (as the rising sun).

[56] ṚV 1.92.1, 1.124.5.

[57] See Gonda 1982. This meaning can be seen already in the late ṚV (10.121.1, 10.129.3,4). See Jurewicz 2003a.

REFERENCES

AJDUKIEWICZ, Kazimierz 1965. *Logika pragmatyczna*. Warszawa: Państwowe Wydawnictwo Naukowe.

AUBOYER, Jeanine 1949. *Le trône et son symbolisme dans l'Inde ancienne*. Paris: Presses Universitaires de France.

BLACKBURN, Simon 1997. *Oksfordzki słownik filozoficzny* (*The Oxford Dictionary of Philosophy*). Warszawa: Książka i Wiedza. (OUP 1994.)

BLAIR, Chauncey J. 1961. *Heat in the Rig Veda and Atharva Veda. A General Survey with Particular Attention to Some Aspects and Problems*. (American Oriental Series 45.) New Haven: American Oriental Society.

EGGELING, Julius (trans.) 1882–1900. *The Śatapatha Brāhmaṇa according to the text of the Mādhyandina school*, I-V. (Sacred Books of the East, 12, 26, 41, 43, 44.) Oxford: Clarendon Press.

ELIZARENKOVA, Tatyana Ya. 1987. Notes on contests in the Ṛgveda. *ABORI* 99–109.

—— 1995. *Rigveda. Izbrannye gimny. Mandaly V-VIII*. Moskva: Nauka.

—— 1999. *Slova i veschi v Rigvede*. Moskva: Izdatel'skaya firma 'Vostochnaya literatura' RAN.

GONDA, Jan 1955–1956. The etymologies in the ancient Indian Brāhmaṇas. *Lingua* 5: 61–83.

—— 1975. *Vedic Literature (Saṃhitās and Brāhmaṇas)*. (A History of Indian Literature, 1.1.) Wiesbaden: Otto Harrassowitz.

GRINTSER, P. A. 1998. *Tajnyj jazyk 'Rigvedy'*. Moskva: Rossijskij gosudarstvennyj gumanitarnyj universitet.

HEESTERMANN, J. C. 1983. Other folks fire. In: Frits Staal, *Agni. The Vedic Ritual of the Fire Altar*, II: 76–94. Berkeley: Asian Humanities Press.

HOLLAND, Dorothy & Naomi QUINN 1987. *Cultural Models in Language and Thought*. Cambridge: Cambridge University Press.

JUREWICZ, Joanna 2001a. *Kosmogonia Rygwedy. Myśl i metafora*. ['The cosmogony of the Ṛgveda. Thought and metaphor.'] Warszawa: Wydawnictwo Naukowe *Semper*.

—— 2001b. Metafora w 'Rygwedzie'. ['Metaphor in the Ṛgveda.'] *Studia Semiotyczne* 23: 175–191.

—— 2003a. Rygwedyjskie pojęcie *ágra* ['The Ṛgvedic notion *ágra*.'] *Studia Indologiczne* 10: 78–97.

—— 2003b. Język tajemny rytuału jako próba definiowania pojęć w starożytnych tekstach indyjskich (brahmany). ['The secret language of the ritual as an attempt to define concepts in ancient Indian texts (Brāhmaṇas).'] *Studia Semiotyczne* 25: 213–227.

KAELBER, Walter O. 1979. *Tapas* and purification in early Hinduism. *Numen* 24.2: 192–214.

KUIPER, F. B. J. 1960. Ancient Indian verbal contest. *IIJ* 4: 217–281.

LAKOFF, George 1987. *Women, Fire, and Dangerous Things. What Categories Reveal about the Mind*. Chicago: The University of Chicago Press.

LAKOFF George & Mark JOHNSON 1980. *Metaphors We Live by*. Chicago: The University of Chicago Press.

LAKOFF George & Mark JOHNSON 1999. *Philosophy in the Flesh. The Embodied Mind and Its Challenge to Western Thought*. New York: Basic Books.

MACDONELL, Arthur A. 1897. *Vedic Mythology*. (Grundriss der indo-arischen Philologie und Altertumskunde III.1.A.) Strassburg: Karl J. Trübner.

MAĆKIEWICZ, Jolanta 1999. Kategoryzacja ą językowy obraz świata. In: Jerzy Bartmiński (ed.), *Językowy obraz świata*: 47–56. Lublin: Wydawnictwo Uniwersytetu Marii Curie-Skłodowskiej.

MALAMOUD, Charles 1996. *Cooking the World. Ritual and Thought in Ancient India*. Delhi: OUP.

OLDENBERG, Hermann 1988. *The Religion of the Veda*. Trans. by Shridhar B. Shrotri. Delhi: MLBD. [German original: *Die Religion des Veda*. Berlin: W. Hertz, 1894.]

RADDEN, Guenter 1992. The cognitive approach to natural language. In: Martin Puetz (ed.), *Thirty Years of Linguistic Evolution*: 513–541. Amsterdam: John Benjamins Publishing Co.

SPARREBOOM, M. 1985. *Chariots in the Veda*. (Memoirs of the Kern Institute 3.) Leiden: E. J. Brill.

SRINIVASAN, Doris 1979. *Concept of Cow in the Rigveda*. Delhi: MLBD.

TOKARSKI, Ryszard 1988. Konotacja jako składnik treści słowa. In: Jerzy Bartmiński (ed.), *Konotacja*: 35–53. Lublin: Wydawnictwo Uniwersytetu Marii Skłodowskiej-Curie.

—— 1990. Prototypy i konotacje. O semantycznej analizie słowa w tekście poetyckim. *Pamiętnik Literacki* 81.2: 117–137.

—— 1991. Poziomy konotacji semantycznej. In: Jadwiga Puzynina & Jerzy Bartmiński, *Język a kultura. Zagadnienia leksykalne i aksjologiczne*, II: 45–51. Wrocław: Wiedza o kulturze.

WEBER, Albrecht (ed.) 1855. *The Çatapatha-Brāhmaṇa in the Mādhyandina-çākhā with Extracts from the Commentaries of Sāyaṇa, Harasvāmin and Dvidevaganga*. (The White Yajurveda, 2.) Berlin: Ferd. Dümmler's Verlagsbuchhandlung – London: Williams and Norgate.

The Upanayana and the 'Repeated Upanayana(s)'

MIEKO KAJIHARA

1. INTRODUCTION

The ritual by which one becomes a Vedic student (*brahmacārín*) is first referred to in the Atharvaveda.[1] Through the ritual, one becomes a student entitled to learn the sacred knowledge of the Veda from his teacher. In the late Vedic texts (the Gṛhyasūtras and the Dharmasūtras), the initiation ritual Upanayana is treated as a major rite of passage, which the male members of the three upper classes (Brāhmaṇa, Kṣatriya/Rājanya, Vaiśya) should go through in their youth.

On the other hand, we find in the Vedic literature that in some cases the initiation ritual can be undergone more than once in one's life. The types of such a 'repeated initiation' and the occasions for their performance are not uniform. The best-known 'repeated initiation' is the Punarupanayana attested in the Dharma texts, but

---

[1] AV(Ś) 11.5.3 / AV(P) 16.153.2 (for this verse, see section 2.1 below). In the early Vedic texts, the initiation of the Vedic student is referred to by the verbs *úpa-nī* [Ā] 'to make someone one's own student' (AV+); *úpa-nī* [P] 'to make someone enter [the *brahmacárya*]' (ŚB 11+); *úpa-i* 'to approach [a teacher], i.e., to become his student' (Br+), 'to enter [the *brahmacárya*]' (Br+), 'to approach a teacher (acc.) for the *brahmacarya* (acc.)' (JUB 1.42.1). The term *upanayana* for the Vedic student's initiation ritual is first attested in the Gṛhyasūtras. Besides *upanayana* (< *úpa-nī*), *upāyana* (< *úpa-i*) is also sometimes used for the ritual (BĀU 6.2.7; KāṭhGS 41.1; MGS 1.22.1; ĀpGS 6.16.4). For the initiation of the Vedic student, see Gonda 1965; 1979; Kane 1974: 268–312; Watase 1993.

there are also some other types of 'repeated initiation' mentioned in the Veda. Why and when should an initiation be repeated, and why such a variety is found? In the present paper, I will investigate these questions by examining the initiation and the 'repeated initiation' of different types in various strata of the Vedic literature. As we will find below, this investigation will lead to a more fundamental question, that is, what kind of functions the Upanayana served in the Vedic social institutions.

2. THE UPANAYANA IN THE TEXTS BEFORE THE GṚHYASŪTRAS

2.1. The Initiation Ritual in the Atharvaveda

The Atharvaveda includes a hymn of praise to the Vedic student, the so-called *brahmacārín* hymn, in its old stratum. It extols the Vedic student, on a cosmic scale, as a great figure whose activities are compared with those of the sun.[2]

In the hymn, the teacher is said to make the *brahmacārín* his embryo when he initiates him:

> *ācāryà upanáyamāno brahmacāríṇaṃ kṛṇute gárbham antáḥ* |
> *táṃ rā́trīs tisrá udáre bibharti táṃ jātáṃ drá̄ṣṭum abhisáṃyanti devā́ḥ* ||
> (AV[Ś] 11.5.3; AV[P] 16.153.2)
>
> The teacher, initiating [him as his own Vedic student], makes the *brahmacārín* an embryo within. He bears him in his womb for three nights. The gods gather to see him when he has been born.

This verse depicts the process of the initiate's being reborn from his teacher as a new figure fit for the *bráhman* after a sort of consecration period (three nights in this case). The idea of the student's rebirth from his teacher after a certain period at the time of his initiation is to be found also in the post-Atharvavedic texts, as we will see below.

---

[2] AV(Ś) 11.5; AV(P) 16.153–155. For this hymn, see Kajihara 1995.

In this hymn, the *brahmacārín* (1) knows the *bráhman* and protects the knowledge of the *bráhman*, (2) serves his teacher, (3) is closely connected with fire, the sun and the heat/asceticism (*tápas*) through the firewood, and (4) is characterized by his girdle (*mékhalā*), hide and mendicancy. In addition to the above direct reference to the initiation, many of his attributes and activities mentioned in this hymn are later found incorporated in the Upanayana of the Gṛhyasūtras as ritual elements.[3]

Besides this hymn, the Atharvaveda also contains throughout its strata several *mantras* which appear to be concerned, directly or indirectly, with the *brahmacārín* rituals including the Upanayana.[4]

2.2. The Initiation Ritual in the Brāhmaṇas

It is in the Brāhmaṇa texts that we first find a more or less coherent procedure of the ritual of the Vedic student's initiation. Two of the Yajurvedic Brāhmaṇas preserve comparatively long passages on ritual procedures of the initiation, in a supplementary book of the Brāhmaṇa of the Vājasaneyins (ŚB 11.5.4), and in a fragment of the Brāhmana of the Kaṭhas (KaṭhB[*u*]).[5]

[3] AV(Ś) 11.5.4 / AV(P) 16.153.4 (*mékhalā;* cf. AV[Ś] 6.133 / AV[P] 5.33); AV(Ś) 11.5.6 / AV(P) 16.153.6 (hide); AV(Ś) 11.5.4, 6, 9, 13 / AV(P) 16.153.4, 6, 8; 16.154.4 (firewood; cf. AV 19.64); AV(Ś) 11.5.9 / AV(P) 16.153.8 (mendicancy; cf. AV[Ś] 6.133.3 / AV[P] 5.33.3).

[4] AV(Ś) 2.13 / AV(P) 15.5–6 (the ritual formulas for putting on a new garment, stepping on a stone, taking away the old garment, wishing for a long life. For this hymn, see Kajihara 2004); AV(P) 20.41.7, 44.1, 48.9, 49.1–3 [20.46.1, 52.9, 53.1–3 in the Orissa mss.] (the formulas for calling for the *brahmacārins*, seizing the initiate's hand, admitting him as his own student, entrusting him to the god Savitṛ. For these formulas in AV[P] 20, see Kajihara 2011; cf. 2014); cf. AV(Ś) 6.133 / AV(P) 5.33 (*mékhalā*); AV(Ś) 6.108 / AV(P) 19.17 (wishing for *medhā́* 'intellectual power'); AV(Ś) 19.64 (putting firewood into the fire).

[5] The Kaṭhas are supposed to have had, in addition to the *Kāṭhakasaṃhitā* which includes Brāhmaṇa-prose portions, a separate *Kaṭhabrāhmaṇa*, which has been lost but for some fragments; see Renou 1947: 144–146, 174, 177; Tsuji 1970: 52, 154 (notes 488–490); Witzel 2004: xi–xiv. For the text of the *Kaṭhabrāhmaṇa* fragments, see Schroeder 1898; Caland 1920; Sūryakānta 1943; Rosenfield 2004; cf. Witzel 1977; 1979; 1980 (*Kaṭhaśikṣā-Upaniṣad*); 2004

It appears that, by the time of these Brāhmaṇa passages, the initiation came to include a series of ritual actions, and became an elaborate ritual close to the Upanayana in the Gṛhyasūtras, though it is quite possible that the extant Upanayana passages in the Brāhmaṇas may not cover all of the ritual at that time. The main procedures of the ritual presupposed in these Brāhmaṇas are:[6]

1) the student declares his entering the *brahmacárya*
2) the teacher asks his name
3) the teacher seizes his hand and admits him as his student
4) the teacher utters the *vyāhṛtis*
5) the teacher entrusts him to the deities
6) he gives him instructions on the student's life[7]
7) he teaches him the Sāvitrī verse.[8]

(*Kaṭha-Āraṇyaka*). The fragment of the *Kaṭhabrāhmaṇa* on the Upanayana is called *Upanayanabrāhmaṇa* (KaṭhB[*u*]; henceforth referred to by the pages and lines of the Sūryakānta's edition).

[6] The major topics occur in the following places:

Major topics	ŚB	KaṭhB(*u*)
The student's entering the *brahmacárya*	11.5.4.1	47.1
The teacher's asking his name	11.5.4.1	47.2
The teacher's seizing his hand	11.5.4.2	
The teacher's admitting him as his student	11.5.4.2	
The teacher's uttering the *vyāhṛtis*		47.3
The teacher's entrusting him to the deities	11.5.4.3–4	48.1
The teacher's giving him instructions	11.5.4.5	49.5
The teacher's teaching him the Sāvitrī	11.5.4.6–15	50.10
Discussion on intercourse and honey	11.5.4.16–18	

[7] 'You are a *brahmacārín*' (*brahmacāry àsi*) (ŚB, KaṭhB[*u*]);
'Drink water' (*apò 'śāna*) (ŚB [twice], KaṭhB[*u*]);
'Do your work' (*kárma kuru*) (ŚB, KaṭhB[*u*]);
'Put firewood [into the fire]' (*samídham ā́dhehi*) (ŚB);
'Do not sleep [in the daytime]' (ŚB: *mā́ suṣupthās*; KaṭhB[*u*]: *dívā mā́ suṣupsīs*);
'Restrain speech' (*vācaṃ yaccha*) (KaṭhB[*u*]).

[8] The Sāvitrī ('a verse dedicated to the god Savitṛ') is a verse regarded as particularly sacred. It is usually ṚV 3.62.10, which is also called Gāyatrī after its meter: cf. JUB 4.28; *Gāyatrībrāhmaṇa* (one of the *Kaṭhabrāhmaṇa* fragments; see Sūryakānta 1943: 118ff.). Though Sāvitrīs of other meters are also occasionally mentioned, that in the *gāyatrī* meter is regarded as the best: see ŚB 11.5.4.13, 14.8.15.8; BĀU 5.14.5; cf. TĀ 2.11.8. The lesson of the Sāvitrī at the

The old idea that the *brahmacārín* is born again at the time of initiation after a period of pregnancy is found also in these Brāhmaṇas, especially in connection with the teaching of the Sāvitrī. The teacher is said to generate the newly-initiated student from his mouth.[9] The *brahmacārín* is said to be born from his teacher, together with the Sāvitrī, after a year or a period considered identical to a year (for example after three nights, as in the Atharvavedic *brahmacārín* hymn).[10]

---

initiation is first referred to in the Brāhmaṇas on the Upanayana without quoting nor specifying the text of the verse (ŚB 11.5.4.6–15; KaṭhB[*u*] 50.10–52.6) (ŚB 11.5.4.13 specifies that the Sāvitrī's meter should be *gāyatrī*). The Sāvitrī lesson at the Upanayana is prescribed in the Gṛhyasūtras of all the schools. Some mention the Sāvitrīs in three different meters for the three upper classes respectively (*gāyatrī, triṣṭubh, jagatī*); see ŚGS 2.5.4ff.; KauṣGS 2.3.2ff.; VārGS 5.26 (with the *pratīkas* of three verses); PGS 2.3.7–10; BDhS 1.2.3.11; cf. MGS 1.22.13, 1.2.3; ĀśvGS 1.22.29 (a Sāvitrī in *anuṣṭubh*; see footnote 27 below); see also Oldenberg's notes on his translation of ŚGS 2.2.1 (on the age of initiation and the meters), 2.5.4–6, 2.7.10 (Oldenberg 1886: 59, 66, 70); Mookerji 1947: 182f.; Kane 1974: 302–304. For the Sāvitrī in various traditions, see Kajihara, forthcoming 2. For the Upanayana and the Sāvitrī, cf. Falk 1988.

9 ŚB 11.5.4.17; cf. 11.5.4.6–11, 12, 14.

10 KaṭhB(*u*) 50.10 *sá vā́ eṣá brahmacārī́ sāvitryā́ sahá prájāyate. tád āhuḥ. saṃvatsaré 'nūcyā́. saṃvatsaré vái rétāṃsi siktā́ni prájāyanta íty.* 'This *brahmacārín* is born together with the Sāvitrī. They say about it: "[The Sāvitrī] should be taught after a year. The emitted semens are born after a year"': cf. ŚB 11.5.4.6 (teaching the Sāvitrī to the initiate after a year is equal to putting speech in a newborn who is born after a year); 11.5.4.7–11; ŚB 11.5.4.12 *tád ápi ślókaṃ gāyanti | ācāryò garbhī́ bhavati hástam ādhā́ya dákṣiṇam, tṛtī́yasyām̐ sá jāyate sāvitryā́ sahá brāhmaṇá íti.* 'On this, they also sing a *śloka*: "The teacher, having laid his right hand, becomes pregnant. On the third [night], he (the initiate) is born as a Brāhmaṇá together with the Sāvitrī".' As for the pregnancy or preparation period before the Sāvitrī lesson, these Brāhmaṇas mention various lengths, which they identify with a year: a year (ŚB, KaṭhB), 6 months (ŚB), 24 days (ŚB), 12 days (ŚB, KaṭhB), 6 days (ŚB), and 3 days (ŚB, KaṭhB). The KaṭhB concludes that one should teach the Sāvitrī after 3 nights (50.12), while the ŚB rejects the *śloka* of the Sāvitrī lesson on the third night (see above) and finally prescribes that the lesson should be on the same day (11.5.4.12).

3. THE UPANAYANA IN THE GṚHYASŪTRAS AND THE DHARMASŪTRAS

All the Gṛhyasūtras and the Dharmasūtras give prescriptions on the Upanayana.[11] The Gṛhyasūtras contain detailed descriptions of the ritual procedure of the Upanayana of their own schools. Among the Gṛhyasūtras, those of the Kaṭhas and the Vājasaneyins, whose Brāhmaṇas preserve passages on the Upanayana (see section 2.2), furnish useful hints as to how the ritual developed, being based on the prescriptions in their Brāhmaṇas, adding to them various ritual actions and rules. In the case of the Vājasaneyins, the Upanayana in their Gṛhyasūtra (PGS) corresponds to that in their Brāhmaṇa (ŚB 11.5.4) roughly as follows:

PGS	Prescribed actions/topics	ŚB
2.2.1–5	Age for initiation; preparation	
2.2.6	The initiate announces his entering the *brahmacarya*	11.5.4.1
2.2.7	Giving him a new garment	
2.2.8–10	Binding a girdle on him	
2.2.11–13	Giving him a staff	
2.2.14	Filling his hand with water (cf. Kajihara 2014)	
2.2.15	Letting him look at the sun	
2.2.16	Touching his heart	
2.2.17–18	Asking his name	11.5.4.1
2.2.17	Seizing his right hand	11.5.4.2
2.2.19–20	Admitting him as a student	11.5.4.2
2.2.21	Entrusting him to the deities	11.5.4.3–4
2.3.1–2	Stepping around the fire; offering oblation	
2.3.2	Giving him instructions on the student's life	11.5.4.5
2.3.3–10	Teaching him the Sāvitrī	11.5.4.6–15
2.4.1–8	Putting firewood into the fire	
2.5.1–8	Mendicancy	
2.5.9–43	Other rules	cf. 11.5.4.18

[11] ĀśvGS 1.19–22; ŚGS 2.1–6; KauṣGS 2.1–3; GGS 2.10; KhGS 2.4; JGS 1.12; KāṭhGS 41; MGS 1.22; VārGS 5; BGS 2.5; BhārGS 1.1–10; ĀpGS 4.10–11; HGS 1.1.1–1.2.8; ĀgGS 1.1.1–4; VaiGS 2.3–8; PGS 2.2–5; KauśS 55–57; ĀpDhS 1.1.1ff.; BDhS 1.2.3; GauDhS 1; VāsDhS 11.49ff.

As for the first lesson of the Sāvitrī, half of the Gṛhyasūtras retain the old custom of the initiate's passing a certain period before the lesson as stated in the Brāhmaṇas.[12]

The most significant feature of the Upanayana in the Gṛhyasūtras and the Dharma texts is that it is treated as a rite of passage to be performed at a specific point in one's life.[13] According to them, the boys of the three upper classes should undergo the ritual in their childhood: the Brāhmaṇas generally at the age of seven or eight, the Kṣatriyas at eleven, and the Vaiśyas at twelve.[14] Especially in the Dharmasūtras, the Upanayana is regarded as the crucial ritual by which one is initiated into the status of a member of the three upper classes. As such, the ritual was allowed only to the youth of those classes, so that it functioned as a device to differentiate the three upper classes from the class that was excluded from it (Śūdra). Those who have the privilege of performing the Upanayana are called *dvija*s 'those who have two births' after the old idea of being reborn at the initiation.[15]

---

[12] ŚGS (1 year / 3 nights / immediately); KauṣGS (do.); JGS (3 nights / immediately); MGS (3 nights / 2 nights / 1 night / 1 year / 12 days / 6 days / 3 days / immediately); BGS (the *sāvitravrata* before the Sāvitrī lesson); BhārGS (1 year / 12 nights / 3 nights / immediately); HGS (3 days / immediately); ĀgGS (3 days / immediately); PGS (1 year / 6 months / 24 days / 12 days / 6 days / 3 days / immediately). Some prescribe also a certain period of *vrata* after the Upanayana: ĀśvGS (3 days / 12 days / 1 year); GGS (3 days); KhGS (3 days); JGS (3 nights); VārGS (12 days / 6 days); BGS (3 days / 3 nights); BhārGS (3 nights); ĀpGS (3 days); HGS (3 days); ĀgGS (3 days); cf. KāṭhGS 41.23; VaiGS 2.7. Some mention the initate's keeping standing for the rest of the day: ĀśvGS, GGS, KhGS, KāṭhGS, PGS (*ity eke*).

[13] Before the Gṛhyasūtras, few mentions are found as to the age for one's first initiation. The *brahmacārín* hymn of the Atharvaveda describes the Vedic student as having a long beard and pouring semen, which imply his maturity (AV[Ś] 11.5.6, 12; AV[P] 16.153.6, 154.2). In ChU 6.1.2, Śvetaketu Āruṇeya is said to have been initiated at the age of twelve.

[14] Mookerji 1947: 174f.; Kane 1974: 274–276; cf. Oldenberg 1886: 59 (on the correspondence between the ages of initiation of the three upper classes and the number of syllables in the meters *gāyatrī*, *triṣṭubh* and *jagatī* 'which are so very frequently stated to correspond to the three castes').

[15] VaiGS 6.7 *dvitīyajanmany ācāryaḥ pitā sāvitrī mātā. dvābhyāṃ janmabhyāṃ dvijo bhavati.* 'At the second birth, the teacher is his father, and the

The initiation ritual in the Atharvaveda and the Brāhmaṇas was not described as a ritual to be performed at a specific age; still, as seen above, it was a crucial epoch-making ritual in one's life, by which he was reborn as a new figure fit for the *bráhman*. This aspect of the initiation ritual in those older texts continues into the Upanayana as a rite of passage in the Sūtra texts.

4. THE INITIATION REPEATED FOR FURTHER LEARNING

4.1. The Initiation Ritual in the Upaniṣads

On the other hand, some late Brāhmaṇas and the Upaniṣads occasionally mention a particular type of initiation ritual that is some-

---

Sāvitrī is his mother. He becomes a *dvija* through the two births.' Cf. BDhS 1.11.21.14 (*dvijanman-*); GauDhS 1.1.9 (1.8) (*dvitīya- janman-*); VāsDhS 2.2 (*dvijāti-*); Manu 2.68 (*dvijāti-*); 2.169–170 (three births of *dvija*); YSm 1.10 (*dvija-*); 39 (*dvija-*); cf. also BDhS 1.2.3.6; ĀpDhS 1.1.1.16–18; VāsDhS 2.3; Manu 2.146–148. The word *dvijá-* is first attested in a late stratum of the Atharvaveda (AV[Ś] 19.71.1). The words *dvijánman-* and *dvijā́-* appear in the Ṛgveda referring to Agni etc. (RV 1.60.1, 140.2, 149.4f.; 6.50.2; 10.61.19). Since the Brāhmaṇas onward, the sacrificer (*yajamāna*) of *soma* rituals is said to become an embryo at the consecration called *dīkṣā* and be reborn at the ritual. It is principally this rebirth at the *soma* rituals that is discussed as the second birth of a man in the Brāhmaṇas and Upaniṣads; for example, JB 1.259 *dvir ha vai yajamāno jāyate. mithunād anyaj jāyate yajñād anyat.* 'The sacrificer is born two times. On one hand, from copulation, and on the other hand, from ritual'; cf. ŚB 11.2.1.1 (cf. ŚB[K] 3.2.4.2) (a man is born three times, first from his mother and father, then when he performs ritual, and then when he dies); JUB 3.8.9 (a man is born three times: from his father, mother and ritual); cf. JUB 3.8.10–3.9.7; 3.11 (three births and deaths); see also Ikari 1989. Some editions and manuscripts of the *Carakasaṃhitā* mention the third birth of physicians on their completing medical training, in CS Cikitsāsthāna 1.4.52 (*vidyāsamāptau bhiṣajas tṛtīyā jātir ucyate*), 1.4.51 (*trijāti-*), 1.4.53 (*trija-*), while the vulgate edition by Trikamji reads *dvitīyā jātir*, *dvijāti-*, *dvija-* respectively; cf. Yano 1988: 235; Scharfe 2002: 262f. According to Dr. Philipp Maas, the readings *dvitīya-* etc. appear to be of archetypal origin and therefore they represent most probably an earlier stage of transmission of the CS than the readings *tṛtīya-* etc. (personal communication. Sep. 2011. I hereby thank him for checking the mss. of the CS for me). For the initiation of medical students, see SuśS 1.2; CS Vimānasthāna 8.9ff.; also Mookerji 1947: 345f.; Gonda 1965: 321f.; cf. Preisendanz 2007.

what different from the Upanayana discussed above. It is an initiation performed by learned and mature scholars. Unlike the Upanayana developed since the Atharvaveda through the Brāhmaṇas to the Gṛhyasūtras and the Dharma texts as a rite of passage, this particular type of initiation mentioned in the late Brāhmaṇas and the Upaniṣads is not one's first initiation performed at a specific point in his life.

This type of initiation is found in the context of stories related to the introduction of new and often esoteric rituals and ritual speculations told in those texts. The most typical pattern is that, when a scholar hears about a novel doctrine which he does not know, he goes to someone who knows it and asks for initiation so that he can learn it from him. A similar pattern is found at the end of some theological debates: the loser asks the winner to make him his pupil and teach him. One of the earliest mentions of this type of initiation is found in the tenth book of the *Śatapathabrāhmaṇa*.[16]

In the stories of these patterns, those who ask for initiation are often famous scholars, or sometimes even gods. They are not very young boys but grown-ups, who have already acquired standard knowledge of the Veda. In other words, this type of initiation found in the Upaniṣads is obviously not one's first initiation in his life, but is a repeated one.[17]

---

[16] ŚB 10.6.1.2–3: the scholars who were discussing the *vaiśvānará* did not reach a solid conclusion and decided to ask Aśvapati Kaikeya for teaching; they went to him with firewood in hand and asked for initiation, saying 'we shall approach you; i.e., become your pupils (*úpa tvāyāma*)' (cf. footnote 20). For this type of initiation found in the late Brāhmaṇas and the Upaniṣads, cf. Watase 1993: 79–89; Scharfe 2002: 297; Kajihara 2003a: 5–9; Kajihara, in press; Kajihara, forthcoming 1; cf. also Heesterman 1968.

[17] Only few Upaniṣads mention one's first initiation. Śvetaketu Āruṇeya is said to be initiated at the age of twelve in ChU 6.1.2 (without a description of the initiation ritual). The initiation of Satyakāma Jābāla by Hāridrumata Gautama, told in ChU 4.4, may be the former's first initiation. There, the following procedure is described:

1) Satyakāma announces his entering the *brahmacarya*, saying 'I shall live the *brahmacarya* at your place (*brahmacaryam bhagavati vatsyāmi*)';

This type of initiation, which I shall call 'the scholars' initiation', could be repeated as many times as needed, whenever one encountered a novel doctrine to learn.[18] Such a doctrine is often introduced as what has been unknown to the traditional Vedic teachers. Probably in relation to this, the people who play the role of the teacher in this kind of stories are not always limited to the Brāhmaṇas who traditionally monopolized the sacred knowledge; sometimes Kṣatriyas or other people teach the scholars.[19]

The ritual procedure of 'scholars' [repeated] initiation' is described as being much simpler than that depicted in the Brāhmaṇas on the Upanayana discussed above (section 2.2). Bringing firewood in hand and/or asking for initiation by words are often the only ritual elements. The following is an overview of the initiation procedure:

---

2) he asks Gautama for initiation, saying 'I would like to approach you (i.e., become your pupil) (*upeyāṃ bhagavantam*)';

3) the latter asks his *gotra*;

4) Satyakāma brings firewood.

It is, however, not the traditional Veda but an esoteric teaching on the *brahman* that Satyakāma learns after this initiation, first from a bull, then fire, a goose, a Madgu bird, and finally from his teacher. This story uses the common motif of the typical Upaniṣadic initiation stories, in which one is said to learn a brand-new teaching from a non-traditional teacher after an initiation.

[18] It is said that Indra approached Prajāpati with firewood in hand (for this ritual action, see below) in order to learn four times in total in ChU 8.7.2ff. Āruṇi (Gautama) asked several teachers for initiation: ŚB 11.4.1.9 (Svaidāyana); KauṣU 1.1 (Citra Gārgyāyaṇi); BĀU 6.2.7 (Pravāhaṇa Jaivali); cf. ChU 5.11 (cf. ŚB 10.6.1); JUB 1.42.1 (Vāsiṣṭha Caikitāneya).

[19] ChU 5.11.7 (King Aśvapati teaches Brāhmaṇa scholars; however, without initiating (*anupanīya*) them; cf. ŚB 10.6.1.2); cf. the non-human teachers of Satyakāma Jābāla in ChU 4.4 (see footnote 17). As to the Kṣatriyas' teaching the Brāhmaṇas, see BĀU 2.1.15; KauṣU 4.18; cf. ChU 5.11.7; BĀU 6.2.7–8; ChU 5.3.6–7; JB 1.22; ChāgU 3. In ŚB 11.4.1.9, a teaching is given without initiation though the teacher is a Brāhmaṇa; cf. ŚB 11.4.2.20. For the background of the Kṣatriya-teaches-Brāhmaṇa stories in the Upaniṣads, see Bodewitz 1973: 215ff.; Watase 1993: 87f.; Bronkhorst 2007: 112–135; cf. Witzel 1987; Sakamoto-Gotō 2000; 2001.

1) Bringing firewood + Asking for initiation:
ŚB 10.6.1.2, 11.4.1.9, 11.5.3.13; GB 1.1.32, 1.2.13, 1.3.8; KauṣU 1.1, 4.18; cf. ChU 4.4[20]
2) Asking for initiation:
ŚB 11.4.2.20, 14.1.1.21; GB 1.1.32, 1.3.14; BĀU 2.1.14, 6.2.7; ChāgU 3[21]
3) Bringing firewood:
ChU 5.11.7, 8.7.2ff.; PraśU 1.1; MuU 1.2.12[22]

---

[20] ŚB 10.6.1.2: Aruṇa Aupaveśi, Satyayajña Pauluṣi, Mahāśāla Jābāla, Buḍila Āśvatarāśvi, Indradyumna Bhāllaveya and Jana Śārkarākṣya ask Aśvapati Kaikeya for initiation with firewood in hand (*samítpāṇi-*) in order to learn the *vaiśvānará*, saying '*úpa tvāyāma*' (cf. ChU 5.11.7; see footnote 22); ŚB 11.4.1.9: Uddālaka Āruṇi asks Svaidāyana for initiation with firewood in hand (*samítpāṇi-*) to learn the answer to the questions the latter asked, saying '*úpa tvāyāni*'; ŚB 11.5.3.13: Śauceya Prācīnayogya asks Uddālaka Āruṇi for initiation, showing firewood, saying '*imā́ni samitkāṣṭhā́ny úpāyāni bhágavantam*', and the latter utters the *vyāhṛtis* to him; GB 1.1.32: Maitreya asks Maudgalya for initiation with firewood in hand (*samitpāṇi-*), saying '*tvām upaiṣyāmi śāntiṃ kariṣyāmi*'; GB 1.2.13, 1.3.8 (*samitpāṇi-*) '*upāyāmo bhavantam*'; KauṣU 1.1: Āruṇi (Gautama) asks Citra Gārgyāyaṇi for initiation with firewood in hand (*samitpāṇi-*) to learn the so-called *devayāna/pitṛyāna* theory etc., saying '*upāyāni*'; KauṣU 4.18: Gārgya Bālāki asks Ajātaśatru Kāśya for initiation with firewood in hand (*samitpāṇi-*) to learn the *brahman*, saying '*upāyāni*' (cf. BĀU 2.1.14; see footnote 21). For ChU 4.4, see footnote 17.

[21] ŚB 11.4.2.20: Śaulbāyana asks Ayasthūṇa for initiation, saying '*úpa tvāyāni*', in order to learn a teaching on *srucs*; ŚB 14.1.1.21: the Aśvins ask Dadhyañc for initiation, saying '*úpa tvāyāva*', to learn the replacement of the head of ritual (in relation to the cryptic Pravargya); GB 1.1.32: '*upāyāmi tv eva bhavantam*'; 1.3.14: '*upayāmi tv eva bhavantam*'; BĀU 2.1.14: Dṛptabālāki Gārgya asks Ajātaśatru Kāśya for initiation, saying '*upa tvāyāni*', to learn the *brahman* (cf. KauṣU 4.18; see footnote 20); BĀU 6.2.7: Gautama (Āruṇi) asks Pravāhaṇa Jaivali for initiation, saying '*upaimy ahaṃ bhavantam*', to learn the so-called *pañcāgnividyā* and the *devayāna/pitṛyāna* theory (cf. ChU 5.3); ChāgU 3: the Ṛṣis ask Kavaṣa Ailūṣa for initiation, saying '*upa no nayasva*', but are refused with the answer '*na hottamān adhama upanetā*'.

[22] ChU 5.11.7: Prācīnaśāla Aupamanyava, Satyayajña Pauluṣi, Indradyumna Bhāllaveya, Jana Śārkarākṣya, Buḍila Āśvatarāśvi and Uddālaka Āruṇi ask Aśvapati Kaikeya for initiation with firewood in hand (*samitpāṇi-*) in order to learn the *ātman vaiśvānara* (cf. ŚB 10.6.1.2; see footnote 20); ChU 8.7.2ff.: Indra and Virocana ask Prajāpati for initiation with firewood in hand (*samitpāṇi-*) to learn the *ātman* (Indra returns to Prajāpati three more times with firewood in hand to learn further); PraśU 1.1: Sukeśan Bhāradvāja, Śaibya Satyakāma,

The firewood is a part of the indispensable belongings that characterize the Vedic student, one of whose principal duties is to take care of fires, as found since the Atharvaveda (see section 2.1). In the initiation ritual in the passages listed here, one's bringing firewood must have symbolized his becoming a student.

In the initiation ritual in these Upaniṣadic passages, neither the old idea of the student's rebirth from his teacher found since the Atharvaveda, nor the Sāvitrī lesson mentioned in the Brāhmaṇas, are referred to. Still, we can find in those passages some trace of the old idea of the teacher's 'pregnancy' period as the preparation time before the initiation. Some of those passages mention that the initiate passes a certain period staying under his teacher after the initiation.[23] The custom of passing a certain period before learning is inherited by the prescriptions of the *vedavrata*s in the Gṛhyasūtras, which I will discuss next.

4.2. The Initiation Ritual in the Gṛhyasūtras' *vedavrata*s

The Gṛhyasūtras prescribe a series of rituals and observances pertaining to the Vedic student and the Veda learning, such as the Upanayana, the Upākaraṇa (the annual ceremony for the opening of each study term), the Utsarga (the annual ceremony for the end of each study term), the *vedavrata*s (various *vrata*s 'vows' for the Veda learning),[24] the Godāna (the ritual of shaving hair and beard),[25] and the Samāvartana (the ceremony of graduation and returning home).

Sauryāyaṇin Gārgya, Kauśalya Āśvalāyana, Bhārgava Vaidarbhi and Kabandhin Kātyāyana ask Pippalāda for initiation with firewood in hand (*samitpāṇi-*); MuU 1.2.12: a Brāhmaṇa goes to a *guru* with firewood in hand (*samitpāṇi-*).

[23] ChU 8.7.2–8.11.3; PraśU 1.1; ChāgU 5; cf. ŚB 14.1.1.27–28; ChU 4.4; ŚB 11.4.2.20; cf. AiĀ 5.3.3; ŚĀ 8.11; JB 3.152.

[24] For the *vedavrata*s, see Kane 1974: 370–373; Gonda 1980: 462–467; Gopal 1983: 306–310; Scharfe 2002: 217–219; Kajihara 2005.

[25] The Godāna is prescribed to be performed when the student is around 16 years old. In many schools, it is incorporated into the learning curriculum, representing one of the *vedavrata*s (GGS 3.1; KhGS 2.5; JGS 1.18; KauṣGS 2.7.15; KāṭhGS 44.1; MGS 1.21.13; VārGS 9.1; BGS 3.2.4, 52ff.; cf. ĀśvGS

In addition to the regular Upanayana which all the Gṛhyasūtras prescribe, some Gṛhyasūtras mention another initiation to be performed for entering the *vedavratas*. This additional initiation is principally a repetition of the regular Upanayana with abbreviated procedures. Some of those Gṛhyasūtras prescribe the repetition of initiation separately at the *vedavrata*: ŚGS 2.11.1ff.; KauṣGS 2.7.1–4; GGS 3.1.1, 10ff.; KhGS 2.5.1, 6ff.; JGS 1.18:16.9ff.; MGS 1.23.24; VārGS 6.2; cf. KāṭhGS 43.1–2.[26] In some other

---

1.18.9; BhārGS 1.10:10.11ff.; ĀpGS 6.16.13f.; HGS 2.1.6.19; ĀgGS 2.2.5: 54.14ff.: cf. also PGS 2.1.25); cf. Oldenberg 1892: 69; Gonda 1965: 351f.; Parpola 1968: 69ff.; Kane 1974: 370ff.; Date 1990; Kajihara 2005.

[26] ŚGS 2.11.1ff.; KauṣGS 2.7.1–4 (Vratādeśana) *atha vratādeśanaṃ. tasyopanayanena kalpo vyākhyāto. na sāvitrīṃ anvāha. daṇḍapradānāntam ity ek[e]*. 'Now, the instruction of the *vratas*. Its proceedings have been explained by the Upanayana. [In this case, the teacher] does not teach the Sāvitrī. Some people say, "[The procedure] ends with handing over the staff".' Cf. Oldenberg 1886: 78ff., also 8f.

GGS 3.1.1, 10ff. (Godāna) *athātaḥ ṣoḍaśe varṣe godānam | ... upanayanenaivopanayanaṃ vyākhyātam | na tv ihāhataṃ vāso niyuktam | nālaṅkāraḥ | nācariṣyantaṃ saṃvatsaram upanayet |* 'Now, after this, in the sixteenth year, the Godāna. ... The initiation [for this] has been explained by the Upanayana itself. In this case, however, a new garment is not used. The adornment is not [used]. One should not initiate one who is not going to carry out [the *vrata*] for a year.' Cf. Oldenberg 1892: 69; Parpola 1968: 69ff.

KhGS 2.5.1; 6ff. (Godāna) *godāne caulavatkalpaḥ | ... | uktam upanayanam | nācariṣyantaṃ saṃvatsaram | aniyuktaṃ tv ahatam | tathālaṅkāraḥ |* 'At the Godāna, a procedure similar to the Caula (the ritual of arranging hair) [is followed]. ... The initiation has been explained [by the Upanayana]. [One should] not [initiate] one who is not going to carry out [the *vrata*] for a year. A new [garment] is not used. Nor adornment'; cf. Parpola 1968: 69ff.

JGS 1.18:16.9ff. (Godāna) *ṣoḍaśe godānakaraṇaṃ. tat keśāntakaraṇam ity ācakṣate. cauḍakaraṇena mantrā vyākhyātā. upanayanena vratādeśanaṃ. na tv iha niyuktam ahataṃ vāsaḥ.* 'In the sixteenth [year], the Godāna ritual. People call it Keśāntakaraṇa (cutting off the hair). The *mantras* have been explained by the Cauḍakaraṇa. The instruction of the *vrata* [has been explained] by the Upanayana. But, in this case, a new garment is not used'; cf. Parpola 1968: 69ff.

MGS 1.23.24 (the *dīkṣā* for learning) *traividyakam upanayanena vyākhyātam.* 'The Traividyaka (the *vrata* related with the three Vedas) has been explained by the Upanayana.' For the *traividyakavrata*, cf. MŚS 4.7.8; KāṭhGS 42; VārGS 7.16; Gonda 1965: 321, 329f.; Witzel 1977: 152f.

VārGS 6.2 (Vratādeśa) *upanayanena vratādeśā vyākhyātāḥ.* 'The instructions of the *vratas* have been explained by the Upanayana.'

Gṛhyasūtras, the prescription of the Upanayana itself includes the rules for repeating it: ĀśvGS 1.22.22ff.; HGS 1.2.6.6–6; ĀgGS 1.1.3:9.20; KauśS 55.4–6.[27]

The initiation ritual for the *vedavrata*s is a 'repeated initiation' performed in order to learn new (and often esoteric) parts of the Veda. As such, it serves the same function as the initiation ritual found in the Upaniṣads discussed in section 4.1. In the initiation

---

Cf. KāṭhGS 43.1–2 (Cāturhautṛka) *athātaś cāturhautṛkam. brahmacāri-kalpena vratam upaiti.* 'Now, then, the Cāturhautṛka (the *vrata* related with the *caturhotṛ*). One enters the *vrata* by the way of the *brahmacārins*.'

Cf. Kane 1974: 392f.; 1973: 98f.; Gonda 1965: 320. For the Godāna as a *vedavrata*, see footnote 25.

[27] The ĀśvGS includes, at the end of the Upanayana (1.19–22), a rite of finishing lessons (Anupravacanīya; 1.22.12–19), the rite of wishing for intellectual power (Medhājanana; 1.22.20–21), and the instruction of the *vrata*s which reads as follows: ĀśvGS 1.22.22ff. *etena vāpanādiparidānāntaṃ vratādeśanaṃ vyākhyātam* | *ity anupetapūrvasya* | *athopetapūrvasya* | *kṛtākṛtaṃ keśavapanam* | *medhājananaṃ ca* | *aniruktaṃ paridānam* | *kālaś ca* | *tat savitur vṛṇīmaha iti sāvitrīm* | 'By this, the instruction of the *vratas*, beginning with the shaving and ending with the entrusting [to the deities], has been explained. Thus is for one who has not been initiated before. Then, for one who has been initiated before. The shaving of the hair [may be] done or not done. So is the Medhājanana. The entrusting [to the deities] is not clearly mentioned. Nor the time [for the ritual]. [He teaches the verse] "*tat savitur vṛṇīmahe*" (ṚV 5.82.1; a Sāvitrī in *anuṣṭubh*; cf. footnote 8) as the Sāvitrī.' Cf. ĀśvGS 1.18.9 (a *vrata* for a year at the Godāna); Gonda 1980: 383.

HGS 1.2.6.6–8 (Upanayana) = ĀgGS 1.1.3:9.20 (Upanayana) *atra sāvitrīṃ vācayati yadi purastād upeto bhavati yady anupetas tryahe paryavete* (*paryapete* ĀgGS) | *sadyaḥ puṣkarasādiḥ* | 'Then he (the teacher) makes [the initiate] recite the Sāvitrī, if he has been initiated before. If he (the initiate) has not been initiated before, [he makes him recite] after three days have elapsed. On the same day, [says] Puṣkarasādi.' Cf. ĀgGS 2.7.1:107.12ff. (Punarupanayana).

KauśS 55.4–6 (Upanayana) *yenāvapad iti sakṛd apiñjūli* | *laukikaṃ ca samānam* (thus Keśava's *Kauśikapaddhati*; *samānām* Bloomfield's ed.) *ā paridhānāt* | *upetapūrvasya niyataṃ savān dāsyato 'gnīn ādhāsyamānaparyavetavratadīkṣiṣyamāṇānām* | (for the last compound, see Caland 1899: 222; Bloomfield's edition reads *ādhāsyamānaḥ paryavetavratadīkṣiṣyamāṇānām*) '[He recites the *mantra* beginning with] "*yenāvapat*" (AV[Ś] 6.68.3) once, without a bunch of stalks (cf. KauśS 53.20–23 [Godāna]). And the same general custom up to putting on [a new garment] (cf. KauśS 54.1–7). [Thus] regularly for one who has been initiated before, for one who is going to give *savas*, for one who is going to settle the fires, one whose time of *vrata* has elapsed, and one who is going to perform the consecration.'

ritual for the *vedavratas*, as in the case of the Upaniṣads, its aspect of being a rite for rebirth does not surface, while the other aspect of being preparations for learning is highlighted. In relation to this, it is noteworthy that in some schools the rules for the Sāvitrī lesson at the initiation for the *vedavratas* are different from those in the regular Upanayana.[28]

The initiation ritual for the *vedavratas* seems to represent a repetition of the Upanayana as the procedure for commencing the lesson of a new text. In addition, it is also possible that the Vedic students did not always complete the whole curriculum of the Veda learning before the Samāvartana, but sometimes learned certain parts of the scriptures after having graduated, by repeating an initiation and passing another period of preparation (*vrata*) in order to learn them.[29]

As the episodes of the learned scholars' initiation in the Upaniṣads discussed in section 4.1 suggest, some of the rituals and

---

[28] In the ŚGS and the KauṣGS, the lesson itself is not given (see above); in the ĀśvGS, another verse is employed as the Sāvitrī (see footnote 27); in the HGS and the ĀgGS, the period before the lesson is abbreviated (see footnote 27).

[29] Some Gṛhyasūtras mention two or three kinds of the *snātaka* 'one who has bathed, i.e., one who has performed graduation ceremony' on the basis of the completeness of his study of the Veda and his *vratas*: the *vidyāsnātaka/veda-snātaka* (a *snātaka* who has finished learning but has not finished the *vratas*), the *vratasnātaka* (a *snātaka* who has not finished learning but finished the *vratas*), the *vidyāvratasnātaka/vedavratasnātaka* (a *snātaka* who has finished both learning and the *vratas*). PGS 2.5.32ff.; cf. AiĀ 5.3.3; GGS 3.5.21f.; JGS 1.19:18.10ff.; ĀpDhS 1.11.30.1–3; BGPS 1.15; Manu 4.31; cf. also BGS 2.6.2ff.; 1.7.1ff.; VārGS 6.29ff. Some texts allude to two kinds of graduation: BŚS 17.39ff.; BhārGS 2.18ff.; ĀgGS 1.3–4; BGPS 1.14.1f.; cf. BGS 2.6.1–16 (for the ritual prescribed in this part, see Kajihara 2011); cf. Heesterman 1968. The rules concerning the Veda learning are not always clear as to for whom they are prescribed; see Einoo 1992: 73, notes 17 & 22. Cf. the *avāntaradīkṣā* ('intermediate consecration', concerned with the study of the Pravargya) in the Śrautasūtras and some Gṛhyasūtras; the *upaniṣadarha-* 'one who deserves the Upaniṣad' (KāṭhGS 10.1f.; MGS 1.7.1f.; VārGS 8.12f.); cf. also ĀpDhS 1.4.13.19f. (Śvetaketu says that one who wants to learn more should live in his teacher's house two months a year even after he settled his own family, and that he himself has done so. This way is rejected in ĀpDhS 1.4.13.21ff.).

speculations taught in the late Brāhmaṇas, the Āraṇyakas and the Upaniṣads were new to the traditional Veda. It may have been a problem for the Gṛhyasūtras how to incorporate those newly increasing teachings into the curriculum.[30]

5. THE INITIATION REPEATED FOR RESTORATION

Both the initiation ritual found in the Upaniṣads (see section 4.1) and that in the *vedavrata* sections of the Gṛhyasūtras (see section 4.2) can be understood as the 'repeated initiation' to be performed for further learning. This kind of 'repeated initiation' is not called by any particular ritual name in the texts. On the other hand, besides them, another kind of 'repeated initiation' with a specific name is found since the late Vedic texts: it is the Punarupanayana ('repeated or renewed Upanayana', often also called Punaḥsaṃskāra) mentioned in some late Gṛhyasūtras and the Dharma texts.[31]

The Punarupanayana is, as its name states, an Upanayana repeated under certain circumstances. The purposes and functions of this 'repeated Upanayana' differ from those we have seen in the cases of the 'repeated initiation' in the Upaniṣads and the *vedavrata*s in the Gṛhyasūtras. Curiously enough, the Punarupanayana is performed mostly on occasions which have nothing to do with the Veda learning.

5.1. The Punarupanayana for the Vedic Students

The Punarupanayana has two sorts according to its performers: one which is performed by the Vedic students and the other whose performers are not limited to them.

---

[30] Watase 1993: 79–91; Scharfe 2002: 294–300; cf. Parpola 1981: 162f.; Falk 1986: 67ff.

[31] Among the Gṛhyasūtras, the VaiGS and the ĀgGS mention the ritual in question. For this ritual in the Gṛhya and Dharma texts, see Gampert 1939: 107ff.; Kane 1974: 392f.; 1973: 98ff.; Gonda 1965: 320; 1980: 383; Falk 1986: 68ff.; Kajihara 2003a; 2003b.

The *Gopathabrāhmaṇa*, one of the latest Brāhmaṇas, tells that the Vedic student should be initiated again (*punarupaneya-*) in case he has neglected his duties:

> If a Vedic student has not carried out [the bringing of] firewood and mendicancy for seven nights, he becomes one who should be initiated again.[32]

According to the Gṛhyasūtras, the Punarupanayana should be performed when one (presumably a Vedic student) has broken certain taboos by eating forbidden food or exposing himself to some pollution.[33]

The Punarupanayana prescribed for the Vedic students can be regarded as a renewal of the Upanayana that has been invalidated as a result of the student's neglecting his duties or breaking prohibitions. The procedure of the Punarupanayana is prescribed to be based on that of the regular Upanayana, yet in a much abbreviated form.[34]

---

[32] GB 1.2.6:38.12 *samidbhaikṣe saptarātram acaritavān brahmacārī punarupaneyo bhavati*; cf. ŚB 11.3.3.7. Taking care of fires with firewood and performing mendicancy are fundamental duties of the Vedic student since the Atharvaveda; cf. sections 2.1 and 2.2 above. On the other hand, the Gṛhyasūtras and Dharmasūtras prescribe that a student who has neglected mendicancy and taking care of fires should perform the *avakīrṇivrata*. KāṭhGS 1.32 (LGS 1.33) = BDhS 1.2.4.7 *bhaikṣasyācaraṇe doṣaḥ pāvakasyāsamindhane | saptarātram akṛtvaitad avakīrṇivratam caret* || 'There is a fault if [a student] has not carried out mendicancy. [There is a fault] if he has not kindled fires. If he has not done it for seven nights, he should carry out the *avakīrṇivrata*'; VaiGS 6.9 (the *avakīrṇaprāyaścitta* is required if he has neglected mendicancy, offering of firewood, bathing, etc.); ĀgGS 2.7.5 (if he has spilt semen, neglected taking care of fires, etc.); Manu 2.187; cf. TĀ 2.18.2. Cf. also ĀgGS 2.7.1: the Punarupanayana should be performed if he has neglected his duties, including the taking care of fires, for a long time.

[33] VaiGS 6.9 (when he has eaten forbidden food); ĀgGS 2.7.1:106.18 (when he has eaten forbidden food, has neglected his duties for a long time, etc.); BGPS 1.12 (when he has eaten forbidden food or has been to certain prohibited districts) ≈ HGŚeṣaS 1.3.18; cf. Gonda 1977: 179f.

[34] VaiGS 6.10 (shaving, the girdle, hide, a staff, *vrata*s and mendicancy are omitted at the Punaḥsaṃskāra); ĀgGS 2.7.1 (eating [of alms], shaving hair and beard, adornment, a garment, the thread, the girdle, addressing, hide, a staff, mendicancy and *vrata*s are omitted at the Punarupanayana); BGPS 1.12.17

5.2. The Punarupanaya Not Limited to the Vedic Students

From the Dharmasūtras onward, the Punarupanayana (Punaḥsaṃskāra) is prescribed in a wider context. Any member of the three upper classes is to perform it when he has violated certain prohibitions, mainly against partaking of *surā* or other impure things. The Punarupanayana is required, for example, when one has drunk *surā* unintentionally (BDhS);[35] when one has eaten food of Cāṇḍālas or Patitas, has drunk liquor other than *surā* intentionally, has drunk *surā* unintentionally, or has drunk urine etc. (VāsDhS);[36] when he has partaken unintentionally of feces and urine, or anything that has been touched by *surā* (Manu);[37] when he has drunk *surā*, semen, feces or urine (YSm).[38]

(shaving, gift, the girdle, a staff, hide, mendicancy and *vrata*s are omitted at the Punassaṃskāra) ≈ HGŚcṣaS 1.3.18.

[35] BDhS 2.1.1.18f. *surāṃ pītvoṣṇayā kāyaṃ dahet* ॥ *amatyā pāne kṛcchrābdapādam caret punarupanayanam ca* ॥ 'When one has drunk *surā*, he should burn his body by hot [*surā*]. If he has drunk without knowing, he should carry out the *kṛcchra* for three months and the Punarupanayana.' Cf. ĀpDhS 1.9.25.3ff. (hot *surā* as penance); GauDhS 3.5.1 (23.1); Manu 11.90ff.; YSm 3.25.3f.

[36] VāsDhS 20.17–20 *etad eva cāṇḍālapatitānnabhojaneṣu tataḥ punarupanayanaṃ vapanādīnāṃ tu nivṛttiḥ* ॥ *mānavaṃ cātra ślokam udāharanti* । *vapanaṃ mekhalā daṇḍo bhaikṣacaryā vratāni ca* । *etāni tu nivartante punaḥsaṃskārakarmaṇīti* ॥ *matyā madyapāne tv asurāyāḥ surāyāś cājñāne kṛcchrātikṛcchrau ghṛtaṃ prāśya punaḥsaṃskāraś ca* ॥ *mūtraśakṛcchukrābhyavahāreṣu caivam* ॥ 'The same (the *kṛcchra* penance) [is required] if he has eaten food of Cāṇḍālas or Patitas. After that, the Punarupanayana [should be performed], but shaving etc. are omitted. And on this, people quote a Mānava *śloka*, "Shaving, the girdle, a staff, mendicancy and *vrata*s – these are omitted at the Punaḥsaṃskāra ritual" (cf. Manu 11.151). And, if he has drunk liquor which is not *surā* intentionally, or has drunk *surā* unintentionally, the *kṛcchra* and *atikṛcchra* [are required], and, after partaking of *ghṛta*, the Punaḥsaṃskāra [is required]. Thus also in the case of eating ordure, urine and semen.'

[37] Manu 11.150 *ajñānāt prāśya viṇmūtraṃ surāsaṃspṛṣṭam eva ca* । *punaḥsaṃskāram arhanti trayo varṇā dvijātayaḥ* ॥ 'When they have partaken unknowingly feces and urine, or anything that has been touched by *surā*, the three classes who have two births should perform the Punaḥsaṃskāra'; cf. Manu 11.146 (one is purified by a *saṃskāra* if he has drunk *vāruṇī* liquor unintentionally); BDhS 2.1.1.21.

[38] YSm 3.255 *ajñānāt tu surāṃ pītvā reto viṇmūtram eva ca* । *punaḥsaṃskāram arhanti trayo varṇā dvijātayaḥ* ॥ 'But when they have partaken unknowingly of *surā*, semen, feces, or urine, the three classes who have two

This Punarupanayana in the wider context is again a renewal of the Upanayana, which has been invalidated as a result of violating certain rules, in this case by the members of the three upper classes in general. In the Dharma texts, the Punarupanayana principally refers to this particular ritual performed for the purpose of restoration and purification, which is not limited to the Vedic students. Its procedure is prescribed in those texts again in a much abbreviated form than the regular Upanayana.[39]

6. CONCLUSION

Being based upon the above discussions, the Upanayana and the 'repeated Upanayana(s)' in the Vedic literature can be summarized as follows:

(1) The Upanayana is the initiation ritual through which a teacher makes someone his own Vedic student. The development of its ritual procedure can be traced from the Atharvaveda through the Brāhmaṇas to the Gṛhyasūtras. The idea of rebirth at the initiation is present already in the early texts, where the teacher is said to give the student a new birth after a certain length of preparation ('pregnancy') period. The student is reborn from his teacher as a new figure fit for the sacred knowledge. Later, in the Gṛhyasūtras and the Dharma texts, the Upanayana is highlighted as a major rite of passage which one should undergo at a specific point in his childhood, so that he is admitted to the three upper classes as their full member (*dvija*).

(2) The initiation ritual for learned scholars narrated in the late Brāhmaṇas and the Upaniṣads is not their first Upanayana, but is the 'repeated' one for the second time or the more in their lives. The scholars repeat the initiation in order to learn the esoteric

---

births should perform the Punaḥsaṃskāra.' Cf. ViSm 51.1–5; GauDhS 3.5.2–5 (23.2–5).

[39] BDhS 2.1.1.20 (shaving, *vratas* and *niyama* are omitted); VāsDhS 20.17–18 (shaving, the girdle, a staff, mendicancy and *vratas* are omitted); Manu 11.150–151 (ditto); ViSm 51.5.

teachings which they have not learned before. This 'repeated initiation of scholars' has a much simpler procedure than the regular Upanayana, and can be performed as many times as needed. In this type of initiation, the idea of rebirth does not appear above the surface, while the function of entitling one to a new learning is focused on. Such a 'repeated initiation' for further learning is also found in the Gṛhyasūtras: the Upanayana is repeated at the *vedavrata*s in an abbreviated form.

(3) The Punarupanayana, which is attested since the late Gṛhyasūtras and the Dharmasūtras, is significantly different from the 'repeated initiation' summerized in (2). It has mostly nothing to do with learning, nor is limited to the students. It is performed when the Upanayana as a rite of passage becomes invalid, that is, when one loses the status of a member of the three upper classes (which he acquired through the Upanayana) because of an encounter with certain sort of impurity. The Punarupanayana renews the Upanayana and restores his status. As such, it serves as a sort of expiation or purification ritual.

(4) From the beginning, the Vedic initiation ritual has been endowed with two aspects. It is a rite of passage which marks a new epoch in one's life with a new birth through it. At the same time, it is a ritual which makes one a student who is entitled to the sacred knowledge. These two aspects are principally not separated from each other. The Upanayana in the Sūtras, in which the aspect of a rite of passage is emphasized, retains the procedure of making one a student. The 'repeated initiation of scholars' in the Upaniṣads, in which the aspect of a ritual for learning is underlined, is often succeeded by a preparation period which would reflect the old idea of the teacher's 'pregnancy'. The Punarupanayana in the late Vedic texts, on the other hand, loses a connection to learning, and enlarges the aspect of a rite of passage, so that it works as a ritual for restoration and purification.[40]

---

[40] Some Vedic rituals are said to be repeated when one has encountered with some misfortune and/or taboo: the Punarādheya (ĀpŚS 5.26.3; cf. TS 1.5.1–4;

ABBREVIATIONS

ĀgGS = *Āgniveśyagṛhyasūtra*
AiĀ = *Aitareya-Āraṇyaka*
ĀpDhS = *Āpastambadharmasūtra*
ĀpGS = *Āpastambagṛhyasūtra*
ĀpŚS = *Āpastambaśrautasūtra*
ĀśvGS = *Āśvalāyanagṛhyasūtra*
AV(P) = *Atharvaveda, Paippalādasaṃhitā*
AV(Ś) = *Atharvaveda*, Śaunaka recension
BĀU = *Bṛhadāraṇyaka-Upaniṣad*
BDhS = *Baudhāyanadharmasūtra*
BGPS = *Baudhāyanagṛhyaparibhāṣāsūtra*
BGS = *Baudhāyanagṛhyasūtra*
BGŚS = *Baudhāyanagṛhyaśeṣasūtra*
BhārGS = *Bhāradvājagṛhyasūtra*
BŚS = *Baudhāyanaśrautasūtra*
ChāgU = *Chāgaleya-Upaniṣad*
ChU = *Chāndogya-Upaniṣad*
CS = *Carakasaṃhitā*
GauDhS = *Gautamadharmasūtra*
GB = *Gopathabrāhmaṇa*
GGS = *Gobhilagṛhyasūtra*
HGS = *Hiraṇyakeśigṛhyasūtra*
HGŚeṣaS = *Hiraṇyakeśigṛhyaśeṣasūtra*
JB = *Jaiminīyabrāhmaṇa*
JGS = *Jaiminigṛhyasūtra*
JUB = *Jaiminīya-Upaniṣadbrāhmaṇa*
KaṭhB = *Kaṭhabrāhmaṇa*
KaṭhB(*u*) = *Kaṭhabrāhmaṇa* (*Upanayanabrāhmaṇa*)
KāṭhGS = *Kāṭhakagṛhyasūtra*
KauṣGS = *Kauṣītakagṛhyasūtra*

ŚB 2.2.3; BŚS 24.18:202; cf. Krick 1982: 514–579); the Punasstoma (PB 19.4; JB 2.83f.; ĀpŚS 22.11.1–8; BŚS 18.46f.; KŚS 22.10.16f.; BDhS 1.1.2.14; 3.10.2ff.; GauDhS 3.1.1ff. (19.2ff.); LŚS 9.4.5; cf. ŚŚS 14.27f.; Gampert 1939: 154f., 162, 196); the Punaściti (TS 5.4.10.3ff.; MS 3.4.5; KS 22.2; ŚB 8.6.3.8–24; ĀpŚS 17.24.11ff., etc.); the Punaryajña (ŚB 4.5.10.6; cf. 8.6.3.16); the Punarvivāha (BGŚS 2.12; VaiGS 6.11–13); cf. Kajihara 2003b.

KauśS = *Kauśikasūtra*
KauṣU = *Kauṣītaki-Upaniṣad*
KhGS = *Khādiragṛhyasūtra*
KS = *Kāṭhakasaṃhitā*
KŚS = *Kātyāyanaśrautasūtra*
LGS = *Laugākṣigṛhyasūtra*
LŚS = *Lāṭyāyanaśrautasūtra*
Manu = *Manusmṛti*
MGS = *Mānavagṛhyasūtra*
MS = *Maitrāyaṇīsaṃhitā*
MŚS = *Mānavaśrautasūtra*
MuU = *Muṇḍaka-Upaniṣad*
PGS = *Pāraskaragṛhyasūtra*
PraśU = *Praśna-Upaniṣad*
ṚV = *Ṛgveda*
ŚĀ = *Śāṅkhāyana-Āraṇyaka*
ŚB = *Śatapathabrāhmaṇa*
ŚB(K) = *Śatapathabrāhmaṇa*, Kāṇva recension
ŚGS = *Śāṅkhāyanagṛhyasūtra*
ŚŚS = *Śāṅkhāyanaśrautasūtra*
SuśS = *Suśrutasaṃhitā*
TĀ = *Taittirīya-Āraṇyaka*
VaiGS = *Vaikhānasagṛhyasūtra*
VārGS = *Vārāhagṛhyasūtra*
VāsDhS = *Vāsiṣṭhadharmasūtra*
ViSm = *Viṣṇusmṛti*
YSm = *Yājñavalkyasmṛti*

REFERENCES

BODEWITZ, H. W. 1973. *Jaiminīya Brāhmaṇa I, 1–65. Translation and Commentary with a Study, Agnihotra and Prāṇāgnihotra.* (Orientalia Rheno-Traiectina, 17.) Leiden: E.J. Brill.

BRONKHORST, Johannes 2007. *Greater Magadha. Studies in the Culture of Early India.* (Handbook of Oriental Studies, Section 2: India, 19.) Leiden: E.J. Brill.

CALAND, Willem 1899. Zur Exegese und Kritik der rituellen Sūtras. XVIII–XXXII. *Zeitschrift der Deutschen Morgenländischen Gesellschaft* 53: 205–230, 388, 696–702 (reprinted in Caland 1990: 44–76).

—— 1920. Brāhmaṇa- en Sūtra-aanwinsten. *Verslagen en Mededeelingen der Koninklijke Akademie van Wetenschappen te Amsterdam, Afdeeling Letterkunde,* 5e Reeks, 4: 461–498. Amsterdam: Koninklijke Nederlandse Akademie van Wetenschappen.

—— 1990. *Kleine Schriften.* Edited by Michael Witzel. (Glasenapp-Stiftung, 27.) Stuttgart: F. Steiner.

DATE, Ranjana 1990. The interpretation of *Agnigodāna. Bulletin of the Deccan College Post-Graduate & Research Institute* 50 (Golden Jubilee Volume): 183–187.

EINOO, Shingo 1992. Gṛhyasūtra bunken ni mirareru gireị-hen'yo ['Some aspects of the ritual development in the Gṛhyasūtras', in Japanese]. *The Memoirs of the Institute of Oriental Culture, University of Tokyo,* 118: 43–86.

FALK, Harry 1986. *Bruderschaft und Würfelspiel. Untersuchungen zur Entwicklungsgeschichte des vedischen Opfers.* Freiburg: Hedvig Falk.

—— 1988. Savitṛ und die Sāvitrī. *WZKS* 32: 5–33.

GAMPERT, W. 1939. *Die Sühnezeremonien in der altindischen Rechtsliteratur.* (Archiv orientální, 6.) Prag: Orientalisches Institut.

GONDA, Jan 1965. *Change and Continuity in Indian Religion.* (Disputationes Rheno-Trajectinae, 9.) The Hague: Mouton.

—— 1977. The Baudhāyana-Gṛhya-Paribhāṣā-Sūtra. In: *Beiträge zur Indienforschung, Ernst Waldschmidt zum 80. Geburtstag gewidmet* (Veröffentlichungen des Museums für Indische Kunst Berlin, 4): 169–190. Berlin: Museum für Indische Kunst.

—— 1979. Upanayana. *Indologica Taurinensia* 7 (Dr. Ludwik Sternbach Felicitation Volume), I: 253–259.

—— 1980. *Vedic Ritual. The Non-Solemn Rites.* (Handbuch der Orientalistik, 2.4.1.) Leiden: E.J. Brill.

GOPAL, Ram 1983. *India of Vedic Kalpasūtras.* 2nd edition. Delhi: MLBD.

HEESTERMAN, J. C. 1968. The return of the Veda scholar (*samāvartana*). In: J. C. Heesterman, G. H. Schokker & V. I. Subramoniam (eds.), *Pratidānam. Indian, Iranian and Indo-European Studies Presented to Franciscus Bernardus Jacobus Kuiper on His Sixtieth Birthday.* (Janua Linguarum, Series Maior 34): 436–447. The Hague: Mouton.

IKARI, Yasuke 1989. Some aspects of the idea of rebirth in Vedic literature. *Studies in the History of Indian Thought* 6: 155–164.

KAJIHARA, Mieko 1995. The *brahmacārín* in the Atharvaveda. *Journal of Indian and Buddhist Studies* 43.2: 1–6.

—— 2003a. Veda-nyūmongirei no futatsu no sou ['The two aspects of Vedic initiation rituals', in Japanese]. *Buddhist Seminar* 78: 1–20.

—— 2003b. Nyūmonshiki to sainyūmonshiki ['The Upanayana and Punarupanayana', in Japanese]. *Journal of Indian and Buddhist Studies* 52.1: 22–24.

—— 2004. The Upanayana and marriage in the Atharvaveda. In: A. Griffiths & J. E. M. Houben (eds.), *The Vedas. Texts, Language & Ritual. Proceedings of the Third International Vedic Workshop, Leiden 2002.* (Groningen Oriental Series, 20): 417–431. Groningen: Egbert Forsten.

—— 2005. Veda gakushū to seikai ['The *vratas* for Veda learning', in Japanese]. In : *Studies in Zen Buddhism (The Zengaku Kenkyū), Special Issue. Aspects of Buddhist Thought and Culture. Essays in Honour of Professor Ensho Kobayashi's 70th Year.* 161–175. Kyoto: Zengaku kenkyūkai.

—— 2011. The "*gṛhya*" Formulas in Paippalāda-Saṃhitā 20. *Zinbun. Annals of the Institute for Research in Humanities, Kyoto University*, 42: 39–62.

—— 2014. Seizing the novice's hand and pouring water into his hands at the Vedic initiation ritual. *Studies in Indian Philosophy and Buddhism* 21: 1–18.

—— in press. The initiation rituals and the *brahmacarya* in the Upaniṣads and the early Buddhist texts [in Japanese]. *The Zinbun Gakuhō: Journal of Humanities. The Institute for Research in Humanities, Kyoto University.*

—— forthcoming 1. The *brahmacārín*, *brahmacárya*, and chastity in the Vedic literature. Paper presented at the 6th International Vedic Workshop, Calicut, January 2014.

—— forthcoming 2. The sacred verse Sāvitrī in the Vedic religion and beyond. Paper presented at the 16th World Sanskrit Conference, Bangkok, June 2015.

KANE, Pandurang Vaman 1973. *History of Dharmaśāstra. Ancient and Mediaeval Religious and Civil Law,* IV. (Government Oriental Series, B.6.) 2nd edition. Poona: Bhandarkar Oriental Research Institute.

—— 1974. *History of Dharmaśāstra. Ancient and Mediaeval Religious and Civil Law,* II.1. (Government Oriental Series, B.6.) 2nd edition. Poona: Bhandarkar Oriental Research Institute.

KRICK, Hertha 1982. *Das Ritual der Feuergründung* (Agnyādheya). Herausgegeben von Gerhard Oberhammer. (Sitzungsberichte der Österreichischen Akademie der Wissenschaften, Phil.-hist. Klasse, 399; Veröffentlichungen der Kommission für Sprachen und Kulturen Südasiens, 16.) Wien: Verlag der österreicheschen Akademie der Wissenschaften.

MOOKERJI, Radha Kumud 1947. *Ancient Indian Education. Brahmanical and Buddhist.* London: Macmillan.

OLDENBERG, Hermann 1886. *The Grihya-Sūtras. Rules of Vedic Domestic Ceremonies*, I: *Śāṅkhāyana-Grihya-sūtra, Āśvalāyana-Grihya-sūtra, Pāraskara-Grihya-sūtra, Khādira-Grihya-sūtra*. (The Sacred Books of the East, 29.) Oxford: Clarendon Press.

—— 1892. *The Grihya-Sūtras. Rules of Vedic Domestic* Ceremonies, II: *Gobhila, Hiraṇyakeśin, Āpastamba, Āpastamba's Yajña paribhāshā-sūtras*. (The Sacred Books of the East, 30.) Oxford: Clarendon Press.

PARPOLA, Asko 1968. *The Śrautasūtras of Lāṭyāyana and Drāhyāyaṇa and Their Commentaries. An English Translation and Study*, I.1. (Commentationes Humanarum Litterarum, 42.2.) Helsinki: Societas Scientiarum Fennica.

—— 1981. On the formation of the Mīmāṁsā and the problems concerning Jaimini, with particular reference to the teacher quotations and the Vedic schools. *WZKS* 25: 145–177.

PREISENDANZ, Karin 2007. The initiation of the medical student in early classical Āyurveda: Caraka's treatment in context. In: B. Kellner, H. Krasser, H. Lasic, M. T. Much & H. Tauscher (eds.), *Pramāṇakīrtiḥ. Papers Dedicated to Ernst Steinkellner on the Occasion of His 70th Birthday*, II: 629–668. Wien: Arbeitskreis für Tibetische und Buddhistische Studien, Universität Wien.

RENOU, Louis 1947. *Les écoles védiques et la formation du Veda*. (Cahiers de la Société Asiatique, 9.) Paris: Imprimerie nationale.

ROSENFIELD, Susan 2004. Kaṭha Brāhmaṇa fragments. A critical edition, translation, and study. Ph.D. thesis, Harvard University.

SAKAMOTO-GOTŌ, Junko 2000. *katháṃ-katham agnihotráṃ juhutha* – Janakas Trickfrage in ŚB XI 6,2,1. In: Almut Hintze & Eva Tichy (eds.), *Anusantatyai. Festschrift für Johanna Narten zum 70. Geburtstag* (Münchener Studien zur Sprachwissenschaft, Beihefte, Neue Folge, 19): 231–252. Dettelbach: Röll.

—— 2001. Zur Entstehung der Fünf-Feuer-Lehre des Königs Janaka. In: Stefan Wild & Hartmut Schild (eds.), *Akten des 27. Deutschen Orientalistentages. Bonn – 28. September bis 2. Oktober 1998. Norm und Abweichung*: 157–167. Würzburg: Ergon.

SCHARFE, Harmut 2002. *Education in Ancient India*. (Handbook of Oriental Studies, Section 2: India, 16.) Leiden: E.J. Brill.

SCHROEDER, Leopold von 1898. *Die Tübinger Kaṭha-Handschriften und ihre Beziehung zum Tāittirīya-Āraṇyaka*, herausgegeben mit einem Nachtrage von G. Bühler. (Sitzungsberichte der Kaiserlichen Akademie der Wissenschaften in Wien, Phil.-hist. Classe, 137.4.) Wien: Gerold.

SŪRYAKĀNTA 1943. *Kāṭhaka-Saṃkalana. Extracts from the Lost Kāṭhaka-Brāhmaṇa: Kāṭhaka-Śrautasūtra & Kāṭhaka-Gṛhyasūtras. Edited with*

Notes. (Meharchand Lachhman Das Sanskrit and Prakrit Series, 12.) Lahore: Meharchand Lachhmandas.

TSUJI, Naoshirō 1970. *Genzon yajur-veda bunken. kodai indo no saishiki ni kansuru konpon shiryo no bunkengaku teki kenkyū* [in Japanese]. (Tōyō bunko ronsō, 52.) Tokyo: Tōyō bunko.

WATASE, Nobuyuki 1993. Brahmacārin zenshi [in Japanese]. *Oriental Culture / Tōyō Bunka* 73: 67–96.

WITZEL, Michael 1977. An unknown Upaniṣad of the Kṛṣṇa Yajurveda: The Kaṭha-Śikṣā-Upaniṣad. *Journal of the Nepal Research Centre* 1: 139–153.

—— 1979. Die Kaṭha-Śikṣā-Upaniṣad [1.1–1.7] und ihr Verhältnis zur Śīkṣāvallī der Taittirīya-Upaniṣad. *WZKS* 23: 5–28.

—— 1980. Die Kaṭha-Śikṣā-Upaniṣad [2.1–7.6] und ihr Verhältnis zur Śīkṣāvallī der Taittirīya-Upaniṣad. *WZKS* 24: 21–82.

—— 1987. The case of the shattered head. *Studien zur Indologie und Iranistik* 13–14: 363–415.

—— 2004. *Kaṭha Āraṇyaka. Critical Edition with a Translation into German and an Introduction.* (HOS, 65.) Cambridge, Mass.: Department of Sanskrit and Indian Studies, Harvard University.

YANO, Michio 1988. *Indo igaku gairon* ['Introduction to the Indian medical science', in Japanese]. *Kagaku no meicho*, II.1. Tokyo, Asahi-shuppansha.

Recording the Four Vedas

GUNI HESTING KIRCHHEINER (†)

I would like to thank Professor Asko Parpola for inviting me to present to this conference the project of recording recitation of the four Vedas, on which I have worked for the last twenty years and which has been recently completed. Parpola has advised and supported me from the very beginning. I also thank Professor Shrikant Bahulkar, who has throughout the project been a truly great help, and who has prepared the catalogue of the recordings. In this paper, I will briefly explain the inspiration behind the project, its purpose and how it was carried out.

The project was actually started in Pune in 1983, but my interest in Indian culture and Indian classical music started long before that. My former husband Erik Kirchheiner was an ethnomusicologist specializing in classical Indian music, and through him I was introduced to India. We visited India together many times, and many Indians visited our home in Denmark, and we arranged many concerts of classical Indian music. After loosing our only child we finally went to India to stay there more permanently, for a number of years.

While living in Pune, I experienced a very traditional version of Indian everyday life. Among other things, I spent many hours listening to different *pūjā*s being performed in our friend's house. The priest was Shri Karambelkar Śāstrī. He was the first person who recited Veda for me. It was a great experience, and I was deeply fascinated. Although I did not understand the words, the

Vedic recitation had a profound impact on me. The Vedas are not only words and wisdom, but also a distinct way of saying these words and presenting that wisdom. To me the presentation, the musical quality and sound of Vedic recitation is an integral and important part of the Vedas themselves. These recitations were simultaneously ancient wisdom and living sound, an expression of both Indian cultural heritage and everyday practice.

Everyday practice changes, however. This became only too apparent to me during a conversation with Karambelkar Śāstrī. I asked him: 'What will happen to the recitation when the old priests are no more?' He replied: 'They will disappear. The young people are not interested. This tradition will not exist in the future.' Yet the Vedas have been handed down from generation to generation for millennia.

But even though everyday practice and tradition change, this does not mean that we should passively stand by and just watch it happen, and thus simply accept that the Vedic recitations and the skill of reciting the Vedas could be lost and forgotten as one generation comes to an end. Although there had been several attempts at recording Vedic recitation, no complete recording of all the four Vedas in their various recensions was available. I decided if possible to do something to preserve this oral tradition, the Vedas as a living sound.

After returning to Denmark I spoke to several friends of mine about the project, and then I approached the Danish Research Council for the Humanities. Professors Søren Egerod and Asko Parpola recommended the project, and the Research Council agreed to finance it.

With the financial side in place, I made it sure that I had the best recording equipment available on the market: a Nagra tape-recorder. After returning to India, I contacted a good friend of mine, Dr Ashok Marathe, who introduced me to Professor Shrikant Bahulkar of the Tilak Maharashtra Vidyapeeth in Pune as the best possible guide. Bahulkar suggested which Vedas to record and who should recite them, introduced me to these Vedic masters and registered the recordings.

With my background of many years in the classical Indian music, I considered it most important to prepare recordings in which it would be possible to hear all the recited words and to avoid disturbance from the outside world. If the sound quality was not good enough, scholars would not be able to use the tapes in future research. Even with the best recording equipment, it is rather difficult to achieve an excellent sound quality. There is generally a high level of noise in the busy cities and towns of India, which can be hard to block out entirely. I realized that I needed a studio for this purpose. A family friend of mine in Pune, Shri Achut Gokhale, placed a room in his house at my disposal. I contacted people who could advise me on how to prepare a studio, and with the help of some friends we succeeded in making arrangement that worked well. These efforts secured very clear recordings. Yet in some parts it is a bit difficult to hear all the words.

The recordings took place in Pune, Gokarna, Sinor and Panjal. They contain a complete set of audio recordings of the Samhitās of the four Vedas in six Vedic schools: the Ṛgveda, the Kṛṣṇa Yajurveda in the Taittirīya *śākhā*, the Śukla Yajurveda in both the Mādhyandina and Kāṇva *śākhā*s, the Atharvaveda in the Śaunaka *śākhā*, and the Sāmaveda in the Jaiminīya *śākhā*. In addition the *Aitareyabrāhmaṇa* and the *Aitareya-Āraṇyaka* of the Ṛgveda and the *Taittirīyabrāhmaṇa* and *Taittirīya-Āraṇyaka* of the Kṛṣṇa Yajurveda were recorded. I had the privilege to meet a number of learned brahmins and Vedic scholars. Through their lives and work, they have contributed to the preservation of the oldest living cultural heritage of India. Many of them recited Veda for me and gave information about Vedic traditions.

As the tradition of Jaiminīya Sāmaveda was not available in Maharashtra, Professor Parpola had recommended to me a Nambudiri family in the Panjal village of Kerala. I visited the family four times before the recordings were finished. It was a great experience to me to meet Shri Itti Ravi Nambudiri. I spent many hours sitting in front of him while recording his strong and beautiful voice.

The recording was completed in 1985, whereafter I returned to Denmark. Afterwards Professor Bahulkar came there to do the demanding job of cataloguing the recordings from tape spools and cassettes. The catalogue was printed in 1999.

In 2000 it became clear to me that I had to have the tapes transferred into CDs. I have seen a lot of tapes lying dusty and forgotten in the archives. They represent many years of hard work done by ethnomusicologists and other scholars, and hardly anybody knows their work. In order to get further financial support, I contacted the Danish Ministry of Research, and they agreed to pay for the conversion of the tapes into 446 CDs. These CDs and the two sets of audiotape with the original recordings have been handed over to the Department of Orientalia and Judaica (led by the Senior Librarian Stig T. Rasmussen), The Royal Library, POB 2149, DK-1016 Copenhagen K.

The Royal Library is presently selling a complete set of the CDs for 25,000 Danish crowns or 3,200 US dollars (plus handling, postage and applicable taxes) to universities, libraries and institutes for research purposes. The recordings are not sold to private people and political and social organizations. Copying is not allowed, and will be followed by legal action. For further information, consult: http://www.kb.dk/en/nb/samling/os/Sydasien/veda.html.

This arrangement was made in order to avoid non-scholarly financial exploitation of the project. Many people do not care much about the Vedas, but more about money. The Danish Research Council and the Danish Ministry of research have financed most part of the work, but I have also spent a lot of my own money, maybe 100,000 Danish crowns or more. For me it has not been a matter of money, but love for the Vedas.

Last time I was in India, I met a priest working in a temple outside Pune. He came from a very well known and respected family with a Sanskrit tradition. His monthly salary was 800 Indian

Rupees, which was far from enough; he and his family were constantly striving to get by. His son too was a priest, but he had found it impossible to make a decent living as a priest; so he had given up on the idea of continuing in this way, and had started another education. I have observed that the social position of priests in India is declining, and generally speaking priests are not much respected. Money and income tend to be an increasingly important parameter for gaining status and respect. Priests are employed by people who have a lot of money, but they tend to consider the *pūjārī* as a kind of servant. I really hope this situation could change, but this does not appear to be in sight. The society is changing very fast and in a more materialistic direction.

The purpose of this project was to contribute to preserving a great and important part of Indian culture. Completing the task proved daunting, and would not have been possible without the help and support of many people and institutions. I am very grateful to all of them.

POSTSCRIPT BY ASKO PARPOLA

Guni Hesting Kirchheiner was born 16 May 1932, and passed away on 12 April 2007, as I was informed by her sister Kirstine Hesting soon afterwards.

In the Veda section of the 12th World Sanskrit Conference, we had a panel 'Fieldwork on Vedic manuscripts, recitation and ritual traditions', and as I considered Guni Hesting Kirchheiner's collection of Vedic recitation an important new resource for research, I invited her to come and give a presentation of her project and its results. Shrikant Bahulkar has had an essential part in this project by helping Guni to select good recitors and by introducing her to them, and not least by preparing the catalogue of the recordings. The booklet in the size of 10.6 x 12.3 cm was printed in Pune in 1999 with the following title: *Veda Recitation: Catalogue of the Recordings Made by Guni Hesting Kirchheiner. Catalogue by Shrikant Bahulkar.* (Page 2 of this print has a dedication to the late

Professor Søren Egerod, pp. 3–6 the preface by Guni Hesting Kirchheiner, and pp. 7–17 the catalogue.)

Professor Bahulkar has in 2004 stated in the internet that she helped Guni Hesting Kirchheiner in his individual capacity, out of genuine academic interest, and care for the preservation of the recitations of renowned Vedamūrtis. No Institute was officially involved in the project, which was undertaken to preserve the tradition and not for making money. On his suggestion, Guni donated a complete set of all the audio recordings to the Vedaśāstrottejaka Sabhā (Pune), of which Bahulkar has been a member of the Executive Council. There have been a number of demands for copies of the recordings, but the Sabhā has respected Guni's copyright and not made them available.

Shrikant Bahulkar has dissociated himself from Guni's CD project, and declared himself in no way responsible for their quality and price, which he considers exorbitant. The Vedaśāstrottejaka Sabhā has initiated a project of recording all the Vedic *śākhā*s and making CDs available at a reasonable price to scholars and lovers of the Veda. Bahulkar has already recorded the Ṛgveda recitation of Vedamūrti Dinakarabhaṭṭa Phaḍke, and Kauthuma Sāmaveda recitation of Pandit Vishvanath Shastri of Tamil Nadu for the Sabhā.

Sōmidēvamma: The Patnī Who Consumes *soma* in the Āndhra Śrauta Tradition

DAVID M. KNIPE

The fragile and dwindling *śrauta* tradition of the Godavari Delta region of coastal Āndhra (see now Knipe 2015) refers to the setting of the fires as *ādhāna*. Having established fires in his *āyatana*, the clay enclosure for *tretāgni* on the floor of the *agnihotra* room of the house (cf. Gonda 1969), the Vaidika Brahman then is eligible to perform *agniṣṭoma*, the initiatory *soma* sacrifice and a rite identified locally as '*yajña*' (cf. Dandekar 1973–83). Having accomplished *yajña*, he is immediately known as 'Sōmayāji', or simply 'Yājulu' in a combinative Vedic/Telugu honorific. He has offered *soma* into the fire and has drunk *soma* and may now affix the title of Sōmayāji or Yājulu to his names.[1] He must be married in order to qualify as *agniṣṭomin*, and therefore his *patnī* as co-sacrificer immediately becomes 'Sōmidēvamma', a title that replaces given names in formal discourse with reference to her. In Telugu economy of speech two syllables are lost, and her name is heard as 'Sōdemma'. If one is so impudent as to ask an *āhitāgni* for the name of his wife, that question is answered by 'Sōdemma'. Only by informally asking a daughter-in-law or granddaughter, perhaps, does one learn that her name is Anasūya, Mahālakṣmi,

[1] For example, Yajñeśvara Yājulu, who later followed his *agniṣṭoma* with the *sarvapṛṣṭha* form of *agnicayana* and later still the *vyūḍha* form of *pauṇḍarīka* and became Yajñeśvara PauṇḍarīkaYājulu.

Subbalakṣmi or Sundari. Although present on the *mahāvedi* for subsequently elected *soma* rituals such as *pauṇḍarīka*, *vājapeya*, *sarvatomukha*, or *āruṇaketuka*, she does not have a personal *graha* or *camasa* cup and does not directly drink *soma* as do the *yajamāna* and most *ṛtvij* priests. Her proximity to *soma* is limited to the offering from the *pātnīvatagraha*.

In *Sacrificed Wife / Sacrificer's Wife*, Stephanie Jamison comments on 'the ritual fact that women do not consume soma': '[I]ngesting a powerful soma directly might harm the woman and the reproductive process' (Jamison 1996: 133). Nevertheless, in the coastal Āndhra tradition, the *patnī* as co-sacrificer does 'consume' *soma* and is therefore called *somapītinī*. How are we to understand the process by which the Sōmidēvamma contains *soma* and yet is not seen to drink it? Is there, in fact, any evidence that she does contain *soma*? Is the coastal Āndhra tradition, one of the last regions of South Asia with continuous *śrauta* practice and the only one to maintain strictly the requisite animal sacrifices, an anomaly or is it consistent with ancient custom?

This essay proceeds out of field data from interviews between September 1980 and March 2000. In 1980 in the river-and-canal-bracketed area known as Konasima, close to the Gautami branch of the spreading Godavari and only a few miles from the Bay of Bengal, a number of Vaidika Brahmans still flourished in *śrauta* traditions. They belong to the Taittirīya *śākhā* and follow Āpastamba, with supplementary reference to Baudhāyana, Bhāradvāja, Āśvalāyana and other Śrautasūtras. At one point nine *āhitāgni*s lived within walking distance of one another. *Agrahāram*s and tiny hamlets only a quarter-mile, or at most three miles apart enabled them to maintain a support network of qualified, experienced *ṛtvij* priests for major rites as well as routine *iṣṭi*s. Three, now going on four, generations of ten families have been tracked in this research, with several of these families long-time lineages of *śrauta* performance that now may be drawing to a close (cf. Knipe 1997: 321–327). Families such as the Bhamidipatis with more than a dozen *āhitāgnis* in the twentieth century may still flourish in Veda, but no longer in *śrauta*.

Today the few Konasima *āhitāgnis* and *patnīs* who remain are aging rapidly. Of this small sample of married pairs who have performed *agniṣṭoma*, all but two ceased *agnihotra* because of the death of one or the other spouse. The average age of those *āhitāgnis* who remain is now 76. Only one pair is still maintaining *nityāgnihotra*, although another intends to rekindle with standard *prayaścittas* after a lapse. Any promise of continuity in *śrauta* lies either with those of a young generation, well trained and certified in Veda but not yet committed to setting the fires, or to those now employed as esteemed Veda Paṇḍita recitants in pilgrimage temples who are eligible, highly qualified, experienced *ṛtvij* priests in all *śrauta* roles, but postponers of *ādhāna* and *agniṣṭoma* for themselves until retirement from T.T.D. (Tirupati-Tirumalai Devasthānam) service affords them an *agrahāram*-like existence (Knipe 1997: 317–319).

To return now to the questions: Is there evidence in the Āndhra tradition that the *patnī*, called *somapītinī*, does contain *soma*? And if so, how does that happen?

One learns a great deal about life after it is all over. Intricate details of funerals – rituals of departure – may reveal significant insights into life experience. Instructive are the special funerary procedures for an *āhitāgni* and *patnī*, with mantras never heard for the *antyeṣṭis* of ordinary, *laukika* Brahmans and others. The day of death and beginning of *āsauca*, ritual impurity (Telugu *maila*) are reckoned not from the moment of physical death but rather from the occurrence of *brahmamedha*, a funerary tradition known to the Taittirīyins, and an ultimate interiorization of Agni. Whoever is first to die – *patnī* or *āhitāgni* – takes their three fires in the cremation pyre, along with all ritual accoutrement except those few items needed for *punardahana*, a second cremation, and two *araṇis* necessary in due course to recreate Agni for the pyre of the surviving spouse. Eight years ago Yajñeśvara Pauṇḍarīka Yājulu, now blind at age 89, cremated his wife of 67 years, years that included 14 children, more than 40 grandchildren, *agniṣṭoma*, *agnicayana*, *pauṇḍarīka*, *śrāvaṇapaśu* and, without exception, yearly *āgrayaṇa*s for the new rice autumn harvest. Knowing full well that his *araṇi*s were waiting for him, carefully wrapped in gunny cloth in the rafters over his head, he still complained with his typical dark humor: 'She took the fires with her! Now I will have to go with kitchen matches!'

Common to most funerary traditions is a strong tension between acceptance of the inevitability of death and separation on one hand, and on the other, a desire to resurrect, re-animate, or at least perpetuate the earthly presence of the deceased. Often in South Asia this is clearly expressed with regard to bones. Perhaps this reflects the tenacity of archaic burial and mound-building traditions that could be older than the gradual adoption of cremation already in the period of Ṛgveda composition. Alongside pastoral symbols such as cremation of the deceased under the opened carcass, hide, limbs or special organs of a cow or goat (ṚV 10.16.2, 7; AVŚ 18.2.8, 58; KauśS 81.25; ĀśvGS 4.1.4, 2.4–8, 3.20–25), or simply the sacrifice of a cow at the time of cremation, there are significant agrarian symbols expressed in subsequent rituals. Treatment of bone and tooth fragments after *asthisaṃcayana* is a case in point. Sprinkling water on the collected bones while reciting mantras beseeching Agni to allow the deceased to join a new body (ṚV 10.16.5–6; AVŚ 18.2.10; KauśS 82.28) suggests symbolic cultivation of life from bones. A possible reinterpretation of *śeṣa* in ṚV 10.16.5 may be the 'remnant' *soma* the poet declares in verse 6 to be 'in' *brāhmaṇa*s (such as the deceased). Agricultural and vegetative metaphors expand with regenerative rituals of seeding and watering of furrows (*karṣū*s) plowed for the bones on or beside the cremation ground, sometimes with a representation of the *agnicit* itself (TS 5.2.5.2–5; ŚB 13.8.2.1–3.13; further, cf. Knipe 2004).

In recent years Godavari *āhitāgni*s have had numerous occasions to perform *brahmamedha*. After a last breath the body is placed lying face up close to the *āyatana*, the clay enclosure for *tretāgni* on the *agnihotra* room floor. In all but the cold months of December and January blocks of ice may be purchased for support, providing limited preservation during the waiting period. It is said that before *brahmamedha* and true ritual death occur there must be time for telegrams to reach relatives, or perhaps for an officiant requested by the deceased to be notified and given transport. This is an acceptable rationale, but possibly under the surface of this delaying of *brahmamedha* for three days there are ancient explanations. For one, a homology between three *soma*-pressing days and a vague three-day journey of the deceased may be expressed in ṚV 10.14.16 (cf. O'Flaherty 1981: 46, nn. 16 and 17). The body is taken up from the floor or ice blocks and stretched directly upon the *āyatana* when the three fires have gone cold, before being set aside for a last rekindling of the *gārhapatya*, and then the other two fires, followed by the milking of the buffalo cow and oblations. *Agnihotra* continues to be performed, by the *yajamāna* if his *patnī* lies beside, or by other *āhitagni*s and the *patnī* if it is the *yajamāna* perched on the threshold of death, and the *patnī* is not too distraught to participate. The body is then bathed twice a day by the living, as if the deceased were still going twice daily down to the riverside to bathe. It is a remarkable instance of the perpetuation of life beyond breath and heartbeat, a reanimation accomplished essentially by proximity to, even absorption into, *tretāgni*. And it is an extraordinary juxtaposition physically – ice on one hand to keep the body from decomposing, three fires on the other hand for revivification.

This suggests an inversion of the *saṃnyāsin*'s vow of dying to this world and interiorizing his three fires. Here, however, this breathless body is not yet 'dead', this person had no intention of stating the vow of *saṃnyāsa*, the fires must remain at this point discrete and separate from each other and, finally, this ritual pertains to the *patnī* as well as the *āhitagni*. It is significant to note that because the breathless body stretched on the *āyatana* from *gārhapatya* across the *vedi* to *āhavanīya* is not 'dead', the *āyatana* itself remains *maḍiga*, in *maḍi*, the Telugu term for the all-important condition of ritual purity.

Finally, the awaited ritual death occurs on the third day with the commencement of *brahmamedha*. The body and three marked pots of embers from each of the three fires, plus a fourth pot for the *aupāsana* fire that will remain after the completed funeral, are all carried in slings to the cremation ground, which invariably is referred to as 'there', never by the textually familiar terms *śmaśāna* or *dahanadeśa*. It is a tidy single-pyre space within sight of, but well away from the *agrahāram*, with three halting places on the ground for group circumambulation and possible goat sacrifice at each. On the pyre the body is covered with ritual implements save only the *araṇi*s (kindling sticks), *juhū* (ladle), *ulūkhala* (mortar) and *musala* (pestle). Despite the well-known dangers of attending funerals, and the terrible onus of proximity to death, usually one or more living *āhitāgni*s of close acquaintance and long-time ritual collaboration are present to pool knowledge of procedures, especially during the two-hour *brahmamedha* near the outset of thirteen days of funerary rituals. They supervise with Sūtra texts, although also present must be the area's one male funerary priest (Apara Brahman) who knows the *brahmamedha*. If it is the *patnī* who has died, and the *āhitāgni* lives, a special female Brahman priestess must come to represent her in the *mūsivāyanam*, a non-textual but essential and apparently quite old, if not specifically ancient coastal Āndhra ritual that captures the *preta*, transforms her to goddess Gaurī and, with the aid of numerous women from both natal and affinal sides, sends her to *gaurīloka* (cf. Knipe 2003: 51–93). As in all *saṃskāra*s it is the women of the household who know and suggest many non-textual details on all these thirteen days.

To return to the cremation, after the pyre has burned down and all have returned to the *agrahāram*, the Apara Brahman (or someone else) extracts a few embers to sustain and protect some distance away in anticipation of *punardahana*. The *asthisaṃcayana* next day, or later, involves collecting bone and tooth fragments from the ashes into a *kumbha*. After a number of preliminary rituals the bone and tooth fragments of the *patnī* or *āhitāgni* are ground into a chalky white powder, either in the ritual mortar (*ulūkhala*) or with two natural stones taken from the cremation ground, then mixed into a paste with ghee for the ritual of *punardahana*. Using the *juhū* ladle, this paste is turned over to Agni for a second burning. The Pitṛmedha, Gṛhya and Śrauta Sūtras provide no reason for this. The *āhitāgni*s say the object of this reburning is the careful removal of every last trace of the *soma* that has fortified the bones throughout a career of sacrifice. And here we are at the heart of the matter, for the bone fragments of the *patnī*, the Sōmidēvamma, must be cleansed by Agni as well as those of the *āhitāgni* who has actually drunk *soma* from his *graha*.

The practice of destroying the *sadas* roof and wall-screens, and of burning or throwing into the river all implements touched by *soma*, is well known. Implements for daily *agnihotra* and routine *iṣṭi*s are retained by the living married pair, but new implements must be made by the carpenters when the next *soma* sacrifice is planned. Bricks from all Godavari *cayana*s are covered over with soil in the agricultural field where the sacrifice occurred, and gradually they return to fragments and dust so that nothing remains to be seen. *Somarasa* is transparently dangerous outside of ritual time and ritual space. Even when *soma* is not the issue in the *agnihotra* room, after the completed funeral of either *patnī* or *āhitāgni* there is only the *aupāsana* fire. The clay *āyatana* for the *vedi* and *tretāgni* have been scraped from the floor of the ritual room with not a mark remaining.

Another uncommon ritual, *loṣṭaciti* or *loṣṭacayana*, is one that clearly replicates the *agnicayana* if such was performed by the *patnī* and *āhitāgni*. It is performed on the thirteenth day, again with the plowing of furrows. There is no space here to deal with other rituals between cremation and *śāntikarma*s and the ritual closing of the house in order to clear it of *dhūḷigali*, Telugu 'dust and wind', the generic hauntings of evil spirits. There still must be an attempt to explain how *soma* comes to be in the body of the Sōmidēvamma. Her funeral ritual discloses the fact that she embodied *soma* without ever having drunk from a *graha* during *somabhakṣaṇa* in the *sadas*. Several lines of inquiry are possible.

One is to consider the lineage of the *patnī*, a pre-pubescent girl when selected for marriage, often from *āhitāgni* stock that sometimes goes back eight generations. In the limited pool of pure Vaidika families, more often than not the bride is a cross-cousin. Could the inheritance of bodily *soma* be a father-to-daughter or other lineage descent?

Another approach involves a non-textual but necessary rite in coastal Āndhra for a wife who dies first. In the *mūsivāyanam*, as it is called in Telugu, a Brahman funerary priestess becomes a surrogate for the deceased *patnī*, locates and incorporates her *preta*, is decorated as a bride with new *maṅgalasūtra* tied by her mother or sister, and then ritually returned to that defining threshold of her original five-day *vivāha* when she moved from her birth house (*puṭṭillu*) to the house of her mother-in-law (*attillu*). Obviously in the case of a Vaidika family there is an evident disjuncture between Telugu matrilocal and Vedic patrilocal traditions, certainly not unique in Vedic dispersal through regional India (cf. Heesterman 1983: 79–81 on sources of fire). The question that arose in publishing the rich details of the hitherto unstudied *mūsivāyanam* ritual (Knipe 2003) was this: If the bride is assumed, as some would have it, to take the husband's blood at marriage (Knipe 2003: 77, 91 n. 45; Harman 1989: 134), does she revert to natal blood in the course of the *mūsivāyanam* when she is turned into a pre-pubescent bride again, a bride without a husband to accompany her on the journey to *gaurīloka*? And the parallel question in the present context would then be, is blood exchange a possible avenue for *soma* to journey from the body of the *āhitāgni* to the body of the *patnī*? In Konasima, Yajñeśvara and Mahālakṣmi were married for 67 years, 51 of them after she became Sōmidēvamma and he became Yājulu. Is husband to wife transfer of bodily *soma* a possible answer?

Still another perspective along this line might consider the fact that the wife, in traditional fashion, eats the leavings on her husband's leaf-plate and so absorbs into her own body his *soma*-imbued 'bodily substance code', to use McKim Marriott's terminology (Marriott 1976; Marriott & Inden 1974: 983–984). Even if they are of the same subcaste, the gender hierarchy prevails in the transaction. This is the explanation for the *patnī*'s *punardahana* given by a potential *āhitāgni*, son and grandson of *āhitāgni*s:

> My mother, the *somapītinī*, ate my father's left-overs. Thus indirect *soma-rasa* was sucked up by her bones and they became strong.

But perhaps a productive way to see the marital relationship is to appreciate symbols that make this pair of sacrificers, *patnī* and *āhitāgni*, a unit. First there is the twice-daily *agnihotra*. One of the many features that seem to distance older *āhitāgni*s and *patnī*s from middle-aged and young Veda paṇḍitas and wives is a special relationship with the fires, usually referred to in the singular in Telugu as *agnihotram*. *Agnihotram* is a secluded household Agni, the deity, and is theologically the cynosure of attention, as if no other god matters in the religious life of the *yajamāna* and *patnī*. It is in many respects a devotional attitude toward *Agnihotram* that characterizes the *āhitāgni* and *patnī* in their lifelong service to and dependence upon the three fires (Knipe 1997: 316, 319–321, 324). In a very real sense it is a triangular bond that exists between the three – husband, wife, fires. To put it another way, it is the consistency of *agnihotram* that has welded the couple into a sacrificing unit. They are one. This is important to recognize in any attempt to understand the substance that is *soma* in the bodily as well as the spiritual lives of *patnī* and *yajamāna*.

Second, although they are of different genders, ages and birth 'houses', their *śrauta* ritual lives began anew simultaneously with the *dīkṣā* for *agniṣṭoma*. It is misleading to believe that textual focus on the *yajamāna* in many Brāhmaṇas and Sūtras, or neglect of rituals and attitudes concerning the *patnī* in contemporary *śrauta* practice and its ethnography, is an accurate depiction of women in *śrauta* life everywhere. In 1,548 pages the Kerala *patnī* in the *agnicayana* is mentioned only in passing, without role or thought, 'crouched under her parasol' behind the *yajamāna*.[2] Although more attention is drawn to the Godavari *yajamāna*, symbolically both were born at the same moment in their approach to *soma* co-sacrifice. Furthermore, each time they prepare for a *soma* ritual they seclude themselves in newly erected, separate but adjacent womb-huts for embryonic gestation,[3] abolishing time and beginning as contemporaries once again (cf. Gonda 1965: 337, 367; Eliade 1958: 53–60).

This is a significant point, supported by other symbols, including the *mekhalā* and *yoktra* fastened respectively by the *adhvaryu* around the waist of the *yajamāna*, and around the waist of the *patnī* (cf. Jamison 1996: 42–50; Gonda 1965: 369–370). This knotting of the *patnī*, only a symbol of the *dīkṣā* in the many ordinary *darśapūrṇamāsa iṣṭi*s performed over the years, is now a definitive admission into *soma*. No matter how many decades have passed since the ritual tying of three-stranded *muñja*-grass cords, the *patnī*s always remember details of this particular event, and some can summon with enthusiasm the mantras recited at the time. As her husband, Kāmeśvara Somayājulu, recalls fervently the procedures of his *upanayana* with *yajñopavita* investiture and the fastening of his *mekhalā* waist-cord when he was a *brahmacārin*, and then again as *dīkṣita*, so too does Satyavati Sōmidēvamma remember with equal pleasure and pride, first, the tying of her *maṅgalasūtra* during their five-day *vivāha* when she was a small girl in 1945, and second, the tying of her *yoktra* in *dīkṣā* readiness for *agniṣṭoma* when she was mother of sons and daughters 22 years later. Clearly

---

[2] Staal 1983: I, 369; plate 45B reinforces the impression that she is a nonparticipant.

[3] On this symbolism, ŚB 3.2.1.6, 11, 15; ĀpŚS 10.11.5.

evident in their faces today is the glow of remembered commitments in those ritual times out of time. As a Vedic student is tied to a schedule of disciplined Veda-learning, and a bride is committed to marriage vows, so in each symbolic 'year' of *dīkṣā* the couple welcomes renewed 'bondage' to a shared ritual life and all its rewards.[4]

The Konasima wives of living or deceased *āhitāgnis*, and those intending to set fires when their Veda paṇḍita husbands retire from temple *pārāyaṇa* service, are divided between those who passively follow along, accepting priestly or spousal directives, and those involved with the same intensity, passion and dedication to grasping *yajña* with the mind and spirit that *yajamānas* possess. In several cases it was the energy, passion and even obsession (*vyasana*) of the wives that first propelled the couple to set the fires.

In the last analysis of Konasima tradition there is recognition of the married pair as co-sacrificers, functioning as a unit, indivisible where *agnihotra* is concerned, and *somarasa* as well. It is not difficult to accept this explanation when one knows of a disabled *āhitāgni*, limbs paralyzed but willful voice still able to mouth the requisite mantras while touching the back or hands of his wife who is the actual performer of all *kriyās* for the ritual (Knipe 1997: 331–332, n. 20). The *karman*, ritual work, is of necessity in that instance a joint effort, but the example is a graphic reminder that sacrifice has been a cooperative venture from the moment of setting the fires. Yajñeśvara Somayājī (Baballa), a Konasima *āhitāgni* who performed *agniṣṭoma* with his wife in 1959, and went on to do the *āruṇaketuka* with Sundari Sōmidēvamma beside him for all twenty days, put the emphasis on offering more than drinking when he defined a *somayājī* as 'one who pours *soma* into the fire'. Understandably, the sharing of giving is also the sharing of receiving.

---

[4] For a contrary view of the symbolism of binding, cf. Smith 1991: 24–27, 32.

REFERENCES

DANDEKAR, R. N. (ed.) 1973–83. *Śrautakośa, Encyclopaedia of Vedic Sacrificial Ritual*, English Section, II.1–2. Poona: Vaidika Saṃśodhana Maṇḍala.

ELIADE, Mircea 1958. *Birth and Rebirth. The Religious Meanings of Initiation in Human Culture*. Trans. by Willard R. Trask. New York: Harper.

GONDA, Jan 1965. *Change and Continuity in Indian Religion*. (Disputationes Rheno-Trajectinae, 9.) The Hague: Mouton.

—— 1969. The meaning of the Sanskrit term *āyatana*. *The Adyar Library Bulletin* 23: 1–79.

HARMAN, William 1989. *The Sacred Marriage of a Hindu Goddess*. Bloomington: Indiana University.

HEESTERMAN, J. C. 1983. Other folks' fire. In: Frits Staal (ed.), *Agni. The Vedic Ritual of the Fire Altar*, II: 76–94. Berkeley: Asian Humanities Press.

JAMISON, Stephanie W. 1996. *Sacrificed Wife / Sacrificer's Wife. Women, Ritual and Hospitality in Ancient India*. New York: OUP.

KNIPE, David M. 1997. Becoming a Veda in the Godavari Delta. In: Dick van der Meij (ed.), *India and Beyond: Aspects of Literature, Meaning, Ritual and Thought. Essays in Honour of Frits Staal*: 306–332. Leiden: International Institute for Asian Studies.

—— 2003. When a wife dies first: The *mūsivāyanam* and a female Brahman ritualist in coastal Andhra. In: Liz Wilson (ed.), *The Living and the Dead. The Social Dimensions of Death in South Asian Religions*: 51–93. Albany: State University of New York Press.

—— 2004. Sowing for the grim reaper: Gardens of the *preta*. In: Maitreyee R. Deshpande (ed.), *Problems in Vedic and Sanskrit Literature*. [Commemorative Volume for Professor Ganesh U. Thite.] Delhi: New Bharatiya Books.

—— 2015. *Vedic Voices. Intimate Narratives of a Living Andhra Tradition*. New York: OUP.

MARRIOTT, McKim 1976. Hindu transactions; diversity without dualism. In: Bruce Kapferer (ed.), *Transaction and Meaning*, 109–142. Philadelphia: Institute for the Study of Human Issues.

MARRIOTT, McKim & Ronald B. INDEN 1974. Caste systems. In: *Encyclopaedia Britannica* (15th edition), III: 982–991.

O'FLAHERTY, Wendy Doniger 1981. *The Rig Veda*. New York: Penguin Books.

SMITH, Frederick M. 1991. Indra's curse, Varuṇa's noose and the suppression of women in Vedic *śrauta* ritual. In: Julia Leslie (ed.), *Roles and Rituals for Hindu Women*: 17–45. Delhi: MLBD.

STAAL, Frits 1983. *Agni. The Vedic Ritual of the Fire Altar*, I–II. Berkeley: Asian Humanities Press.

Towards a New Edition of the *Baudhāyanagṛhyasūtra*

TIMOTHY LUBIN

This article reviews the current state of research on the *Baudhāyanagṛhyasūtra* (BGS) in preparation for a new critical edition and translation. One of the longest and most important, yet most neglected, of the codes (*sūtra*) of domestic ritual, its text poses complex problems that can only be answered through a new collation of a much wider range of manuscripts than have been used in earlier editions. First, the BGS and its appendices, the *Baudhāyanagṛhyaparibhāṣāsūtra* (BGPS) and the *Baudhāyanagṛhyaśeṣasūtra* (BGŚS), are situated in relation to the rest of the Baudhāyana Kalpa literature. The question is raised whether its prolixity and its inclusion of mantras in full should automatically be taken to indicate the BGS's greater antiquity relative to the Gṛhyasūtras of other schools. The fact that the *Baudhāyanaśrautasūtra* (BŚS) is also known for being less concise, even to the point of containing Brāhmaṇa-type passages, has generally been treated as proof of its being one of the first Sūtras to be composed. Yet if the Gṛhyasūtras as a class came into being as a secondary development, even the oldest of them could have adopted a more mature Sūtra style. Various possible explanations are considered: (a) the BGS was composed in tandem with, or only shortly after, the BŚS; or (b) the BGS is in fact much younger that the BŚS, but was deliberately made to resemble its *śrauta* prototype, which remains one of the earliest Śrautasūtras; or (c) prolixity and full citation of mantras were a stylistic preference of the Baudhāyana school, and so cannot inform us about relative chronology. Some observations about the form and content of the Sūtra are adduced to support the view that even if the BGS were one of the first Gṛhyasūtras to be composed, the form in which it is attested today shows many signs of relative lateness. Finally, a survey is offered of the manuscript and other source material available for collation, including some new manuscripts photographed by the author.

The BGS is one of the longest and most important – and yet, curiously, one of the more neglected – of the codes of domestic ritual. Caland's lament of a century ago of the neglect of the *Baudhāyanasūtra* as a whole applies still to the GS and its appendices. There have been four[1] different editions produced in India, two in Grantha script and two in Devanagari, but scholarship has relied exclusively on the Mysore edition (by preference the corrected 1920 version), which records some variant readings. The new but hard-to-find four-volume edition from Honnavar, Karnataka (1986–89), which includes a new commentary, unfortunately shows a high number of errors. Moreover, there has been no translation of the BGS, aside from a few selections from the *Gṛhyaśeṣasūtra* that were translated into English in 1922.[2] In this article I will comment on some of the matters that have already been raised regarding this text, including arguments about its character and age relative to other Gṛhyasūtras, and will propose some tentative answers. A final section will briefly review the materials available for a new edition.

[1] Or five: the *New Catalogus Catalogorum* refers to a 1920 edition from Poona that is listed in 'A Printed List of Printed Books and Manuscripts in the Veda Sastra Uttejaka Sabha, 608, Sadashiv Peth, Poona', by Vaidya Pancanan Krishna Sastri Kavade, 1925. I have not been able to lay eyes on this edition, nor on the list in which it is mentioned. For the *Pitṛmedhasūtra*, which I will not edit, we have also Caland's edition of 1896.

[2] Harting 1922.

THE COMPONENTS OF THE BAUDHĀYANA CORPUS

There have also been hardly any studies of this Sūtra,[3] though it is vital for understanding the Vedic domestic ritual cult. The Baudhāyana school is accorded a position of great historical importance in the ritual traditions of the Yajurveda, and it continues to be prominent today in its longtime home in south India. The BGS proper has been transmitted with more than one layer of supplements, the *Baudhāyanagṛhyaparibhāṣā(sūtra)* and the *Baudhāyanagṛhyaśeṣasūtra* (or *Gṛhyapariśiṣṭa*).[4] The fact that we possess such a full set of Kalpasūtras of this school provides an excellent opportunity to observe in detail the textual elaboration of norms of religious observance within a single tradition.

One interesting case is the description of the *samāvartana*, the graduation ceremony at the end of the regimen of Veda study. Although this *gṛhya* topic is generally broached in Gṛhyasūtras in other schools, the Baudhāyana case is unique: the *samāvartana* rite has been included, for no obvious reason, in (Caland's edition of) the BŚS (17.39–44). When the subject comes up in its 'natural' place at BGS 2.6, the edition and most manuscripts have a brief allusion to the prior passage in BŚS (*vedam adhītya snāsyann ity uktaṃ samāvartanam*, 'The *samāvartana* has been described in the passage beginning "Having studied the Veda, one who is going to bathe" ...'). The BGS then proceeds to describe a variant of the rite, which differs mainly in having inserted into its middle a series of offerings to be accompanied by mantras from the *Taittirīya-Upaniṣad* (TU 1.4[d–i]), which are intended to conjure up fame, fortune, and many eager students for a teacher.

Kajihara, who has discussed this passage most recently, notes that BGS 2.5 is also unusual among Yajurvedic Sūtras in rubricating Upaniṣad mantras, viz., TU 1.4[a–c], in its format for the *upa-*

[3] In the last thirty years, there is only pieces by Gonda (1977a: 582–590; 1977b) that summarize its contents. Now there is also Kajihara 2002: 343–355.

[4] Manuscripts and editions often include the *Baudhāyanapitṛmedhasūtra* in the *gṛhya* corpus.

nayana.[5] She suggests that the composite *samāvartana* rite of BGS 2.6, which along with the *upanayana* as described in 2.5 completes the sequential deployment of the mantras from TU 1.4, was devised in order to ensure that the TU be included as 'required reading' for *brahmacārins*, or at least that it be accepted as *śruti*, during a period in which the boundaries of 'Veda' were expanding in all schools (Kajihara 2002: 353–355).

The situation is complicated by the fact that the older passage prescribing the rite actually does occur in some manuscripts of the BGS,[6] and in any case, it is reintroduced into the *gṛhya* canon as BGPS 1.13. It is worth remembering that the *samāvartana* section in the published BŚS appears in the so-called *Uttarā tatiḥ*, a collection of supplemental topics appended to the Śrautasūtra. In fact, only one of Caland's BŚS manuscripts (the 'Mackenzie manuscript') includes the *samāvartana* passage, and all the other manuscripts that he collated for this section were of the BG(P)S or of *gṛhyaprayoga*s! It may be better to treat this passage as a freestanding set of rules, codified earlier than the other *gṛhya* rites of this school and known to the redactor(s) of the BGS, but which somehow got bundled in, perhaps accidentally, with the Śrautasūtra in one case, and otherwise later found a more suitable home in the BGPS.

Another point of overlap between the Śrauta- and Gṛhyasūtras is the almost verbatim repetition of the section on the *avāntaradīkṣā* (BŚS 9.19–20), the consecration for the *pravargya* rite, as BGS 3.4, where it stands alongside the so-called '*vedavrata*s' for

---

[5] Kajihara 2002: 353–355. Witzel (1979–80) was the first to notice the use of TU 1.4 in the BGS in his studies of the parallel *Kaṭhaśikṣā-Upaniṣad*.

[6] Caland (BŚS edition, vol. II, p. iii) cites 'Hultzsch's manuscript' as showing at BGS 2.6.1 the same reading as BGPS 1.13.1: *vedam adhītya snāsyann ity* (sic) *upakalpayata* ... (*ity* must have been inserted here by mistake, by attraction to his preceding quotation of the usual reading of BGS 2.6.1; Caland 1903: 8 shows the correct reading). At least one of the Grantha manuscripts I have examined, ms. no. 259 in the ÉFEO collection, likewise has this 'original' *samāvartana* passage at BGS 2.6.1ff.

the study of esoteric portions of the Taittirīya canon. Its pertinence there derives from the fact that the *avāntaradīkṣā* serves to renew and strengthen the *śukriyavrata* (first broached at BGS 3.2.27 for the study of the Saumya portion of the canon) at the time when the study of the *pravargya* mantras (*Taittirīya-Āraṇyaka* 4, with exegesis in TĀ 5) is taken up.[7]

The fascinating appendices to the BGS deserve much more study in their own right.[8] Although undatable in strict terms, the contents of the BGPS and BGŚS (the latter comprising more than half of the *gṛhya* material) are surely of various ages, in most though not all cases later than the BGS proper. They expand upon and provide more detailed prescriptions for rites presented in the BGS, and provide a rubric for many other rites, such as the cult of images of Rudra and Viṣṇu. But at several points they also serve as a commentary on the BGS, offering nuanced discussion not only of ritual matters but of ethical (and perhaps 'spiritual') questions as well, asking, for example (BGPS 1.1.18–28): What forms of pious observance count as 'sacrifice' or 'worship' (*yajña*)? What constitutes a brahmin: birth alone or proper practice?

The only study dedicated entirely to the BGPS remains the article by Gonda (1977b), which enumerates the contents of the text in detail.[9] Caland earlier described it as partly a *gṛhyabrāhmaṇa* and partly a *gṛhya* analogue of the *Karmāntasūtra*, that is, a collection of additional details relevant to rites treated in the BGS proper.[10] In

7 BGS 3.4.16: ... *agne vratapate śukriyaṃ vrataṃ cariṣyāmi* ... On the *avāntaradīkṣā*, see Kashikar 1976: 66–67; Houben 1991: 21–25, 34–36, and 131.

8 *Pariśiṣṭa*s of the Vārāha tradition earlier attracted the interest of Pierre Rolland (1969; 1972).

9 There is now also Lubin 2016a (on BGPS) and 2016b (on BGŚS, in part).

10 Caland 1903: 12. Notwithstanding Gonda's caveats on this point (1977b: 187–188), the BGPS indeed introduces important exegetical arguments within the framework of a Sūtra. Lubin 2016a gives an English translation of the verses, along with further remarks on the *āśrama* doctrine implicit in this section of the text.

many ways, the BGPS stands midway between the BGS and the *Baudhāyanadharmasūtra*. In the first section, we find an awareness of the *āśrama*s – not yet sequential, it would seem, and thus in harmony with the older core of BDhS – and those of *brahmacarya* (1.1) and *gārhasthya* (1.2) are explained in light of the doctrine of the 'Three Debts' (an idea introduced in *Taittirīyasaṃhitā* 6.3.10.5). Further on, a versified eulogy of the *pākayajñas* (the *gṛhya* sacrifices) is quoted to support the idea that they are the ultimate basis, the 'tree', even of the *śrauta* cult (1.6.11–22).[11] The provision for analogues of the *śrauta* rites that can be performed by a *gṛhya* ritualist (2.1.28–38), and the claim that one may make any offering so long as it is done with faith (*śraddhā*) (2.1.47) help to legitimate *gṛhya* piety.

BGŚS 2.8 gives additional provisions for the initiation of *rājanya*s and *vaiśya*s – precisely the groups targeted by the more embracing doctrine of initiation. The itinerant chapter on *samāvartana* from BŚS 17.39–44 is repeated here (BGŚS 1.13) almost verbatim; it is followed (1.14) by rules for performing the *samāvartana* of a *vratasnātaka* ('one who has completed the *vrata* of *brahmacarya*, but has not actually learned the Veda'; this recalls BGPS 1.16.1, which distinguishes three classes of *snātaka*). This provision calls attention to the fact that completion of the regimen of *brahmacarya* need not imply a complete mastery of the Veda, especially given the fact that initiation was being promoted as an obligation for all males of the three upper *varṇa*s, and not merely the natural province of brahmins.

Many sections of the BGŚS, including some of those translated by Harting, which prescribe rites for the worship of images of Rudra and Viṣṇu, are evidently post-Vedic. These sections give us a dynamic view of efforts by Vaidikas to broaden the scope of 'orthodox' practice by assimilating the cult of images into the

[11] These verses are translated by Caland (1903: 34–35). The term *āśrama* even occurs here at 1.6.21. On the evolution of the '*āśrama* system', see Olivelle 1993, esp. chapter 3.

framework built around the fire cult and the Vedic liturgical texts.[12] Some traces of the early development of cults of personal salvation can be recognized, as in the case of the *nārāyaṇabali* (BGŚS 3.20–21, framed by the *jīvaśrāddha*, 3.19, and *ātmaśrāddha*, 3.22).[13] Critical editing of the BGŚS, especially in comparison with similar material in the *Vaikhānasasmārtasūtra* and the *Atharvavedapariśiṣṭas*, may help to clarify trends in the intermediate phase between the composition of the Gṛhyasūtras and the formation of 'classical Hindu' institutions such as the Dharmaśāstra and the various deity cults.

STRATA AND DATING: FORM AND CONTENT

In its Gṛhyasūtras, as in other respects, the Baudhāyana tradition stands apart from that of other Vedic schools. As in the case of the BDhS,[14] the Baudhāyana *gṛhya* corpus is a composite, lacking the structural integrity and evenness of style of, say, the *Āpastambagṛhyasūtra*. Even in the BGS proper, BGS 4, the *prāyaścittapraśna*, ought to be treated as an appendix to the first three *praśnas*, the core.

What can we say about the position of the BGS relative to other Yajurveda Gṛhyasūtras, and to the rest of the Sūtra literature as a whole? The fact that BŚS is known for being less concise than most other Śrautasūtras – repeating lengthy phrases, registering

[12] The presence even in the BGS proper of ritual features he deemed to be later innovations led Bhandarkar (1883: 34) to conclude that this work was later than the *Āpastambagṛhyasūtra* and the *Bharadvājagṛhyasūtra*.

[13] Cf. VaiSmS 7.4 and 10.9–10; *Āgniveśyagṛhyasūtra* 3.11.4. For a study of this rite and its historical development, see Krick 1977, esp. pp. 72–91.

[14] Bühler (1882: xxxiii–xxxv) finds it likely 'that Baudhâyana's original Dharma-sûtra consisted, like Âpastamba's, of two Prasnas only', with *praśnas* 3 and 4 representing successive additions by members of the school. Olivelle (1993: 86–87; 2000: 610) identifies the last two *khaṇḍas* of the second *praśna* (2.17–18) as an interpolation as well, and refers to these, and the subsequent *praśnas* as 'Deutero-Baudhāyana', to distinguish it from the older material.

divergent views on many points, quoting *brāhmaṇa* passages[15] and even entering into *brāhmaṇa*-like discussions of its own – has generally been treated as evidence that it was one of the first Sūtras to be redacted. Indeed, in this respect, it is almost the opposite of the ĀpGS, which is concise in the extreme. Winternitz has also observed that the ĀpGS sometimes prescribes rules directly in contrast to Baudhāyana's views, which are cited with closely similar wording and attributed obliquely to *eke* ('some [authorities]'),[16] and thus must already have been known to the Āpastambins, who wished to establish their own views on these points. From this both Winternitz and Bühler conclude that BGS is older than the ĀpGS (Bühler 1897: xxiii).

Yet if the Gṛhyasutras as a class came into being as a secondary development, even the oldest of them might have adopted the more

---

[15] Recognizing that quotations in Vedic texts are useful for showing the relationships between texts within a school, and between schools as well, Makoto Fushimi has pointed out that particular markers may be used to distinguish different types of quotation. He found that *ity uktam* in the ĀpŚS usually indicates a quotation from the TS; *iti vijñāyate* usually indicated that the quotation was from other, usually unnamed, Vedic sources (including TB and TĀ, which are thus put on a par with several non-Taittirīya works) (Fushimi 1998: 1). In the BGS, such expressions also occur, but their usage appears to be less systematic. The phrase *ity uktam* is used only once (BGS 2.6.1), to refer to the *samāvartana* passage printed as part of the BŚS and in the BGŚS (discussed above). Here and there, a passage of *brāhmaṇa* is quoted with special notice: e.g., BGS 1.3.8 quotes the words *yat saha sarvāṇi mānuṣāṇi* ('if [he were to collect the weapons of worship] all together, they would have men [as their divinity]', TS 1.6.8.2) with the remark *ity etasmād brāhmaṇāt*. Elsewhere, though, the BGS generally marks quotations of whatever sort with the word *iti* alone. It is thus in marked contrast that the BGPS and BGŚS imitate the BŚS in introducing quotations of *brāhmaṇa* (whether from TS, TB, or TĀ, or in some cases, from an unknown source) with the phrase *atha vai bhavati*. Throughout the *gṛhya*-corpus quotations of Brāhmaṇa-type passages are sometimes marked by (*iti*) *vijñāyate*, 'it is recognized [by authorities]' (Gonda's gloss, 1977b: 171); these may be from the TS, TB, TĀ, or from another source. The word *vijñāyate* may precede or follow the quotation, and the word *iti* is sometimes omitted. On the BGS's citing of the authority of rival schools, I will have more to say below.

[16] Thus ĀpGS 5.4–5, 7.20–21, 11.17, and 21.2 vis-à-vis BGS 1.4.25, 2.6.21, 2.5.17, and 2.11.5–6, respectively (Winternitz 1892: 8; I here supply the correct references to the edited BGS).

compressed style that becomes typical of Sūtras. Various explanations are possible: (a) that the BGS was composed in tandem with or only shortly after the BŚS; (b) that the BGS is in fact much younger that the BŚS, but was deliberately made to resemble its *śrauta* prototype; or perhaps (c) that prolixity and the full citation of mantras were a stylistic preference of the Baudhāyana school, and so cannot inform us about relative chronology.

Caland observed that the BGS presupposes the BŚS, and that the BGPS stands in the same relation to the BGS as the *Karmānta-sūtra* to the BŚS. It is certainly unlikely that the entire Kalpasūtra was composed, or even redacted once and for all, by a single individual; rather it was the product of a school that identified itself with the *pravacanakāra* Baudhāyana. This special status and authority attributed to Kāṇva Baudhāyana by the later tradition, even by authors outside the Baudhāyana school, is one of the factors cited by those who would date the entire Kalpasūtra as relatively early.[17]

Several points might be mentioned in support of the view that the BGS was composed somewhat later than the BŚS. First, one of the distinctively archaic features of the Baudhāyana tradition, as Caland showed, is the appearance of tmesis in the Sūtras, a trait rarely found in the other Yajurveda Sūtras.[18] However, all of the forty examples that he cites are drawn from the BŚS. It might be argued that such linguistic differences reflect differing registers of the language, rather than different periods of composition, with the *śrauta* rules being presented in a deliberately archaic idiom, while the domestic rules are expressed in a less stilted manner. Yet in other respects the characters of the different parts of the Kalpasūtra

[17] Thus, Mahādeva opening his commentary on HŚS, gives Kāṇva Baudhāyana the epithet *pravacanakartā*, and lists Bhāradvāja, Āpastamba, and Satyāṣāḍha Hiraṇyakeśin as *sūtrakārins* who followed him; cf. BDhS 2.5.9.14. BGS 3.9.6 also thus names 'Kāṇva Baudhāyana Pravacanakāra' in a list of figures honored in the *sarpabali*.

[18] Comparing parallel passages from the ĀpŚS and the HŚS, he uses this criterion to show that the *Āpastamba* is older (Caland 1903: 48).

are similar; in fact, there is a general effort to interlink the various classes of Sūtra, and to demonstrate that the *gṛhya* rites are just as serious business as the *śrauta* rites. So it seems unlikely that the archaic linguistic features of the Śrautasūtra are merely a conscious affectation.

What are we to conclude from the tendency of the Baudhāyana Sūtras (*gṛhya* as well as *śrauta*) to present repetitive passages verbatim, and mantras *sakalapāṭhena*? Caland has considered this question, and is inclined to see this as indicating that the rules were for a time transmitted orally, or to put it another way, that the Baudhāyana Sūtra retains the character of a *pravacana*, the first authoritative expounding of the ritual, still preserving marks of its oral presentation (Caland 1903: 10). Indeed, such unabbreviated repetitions found in Buddhist texts have been regarded as signs of their earlier oral transmission. For further 'convincing proofs' of this, Caland notes the use of deictic expressions ('*this* one, in *that* direction') and the demonstrative adjective *ayam* in places where later Sūtras provide more specific indications (Caland 1903: 3–4). The presence in the Sūtra of Brāhmaṇa-like arguments has also been treated as a mark of antiquity.

The BGS in this respect is often like the BŚS. Individual stanzas and *yajus* formulas are given in full, while only groups of contiguous stanzas tend to be cited by *pratīka*. While other Yajurveda Gṛhyasūtras – namely, the *Āpastamba*, *Kāṭhaka*, and *Vaikhānasa* – and *Gobhila* (and *Khādira*) of the *Sāmaveda*, compiled *mantrasaṃhitās* for the *gṛhya* ritual by analogy with the *śrautasaṃhitās*,[19]

[19] These are all available (the YV Mantrapāṭhas in accented form) in the following editions: *Āpastambamantrapāṭha*: see Winternitz 1897 and Srînivâsâchârya 1902; *Kāṭhakamantrapāṭha*: Caland 1925: 291–310; *Vaikhanasamantrapraśna*: Nārāyaṇa Bhaṭṭa Pākayājin 1910 and Mysore ORI mss. A297 and P1359/2 (on the latter of which see Caland 1929: x–xi); *Mantrabrāhmaṇa*: Stönner 1901; Jörgensen 1911. Caland (1929: xi) finds that the VaiMP must have been composed 'either later than the Gṛhya-text or, at least, at the same time'; Oldenberg (1892: 3–11) argues that the Gobhilas' *Mantrabrāhmaṇa* must have been composed in tandem with the GGS, whereas Knauer (1886: 24ff.) felt the GGS presupposed the MB.

the BGS does not presuppose the existence of such a collection (although it does cite by *pratīka* sequences of stanzas found in the TS).

Not only its form and structure but also its content give indications that the BGS in its extant form cannot be regarded as old compared to other Gṛhyasūtras. The treatment of the *upanayana* (initiation into Veda-study) provides a valuable index of the relative age of the Gṛhyasūtras. Elsewhere, I show that the early descriptions of this rite have the marks of having been made to conform – to a greater or lesser extent – to a common scheme, namely, the 'classical' scheme canonized in the *Mānavadharmaśāstra*. A hierarchical pattern of ages and seasons for the initiation, types of staff and garment, modes of alms-collecting, and so forth, begin to appear, falteringly, in the Gṛhyasūtras of most schools, apparently displacing the older conventions particular to each school.[20] It is clear that, in earlier times, it was generally assumed that initiates would be of brahmin birth (though initiates of other *varṇa*s were not necessarily excluded). The Gṛhyasūtras take pains to assert that, in principle, every able *kṣatriya* or *vaiśya* must undertake *brahmacarya* in order to be considered Ārya. Yet while prescribing *brahmacarya* for the classes of non-brahmins, certain markers of hierarchical difference within the Ārya sphere were needed.

This system represents an effort within priestly circles to inculcate a reverence for Veda mantras, and so for the authority of brahmin knowledge more generally, outside of *śrauta* contexts. The result was a new insistence that *upanayana* and Veda-study were a duty of all male *kṣatriya*s and *vaiśya*s, and the definitive criterion of Ārya status.

The extant Gṛhyasūtras fall along a spectrum, from those that take little or no cognizance of this system (e.g., *Kāṭhaka*, *Mānava*), giving rules that do not make these distinctions, to those that present the system in its full form. Between these extremes, we

---

20 This argument is presented in more detail in Lubin 2005 and forthcoming.

TABLE: Comparison of *varṇa* Distinctions in the *upanayana* according to the Gṛhyasūtras

	B	M	Kā	H = Āg	Vā	Bh	Āp	Vai	Pār	Āśv	Ś	Kauṣ	G	Kh	Jai	Kauś
garbha-	yes	no	no	no	yes	yes	yes	yes	opt (br)	opt (br)	yes	yes	yes	no	no	—
age	8:11:12\ *kāmyāni*	7/9	7:9:11	7:11:12	8/6/7/5: 11:12 kṣ	8/9:11: 12	8:11:12	5/8/9:11 :12	8:11:12\ any	8:11:12	8/10...	8/10...	8:11:12	8:11:12	7/5/9...	—
patita	16 ...	16 ...	16 ...	—	16 ...	16 ...	—	16 ...	16 ...	16 ...	16 ...	16 ...	16 ...	16 ...	16 (:-:-)	—
ajina	k:r:b\k=	k	e:vy:r	k:r:b	k	e.r:b	x	k:r:b	e:r:aj/g\g =	e:r:aj	e:r:g	e:r:g	e:r:aj	—	e:r:aj\e=	e:r:aj/av
vāsas	x	x	x	x	—	x	x...	—	ś:kṣ:āv	k:m:h	x	k:m:h	kṣ/ś:kp: āv\any)	—	kṣ/ś=	kṣ/ś=
mekhalā	m:mū+j: āvi/m\=	m	m:nū+j: [ū]	m:j:āvi	m:j:śa	m:mū:sū	m(:-:-)	m:mū:śā	m:j:mū/. . (*raśanā*)	m:j:āvī	m:j:ū	m:j:ū	m:kāśa:t (*raśanā*)	—	m:mū:t +m/m=	m:mū/j: ks,.auma
daṇḍa	p/b:n/r:b ā/u\any	yajñ. vṛ.	p:a:n	b/p:n:u	p:n:a	b/p:n:u	p:n:bā/u \=	p/b:n:u	p:b:u	p:u:b	p/b:n:u	p/b:n/kh :u	pārṇa:b: a	—	p/b:n:u\ p=	p:a:n
- height	—	—	—	—	—	—	—	k:l:n	k:l:gh\=	k:l:p\=	ṗ:l:k\=	ghr:l:k\ =	—	—	p(=?)	—
season	v:g:ś:var \any=	—	—	v:g:ś	—	v:g/h:ś:v ar*śiśire*=	v:g:ś	v:g:ś	—	—	—	—	—	—	—	—
bhikṣā	x3	x	x	x	x3	x	x	x3	x3	x	x	x	x	x	x3	x3

Key to Symbols:

– Colons separate the prescribed forms for each *varṇa* in the order brahmin:*kṣatriya*:*vaiśya*(:*rathakāra*)
– An oblique signifies an option within a class
– A reverse oblique signifies an option for all classes without distinction
– Equal sign means 'the same for all'
– 'x' means that element is mentioned, but no distinctions by class are made
– An ellipsis means that the rest of the classes follow the usual pattern
– An m-dash means that the category is not mentioned

Key to Abbreviations:

garbha-: (as in *garbhāṣṭame*, etc.) age to be calculated from conception rather than birth; opt(br) = when the age of the brahmin is given, it is noted that calculating from conception is optional.

ajina: e = *eṇī* (black antelope), r = *ruru* (spotted deer), aj = *aja* (goat), av = *avi* (sheep), b = *bakra* (goat), g = *go* (cow), vy = *vyāghra* (tiger).

vāsas: k = *kāṣāya* (rust red), m = *māñjiṣṭha* (madder red), *hāridra* (yellow); kṣ = *kṣauma* (linen), ś = *śāṇa* (hemp), kp = *kārpāsa* (cotton), āv = *āvi* (wool).

mekhalā: m = *muñja* grass, mū = *mūrva* grass, j = *jyā* (bowstring [of *mūrva* grass?]), *āvī* or ū = *ūrṇa* (wool), śā = *śāṇa* (hemp), t = *tāmala* bark, sū = *sūtra* (cotton thread).

daṇḍa: p = *palāśa*, b = *bilva*, u = *udumbara*, n = *nyagrodha*, bā = *bādāra*, a = *aśvattha*, yajñ. vṛ. = the wood of any tree suitable for use in worship.

height of *daṇḍa*: k = *keśa* (hair), l = *lalāṭa* (forehead), p = *prāṇa* (breath = mouth?), ghr = *ghrāṇa* (nose).

season: v = *vasante* (spring), g = *grīṣme* (hot season), ś = *śaradi* (autumn), h = *hemante* (cold season), var = *varṣāsu* (rainy season), śi = *śiśire* (cold season).

bhikṣā: x3 = using the word *bhavati* in first, second, and third position in the three-word petition for alms, respectively; Kauś. specifies the number of houses each class may visit as well: 7:3:2.

find several cases in which the patterns are applied partially and often inconsistently (see Table). The vector is toward consistency across schools, and culminates in Manu's catholic synthesis.

By this standard, then, the BGS must be judged to have been kept 'up-to-date' in adopting the system of distinctions in a very thorough form: The ages 8:11:12 for initiation of brahmins, *kṣatriyas*, and *vaiśyas*, respectively, with 16:22:24 as the latest possible ages, are prescribed for members of different *varṇas*, as well as different animal skins, materials for the *mekhalā*, woods for the staff, seasons for the initiation rite, and word-orders for the alms-request. Only in the material for the garment is no distinction by *varṇa* made (and in the height of the staff, which is not discussed at all). Moreover, BGS 2.5 adopts the method of calculating from conception (rather than from birth) the age suitable for initiation. I argue elsewhere (Lubin 2005; forthcoming) that this peculiar method, used only in this context, may have been introduced in order to reconcile the new system, which requires the use of the number eight corresponding to the number of syllables in a *gāyatrī pāda*, with an older custom of initiating youths at the age of seven, which continues to be the first age cited by four Black Yajurveda schools (*Mānava*, *Kāṭhaka*, *Hiraṇyakeśin*, and *Āgniveśya*) as well as *Jaimini* – none of whom calculate age from conception, and none of whom mention the number eight.[21] In this way, a seven-year-old can be treated as aged 'eight from conception' (*garbhāṣṭame*).[22] *Baudhāyana*, however, simply presents the new standard format of 8:11:12, counting from conception (though he lists seven as the first optional age, for 'one who desires *brahmavarcasa*').

---

[21] For *Kāṭhaka*, *Hiraṇyakeśin*, and *Āgniveśya*, this is the only age assigned to the brahmin; *Mānava* and *Jaimini* offer other options. Seven is also given as an option by *Vārāha*.

[22] Though no rationale is ever provided, another possible reason for calculating so in this context is possible. Since the initiation marks a new birth process, beginning with conception in the teacher's 'womb' (ŚB 11.5.4, etc.), it is appropriate to count years from the last, merely bodily conception. However this symbolical rationale need not exclude a more practical one, which may still be primary.

Another sign of late redaction is the use of *yajñopavīta* to refer to an actual thread rather than to a special manner of wearing the upper garment: thus BGS 2.5.7 prescribes that the teacher, while placing the thread on the initiate (*yajñopavītaṃ pramuñcan*), should make him recite a mantra praising the thread as the 'supreme purifier'. This *triṣṭubh* stanza is a Sūtra-period confection, and is not found, for instance, in the *Āpastambamantrapāṭha*.

Other arguments for its being early, such as its being the basis for 'later' dissensions such as those of *Āpastamba*, cited above (footnote 15) must be considered in light of the fact that such polemics appear also in BGS. In fact, the last of the examples mentioned by Winternitz supplies its own counterargument: It is in fact BGS 2.11.5 that alludes to *Āpastamba*'s view when it states: *yonigotraśrutavṛttasaṃpannān asaṃbandhān ity eke*, 'Some say: [brahmins] not related to him, who possess [good] birth, *gotra*, learning, and conduct' (cf. ĀpGS 21.2: *śucīn mantravato yonigotramantrāsaṃbandhān ... bhojayet*, 'He should feed ... pure, mantra-knowing [brahmins] not related to him by blood or by *gotra* or by mantras [i.e., such as his teachers or pupils]').[23] Indeed, it is one of the BGS's characteristics that it is replete with quotations from and disputations with other authoritative texts, including *Āpastamba*: thus, on the subject of the tuft of hair left during the *caula* rite, BGS 2.4.17–18 appears to quote ĀpGS 16.6: *yatharṣi śikhāṃ nidadhātīty eke* ('Some say, "He arranges the tuft in the manner of the Sages."').[24]

In short, even leaving aside the various passages on this subject that come in the BGPS and BGŚS, we must conclude that the BGS proper acquired its final form relatively late. Hence, any *pravacana*-like traits that it has should be regarded as no more than

---

[23] In fact, the wording is close enough to wonder whether *Āpastamba* might originally have read, with *Baudhāyana*: *yonigotraśrutavṛttasaṃpannān asaṃbandhān* (or *yonigotramantrasaṃpannān asaṃbandhān*) with the loss of *–saṃpannān* arising through eyeskip.

[24] ĀpGS 16.6: *yatharṣi śikhā nidadhāti*. The difference in reading *śikhāṃ* for *śikhā[ḥ]*, 'tufts' is not significant. Other examples are not lacking.

a stylistic idiosyncrasy of the Baudhāyana school – or at most as vestiges of its earliest phase – and not as an indication of the antiquity of the text as a whole.

MATERIALS FOR A NEW EDITION

Just as Caland's edition of the BŚS began to appear in 1904, L. Srinivasachar's edition of the BGS, with the BGPS, BGŚS, and *Baudhāyanapitṛmedhasūtra* was published in Mysore; the work appeared again in 1920, now listing R. Shama Sastri as editor, although this was simply a somewhat corrected revision of the 1904 edition. This edition (or the retypeset reprinting of 1983, which adds rather than removes errors from the text) is still the one cited by scholars, but in several respects there is room for improvement. First, only manuscripts available in Mysore were used. The apparatus is so slight that one suspects that many important variants may have been passed over in silence according to the judgment of the editor. Only three complete manuscripts were used, two in Grantha script and one in Devanagari, plus two incomplete manuscripts, one in Telugu script and a Devanagari manuscript with a modern *vyākhyā*. The 1920 edition is marred by misprints, some of them important ones.

One of the things a new edition can offer is comparison of a much wider range of manuscripts. I have collected already copies of forty-six complete or partial manuscripts, of diverse provenance, and in addition to examples of their testimony mentioned above, I add here remarks on some of them. Most of these are in the Grantha script, reflecting the prominence of the Baudhāyana school in the Tamil region, but the Devanagari, Nandinagari, Telugu, Kannada, Malayalam, and (indirectly, through a transcription) Tigalari scripts are represented as well. Many of these manuscripts have not been used in any of the earlier editions: this is certainly the case with the manuscripts belonging to the Institut français de Pondichéry and to the Pondicherry Centre of the École française d'Extrême-Orient. The latter collection, most of which was obtained as a group from Tirunelveli District in the extreme south of Tamil Nadu, includes six Grantha palm-leaf manuscripts of most or all of the Sūtra. The IFP also has a complete Grantha copy of the Sūtra (M35177), plus a few partial ones.

My Devanagari manuscripts include a paper manuscript kept in the National Archives, Kathmandu (NGMPP A522/6). This manuscript includes the BGS proper, as well as the BGPS, most of the BGŚS (and three *adhyāyas* of the *Pitṛmedhasūtra*). The Taittirīya school has since late Vedic times been restricted to south India, aside from a presence attested in Assam (ca. 600 CE),[25] but there are references to Taittirīya priests in Nepal since at least ca. 750 CE;[26] there has long been a tradition of having south Indian brahmins participate in ritual service in Nepal. The Nepali manuscript does not appear old from the palaeographic point of view, and it may belong to the group of Taittirīya manuscripts from the Konkan or Karnataka, associated with the Bhaṭṭas of Paśupatināth who came to Nepal after King Jagajjaya Malla removed the Nambudiris around 1730.[27]

My manuscripts are Mysore ORI nos. P303/2 (Nandinagari PL) and B353 (Kannada script on paper); Trivandrum, no. 1413 (Grantha PL); not yet in hand is an incomplete Grantha ms. from Tanjore (11784–86). I am informed that an edition of it was in preparation at the Vaidika Saṃśodhana Maṇḍala, Pune, but I do not know its status.

---

[25] Recorded in the Nidhanpur inscription of Bhāskaravarman; see Witzel 1980: 130.

[26] Witzel (2000: 256 and n. 12) cites the Nārāyaṇ Caur inscription of ca. 750, which alludes to a *taittirīśākhāgoṣṭhī*; he also notes a Nepalese manuscript of the *Śivadharmaśāstra*, that was copied by one Ratnasiṃha residing in the *taittirīya-śālā* in Kathmandu in 1026. Witzel (1985; 1994; 2000: 256, n. 13) provides references to south Indian brahmins officiating in other north Indian locales.

[27] Witzel 2000: 285, 293. Although Witzel (2000: 289) in a brief note describes this manuscript as including a commentary, the microfilm made for me by the National Archives in Kathmandu, comprising 101 folios, shows the *mūla* text alone.

I have also been able to turn up some previously unknown material. During a recent field trip I photographed a manuscript in Malayalam script belonging to Kaimukku Sreedharan Nambuthiri of Kaimukku Mana, near Irinjalakuda,[28] as well as an early-20th-century Devanagari transcription of a palm-leaf written in the Tigalari script, belonging to Subrahmanya Bhatt of Gokarn. Meanwhile, Ikari's work in bringing to light new manuscripts of (fragments of) the *Vādhūlagṛhyasūtra*, promises to clarify further the relation of the Baudhāyanas to adjacent Vedic schools, and may help in settling textual questions.[29]

Caland 100 years ago lamented the lack of a BGS commentary.[30] Despite the availability of *prayoga*s and *paddhati*s of this school, the Baudhāyanīyas that I have spoken with know only one commentary, the *Śiṣṭivyākhā*, which remains unpublished.[31] This short work covers only the first three *praśna*s of the Sūtra, although one of my manuscripts, a Nandinagari palm leaf from Mysore, begins with a discussion of *pravara* (the appointment of priests).[32]

---

[28] I know of only two other Malayalam manuscripts of the Sūtra: ms. L. 179 of the University Manuscript Library, Trivandrum (the other five BGS manuscripts in that collection being in Grantha or, in one case, Devanagari script), and ms. R. 4692(a) in the GOML, Madras, a paper manuscript including the *Paribhāṣā-* and *Śeṣasūtras*. Both of these are available to me in photographs.

[29] Four privately owned manuscripts of the *Vādhūlagṛhyasūtra*, along with other relevant materials, have been identified and photographed by Yasuke Ikari during field surveys in Kerala in 1992 and 1994 (Ikari 1995: 3–4; 1998: 5, 13–17).

[30] Caland (1903: 15) mentions a report by Hultzsch of the discovery of a commentary; this is presumably no. 668, a 58ff. palm leaf from Thiruvaiyaru, listed by Hultzsch (1896: 2).

[31] I am informed that an edition of it is currently being prepared by the Vaidika Saṃśodhana Maṇḍala, Pune.

[32] This manuscript of the *Śiṣṭi* (no. P303/2) begins with a 13-leaf section on *pravara*. On f. 14, where the commentary on BGS *praśna* 1 starts, a newer pagination using Arabic numerals in chalk and pen begins (with f. 14r as '1'); this may have been added by the writer of a Telugu transcript on paper, which omits the *pravara* section; this transcriber worked either from P303/2 or from the same prototype, since, for instance, they both show a space near the end (42r6/72r8) where the source manuscript had illegible or broken-off characters, or a lacuna. B353 supplies a conjecture, with is underlined in the Telugu. In any

In any case, the fact that that the author of the *Śiṣṭi* ignores the fourth *praśna* of the BGS, which is a collection of *prāyaścitta*s (expiations for defects in the performer or the ritual performance), suggests that he regarded it as secondary, e.g., as a *pariśiṣṭa*.

Apart from the *Śiṣṭivyākhyā*, the Sarasvatī Bhavan in Banaras lists in its collection a single manuscript of a *bhāṣya* by Vopanabhaṭṭa, but I have not yet been able to consult it. Some help in constituting the text may also be provided by *Bodhāyanapūrvāparaprayoga*, which sometimes quotes from the Sūtra.[33] The *Bodhāyanīyabrahmakarmasamuccaya*, a contemporary *prayoga*, provides a rich exposition of how contemporary Baudhāyanīyas put the rules into practice.

REFERENCES

Editions of Select Texts

BGS, BGPS, BGŚS = *Baudhāyanagṛhyasūtra* (including appendices)

1904 *The Bodhâyana-grihya-sûtra*. Ed. by L. Śrînivâsâchârya. (Government Oriental Library Series, Bibliotheca Sanskrita, 32.) Mysore: Government Branch Press.

1905 *Maharṣibodhāyanapraṇītaḥ smārtakalpasūtragranthaḥ*. Ed. by Maṇakkāl N. Muddu Dīkshita. Cennanagara [Madras]: Jñānasāgara Press. (Full t.p.: *Akhilaśrautasmārta satkarmācaraṇālaṃkarmīṇānāṃ śiṣṭajanānām atyantāpekṣaṇīyaḥ, pūrvāparaprāyaścittaparībhāṣādivividhaviśeṣavipulaḥ. Śrīmadāoāryavarma. Maharṣibodhāyanapraṇītaḥ smārtakalpasūtragranthaḥ. Ayaṃ kila maṇakkāl grāmavāstavyena kalpasūtraviśāradena śrīrāmaśarmaparanāmnā muddudīkṣitena anekavividvajjansāhāyyapūrvaṃ samyakpariśoddhya cennanagaralalāmabhūtāyām.*) (Grantha script.)

1920 *Bodhāyanagṛhyasūtram / The Bodhâyana Gṛihyasutra*. Ed. by R. Shama Sastri. (Oriental Library Publications, Sanskrit Series, 32/55.) Mysore: University of Mysore/Government Branch Press; reprint: 1983. [Corrected version of the 1904 edition.]

---

case, the secondary pagination of P303/2 and the shorter text of B353 suggests that the *pravara* discussion was not always considered an integral part of the *vyākhyā*.

[33] See the 1930 edition in the bibliography, as well as the 1903 edition of the *Aparaprayoga*.

1920 Poona. (?) [Mentioned in A Printed List of Printed Books and Manuscripts in the Veda Sastra Uttejaka Sabha, 608, Sadashiv Peth, Poona, by Vaidya Pancānan Krishna Sastri Kavade, 1925.]

1986–89 *Sri Gṛhyasūtram Bodhāyanācāryapraṇītam; vidvānmaṇḍalyā sampāditam; Rāmacandraśāstrī-Sūri-viracitayā 'Sañjīvinī'-samākhyayā vyākhyayā samalaṅkṛtam; Bhalacandraśāstrinām viśiṣṭabhūmikāsahitam; Anantabhattai saṃśodhitam / Classical manual for Hindu domestic ceremonies, according to the Baudhayana school in the Taittiriya recension of yajurveda*, 4 vols. [second title in vols. 2–4 only]. Honnavar, Karnataka: Śri Subrahmaṇyaprācyavidyāpīṭham.

BGPrayoga = *Baudhāyanagṛhyaprayoga*

1903 *Bodhāyanagṛhyoktāparaprayogākhyo 'yaṃ granthaḥ*. Ed. by Īśvara Yajvā & Rāmakṛṣṇa Śāstrī. Palghat: Vāṇīvilāsa Press. (Grantha type.)

1930 *Bodhāyanapūrvāparaprayogaḥ*. Kumbakonam: Grantha Pratiṣṭhānam, Śrīmahārājasaheb Śrigovindadīkṣitapuṇyasmaraṇasamitiḥ; reprints: 1985, 1998. (Grantha type.)

BPitS = *Baudhāyanapitṛmedhasūtra* (see also the editions of BGS)

1896 *The Pitṛmedhasūtras of Baudhāyana, Hiraṇyakeśin, Gautama edited with critical notes and index of words*. Ed. by Willem Caland. (Abhandlungen für die Kunde des Morgenlandes, 10.3.) Leipzig: F. A. Brockhaus; reprint: Nendeln: Kraus Reprints, 1966.

1911 *Bijdrage tot de kennis van het Hindoesche doodenritueel*. Ed. by C. H. Raabe. Leiden: Brill.

BŚS = *Baudhāyanaśrautasūtra*

1904–23 *The Baudhāyana Śrauta Sūtra*, 3 vols. Ed. by Willem Caland. (Bibliotheca Indica, Work 163.) Calcutta: Asiatic Society.

BDhS = *Baudhāyanadharmasūtra*

1922 *Das Baudhayana-Dharmasutra*. 2nd edition. Ed. by E. Hultzsch. (Abhandlungen für die Kunde des Morgenlandes, 16.) Leipzig: F. A. Brockhaus.

1972 *The Baudhayana-Dharmasutra with the 'Vivarana' Commentary by Sri Govinda Svami and Critical Notes by M. M. A. Chinnaswami Sastri*. Ed. by Umesa Chandra Pandeya. (Kashi Sanskrit Series, 104.) Varanasi: Chaukhamba Sanskrit Sansthan.

2000 *Dharmasūtras: The Law Codes of Āpastamba, Gautama, Baudhāyana, and Vasiṣṭha*. Ed. and trans. by Patrick Olivelle. Oxford: OUP.

BBKS = *Bodhāyanīyabrahmakarmasamuccaya*

1970 *Bodhāyanīyabrahmakarmasamuccayaḥ*. By a committee consisting of Gaṇapati Subrahmaṇya Dīkṣita, Rāmacandra Gaṇeśabhaṭṭa Koḍlekere, Parameśvara Rāmakṛṣṇaśarmā Bailakerī, Śrautī Subrāya Gaṇeśabhaṭṭa Koḍlekere, and Rāma Veṃkaṭaramaṇa Paṃḍita; with an introduction ('Upodghātaḥ') by C. G. Kashikar (ff. 2r–8v). Gokarn: Śrī-Medhā-Dakṣiṇāmūrti-Saṃskṛta-Vidyāpīṭha, śake 1892, īsavīya san 1970.

MB = *Mantrabrāhmaṇa* (*Sāmaveda*)

1901 *Das Mantrabrāhmaṇa. 1. Prapāṭhaka*. Ed. by Heinrich Stönner. Halle: [s.n.].

1911 *Das Mantrabrāhmaṇa. 2. Prapāṭhaka*. Ed. by Hans Jörgensen. Darmstadt: Wintersche.

ĀpMP = *Āpastambamantrapāṭha*

1897 *The Mantrapāṭha, or The Prayer Book of the Āpastambins edited together with the commentary of Haradatta*, vol. 1. Ed. by M. Winternitz. Oxford: Clarendon Press. [The promised second volume, intended to comprise a translation of the mantras, plus Haradattamiśra's commentary, never appeared.]

1902 *Kṛṣṇayajurvedīyaḥ ekāgnikāṇḍaḥ Haradattamiśraviracitavyākhāsahitaḥ / The Ekágnikáṇḍa of the Krishna-Yajur-Veda with the Commentary of Haradattamiśra*. Ed. by L. Srînivâsâchârya. (Government Oriental Library Series, Bibliotheca Sanskrita, 28.) Mysore: Government Branch Press.

KāṭhGS = *Kāṭhakagṛhyasūtra*

1925 *The Kāṭhakagṛhyasūtra, with Extracts from Three Commentaries, an Appendix and Indexes*. Ed. by Willem Caland. (Śrīmaddayānanda Mahāvidyālaya Saṃskṛtagranthamālā, 9.) Lahore: Research Department, D.A.V. College.

VaiMP = *Vaikhānasamantrapraśna*

1910 *Śrīvaikhānasamantrapraśnaḥ, sasvaraḥ praśnacatuṣṭayātmakaḥ* .... Ed. by Nārāyaṇa Bhaṭṭa Pākayājin. Kumbakonam: Śāradāvilāsamudrākṣaraśālā. (Grantha type.)

1945 [cover title:] *Śrīvaikhānasa maṃtrapraśnaḥ* ...; [t.p.:] *Śrīvaikhānasagraṃthamālā saptamakusumam dvitīyamudraṇam. sakalamunilōkavaṃditadivyacaraṇana inayuga ēna śrīmadvikhanomunīṃdreṇa saṃgṛhīte apauruṣēyē Śrimati Śrīvaikhānasamantrapraśnāṣṭakē prathamādicaturthapraśnātmakō 'yaṃ bhāgaḥ vidvadbhir yathāmati pariśōdhitaḥ*. Ed. by Di. Raṃgācāryaḥ & Pa. Paṃ. Pa. Si. Bhiṣagvaraḥ. Madras: Sri Gopalakrishna Press. (Telugu type.)

VaiSmS = *Vaikhānasasmārtasūtra*

1929 *Vaikhānasasmārtasūtram: The Domestic Rules and Sacred Laws of the Vaikhānasa School Belonging to the Black Yajurveda*. Ed. by W. Caland. (Bibliotheca Indica, Work 242.) Calcutta: Asiatic Society of Bengal.

Secondary Sources

BHANDARKAR, R. G. 1883. *Report on the Search for Sanskrit MSS. in the Bombay Presidency*, II: *1882/1883*. Bombay: Govt. Central Press.

BÜHLER, Georg 1882. *The Sacred Laws of the Âryas*, II: *Vasishtha and Baudhâyana*. (Sacred Books of the East, 14.) Oxford: Clarendon Press.

—— 1897. *The Sacred Laws of the Âryas*. I: *Âpastamba and Gautama*. 2nd revised edition. (Sacred Books of the East, 2.) Oxford: Clarendon Press.

CALAND, Willem 1903. *Über das rituelle Sūtra des Baudhāyana*. (Abhandlungen für die Kunde des Morgenlandes, 12.1.) Leipzig: F. A. Brockhaus.

—— 1925. [See primary sources under KāṭhGS]

—— 1929. [See primary sources under VaiSmS]

FUSHIMI, Makoto 1998. Brāhmaṇa Passages in Āpastamba-Śrautasūtra. *Electronic Journal of Vedic Studies* 4.1: 1–19.

GONDA, Jan 1977a. *The Ritual Sūtras*. (A History of Indian Literature, 1.2.) Wiesbaden: Otto Harrassowitz.

—— 1977b. The Baudhāyana-Gṛhya-Paribhāṣā-Sūtra. In: *Beiträge zur Indienforschung. Ernst Waldschmidt zum 80. Geburstag gewidmet*: 169–190. Berlin: Museum für Indische Kunst.

HARTING, P. N. U. 1922. *Selections from the Baudhāyana-Gṛhyapariśiṣṭasūtra*. Utrecht: [s.n.].

HOUBEN, Jan E. M. 1991. *The Pravargya Brāhmaṇa of the Taittirīya Āraṇyaka*. Delhi: MLBD.

HULTZSCH, E. 1896. *Reports on Sanskrit Manuscripts in Southern India, no. 2*. Madras: Government Press.

IKARI, Yasuke 1995. Vādhūla Śrautasūtra 1.1–14 [Agnyādheya, Punarādheya]: A new critical edition of the Vādhūla Śrautasūtra, I. *Zinbun: Memoirs of the Research Institute for Humanistic Studies, Kyoto University* 30: 1–129.

—— 1998. A survey of the new manuscripts of the Vādhūla school – MSS. of K_1 and K_4. *Zinbun: Memoirs of the Research Institute for Humanistic Studies, Kyoto University* 33: 1–30.

KAJIHARA, Mieko 2002. *The Brahmacārín in the Veda. The Evolution of the "Vedic Student" and the Dynamics of Texts, Rituals, and Society in Ancient India.* Doctoral dissertation, Harvard University.

KASHIKAR, C. G. 1976. The Avāntaradīkṣā of Pravargya. *Bulletin of the Deccan College Post-Graduate and Research Institute* 35.3–4: 66–72.

KNAUER, Friedrich 1886. *Das Gobhilagṛhyasūtra herausgegeben und übersetzt.* Zweites Heft: *Uebersetzung*. Dorpat: Mattiesen.

KRICK, Hertha 1977. Nārāyaṇabali und Opfertod. *WZKS* 21: 71–142.

LUBIN, Timothy 2005. The transmission, patronage, and prestige of Brahmanical piety from the Mauryas to the Guptas. In: F. Squarcini (ed.), *Boundaries, Dynamics and Construction of Traditions in South Asia* (Kykéion studi e testi, I: Scienze delle religioni, 3): 77–103 Firenze: Firenze University Press.

—— 2016a. Baudhāyanīya contributions to Smārta Hinduism. In: Jan E. M. Houben, Julieta Rotaru & Michael Witzel (eds.), *Vedic Śākhās: Past, Present, Future. Proceedings of the Fifth International Vedic Workshop, Bucharest 2011* (HOS, Opera Minora). Cambridge, Mass.: Harvard University.

—— 2016b. The Vedic *Homa* and the Standardization of Hindu *Pūjā*. In: Richard K. Payne & Michael Witzel (eds.), *Homa Variations. The Study of Ritual Change across the Longue Durée* (Oxford Ritual Studies): 143–166. New York: OUP.

—— forthcoming. The householder ascetic and the uses of self-discipline. In: Peter Flügel & Gustaaf Houtman (eds.), *Asceticism and Power in South and Southeast Asia*. London: RoutledgeCurzon.

NĀRĀYAṆA BHAṬṬA PĀKAYĀJIN 1910. [See primary sources under VaiMP]

OLDENBERG, Hermann 1892. *The Grihya-Sûtras. Rules of Vedic Domestic Ceremonies*, II. (Sacred Books of the East, 30.) Oxford: Clarendon.

OLIVELLE, Patrick 1993. *The Āśrama System. The History and Hermeneutics of a Religious Institution*. New York: OUP.

—— 2000. [See primary sources under BDhS]

ROLLAND, Pierre 1969. Deux pariśiṣṭa de l'école Vārāha. *JA* 257: 265–272.

—— 1972. Un fragment médical "védique": La premier khaṇḍa du Vārāhapariśiṣṭa Bhūtotpatti. *Münchner Studien zur Sprachwissenschaft* 30: 129–138.

WINTERNITZ, M. 1892. *Das altindische Hochzeitsrituell nach dem Āpastambīya-Gṛihyasūtra und einigen anderen verwandten Werken.* (Denkschriften der kaiserlichen Akademie der Wissenschaften, Philosophisch-historische Klasse, 40.) Vienna: F. Tempsky.

WITZEL, Michael 1979–80. Die Kaṭha-Śikṣā-Upaniṣad und ihr Verhältnis zur Śikṣāvallī der Taittirīya-Upaniṣad. *WZKS* 23: 5–28; 24: 21–80.

—— 1985. Regionale und überregionale Faktoren in der Entwicklung vedischer Brahmanengruppen in Mittelalter (Materialien zu den vedischen Schulen, 5). In: H. Kulke & D. Rothermund (eds.), *Regionale Tradition in Südasien* (Beiträge zur Südasienforschung, 104): 37–76. Wiesbaden: Steiner Verlag.

—— 1994. The Brahmins of Kashmir. In: Y. Ikari (ed.), *A Study of the Nīlamata. Aspects of Hinduism in Ancient Kashmir*: 237–294. Kyoto: Institute for Research in Humanities, Kyoto University.

—— 2000. Medieval Veda tradition as reflected in Nepalese manuscripts. *Journal of the Nepal Research Centre* 12: 255–300.

Dakṣiṇā in Vedic Sacrifices

MANJULA DEVI

Dakṣiṇā – the 'honorarium' or 'fee' presented by the sacrificer to the priests – plays a significant role in Vedic sacrifices. *Dakṣiṇā* is highly eulogized in Vedic texts. A whole hymn (ṚV 10.107) is attributed to her praise in the Ṛgveda. This paper attempts to trace the significance of the *dakṣiṇā* in Vedic sacrifices.

The word *dakṣiṇā* is derived from the root *dakṣ-* 'to prosper' with the addition of the suffix *inan.*[1] Yāska explains the term *dakṣiṇā* in his *Nirukta* (1.7) by stating that the term *dakṣiṇā* is derived from *dakṣ-* meaning 'to cause to accomplish': it causes the imperfect to be accomplished *(dakṣiṇā dakṣateḥ samardhayati karmaṇaḥ vyṛddhaṃ samardhayatīti).* So whatever fails in a sacrifice the sacrificer invigorates by means of giving *dakṣiṇā* to the priests; thereupon the sacrifice becomes successful. Cf. *Śatapatha-brāhmaṇa* (ŚB 2.2.2.2), according to which 'the gods made it successful by means of *dakṣiṇā*s; it is called *dakṣiṇā* because they made it successful by means of *dakṣiṇā*s' (*taṃ devā dakṣiṇābhir adakṣayaṃs tad yad enaṃ dakṣiṇābhir adakṣayaṃs tasmād dakṣiṇā nāma*). *Taittirīyabrāhmaṇa* (TB 3.11.8.8) states: 'One who accepts the sacrificial fee is competent to accomplish everything' (*dakṣate ha vai dakṣiṇāṃ pratigṛhya*). In his commentary on ṚV 2.12.11, Sāyaṇācārya too has said (that the *dakṣiṇā* is so called

[1] Cf. Bhaṭṭojī Dīkṣita's *Siddhāntakaumudī*, Uṇādiprakaraṇa 2.50: *drudakṣibhyām inan.*

because it makes the sacrifice to go forward (*dakṣaṃ utsāhanaṃ karotīti dakṣiṇā*).

But Yāska has furnished also a different interpretation of the term *dakṣiṇā* by stating in *Nirukta* 1.7: 'or else, it refers to the southern direction of space on account of the (*dakṣiṇā*'s) arrival in the sunwise direction' (*api vā pradakṣiṇāgamanād diśaṃ abhipretya dakṣiṇā*). This is connected with the procedure of bringing the honoraria to the sacrificial place for distribution among the priests. Skandasvāmin comments this passage of the *Nirukta* as follows:

> *api vā dānakāle dakṣiṇasyāṃ vediśroṇyām agreṇa gārhapatyaṃ dakṣiṇena sado dakṣiṇā nīyate | tataḥ pradakṣiṇāgamanād diśaṃ dakṣiṇām abhipretya dakṣiṇeti*
>
> Or else, when the moment comes for the distribution of the sacrificial fee, the objects of which it consists are brought to the southern (*dakṣiṇā*) border of the altar (*vedi*) along the route that goes east of the *gārhapatya* fire and south of the *sadas* shed

As the sacrificial gifts are moved to the right by circumambulation (*pradakṣiṇam*), these are called *dakṣiṇā* and the term definitely refers to the southern quarter. It is clearly stated in the Brāhmaṇas that the gifts which chiefly consist of cows stand south of the altar, e.g., ŚB 11.1.6.22: 'that is why the (cows brought as) sacrificial gifts stand by to the south (of the altar); they drive them from the south' (*tasmād u dakṣiṇata eva dakṣiṇā upatiṣṭhante dakṣiṇato 'bhyavājanti*).[2]

According to the *Aitareyabrāhmaṇa* (AB 6.35), a sacrifice without a *dakṣiṇā* is futile (*yajño 'dakṣiṇo riṣyati*). 'They say that no offering in a sacrifice should be made without a *dakṣiṇā*', states ŚB 11.1.3.7 (*nādakṣiṇaṃ haviḥ syād iti hy āhuḥ*). Therefore Dakṣiṇā is the mate of the sacrifice: according to ŚB 9.4.1.11, 'the Sacrifice is a Gandharva and the offering-gifts are his Apsarases' (*yajño gandharvas tasya dakṣiṇā apsarasa iti*). *Vājasaneyisaṃhitā*

---

[2] See also *Ṣaḍviṁśabrāhmaṇa* (ṢB 2.10.14).

(VS 18.42) states that the *dakṣiṇās* are called *stāvāḥ*. The commentator Mahīdhara explains that those (sacrificial fees) by means of which the sacrifice and the sacrificer are praised, are *stāvāḥ* (*stūyate yajño yajamānaś ca yābhis tāḥ stāvāḥ*). ŚB 9.4.1.11 also categorically states that 'the sacrifice is praised by means of the sacrificial gifts, and whoever gives sacrificial gifts, he is praised' (*dakṣiṇā vai stāvā dakṣiṇābhir hi yajñaḥ stūyate 'tho yo vai kaś ca dakṣiṇāṃ dadāti stūyata eva saḥ*). Evidence for this are the *dānastutis* of the Ṛgveda, such as ṚV 1.126, which contain the praises of rich priestly rewards.

The sacrificer is enjoined to give sacrificial gifts according to his capacity: if he is not financially sound, he should spend only what he can afford, for no oblation should be made without an honorarium (ŚB 11.1.4.4 *tatro yac chaknuyāt tad dadyān nādakṣiṇaṃ haviḥ syād iti hy āhuḥ*). The sacrificer may give more according to the depth of his faith.[3] AB 6.35 observes:

> *dakṣiṇā vai yajñānāṃ purogavī yathā ha vā idaṃ ano 'purogavaṃ riṣyaty evaṃ haiva yajño 'dakṣiṇo riṣyati tasmād āhur dātavyaiva yajñe dakṣiṇā bhavaty apy alpikāpi*
>
> Dakṣiṇā is the ox that goes in front of sacrifices. Just as a carriage without the foregoing ox is useless, likewise a sacrifice without a fee is useless. So, a fee, however small, must be given in a sacrifice. (AB 6.35)

Gopathabrāhmaṇa (GB 1.1.33) rightly remarks: 'Where there is a sacrifice there is the sacrificial fee and where there is a fee there is the sacrifice' (*yatra hy eva yajñas tad dakṣiṇā yatra vai dakṣiṇās tad yajña iti*).

The sacrifice is regarded as a sure means to attain both worldly and otherworldly possessions. The sacrifice goes to the world of the gods, and the fee which he gives to the priests accompanies it; holding on to the sacrificial fee, the sacrificer also goes to heaven (ŚB 4.3.4.6 *so 'syaiṣa yajño devalokam evābhipraiti tadanūcī*

---

[3] See ŚB 2.2.2.5 *dadyāt tv eva yathāśraddhaṃ bhūyasīs tad yad dakṣiṇā dadāti.*

dakṣiṇā yaṃ dadāti saiti dakṣiṇām anvārabhya yajamānaḥ). While presenting gold as a sacrificial fee to the Firelighter priest in a Soma sacrifice, the sacrificer urges the fee to go to the gods by reciting the Yajurvedic hymn *asmadrātā devatrā gacchata*, etc. In the prayer of that hymn, the sacrificer wishes that there may be a place for him in the world of the gods (cf. ŚB 4.3.4.20). Thus, aimed at the attainment of a heavenly abode the sacrificer performs the sacrifice and offers the sacrificial fee.

Besides, the priestly class is highly honoured with the presentation of the fee. According to AB 2.32, the whole sacrifice is established in the priest (*ṛtviji hi sarvo yajñaḥ pratiṣṭhitaḥ*). The Vedic texts are full of references to the civilities to be paid to the priestly class. They occupied a unique position in the society of the Vedic age. According to Vedic texts, the priest should aim at the attainment of pre-eminence in the sacred knowledge.[4] TS 6.6.1.4 states that 'a Brahmin who is learned in the Vedic scriptures becomes a *ṛṣi* born of *ṛṣi*s' (*eṣa vai brāhmaṇa ṛṣir ārṣeyo yaḥ śuśruvān*); in other words, learning is the criterion of sagehood. A Brahmin who is well-versed in Vedic studies is entitled to perform the sacrifice and to receive the sacrificial fee. Who is not entitled to perform a sacrifice but officiates as a priest should renounce the fee and be duly expiated.[5] The Brahmins are often declared to be the gods on earth, that is, to personify gods.[6] ŚB 4.3.4.4 categorically states:

> *dvayā vai devā devāḥ | ahaiva devā atha ye brāhmaṇāḥ śuśruvāṃso 'nūcānās te manuṣyadevās teṣāṃ dvedhāvibhakta eva yajña āhutaya eva devānāṃ dakṣiṇā manuṣyadevānām ... āhutibhir eva devān prīṇāti, dakṣiṇābhir manuṣyadevān*

[4] See TB 3.8.13.1 *ā brahman brāhmaṇo brahmavarcasā jāyatām ity āha*; VS 22.22 *brāhmaṇa eva brahmavarcasaṃ dadhāti*.

[5] *Sāmavidhānabrāhmaṇa* 1.5.11 *ayājyayājane dakṣiṇās tyaktvā māsaṃ caturthe kāle bhuñjānaḥ kānī ity etad gāyet*.

[6] E.g., TS 1.7.3.1 *ete vai devāḥ pratyakṣaṃ yad brāhmaṇāḥ*.

> Indeed, there are two kinds of gods. The gods are the gods and the Brahmins who have studied and teach sacred lore are the human gods. The sacrifice is divided into two between these two: the sacrificial offerings are for the gods and the sacrificial fee is for the human gods. The gods are pleased by the sacrificial offerings and by the fee the human gods ... he satisfies the gods with oblations, the human gods with sacrificial gifts. (Cf. also ŚB 1.1.28).

It is also remarked in ŚB 12.4.4.6 that a Brahmin descending from a *ṛṣi* represents all the deities (*brāhmaṇo vā ārṣeyaḥ sarvā devatāḥ*). Thus the priestly class is exalted even above the gods.

On the other hand, it is to be noted that a priestly greed for sacrificial fees is condemned in Vedic texts. ŚB 9.5.2.16 distinctly instructs: 'There should be no bargaining as to the sacrificial fee, for by bargaining the priests are deprived of their place in the highest region' (*dakṣiṇāsu tv eva na saṃvaditavyaṃ saṃvādenaiva ṛtvjijo 'lokā iti*). The priest is also ordained not to accept a sacrificial fee that has been refused by another priest.[7] But should he receive it, he should give it to an adversary whom he does not like.[8] Thus the Vedic texts caution the priests to follow a code of conduct though they are honoured with lucrative honoraria.

The officiating priests alone are entitled to accept the sacrificial fee and not any persons who are not officiating priests.[9] The officiating priests are to get the fee according to their shares as laid down in Vedic texts. The entire fee is divided into four shares that are distributed among four graded priestly groups, the *bhāginaḥ, ardhinaḥ, tṛtīyinaḥ* and *pādinaḥ*.[10] The principal priests are called *hotṛ, adhvaryu, brahman* and *udgātṛ* and they receive each 12% of the whole amount, and as such they are called *bhāgin*. The four priests called *maitrāvaruṇa, pratiprasthātṛ, brāhmaṇācchaṃsin* and *prastotṛ* are called *ardhin*, which means they enjoy half of the

---

7 ŚB 3.5.1.25 *tasmān nivṛttadakṣiṇāṃ na pratigṛhṇīyāt*; AB 6.35 *tasmād āhur na nivṛttadakṣiṇāṃ pratigṛhṇīyāt*.

8 AB 6.35 *yadi tv enāṃ pratigṛhṇīyād apriyāyaināṃ bhrātṛvyāya dadyāt*.

9 ŚB 4.3.4.5 *tasmād ṛtvigbhya eva dakṣīṇā dadyān nānṛtvigbhyaḥ*.

10 Cf. Karka on *Kātyāyanaśrautasūtra* (KŚS 10.2.24) *ṛtvijaḥ prakṛtyaivaṃ śrūyante bhāgina ardhinas tṛtīyinaḥ pādina iti*.

share of the principal priests, that is, 6% each. The four priests called *acchāvāka*, *neṣṭṛ*, *āgnīdhra* and *pratihartṛ* are known as *tṛtīyin*, as they get one third of the principal priests' share, that is, 4% each. The four priests called *grāvastut*, *unnetṛ*, *potṛ* and *subrahmaṇya* get 3% each, that is, one fourth of the principal priests' share and therefore are called *pādin*.[11] According to the *Jaiminīya-Upaniṣadbrāhmaṇa* (JUB 3.17.5), however, 'formerly they brought half of the fee to Brahman and the remaining half to the other priests' (*ardhā ha sma vai purā brahmaṇe dakṣiṇā nayantīti ardhā itarebhyaḥ ṛtvigbhyaḥ*).

In the Vedic age, the sacrificial fee principally consisted of cows. Herds of cows that people kept were so big that they were given away in hundreds and thousands as fees. The *Kātyāyana-śrautasūtra* (KŚS 15.4.51) mentions that hundred thousand cows were offered as a fee in the sacrifice of royal consecration, the *rājasūya* (*śataṃ sahasrāṇi dakṣiṇā*). It is, of course, remarkable that the Vedic seers exaggerated the quantity of gifts bestowed on the priests. 'Cow is offered as a *dakṣiṇā,* because the *dakṣiṇā* as well as the cow grants all desires of man', explains ŚB 2.2.1.21 (*dhenur iva vā iyaṃ manuṣyebhyaḥ sarvān kāmān duhe*). The word *vara* may stand for the cow as a sacrificial fee: Sāyaṇācārya in his commentary on TB 3.12.5.7 (*varo dakṣiṇā*) states: *varaśabdena gaur abhidhīyate | gaur vai vara ity āpastambenābhidhānāt | sā hi vara iti śruteś ca.*

Anvāhārya is often mentioned as a sacrificial fee in Brāhmaṇa texts. It is a mess of food cooked with rice. The term *anvāhārya* is derived from *anu+ā+hṛ-* with the suffix *ṇyat* added to the root. The sacrificer redeems the oblation with the mess of rice and he thereby supplies or makes good whatever may be wanting in the sacrifice; therefore, it is called *anvāhārya*.[12] According to

---

[11] Cf. KŚS 10.2.24 *yathārambhaṃ dvādaśa dvādaśādyebhyaḥ ṣaṭ ṣaḍ dvitīyebhyaś catasraś catasras tṛtīyebhyas tisras tisra itarebhyaḥ.*

[12] ŚB 11.1.8.6 *āhutim evānvāhāryeṇa niṣkrīṇāti tad yad etadd hīnaṃ yajñasyānvāharati taṣmād anvāhāryo nāma*; cf. also TS 1.7.3.1.

Sāyaṇācārya's commentary on ŚB 11.1.8.6, the *anvāhārya* takes away the guilt incurred by the sacrificer due to mistakes during the sacrifice (*anvāharati doṣajātam anena śamayatīti*). Thus the *anvāhārya* mess of rice serves the purpose of *dakṣiṇā* very well.

ŚB 4.3.4.7 mentions four kinds of objects used as *dakṣiṇā*: gold, the cow, clothing and the horse (*catasro vai dakṣināḥ | hiraṇyaṃ gaur vāso 'śvaḥ*). Gold is given as a sacrificial fee for the well-being of the sacrificer.[13] Gold weighing a hundred grains (*śatamānam*) is offered as a fee in various sacrifices. ŚB 13.1.1.4 justified this as follows:

> *śatamānaṃ bhavati śatāyur vai puruṣaḥ śatendriya āyur evendriyaṃ vīryam ātman dhatte*
>
> Man has a life of a hundred years and he possesses a hundred energies. The sacrificer who offers *śatamāna* gold as a fee in the sacrifice is able to procure for himself life, energy and vigour.

In addition to the four principal kinds of gifts, the sacrificer may offer many other objects to regale the priests. Among them are animals, chariots, clothes, food, utensils, agricultural equipments and so on.[14]

The priests perform the sacrifice accurately and in recognition they earn the honorarium as their livelihood. AB 6.3 rightly observes that the sacrificial fee procures food for the priest (*annaṃ dakṣiṇā*). *Dakṣiṇā* is also called *pitu* (AB 1.13 *dakṣiṇā vai pitu*). According to Yāska (*Nirukta* 9.24), the word *pitu* is a synonym of *anna* and derived from the root *pā-* 'to protect' or from the root *pā-* 'to drink' or from the root *pyai-* 'to swell' (*pitur ity annanāma | pāter vā pibater vā pyāyater vā*).

Thus, the sacrificer is inspired to give away his personal property to the priests as *dakṣiṇā*. The institution of *dakṣiṇā* benefits both the bestower and the receiver and thereby promotes peace and social harmony. It also serves as an ethical regulation by teaching

---

[13] TB 1.6.1.7 *hiraṇyaṃ dakṣiṇā samṛddhyai.*

[14] See ṚV 10.107.2,7; AV(Ś) 6.71.1; TS 1.8.7.1; TB 1.6.1; TĀ 1.32.3.

that the purpose of wealth is its proper distribution in the society, where the sacrificer is trained to look beyond himself. This sense of parting with material possessions as against foolish hoarding of wealth enables the sacrificer to find the path of Truth: 'By means of the sacrificial fee the sacrificer attains faith, and Truth is attained with faith' (*dakṣiṇā śraddhām āpnoti śraddhayā satyam āpyate*), declares the *Vājasaneyisaṃhitā* (19.30). Explaining the term *satya* in this present context, the commentators Uvaṭa and Mahīdhara state that *satya* is the knowledge of Brahman.[15]

To conclude: the ritual of offering *dakṣiṇā* bears an expiatory function in addition to serving as spiritual experience and as social participation.

REFERENCES

AB = *Aitareyabrāhmaṇam*, I–II. Ed. by M. Haug. Bombay: Government Central Book Depôt, 1863 (reprint: Delhi: Bharatiya Publishing House, 1976).

AV(Ś) = *Atharavavedasaṃhitā (Śaunakaśākhā)*, Ed. by S. D. Satavalekara. Pardi śaka 1865 (śaka).

GB = *Gopathabrāhmaṇam*. Ed. by R. L. Mitra & H. Vidyabhushan. Calcutta: The Asiatic Society of Bengal, 1872 (reprint: Delhi: Indological Book House, 1972).

JUB = *Jaiminīya-Upaniṣadbrāhmaṇam*. Ed. with translation and notes by Hanns Oertel. *JAOS* 16 (1896):79–260.

KŚS = *Kātyāyanaśrautasūtram*. Ed. with the commentary of Karka by P. N. Paṭṭābhirāma Śāstrī. New Delhi: Shri Lal Bahadur Shastri Kendriya Sanskrit Vidyapeetha, 1982–83.

Nirukta = *Niruktam* by Yāska, I–III. Ed. with Nighaṇṭu by L. Sarup. Oxford: Oxford University Press (I–II) & Lahore: University of the Punjab (III), 1920–27 (reprint: Delhi: MLBD, 1984).

ṚV = *Ṛgvedasaṃhitā*. Ed. with the commentary of Sāyaṇācārya by N. S. Sontakke & C. G. Kashikar. Poona: Vaidika Saṁśodhana Maṇḍala, 1933–51.

ṢB = *Ṣaḍviṃśabrāhmaṇam*. Ed. with the commentary of Sāyaṇācārya by Jibananda Vidyasagara. Calcutta: Saraswati Press, 1881.

[15] Uvaṭa: *satyaṃ jñānam anantaṃ brahma*; Mahīdhara: *śraddhayā satyaṃ jānam anantaṃ brahmāpyate prāpyate*.

ŚB = *Śatapathabrāhmaṇam (Mādhyaṃdinaśākhā)*. Ed. with the commentaries of Sāyaṇācārya and Harisvāmin by S. Sharma et al. Delhi: Nag Publishers, 1990.

Transl. J. Eggeling. Oxford: Clarendon Press, 1882–1900 (reprint: Delhi: MLBD, 1966).

Siddhāntakaumudī = *Vaiyākaraṇasiddhāntakaumudī* of Bhaṭṭojī Dīkṣita. Ed. (*kṛdantaprabhṛtisamāptiparyantā*) by G. Sharma & P. Sharma, Delhi: MLBD, 1961.

SVB = *Sāmavidhānabrāhmaṇam*. Ed. with the commentary of Sāyaṇācārya by B. R. Sharma, Tirupati: Kendriya Sanskrit Vidyapeetha, 1964.

TĀ = *Taittirīyāraṇyakam*. Ed. with the commentary of Bhaṭṭabhāskaramiśra by A. M. Shastri & P. K. Rangacarya. Mysore: Government Oriental Library, 1900–02 (reprint: Delhi: MLBD, 1985).

TB = *Taittirīyabrāhmaṇam*. Ed. with the commentary of Sāyaṇācārya by P. Kumar. Delhi: Nag Publishers, 1998.

TS = *Taittirīyasaṃhitā*. Ed. with the commentaries of Bhaṭṭabhāskaramiśra and Sāyaṇācārya by N. S. Sontakke & T. N. Dharmadhikari. Poona: Vaidika Saṁśodhana Maṇḍala, 1970–2010.

VS = *Vājasaneyisaṃhitā (Mādhyaṃdinaśākhā)*. Ed. with the commentaries of Uvaṭa and Mahīdhara by J. L. Shastri. Delhi: MLBD, 1978.

Why Perform Vedic Sacrifice in the 21st Century? Notes on Recent Vedic Ephemera

FREDERICK M. SMITH

INTRODUCTION[1]

It is easy to repeat the observation that the dwindling numbers of Vedic ritualists who perform *śrauta* sacrifices do so out of a sense of cultural preservation, maintenance of traditional hobbies, etc. While that may be true, I would like to add a few other observations, based on my own notes and queries that grow out of more than twenty-five years of 'Vedic fieldwork', during which I have had extensive contact with *śrauta* ritualists in Maharashtra, Gujarat and South India. Some of the viewpoints of these ritualists are predictable, but their thinking on topics critical to their lives and practices is unexpectedly broad, ranging from issues of authenticity and self-actualization to notions of cosmogonic reality, divine inspiration, worldly rectification, science real and imagined, social responsibility, and enactment of *vidhi* or injunction derived from esoteric, and therefore empowering, understanding of the Vedas.

---

1 A slightly revised version of this essay is in press to appear in the Frits Staal Memorial Volume edited by George Thompson and Richard K. Payne. The author has kindly conceded to our wish to publish here this original version presented at the 12th World Sanskrit Conference. We think the paper deserves to be widely known and that its duplicate appearance should not do any harm – in any case, the possible blame for it belongs to us, not to Fred Smith. [AP & PK]

A cursory glance at the history of Indology reveals that Western and Western-trained scholars have been deeply suspicious – and have often been hastily dismissive – of modern Vedic education and ritualism. The early Indological suspicion resulting from religious bias, clothed as intellectual bias, has been replaced with positivist presuppositions that leave little room for the viewpoints and logic of classical dharma and ritual texts, which up to the present have continued to influence *śrauta* ritualists more strongly than Western positivism. It is for this reason that the motivations of modern ritualists – and the contemporary literature, ephemeral though it is, through which these are often revealed – have not become the subject of scholarly analysis. The issue, however, is not so simple as extracting a few standard ideas from Vedic or Purāṇic textuality and ascribing them to modern ritualists. It is more complex than this, to a great extent because the present era of multi- and cross-cultural influence leaves no area of 'traditional' Indic activity and thought isolated or unaffected. With this caveat, then, we must take seriously the claims and rationale of contemporary Vedic 'traditionalism' in theorizing about the socio-religious praxis of modern ritualists, which is never as 'traditional' as they might sometimes wish. In doing so, we must distinguish this traditionalism within (and from) its political trappings, and try to determine what may be of lasting value for it (as well as for us).

We may ask a number of questions in addition to the issues posed above, aware that in the brief space of this essay we will have little opportunity to do more than point towards a few answers. How, for example, do modern ritualists, including passive ones, namely patrons who perform or have the sacrifices performed for them, view their religious objectives and responsibilities? How do they view their social objectives and responsibilities? What forms of social responsibility and caste relations do they objectivize? How has the authority traditionally accorded to brahmans stood the tests of modernity? Have the various pressures of modernity to behave in a more socially inclusive manner dented this traditional stance? To all these questions, there may be as many answers as there are Vedic ritualists and patrons. Have the rituals become unrecognizably compromised as a result of this peculiar modernity, or have the adaptations and accommodations to modern social and political realities allowed the rituals to survive in a manner that reflects roughly the same quality and quanta of change that may be found in other historical periods? Do today's Vedic ritual forms follow, consciously or otherwise, the creative impulse of the Arya Samaj and other reformist groups in the nineteenth century? Finally, and perhaps most importantly, how are these questions addressed in ephemeral, even disposable literature produced by these ritualists for public consumption at the time of the performance of *śrauta* sacrifices? These are only some of the questions that may be asked of the modern performances of Vedic ritual.

I will here deal – again, all too briefly – with two models of Vedic ritualism in the late twentieth and early twenty-first centuries. First, we will look at some of the cultural practices of three *śrautins* of contemporary Maharashtra who have performed a large number of complicated soma sacrifices, as well as at the ephemera produced by them. Second, we will look at three *śrautins* of the Puṣṭimārga, a sect of Kṛṣṇa devotion primarily found in western India (Gujarat, Rajasthan, Mumbai), the rationale they resort to for their performances, and the literary ephemera they have produced. For the latter, it will be helpful to examine a revealing precedent from the sixteenth century in the form of a fragment of a Vedic commentary. What we will see here are examples of how this literary ephemera augments performance, how even the most seemingly innocuous material is qualitatively interpretive and commentatorial, and how the pressures of modernization have influenced modern ritual thinking. As several of the articles in the second volume of Frits Staal's *Agni* demonstrated more than twenty years ago, many of the modern innovations and reinterpretations are perhaps not so modern.

THE CONTEMPORARY CULTURE OF *ŚRAUTA* RITUAL IN MAHARASHTRA

I have dealt with the topic of *śrauta* ritual in Maharashtra in an earlier paper (Smith 2001), discussing current trends and the performance histories of recent *śrautins*. Here I would like to add just a bit to what I said in that article, addressing my concerns to the issues cited above. The most prominent *āhitāgnis* of the last twenty-five years in Maharashtra were Nārāyaṇ Govind (Nānā) Kāḷe of Barsi (Solapur District, b. 1932), Raṅganāth Kṛṣṇa Selūkar of Gangakhed (Parbhani District, d. 2002) and Mahādev Viṣṇu (Nānā) Atre of Solapur (1911–1994). These three *āhitāgnis* have performed a large number of *soma* sacrifices, many, perhaps even most, of them exotic even by the standards of *śrauta* ritual. For their performances, these men of relatively modest means required large endowments. Among them, Śrī Kāḷe is the wealthiest and most independent, as the owner of a fairly large tract of productive farmland a few kilometers from Barsi. Though all three were completely dedicated to the performance of *śrauta* ritual, Śrī Kāḷe was the only one with his own Vedic memory school (*pāṭhaśālā*). He has thus been able to draw increasingly on his own students (three of whom are his sons, who have studied different Vedic texts, one the *Ṛgveda*, one the Taittirīya *Yajurveda*, and the third the Rāṇāyaṇīya branch of the *Sāmaveda*) for officiating duties. Keeping the performances very much under his control, and with less need to appeal to outside sources for funding, he has been able to perform his *somayāgas* with *pratyakṣapaśu* or offering of 'actual animal' parts rather than substitutes, as was the practice of Śrī Selūkar and Śrī Atre.[2]

These three *āhitāgnis* produced items of ritual ephemera with every major sacrifice they performed, in addition to performance manuals (*prayogas*) produced by the late Paṇḍit Viśvanāth Śrauti

[2] This is one of the most contentious issues among the ritualists of Maharashtra (and elsewhere in India). See Houben 1999; Gune 1994.

of Nellore for Śrī Atre and Śrī Selūkar, including, for example, *prayogas* for an *ātreyacatūrātra* for Śrī Atre[3] and a *gavāmayana* for Śrī Selūkar.[4] I will here present two *nimantraṇapatras* or letters of invitation to different *somayāgas*.

The *mahāvrata* Performed in Bhopal in 1985

The first is an invitation distributed by Śrī Atre in 1985 to attend a *mahāvrata*, a complicated sacrifice with much of interest, including music and lewd dialogue and sexuality (the dialogue was toned down and the sexuality not enacted at all). In origin the *mahāvrata* was probably a seasonal festival that was integrated with a *soma* sacrifice.[5] It was performed in Bhopal in May 1985 as a purificatory ritual in the wake of the lethal Union Carbide gas leak on 4 December 1984 that killed thousands of local residents and injured probably tens of thousands of others. The *nimantraṇapatra*, which has pages in Hindi, Marathi and English, reads:

> *kṣetre 'smin pālite bhoje janādaivāt kilādhunā* |
> *pīḍitā viṣavātena dhyāyo hy atra sadāśivaḥ* |
> *taṃ devaṃ ca mahādevaṃ mahāvratena toṣaye* |
> *yajñena tārkṣyarūpena svasti me 'stu sadā bhuvi* ||
>
> 'Mahavrata Maha Somayaga' in Bhopal.
>
> This region, the kingdom of great king Bhoja, had the misfortune of facing a serious calamity. Today the people are troubled and are suffering because of the air which is polluted by poisonous gases. Now, as a redress, we shall perform here a great yajnya. This yajnya is an antidote to the poisonous gases. This great Somayaga will heal the atmosphere. Let this Somayaga do good to all of us wherever we are on the face of this planet.
>
> This 'Mahavrata Maha Somayaga' is being performed on the Supreme Command of Parama Sadguru by Yajamana Shri Mahadev Vishnu Atre

---

[3] For *ātreyacatūrātra*, see ĀpŚS 22.18.12–15.

[4] *Prayogas* for Śrī Selūkar were always problematic because he was a Mādhyandina Śuklayajurvedin following the Kātyāyana *śākhā* of ritual praxis, while the entire *ādhvaryava*, including Viśvanāth Śrautī, were Taittirīya Kṛṣṇayajurvedins belonging to the Āpastamba *śākhā*. Reconciling these in performance created nearly intractable problems that I cannot address here (but see Smith 2001). For the *gavāmayana*, see Hillebrandt 1897: 157.

[5] Cf. e.g., Hillebandt 1981: II, 128.

Somayajee for the welfare of the gas stricken people and also for the benefit of the whole world.

It is decided to perform the Yajnya at the Madhav Ashram, Sehore Road, Bairagarh, Bhopal in the immediate and distinguished presence of Parama Sadguru Shri Gajanan Maharaj (Shivapuri, Akkalkot, Maharashtra) from May 15 to May 20, 1985 – Vaisakha Krishna Ekadasi Wednesday to Pratipada Monday, Uttara Praushtpada Nakshatra in the Jyeshta month of Shri Krodhanam year.

The Maha Yajnya will be held according to Srouta method for the welfare of the world and for the removal of the sufferings of the people.

We request all devotees to extend their cooperation by timely participation and deserve to receive the blessings of Yajnya Narayana.

The invitation does not mention the Bhopal gas leak except in the Sanskrit verse at the beginning, which states that Śiva should be propitiated by this *mahāvrata* sacrifice because poison gas has afflicted the city that, because of the good fortune of its people, has earned the protection of King Bhoja. Both the invitation and the sacrifice were thus embedded in the local political and religious context in several ways:

1) They offered a uniquely 'Indian' solution to a catastrophe inflicted by the excesses of westernization (though to be fair, the *yajña* as a political countermeasure was underplayed in favor of the message of *yajña* as a spiritual and environmental corrective to these excesses).[6]
2) The blessings of the *yajamāna*'s guru, Gajanan Maharaj of Akkalkot, were declared paramount in bringing about the goals of the sacrifice.[7]
3) The deities Śiva and Yajñanārāyaṇa were invoked. This conferred on the sacrifice link with local religious culture. In all likelihood no one in Bhopal had ever witnessed a Vedic *soma* sacrifice.

---

[6] Neither Atre, the *yajamāna*, nor Gajanan Maharaj were involved in Hindutva politics.

[7] Gajanan Maharaj was well-known in Maharashtra (and elsewhere) for advocating a '*laukika*' *agnihotra* for his lay, non-initiated, non-brahman, even non-Indian, followers.

4) The invitation appealed to Hindu ethical sensibilities in declaring that *śrauta* ritual was effective in 'the removal of the sufferings of the peoples'.
5) Identifying the sacrifice's commencement on an auspicious day (*tithi*) and under an auspicious lunar asterism (*nakṣatra*) further contextualized it in the realm of Hindu ritual.

Thus, the *mahāvrata* could be identified as an auspicious and special ritual performance that should be supported.

The *aptoryāma* Performed in Beed in 1983

The next example is an invitation in mixed Sanskrit and Marathi to an 'Aptoryāma Somayāga Mahāyajña' performed in Beed, a mid-size industrial town in Parbhani district, by Śrī Selūkar in April 1983. The sacrifice was a *dvisāhasracayana* with *sarvastoma*, meaning that it was a double *agnicayana*, with ten layers of bricks rather than five, featuring the chanting of a large number of *sāmans*. First, Śrī Selūkar, the putative author of the invitation, announces that by the grace of the supreme God (*parameśvarasya paramayā kṛpayā*) he has decided to perform an *aptoryāma yāga*. He supplies the date or commencement (*Caitra śukla dvitīyā śake* 1905 *śukravār*) and the location. He continues that the supreme God, the enjoyer of sacrifices (*yajñabhoktā*), having become satisfied by our sacrificial performance (*yajñānuṣṭhānena*) will bestow on us wealth and enlightenment (*abhyudaya-niḥśreyasaḥ*), as well as the grace that allows us to realize the highest goals of life (*paramapuruṣārthasiddhiḥ*).

He explains that according to the correct Vedic viewpoint (*iti vaidikadharmasya siddhāntaḥ*) *yajña* is a *pūjā* to Agni and Sūrya, the two great deities who consist of brilliance (*tejas*). The mantras and invocation of Agni reach Sūrya, and through him are relayed to Sūryanārāyaṇa or Viṣṇu in the form of the sun. From Sūryanārāyaṇa, the mantras and invocations reach all the gods. Finally, the highest deity internal to all, the deity responsible for *sacchidānanda* (being-consciousness-bliss) is satisfied. This is verified by a 'well-known *smṛti*', which says that an offering properly made to Agni will approach Sūrya, who then gives birth to rain, after which rain becomes food and food becomes offspring (*agnau prāstāhūtiḥ samyak ādityam upatiṣṭhate* | *adityāj jāyate vṛṣṭiḥ vṛṣṭer annaṃ tataḥ prajā* ||).

The Gods themselves, he explains, obtain their character (*devatvam*) and divinity (*divyatvam*) through the sacrifices. Lord Rāmacandra demonstrated through his protection of Viśvāmitra's sacrifice that the institution of Vedic ritual should be supported by *dakṣiṇā*, fees paid by the patron to the ritualists. Furthermore, Śrī Selūkar explains, Bhagavān Gopālakṛṣṇa performed his sacred duty by removing the dirty vessels of the Brāhmaṇas at the time of the Rājasūya of the Pāṇḍavas.

The institution of sacrifice, he says, has been propagated by the Veda for the complete development of man; but today this has been forgotten. Everyone should agree that man once enjoyed the happiness of divinity through the observance of these Vedic rituals. Life today, he continues, can definitely be nourished and protected by the performance of these great sacrifices. Just as only one's own cherishing mother can protect her children and wish them greatness and prosperity, similarly only 'Vedamātā' has the ability to confer on all people the capacity for divinity. On the greatness of the Veda, he says, Jñāneśvara sings the following: *pai ahitā pāsonī kāḍhitī* | *hit deūnī vādhavītī* | *nāhī śrutīparautī* | *māūlī yā jagī* | (Jñāneśvarī 16.459) 'There is no mother like the Vedas who takes away the bad and lets the good flourish.'[8] It then announces that Śrī Raṅganāth Kṛṣṇa Selūkar will perform the Aptoryāma Somayāga in Beed from April 4 to 15, 1983 with this religious ideal in mind.

The leaflet continues, explaining that the principal offering to Agni in this *yāga* is the juice of the plant called *soma*. Thus, we

---

Thanks to Christian Novetzke for the translation. It is part of Jñāneśvar's commentary on *Bhagavadgītā* 16.24 (Jñāneśvarī 16.462). Cf. the 'rendering' or Swami Kripananda: 'The Vedas protect us from evil and give us what is good. There is no mother in the world who is better than they are' (Kripananda 1989: 272).

have the well-known name 'Somayāga'. It then notes that, great authorities on the *yajñakarmakāṇḍa* from all over India and the West, including America, Germany and other Western countries (*pāścātyadeśāt*) will be coming. Also coming will be great priests, brahmans, Vedic scholars, experts in Mīmāṃsāśāstra, lecturers, *kīrtankārs*, devotees, observers of dharma and others with great spiritual experience (*mahānubhāvāḥ*). They will come from major pilgrim centers, including Kashi, Gokarna, Kurukshetra, Madras, Prayag, Pandharpur, Nasik and Tryambakeshvar. They will all be gathering according to Vedic injunction in order to contribute and share their knowledge as well as to perform the sacrifice, lecture and sing religious songs.

The leaflet then states that 'this Mahāyajña is undertaken with the co-operation of the great dharma abiding people of India', and that

> the following great *vidvāns* will be coming:
> 1) *adhvaryu* – Vedamūrti Viśvanāth Śrautī and his learned co-workers from Nellore.
> 2) *hotā* – Vedamūrti Keśavaśāstrī Joglekar and other officiants from Gokarṇa.
> 3) *sāmagāna* – Vedamūrti Naṭarāj Ghanapāṭhī and his learned co-workers from Madras.
> 4) Vedamūrti Nārāyaṇa Śāstrī Bhānose and a few other officiants from Nasik.
> 5) Pradhānaravacanakāra (featured lecturer) – Vedamūrti Paṇḍita Yudhiṣṭhira Mīmāṃsaka from Bahālgaḍh, Sonīpat (Haryāṇā).
> 6) Pradhānapravacanakāra – Svāmī Satyaprakāśa Sarasvatī from Allahabad.
> 7) Pravacanakāra – Vedamūrti Narendra Brahmacārī of the Ārya Sāmaj.

The leaflet concludes formally: 'You are hereby invited to assist in serving and awakening Dharma by gathering for this *yajña*.'

This attractive announcement conveys the same messages to the target audience of prospective donors that we saw in Śrī Atre's *mahāvrata* invitation.[9] In invoking the statement from the 'well-known Smṛti', Śrī Selūkar assented to the message that Vedic ritual is of benefit to the environment. This message is not the brainchild of Gajanan Maharaj alone, but is found often elsewhere India as well.[10] The addition of the names of some of the best-known Vedic families in the area was also undoubtedly attractive to a few potential donors. The name of the elderly Yudhiṣṭhira Mīmāṃsaka, perhaps the best-known Vedic scholar of his time within the Arya Samaj, might have also contributed to the cachét of the performance. What is missing from these announcements, and which would have been less appealing, are explanations of the mechanics of *śrauta* ritual, though many of the dozens of announcements I have collected over the years do in fact have daily schedules of ritual events.

---

[9] Both Atre and Selūkar occasionally experienced financial difficulties, going into substantial debt due to the expenses incurred in their sacrifices. I was in attendance at one of Atre's *somayāgas* when he was unable to pay the proper *dakṣiṇā* at the *dakṣiṇādāna* rite during the afternoon pressing on the *sutyā* day. The *ṛtviks*, led by Viśvanāth Śrautī, went on strike, in the form of a siesta, until Atre could secure the promise of a bank loan from a friendly banker in Solapur a couple of hours later.

[10] Note the following, from an invitation to an *agniṣṭoma* in Kerala in April 2003. The 'Jt. Convenor & International Correspondant, Somayaagam 2003 Committee', P. Vinod Bhattathiripad, writes:

'The word "Yaagam" in Kerala-context is the same as "Yajna" in other states. The attractions of the Somayaagam in Kerala is that all Rithwiks learn all manthras by heart and chanted in the traditional style, with vedic accents like Udaatha, Anudaatha and Svarita as well as the special hand gestures ("Mudra") that accompany special features of Vedam recitation. This method of vedic recitation is believed to release maximum positive energy for purifying the environment. It is well known that large quantity of fumes arising out of burnt ghee, seeds and vast quantity of appropriate herbals, cleanse the environment ... The goal of all Yaagams is the prosperity of the people at large by energizing and protecting the environment. The Sun is considered as the main source of energy supply, and fire is considered as a representation of the Sun's energy. According to the ancient texts on Yaagam, any offer to Fire as a god, is actually an offer to Sun. Any such offer is either to enrich energy in the environment or to destroy the undesirable elements in the environment, and thus, in both ways, environment is protected.'

PUṢṬIMĀRGĪ *ŚRAUTA* RITUAL

Three Puṣṭimārga *ācāryas* who have taken up the *śrauta* fires in the last twenty-five years have produced some of the most extensive ritual ephemera I have encountered. These *āhitāgnis* are the following: First, Gosvāmī Raṇachoḍācārya Mahārāj of Kota (1930–1989), otherwise known as Prathameśjī, because he was the lineage holder of the first (*prathama*) house of the seven Puṣṭimārga houses or lineages, making him one of the most important and influential members of the Vallabh *sampradāya*. He was the first member of this sect of Kṛṣṇa devotion to set the Vedic fires (he performed his *ādhāna* in 1979) in more than two centuries, reviving the practice of *śrauta* ritual in the *sampradāya*. Indeed, Vallabhācārya himself (1479–1531) descended from a family of Tailāṅga *somayājins*, and his first few generations of descendants were *āhitāgnis*. The second modern Puṣṭimārgī *ācārya* to set the Vedic fires was Gosvāmī Vallabharāyjī of Surat (sixth house), who performed his *ādhāna* in 1984 on the inspiration of Prathameśjī. The third was Gosvāmī Gokulotsavajī Mahārāj of Indore (second house), who performed his *ādhāna* in 1991. All of them have performed the *vājapeya*, and both Prathameśjī and Gokulotsavajī have performed the *agnicayana*. All of their performances have been under the direction of Agnihotram Ramanuja Tatachariar of Chennai, primarily because he is a Vaiṣṇava (though he is known to have offered *pratyakṣapaśu* himself), but also because he follows the ritual of the Āpastamba *śākhā* of the Taittirīya recension of the Kṛṣṇayajurveda, the same *śākhā* followed by the extended family of Vallabhācārya. But it is Vaiṣṇava theology rather than reflection on the mechanics of Vedic ritual that is most vividly profiled in the Vedic writings – and indeed in the Vedic performances – of these Puṣṭimārgī *āhitāgnis*.[11] This, however, is not as much of a modern innovation as one might think, as we shall see.

---

[11] See Smith 2000.

While the ephemera examined above do not address the issue of non-violence and animal sacrifice, it was always a major issue, as mentioned. Indeed, for more than eight hundred years, since Rāmānuja (12th century) and Madhvācārya (1238–1317), it has been the single issue that has sequestered Vaiṣṇava *śrautins* from others. More recently, however, Śrī Selūkar and Śrī Atre, both non-Vaiṣṇavas, were vehemently against it, under the influence of Gajanan Maharaj's opposition, while Śrī Kaḷe has strongly advocated it. Some of the more extensive ephemeral literature addresses this issue, though it is not usually present in leaflets or letters of invitation. The *śrautins* of the Puṣṭimārga, *ācārya*s in the highest positions of authority in their sect, are Vaiṣṇavas with a long history of adherence to the strictest rules of personal purity, vegetarian cooking and opposition to animal sacrifice.[12] This is not neglected by three late twentieth-century Puṣṭimārgī *śrautin*s, who have often supported their religious lifestyles as Vaiṣṇava *śrautins* with devotional explications of Vedic statements such as 'Viṣṇu is the sacrifice' (cf. ŚB 5.2.3.6 *yo vai viṣṇuḥ sa yajñaḥ*; 5.4.5.1 *eṣa viṣṇur yajñaḥ*). This position will be best illustrated if we reach back to the sixteenth century for an important precedent to this element of Puṣṭimārga sacrificial ideology.

This precedent is drawn from the early literature of the Vallabha tradition. In his commentary on Vallabhācārya's brief treatise called *Siddhāntamuktāvalī*, verses 17–19, Viṭṭhalnāthjī, the second son of Vallabhācārya, who is accorded equal status in the Puṣṭimārga with his father, interprets at length ṚV 1.156.3, a verse from a hymn to Viṣṇu by Dīrghatamas Aucathya:

> *tám u stotāraḥ pūrvyáṃ yáthā vidá ṛtásya gárbhaṃ janúṣā pipartana* |
> *ā́sya jānánto nā́ma cid vivaktana mahás te viṣṇo sumatiṃ bhajāmahe* ||
>
> O singers, from your very birth you have satisfied him, the ancient source of cosmic order, to the best of your knowledge. You, understanding merely his name, have spoken it out. May we, O Viṣṇu, the mighty one, share in your benevolence.

---

[12] Cf. Bennett 1993: 88ff., 124–136.

Viṭṭhalnāthjī interprets this verse as demonstrating the superiority of the path of *bhakti* over the path of knowledge. His gloss on the first half of the verse (occasionally paraphrased) is as follows:

> O singers, you speak of Him in the true sense of the term, which puts you on an equal footing with Him.

Viṭṭhalnāthjī then puts the following in the mouth of the Lord himself:

> You are dedicated to describing the greatness of me, the highest Lord who is well known in the world and the Vedas, whose original form was the cause of everything (as the Lord who brought the *akṣarabrahman* into being), of me, the womb which has within it the Veda as the manifestation of true speech.

Viṭṭhalnāthjī changes registers here and adds his own thoughts:

> You are describing this greatness right from your birth, O singers; it is your full time occupation. By always praising his glories you have satisfied him.

The sub-commentator on this work, Puruṣottama, the greatest and most learned commentator on Vallabha's work (1657 or 1668 to 1725), explains that when the Lord is in a state of *ātmarati*, an undistracted condition of enjoyment prior to manifestation and prior to time and space, the Veda remains within him. Indeed, during the period of cosmic dissolution the Veda remained within Kṛṣṇa's belly. His authority for this statement is the *Bhāgavata-purāṇa* (11.14.3, also 11.21.42–43).

Viṭṭhalnāthjī now interjects his own thoughts on this *śruti*. The singers referred to here are called *yáthā vidáḥ* because they know Puruṣottama, the Supreme Lord, in his true form, which is to say they are complete knowers of the Veda. *Śruti* is telling these sages of pure knowledge that because they are born for this purpose, they should understand that their bodies, external sense organs, breaths, internal sensory organ (*antaḥkaraṇa*), and their very lives must be dedicated to worshipping and satisfying the Lord alone. The *śruti* itself is thus enjoining these sages to enter the path of *bhakti*. In this way, the fruitfulness of knowledge is in devotion to the Lord. Keeping this in one's heart, says Viṭṭhalnāthjī, one should understand that in the second part of this *śruti* the Lord in the form of the Veda addresses those who are incapable of offering their bodies, senses, etc., to the Lord.

Viṭṭhalnāthjī continues:

> Fully comprehending that divine speech (*śabdabrahman*) is name, know that the Lord exists in two aspects: name and embodied form (*mūrtisvarūpa*). Though you may merely understand the name, and not yet have realization of the form of the Lord, you should at least recite the names of the Lord, which are the very form of divine speech. You should thus speak those names that are alone relevant. *Śruti* is requesting that even if one does not know much about the Lord's greatness and other supreme qualities of beauty, omniscience, etc., one should at least recite His name. In this way, knowledge of the supreme qualities of the Lord's form will arise. The name thus develops into the form. The name, which embodies *saccidānanda*, indicates this. Beyond this, if knowing the complete body of divine speech is impossible, then simply utter the names of the Lord without singing entire Vedic hymns. If one cannot even master this, then the *śruti* instructs one to find a guru and at least gain a nodding familiarity with the idea and form of *brahman*. We should know that the form of the guru is free of shortcomings and full of great attributes. Let us know, O Viṣṇu, that the guru is your own form and allow us to enter the service of the guru knowing him as your own form. By his divine aura (*svatejasā*), the guru destroys the ignorance of others.

In this way, Viṭṭhalnathjī has intellectually valorized and made ritually relevant the Vedic utterance of Dīrghatamas Aucathya by conferring on it a sectarian reading.[13]

Now, let us oscillate back to the twentieth century. As elucidated by Gokulotsavajī, following one of the other Puṣṭimārgī *āhitāgnis*, Gosvāmī Vallabharāyjī, the understanding of Vedic ritual is first derived from the Pūrvamīmāṃsā, because it is from there that the doctrines of heaven (*svarga*) as the goal of the rituals

---

[13] Viṭṭhalnāthjī is not alone in this. Nīlakaṇṭha Caturanara, in his *Mantrakāśīkhaṇḍa*, analyses ṚV 1.122.14 along similar lines; see Minkowski 2002.

and the eternality and *apauruṣeyatva* of the Veda are systematized. Then, extrapolating from Vallabhācārya's Śuddhādvaita, *svarga* is recognized as a Vedic expression of divine bliss (*ātmasukha*) and the Veda and Vedic ritual are identified as the *akṣarabrahman*, the eternal body of Kṛṣṇa.[14] Thus, through this progression of theological resonances, the performance of Vedic ritual is reclaimed as *sevā*, or divine service, to the supreme Lord. I might mention here another interpretation of the sixteenth century. K. Kunjunni Raja mentions in an article in Staal's *Agni*, Volume 2, that Melputtūr Nārāyaṇa Bhaṭṭa, the early sixteenth-century author of the well-known Malayalam *Nārāyaṇīyam*, states in his *Rājasūyaprabandha* that the bricks called *yaśodā*, 'fame-giver', in the *agnicayana* are symbolic of Yaśodā, the foster mother of Kṛṣṇa.[15]

I have a forty-four page pamphlet (the pages are unnumbered) in Hindi, an excellent example of Indian religious literary ephemera, titled *Somayajña Mahotsava* (Calcutta: Antarrāṣṭrīya Puṣṭimārgīya Vaiṣṇava Pariṣad, 1988), issued on the occasion of an *agnicayana* performed by Prathameśjī and containing a six-page spirited defense (unsigned, but seemingly by him) of the performance of *somayāgas*. This is preceded by twenty pages containing well-known hymns by Vallabhācārya and Viṭṭhalnāthjī. It appears that the intent of the booklet was to provide casual viewers of the *agnicayana* with new copies of these well-known hymns, with the extra bonus of reading Prathameśjī's brief tract on Vedic ritual.

I also have in my collection a fifty-page commemorative magazine in Gujarati and Hindi (with a large number of advertisements in English), titled *Śrī Virāṭ Somayajña Mahotsav Smaraṇikā*, released on the occasion of a *vājapeya* performed by Gokulotsavajī Mahārāj in New York City in July 2000.[16] The magazine contains a

[14] ŚB Cf. Go. Śrī Vallabharāyjī, *Vaiṣṇavbhāvpracūr vājapeya yāga (svarūp aur mahattva)* (Surat 1989); and *Somayāgkā śāstrīya paricay* (Surat 1983), especially pp. 30ff.

[15] Cf. Kunjunni Raja 1983: 309.

[16] For my remarks on his *agniṣṭoma* performed in London in July 1996, see Smith 2000.

number of short articles, including a brief biography of Gokulotsavajī (who, besides being a *śrautin* and a descendant of Vallabhācārya, is one of India's best known *dhrūpad* vocalists, with many CDs to his credit) and an article on the history of *soma* sacrifice (*Somayajñano Itihās* by Bhāratī Rājeś Śāh) that argues for its consistency with recitation of sacred texts, that it is an ancient expression of well-known and commonly practiced dharma, and is the revelation of Yajñanārāyaṇa. Also included are a brief article by Gosvāmī Śrī Śyām Manoharjī from Mumbai (*Kumbhparv evaṃ Somyāg*), currently the best-known Sanskrit paṇḍit in the Puṣṭimārga, arguing that Vallabhācārya himself has accepted Vedic ritual as a legitimate practice with a history in the *sampradāya*; two relatively lengthy unsigned articles giving general points of Vallabhācārya's teachings drawn from stray verses in his *Ṣoḍaśagranthāḥ*[17]; and an unsigned article titled 'Why Perform Soma Sacrifice?' (*Somayajña kyā hai*). A few points argued in this article's are: (1) that *somayajña* is the highest form of Indian culture; (2) that Śrī Kṛṣṇa in the Gītā states that *soma* is the essence of all mood (*rasa*); (3) that the statement from the *Taittirīya-Upaniṣad* (2.7), *raso vai saḥ, rasaṃ hy evāyaṃ labdhvānandī bhavati* ('this is indeed *rasa*; having obtained that *rasa*, one becomes filled with bliss') must be interpreted as a Vedic argument for identifying Kṛṣṇa with both the essence of sacrifice and the highest state of *bhakti*, which the commentators on Vallabhācārya's work recognize as a *rasa*; (4) that in the Sarvottamastotra, an oft-recited Puṣṭimārga hymn listing the names of Vallabhācārya, he is given the designations *yajñabhoktā* ('enjoyer of sacrifice') and *yajñakartā* ('performer of sacrifice'). Thus, Gokulotsavajī Mahārāj is depicted as an exemplar in the Puṣṭimārga: he manifests the highest realms of Indian culture and realizes the highest states of *bhakti* through the same Vedic means that Vallabhācārya himself practiced five hundred years ago. The *somayajña*, then, should

---

[17] See e.g., Redington 2000; Smith 1998; 2005.

be supported by good *bhaktas*, who are directed to revere other good *bhaktas* whenever possible.[18]

THE ART OF SACRIFICE

Let us look briefly at the artwork that adorns the covers of two of the three examples of ritual ephemera we have discussed, the Invitation to Śrī Selūkar's *aptoryāma* (FIGURE 1) and the souvenir magazine for Gokulotsavajī Mahārāj's *vājapeya* (FIGURE 2). The full color cover of the latter is strikingly different from that of the former, expressing differences in the ritual outlooks of the Puṣṭimārgi and the Maharashtrian *śrautins*. The front of the *aptoryāma* invitation is replete with Vedic images, including the five fires and *vedi* employed by *śrautins* of the Kātyāyana *śākhā* to which Śrī Selūkar belonged, a banner reminiscent of a renunciant's staff and a sunburst with the syllable *om* inscribed on them, and Sanskrit mantras bordering these images on all sides in a manner often found on yantras. The souvenir magazine issued on the occasion of Gokulotsavajī Mahārāj's New York *vājapeya* has a small picture of Gokulotsavajī in the upper left, next to the Gujarati title, while the greatest amount of space depicts the baby Kṛṣṇa on the right, flute in hand, looking up, and on the left Vallabhācārya emerging translucently from a three-tiered sacrificial fire, surrounded by leaping flames. This harks back to his birth and death narratives, both celebrations of fire that hold great mythic power in the Puṣṭimārga.

His birth, the story goes, was prophesied by Viṣṇu himself, who emerged from the fire altar of Vallabha's distant ancestor, Yajñanārāyaṇa Dīkṣita, a Tailāṅga brahman from Andhra Pradesh, informing him that he, Viṣṇu himself, would take birth in his family once he and his descendents performed a hundred *soma* sacrifices. Eventually Lakṣmaṇa Bhaṭṭa, five generations later. and settled in Varanasi, performed the hundredth *soma* sacrifice. Shortly there-

[18] That the *vājapeya* itself was riddled with insuperable problems is not the point here; I shall address this in a future publication.

FIGURE 1. *Cover of the Invitation to Śrī Selūkar's aptoryāma.*

after, Lakṣmaṇa Bhaṭṭa and his pregnant wife Illamagāru were forced to flee Kāśī in the wake of rumors of invading Muslims. In the weariness of their flight back to their ancestral home in Andhra Pradesh, Illamagāru, in the Champa forest in Raipur district of the present-day Madhya Pradesh, gave birth prematurely to a son, apparently stillborn, on the eleventh day of the dark half of the month of Vaiśākha. The couple wrapped the child in cloth and left him in the hollow of a *śamī* tree before continuing on their journey. The next morning, however, in response to a dream, Illamagāru led her husband back to the site of the delivery and there discovered a newborn babe cheerfully playing, encircled by flames, with a halo around his head.

FIGURE 2. *Cover of the souvenir magazine for Gokulotsavajī Mahārāj's vājapeya.*

The tale of his death was equally important to the significance of ritual fire. Soon after his *saṃnyāsa* initiation, probably in the year 1531, Vallabhācārya set out for Varanasi, and after a journey of eighteen days arrived and settled into a hut on Hanumān Ghāṭ where he sat in undistracted contemplation for a week. His family and followers knew that his days were numbered, that he clearly intended to leave this world; nevertheless, they respected his desire for solitude. After a final written exhortation to his disciples to maintain their devotion to Kṛṣṇa, Vallabhācārya rose from his seat and entered the Ganges singing to himself the Gopīgīta (*Bhāgavatapurāṇa* 10.21) and the Yugalagīta (*Bhāgavatapurāṇa* 10.35), which express separation and union with the Lord, respectively. Then, as Vallabhācārya gazed transfixed as if beholding the Lord, a flame arose from the waters in the form of the Lord and swept Vallabhācārya away forever, with several thousand people as witness.[19]

CONCLUSIONS AND COMMENTS

The central concerns of the diminishing *śrauta* communities are, first, the mere survival of *śrauta* ritual, and second, the authenticity of the survival, which, we have seen, varies according to the religious ideologies of the ritualists. I have dealt with this question of authenticity in an earlier essay (Smith 2001), and cannot deal further with that issue here. In general I can repeat, however, that whether or not compromise, adaptation, or innovation undermines and eventually destroys the fabric or 'authenticity' of the Vedic traditions, or merely distributes their legitimacy differently, is very much a matter of debate.

The knowledge of these ritualists is so vast, precise, contextualized and difficult to sustain that almost no one would want to undertake their mastery, or would be able to even if they so desired, outside the communities of *vaidika*s themselves. In most cases, the textual and performative knowledge of *śrauta* ritual, including context-sensitive knowledge that is transmitted along with it, such as gestures, preservation practices, strategies of textual organization, and so on, can be comprehended only by a few highly trained members of these communities. Thus, these traditions can be, in the end, directed towards only a few individuals within these communities. This renders the practice of this traditional knowledge incomprehensible or meaningless outside of these

[19] No single account of Vallabhācārya's life is available from within the tradition. The usual sources are the comparatively recent Gujarati *Vallabhākhyān* by Gopaldas; the *Śrīvallabhadigvijaya*, a Sanskrit work by Yadunāthjī, one of Vallabhācārya's grandsons; and several works in Brajbhāṣā by various descendents of Vallabhācārya. These include the Śrī *Ācāryajī Mahāprabhun kī Nijvārtā Gharū Vārtā* by Harirāyjī, one of Vallabhācārya's great grandsons, and the *Caurāsi Baiṭhak Caritra* by Gokulnāthjī, another of Vallabhācāya's grandsons.

small groups. The production and practice of this knowledge is not just religious, but social as well. In this way, Vedic ritual is multivalent; it is the repository of a number of levels of meaning. Thus, introducing it to the outside world is fraught with danger, from promises of inter-caste or extra-community inclusion that are practically impossible to fulfill, to fears of dissipation of the knowledge, to guardedness against destruction of personal purity. Increasingly, I find that the ritualists are not opposed to the idea of brahmanical power breaking down, though family and community loyalty require that most of them maintain to some extent both the ritual and the business of ritual. The few cases we have briefly examined here bear out the range of options and choices open to modern-day Vedic ritualists, and the dangers inherent in them.

Śrauta ritual has always possessed a certain amount of cultural cachét. This is already clear in the early and middle Vedic literature. Both the Vedic literature and the late first millennium BCE or early first millennium CE Sanskrit epics demonstrate handily that *śrauta* ritualists, whether brahman or kṣatriya, were widely revered. Brahmans in the epics are almost always depicted as performing sacrifices, and the sacrifice provided an array of tropes on which the epics were constructed. It is likely, however, that even in the first millennium BCE, *śrauta* ritualists were a tiny, if visible, segment of the population. In the Brāhmaṇa texts, the epics, and elsewhere in Indic literature, the *śrauta* rituals were romanticized disproportionately to the actuality and possibility of performance. This legacy of romanticizing, of manipulating the cachét of *śrauta* ritual, continues up to the present. This is not to say that *śrautin*s of two or three millennia ago were not sincere in their beliefs and practices, just as today's *śrautin*s are sincere – indeed, they are disarmingly sincere in their view that these rituals are beneficial not only to the sacrificer as a means of bringing about material prosperity and spiritual fulfillment (see above: *abhyudayaniḥśreyasaḥ*), but were also 'a powerful means of promoting social solidarity and progress', to quote the late R. N. Dandekar (1958: 6). It is clear from the invitations examined above that this same sentiment exists today.

The study of Vedic ritual has advanced considerably in the last twenty-five years. Among the themes that emerge from these studies is the intimate link between performance and preservation: in spite of a stable initial level of textuality, the ritual was constantly modified, albeit subtly, due to both external pressures and internal reinterpretations. Among the external contributors were geographical relocation or redistribution of the ritual communities, climactic and environmental change that forced substitutions in the materials of sacrifice, and accretions of sectarian ritual that emerged from the Purāṇic or Āgamic religion. Internally, modifications were due to the influence of other Vedic *śākhā*s, vague or elliptical *śruti* and Śrautasūtra passages that lent themselves to scholastic reinterpretation within a *śākhā*, and a growing reliance on epiphenomenal interpretation, such as that offered by the Pūrvamīmāṃsā (cf. Smith 1987) or the *Bhāgavatapurāṇa*. A further item of significance is the loss in the consciousness of *yājñika*s throughout India of a sense of an 'original meaning' of the sacrifice. This paved the way for epiphenomenal interpretations such as those of Viṭṭhalnāthjī on ṚV 1.156.3. These, then, were the dynamic elements that effected subtle but important shifts in the astonishingly stable and durable institution of Vedic sacrifice.

It is also important to recognize that the Vedic traditions shifted away from *śrauta* performance, as only a select few *vaidika*s who memorized the *saṃhitā* texts actually performed the *śrauta* rituals. The great majority served as temple priests or performed domestic ritual, while a few others became paṇḍits or Sanskrit teachers. Whereas the performance of rituals and the memorization of primary texts appear to have been the most important, if not always the sole, platforms on which the Vedic traditions operated until more or less the fifth century BCE, after that time the production of Vedic knowledge became much more diffuse, inclusive of not just the preservation of primary texts and ritual performance, but of ancillary matter such as *vedāṅga*s and systematic philosophy.

Before the twentieth century, modifications within the Vedic ritual traditions occurred inside the boundaries set by the traditions themselves. Few outside the elite circles of *śrauta* ritualists, not even other Sanskrit paṇḍits, would have read *śrauta prayoga*s and *paddhati*s (though many other ritual *prayoga*s were read by others, including those describing various *pūjā*s and Tantric rituals). Finally, when the old patronage systems consisting of local kings and brahman *agrahāram*s dried up, *śrautin*s were forced into a kind of commodification that ran counter to their history. This loss of historical status meant, essentially, opening up their knowledge, or at least some credible version of it, to the public. With the decline of the British Empire and the rise of India as an independent modern democratic country, cultural elites functioned almost entirely outside governmental (read: royal) agencies for the first time. Thus, patronage was for the first time sought largely from business classes, which increasingly cut across caste boundaries. It is out of this necessity that most of the ephemera that I have collected emerges.

I do not claim to have a complete collection of this ephemera, consisting mostly of leaflets, posters and small to medium-sized booklets or magazines such as the souvenir booklet put out at the time of the New York City *vājapeya*. Most of this material is too ephemeral or transient to warrant putting forth a great effort to collect it in large quantities; indeed, much of it is designed to be disposable. It was not, in fact, generated with a sense of posterity or permanence, to be a part of any religious or ritual canon. That these materials were written in English and a number of regional languages including Hindi, Gujarati, Marathi, Tamil, Telugu and Malayalam, but rarely in Sanskrit (I have one example of an explanatory manual written in Marathi by Nānā Kāḷe that was then translated into Sanskrit), testifies to the absence of canonical consciousness. Nevertheless, as we hope to have shown here, a great deal can be learned from it about the ideologies of contemporary Vedic ritual performance, and much more still can be read into the performance of Vedic ritual historically if we can prudently connect this ephemera with earlier genres of ritual literature.

REFERENCES

BENNETT, Peter 1993. *The Path of Grace. Social Organization and Temple Worship in a Vaishnava Sect.* Delhi: Hindustan Publishing Corporation.

DANDEKAR, R. N. 1958 *Śrautakoṣa*, I. (English section, 1.) Poona: Vaidika Saṁśodhana Maṇḍala.

GUNE, Jayashree 1994. Paśu-sacrifice in the Sūtras. *Annals of the Bhandarkar Oriental Research Institute* 74: 153–167.

HILLEBRANDT, Alfred 1897. *Ritual-Literatur. Vedische Opfer und Zauber.* Strassburg: Trübner (Reprint: Graz: Akademische Druck- u. Verlagsanstalt, 1981).

—— 1981. *Vedic Mythology*, II. English translation by S. Rajeswara Sarma. Delhi: MLBD. [Original: *Vedische Mythologie*, II. 2nd revised edition: Breslau 1929.]

HOUBEN, Jan E. M. 1999. To kill of not to kill the sacrificial animal (*yajña-paśu*)? Arguments and perspectives in Brahmanical ethical philosophy. In: Jan E. M. Houben & Karel R. van Kooij (eds.), *Violence Denied. Violence, Non-Violence and the Rationalization of Violence in South Asian Cultural History*: 105–183. Leiden: E.J. Brill.

KRIPANANDA, Swami 1989. *Jnaneshwar's Gita.* Albany: State University of New York Press.

KUNJUNNI RAJA, K. 1983. Sanskrit and Malayalam references from Kerala. In: Frits Staal, *Agni. The Vedic Ritual of the Fire Altar*, II: 300–310. Berkeley: Asian Humanities Press.

MINKOWSKI, Christopher Z. 2002. Nīlakantha Caturdhara's *Mantrakāśīkhaṇḍa*. *JAOS* 122.2: 329–344.

REDINGTON, James D. 2000. *The Grace of Lord Krishna. The Sixteen Verse-Treatises [Ṣoḍaśagranthāḥ] of Vallabhacharya.* Delhi: Sri Satguru Publications.

SMITH, Frederick M. 1987. *The Vedic Sacrifice in Transition. A Translation and Study of the Trikāṇḍamaṇḍana of Bhāskara Miśra.* Poona: Bhandarkar Oriental Research Institute.

—— 1998. *Nirodha* and the *Nirodhalakṣaṇa* of Vallabhācārya. *Journal of Indian Philosophy* 26.6: 589–651.

—— 2000. Indra goes West: Report on a Vedic soma sacrifice in London in July 1996. *History of Religions* 40.3: 247–267.

—— 2001. The recent history of Vedic ritual in Maharashtra. In: Klaus Karttunen & Petteri Koskikallio (eds.), *Vidyārṇavavadanam. Essays in Honour of Asko Parpola*. (Studia Orientalia, 94): 443–463. Helsinki: The Finnish Oriental Society.

—— 2005. The hierarchy of philosophical systems according to Vallabhācārya. *Journal of Indian Philosophy* 33.4: 421–453.

Somayajña Mahotsava. Calcutta: Antarrāṣṭrīya Puṣṭimārgīya Vaiṣṇava Pariṣad, 1988.

Śrī Virāṭ Somayajña Mahotsav Smaraṇikā. New York: Shri Nidhi Universal, Inc, 2000.

VALLABHARĀYJĪ, Go. Śrī 1983. *Somayāgkā śāstrīya paricay*. Surat: Ṣaṣṭhī Pīṭh.

—— 1989. *Vaiṣṇavbhāvpracūr vājapeya yāga (svarūp aur mahattva)*. Surat: Ṣaṣṭhī Pīṭh.

APPENDIX

The Closing Address of the 12th World Sanskrit Conference

ASKO PARPOLA

Many participants of this conference took part also in the 11th World Sanskrit Conference held in Turin in April 2000. I am quite sure that my own feelings of gratitude to Professor Oscar Botto and his team for their overflowing hospitality in Turin reflect the feelings of all of us who took part in that conference. I cannot suppress my admiration for Professor Botto's ability to arrange that conference at a very short notice when the people who had wanted to hold it elsewhere unexpectedly announced their inability to carry out their plan. This was already the second time Professor Botto organized the World Sanskrit Conference – I had the pleasure of participating in the 1975 meeting at Turin as well – and the International Association of Sanskrit Studies has done well in expressing its gratitude to Oscar Botto by electing him as an Honorary Vice President of the Association.

As the Chairman of the organizing committee of the present conference it is my pleasure to thank, first of all, our sponsors, without whose benevolence it would have been impossible to hold this conference. The Academy of Finland covered one third of our budget, which is the maximum subsidy that this state institution is allowed to grant. Another major sponsor was the University of Helsinki, which without hesitation accepted our application for covering the rent of the rooms we needed and for a reception by the rector. We thank the Mayor of the City of Helsinki, Ms Eeva-Riitta Siitonen, and His Excellency the Ambassador of India to Finland, Shri O. P. Gupta, for the receptions that they kindly offered to us. We got minor but still substantial contributions also from the Finnish Cultural Foundation, the International Association of Sanskrit Studies, and through the efforts of its former and present treasurers, Professors Colette Caillat and Bruno Dagens, also from the UNESCO. The Scandinavian Airlines System, the official airlines of the conference, granted us free travel to a couple of participants.

In spite of our best efforts, our budget unfortunately came only to a fraction of the vast resources that Professor Botto could tap for the Turin conference(s). We have tried to utilize our funds to the maximum, but one inevitable consequence was that we could not sponsor the participation of delegates from India and other countries to the extent we would have liked.

Nevertheless, and in spite of the fact that the submitted papers were screened in advance to ascertain that they fulfilled the required quality criteria, the number of participants exceeded our expectations. We thank all of you for your willingness to come here and to enrich this scholarly meeting with your valuable contributions, comments and discussions. I would like to mention specifically Professor Stephanie Jamison, our keynote speaker.

I am very grateful to the other members of the organizing committee and to all our session chairmen for their encouraging and obliging response when I approached them for help in organizing the various sections of this conference, and for agreeing to edit the resulting proceedings in the publication series of the conference. They have done a great job, and I trust that with their kind help we can bring the whole process to a successful conclusion.

At this junction I would like to express our gratitude to Motilal Banarsidass Publishers Private Limited, one of our important sponsors not yet mentioned, who are now celebrating their centenary years, as you have heard, and seen in the conference bags donated by them. Motilal Banarsidass has kindly agreed to publish the proceedings of our conference at very reasonable sales prices, which will guarantee these publications a wide circulation, given also the good international distribution of this major publisher of Sanskrit and Indological studies.

I urge all participants to send their contribution in the final form as soon as possible, and in any case not later than the end of this year, to the Conference Secratary, Petteri Koskikallio. With regard to the references and bibliography, please observe the guidelines given in the conference programme, and submit your contribution both on paper and, if possible, on a computer disk or by e-mail. Petteri Koskikallio will send the contributions further to the section chairmen for editing.

I thank CongresZon and especially Iina Ojala for smooth and effective collaboration in managing the hotel reservations of the delegates and for arranging their post-conference tours.

I am sure you all will join me in thanking our devoted graduate and post-graduate students, who have made a really most essential contribution to this conference. Indeed, it would have been impossible to carry out this conference without their untiring practical help at every turn. I hope they also profited from this experience and that we shall be seeing them as active participants in the forthcoming World Sanskrit Conferences. The names of these our voluntary assistants have been printed in the programme, but I would like to repeat them here. I thank Gunta Ahlfors, Tiina Hyytiäinen, Mari Jyväsjärvi, Maria Kekki, Juha Laulainen, Jussi Nyblom, Thupten K. Rikey, Ilmari Saarilehto, Heini Salminen, Jaakko Takkinen, Katarina Turpeinen, Mikko Viitamäki and Riika Virtanen. Special thanks are due to Juri Ahlfors for his assistance with the technical equipment in demanding circumstances.

Last but certain not least, my grateful thanks go to the Conference Secretary, Petteri Koskikallio, who has borne the heaviest load of the arrangements at every stage, and very effectively and skilfully seen them carried through. I could not imagine any better man in this demanding role. *Dhanyavādaṃ karomi*.

We do hope you have enjoyed the conference as much as we have enjoyed your presence here. Please reconvene on the ground floor of the University at three o'clock for the last item on our programme, the excursion to the fortress island of Suomenlinna and the farewell dinner there. Thank you!

Finally, our best wishes for the next World Sanskrit Conference in Edinburgh in July 2006.

INDICES

(Italicized page numbers refer to the footnote section)

1. General Index

2. Sanskrit Words (including names and parts of compounds)[1]

[1] Not included in the Sanskrit index are the many ancient persons in notes on pp. 279–282, 285, nor modern persons with Sanskritic names.